elementary
computer programming
in fortran iv

2nd edition

elementary computer programming in fortran iv
2nd edition

boris w. boguslavsky
louisiana state university

reston publishing company, inc.
a prentice-hall company
reston, virginia

Library of Congress Cataloging in Publication Data

Boguslavsky, Boris W
  Elementary computer programming in FORTRAN IV.
  Second edition

  Includes index.
  1. FORTRAN (Computer program language) I. Title.
QA76.73.F25B63 1980   001.64'24   79-25470
ISBN 0-8359-1648-0

10 9 8 7 6 5 4 3 2

Printed in the United States of America.

preface
to the second edition

Computers have become an ineradicable part of our lives, as if anyone needs to be told. Witness the spate of computer jokes that have replaced the Polish jokes since the election of Pope John Paul II. Some of them have even acquired an ethnic tint in reverse. Sample: Why does it take five Americans to multiply six by nine? One to punch the keys, and four to fix the equipment.

Ubiquitous as they are, computers seldom get good press. Just as rare incidents of crime get instant play in the media while predominantly good and uneventful behavior receives scant attention, computer failures and computer "mistakes" get the publicity while the enormous benefits that flow from the use of the computers seem to be known only to their users.

Few people realize that *computers do not make mistakes;* mistakes are being made by the people who use them. To paraphrase an old joke: Doctors bury their mistakes; mistakes bury computers. Manufacturers of faulty computers go bankrupt.

To any professional an ability to communicate with a computer has become, aside from his field of competency, a skill next in importance to reading. Whether his work has to do with men, maps, machines, or money, it requires him to seek information, to provide information, to make calculations, to set up records. All these tasks are simplified and speeded up by computers. Computers reach him even at home, in the form of tape-recorded messages, bills, and junk mail.

Gibbon said, way back in 1776: "All that is human must retrograde if it do not advance." To stay abreast of the developments in today's world, we must gain familiarity with computers. Better yet, we must learn to use computers. Fortunately, any one who can read can learn to program a computer, that is, to make the computer answer questions. All that is needed is a textbook that presents the art of writing instructions to the computer in short, easy-to-understand steps. Of course, access to a computer will make the reader's progress more rapid and tangible.

To provide such a textbook, I have revised the first edition of my ELEMENTARY COMPUTER PROGRAMMING IN FORTRAN IV to make the material clearer, simpler and easier for a beginner to assimilate. At the same time I have added material to make the book interesting to a programmer with some experience. To keep the book from becoming too long and unwieldy, I have deleted the chapters on graphics and magnetic tape and disc. The material on graphics, in greatly expanded form, will be published in a separate book. To make it easier for a student to check his or her progress, I have provided answers to every odd question and problem in the textbook.

I close with words of appreciation to two members of the System Network Computer Center at the Louisiana State University. They are Robert L. Jenkins, manager of computer services, and Malcom D. McNaylor, manager of computer systems. These two gentlemen are walking encyclopedias of computer science. Time and again they pulled me out of the depths of my dilemmas, and they did it with speed, courtesy, and, last but not least, with a clear explanation. These two men are not only capable scientists: they are excellent teachers.

Boris W. Boguslavsky

contents

chapter 1

digital computers-FORTRAN

1-1. introduction

A digital electronic computer is an automatic device that (1) accepts (a) data and (b) instructions on how to manipulate these data, and stores both in its magnetic memory in the form of digits; (2) performs step-by-step operations on the data in accordance with the instructions; and (3) issues the results of these operations. The *data* consist of the related items of information pertaining to a field of activity or study, such as the payroll of an industrial plant, the dimensions of a structure, or the grades received by students in an examination. The sequence of instructions that guide the computer in the processing of the data is called a *program*. A program is written by a person, called a *programmer*. It is the purpose of this book to teach you to become a computer programmer.

A competent programmer can usually write a short program directly. Longer or involved programs often require a carefully laid plan. A plan may be in the form of either an *algorithm** or a *flow chart*. An algorithm may be defined as a finite sequence of unambiguous steps that lead to a desired result. A flow chart is a graphical representation of the operations that bring forth a result. An algorithm and a flow chart to find the sum of any two numbers, and a program that parallels them may be written as follows:

---

* From the name of the Arab mathematician, al-Khwarizmi, 780-850 A.D.

Algorithm	*Flow Chart*	*Program*
1. Given any two numbers, record or store them under the names J and K	Read values of J and K on a data card	READ J, K
2. Add the numbers stored at J and K, and store the sum under N	Find the sum N = J + K	N = J + K
3. Write the number stored at N	Write the sum N	WRITE N

If the numbers 7 and −2 accompany the program as the data, the machine will take the path described in the algorithm, or the flow chart, or the program, and will print the result, 5.

A program is prepared for every different problem that is submitted to the computer for a solution. The computer is only a machine: presenting to it, as the data, two numbers, such as 7 and −2 above, does not cause the computer to calculate their sum, 5, unless it receives an appropriate instruction, such as N = J + K. Conversely, the computer executes the instruction N = J + K only if the values of J and K are *defined,* that is, if it receives the values of J and K. Finally, the computer does not print the result unless it receives a command to do so, such as WRITE N.

A program is usually written on a coding sheet, such as is shown in Fig. 1-1, employing the notation of numbers, letters of the alphabet, punctuation marks, mathematical and other symbols, and blanks. The ten numerical digits (0 to 9) and the 26 alphabetical characters are usually referred to as the *alphameric* (or *alphanumeric*) characters; all the other marks and symbols are called *special* characters, and most commonly include:

$$+ \quad - \quad * \quad / \quad = \quad , \quad . \quad (\quad) \quad ' \quad blank$$

11	12	13	14	15
A	+		B	

The special character *blank* is simply a blank space on the coding sheet; in the illustration shown above, right, blanks occupy spaces 12 and 14; a blank is a character, as much as A, +, and B. If the information containing blanks is printed on plain paper, as will happen in many places in this textbook, the blanks may be indicated by the symbol ⌃; thus the illustration above may be printed A⌃+⌃B.

Three additional special characters, $ (dollar), # (pound), and @ (at), are also known as *national* characters.

For their interpretation by the computer, the alphameric and special characters are transformed into magnetic spots on tape or disks coated with iron oxide or into holes punched on paper tape or cards. Figure 1-2 shows a typical card punched with holes that are coded to represent X = 2.4.

The punched card is the most commonly used medium for recording in-

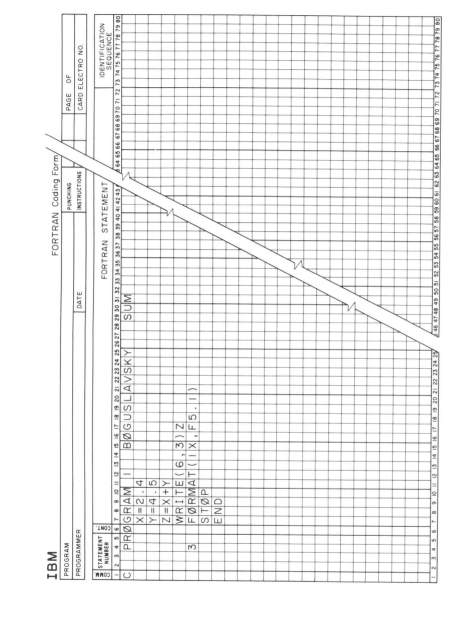

Figure 1-1

3

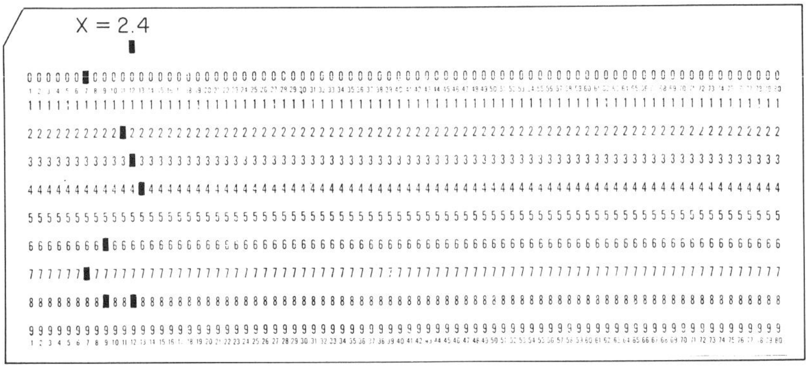

Figure 1-2

formation for a computer because, when additions or corrections have to be made, individual cards can be easily inserted into or removed from a deck of cards. For instructing beginners in the science of computer programming, exclusive reliance is made on punched cards, because mistakes abound in the beginners' work.

A simplified example of a program and the accompanying data are shown on four lines of a coding form in Fig. 1-3.

For submission to the computer, these four lines will be punched on four cards, one line per card (a card may contain only one line of information). The program shown will be encoded on the first three cards, and the data on the fourth.*

When the cards are presented to the computer, the machine will read the program on the first three cards, will scan the data card and interpret 6.0 as P, 4.4 as Q, and 4.0 as R, will add P and Q ($6.0 + 4.4 = 10.4$), will subtract R from P ($6.0 - 4.0 = 2.0$), will divide the sum by the difference ($10.4/2.0 = 5.2$), and will print the result (5.2) on a sheet of paper.

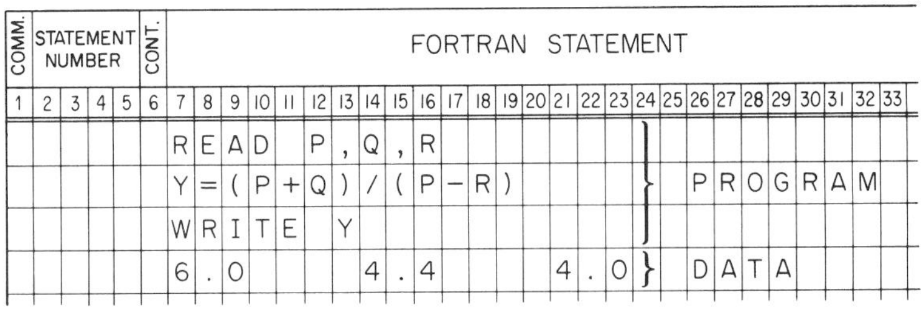

Figure 1-3

---

* Additional cards required to establish unfailing communication with the computer will be described later in the book.

More complex problems are handled by the computer in a similar fashion; the only difference is that there are more cards, both for the data and for the instructions that guide the computer in processing the data.

1-2. digital and analog computers

Article 1-1 began with a definition of a *digital* electronic computer. Modern electronic computers are divided into two basic types: *digital* computers and *analog* computers.

A digital computer is a device that receives information in the form of discrete electrical pulses transmitted in coded combinations, stores these pulses in its magnetic memory as strings of only two digits, 0 and 1, and, when these strings represent numbers, operates on them; because the computer preserves the effects of all the pulses, the values stored in the computer and the results obtained by it are *exact* (within the range of the machine).

An analog computer operates on numbers that are represented in a continuous form by measurable amounts of current or voltage: the larger the current or voltage, the larger the number. Since measurements of the currents or voltages, and therefore of the numbers, are made by ammeters or voltmeters, which can be read only approximately, the results supplied by an analog computer are never precise; however, their accuracy is generally sufficient for most purposes.

The difference between a digital computer and an analog computer is comparable to the difference between a beam balance with pans and a spring balance. In the beam balance the weight of an object placed on one pan is found by adding together the discrete known weights placed on the other pan; in the spring balance, such as a bathroom scale, the weight is found by reading a number corresponding to a measured deformation of the spring.

This text will be devoted exclusively to digital computers.

1-3. programming

Although the program and the associated data are always submitted to the computer together, they seldom have the same origin, and their respective developments may be widely separated in time and place. A problem and its data may originate with a scientist, a businessman, or even a schoolboy who has learned the ages of his classmates and wants to determine the average age of the class. The program, on the other hand, which will guide the computer through the solution of the problem, is usually prepared by a programmer, the person who can devise the requisite algorithm or flow chart and who knows the details of communication with the computer in a language that it accepts. For instance, a competent programmer will not permit the second statement of the program shown in Fig. 1-3 to be written

$$Y = \frac{P + Q}{P - Q}$$

that is, in two lines and without parentheses: such a statement cannot be punched in a single line on a card. Again, the programmer will not allow symbols such as Δ or π to appear in a program, because these symbols are not to be found among the alphameric and special characters that can be punched on a card; he would replace Δ by DELTA and π by PI (or PIE).

The computer—strictly speaking, the computing system—is designed to accept a fixed number of symbols and of combinations of these symbols; therefore, it can function only when only these symbols and these combinations are presented to it. The programmer is the person who can digest the problem presented to him by a scientist or a schoolboy and write logical instructions to the computer, using the symbols or combinations of symbols and procedures that are acceptable to the computer.

1-4. FORTRAN IV (four) language; compiler

Although the program of Fig. 1-3 appears to be written in the ordinary English language in combination with a mathematical expression, actually it is written in a specialized and rigidly formulated language—a *programming language*—called FORTRAN IV (there were earlier versions of FORTRAN). This language was invented to simplify writing computer programs.

There are two languages involved in the solution of a problem by a computer: (1) the language of the programmer, a human being, who prepares the program, that is, the sequence of instructions that guide the computer; and (2) the language of the computer, a machine, which must interpret and execute the instructions of the program.

The language of a computer is called a *machine language*. A machine language consists of a limited number of one-step instructions that a computer is designed to interpret and execute. Generally a machine-language instruction consists of two parts: (1) an order to perform an operation and (2) the location of the item of information that is to be operated on; both the operation and the location are identified in a numerical code. A programming-language instruction, such as $X = A + B$, is broken down, in the machine language, into a sequence of three steps, GET A, ADD B, STORE AT X, all expressed as two-part numbers.

These numbers enter the computer expressed in terms of only two digits, 0 and 1. These two digits can be represented in a machine by the electromagnetic effects of an electric current flowing in the one or opposite directions along a wire. Since only two directions are possible, only 0 and 1 can be represented by their effects. Therefore the computer can read instructions and operate on data only if they are presented to it in the form of numbers such as 0101 or 1000101. (Numbers expressed in terms of 0 and 1 are called *binary* numbers; a description of the binary system of numbers is given in Appendix C.)

The programmer, being only human, cannot write a program using only 0's and 1's without making mistakes or, worse, losing his mind. Therefore he uses a programming language, such as FORTRAN. FORTRAN is a problem-oriented programming language, that is, a language that, instead of reflecting the machine-language idiosyncrasies of a particular computer, enables the programmer to write the solution of a problem utilizing familiar English words and mathematical expressions. FORTRAN is a most widely used problem-oriented programming language.* FORTRAN is a coined word, formed by joining the first syllables of FOR*mula* TRAN*slation.*

The program written by the programmer in a programming language is called the *source program,* and the language itself (FORTRAN) is called the *source language;* the program written in the machine language is called the *object program* and the machine language is called the *object language.*

A source program written in a programming language, such as FORTRAN, must be translatable into the machine language. This must be so, because a gap exists between the source program that the programmer writes and the object program that the computer reads and executes, just as a gap exists between programs written in English and French. The gap in the latter case is filled by a translator or a dictionary; the gap between the source program and the object program is filled by a *compiler.*

A compiler is a special *program,* written in the machine language, which is loaded into the computer ahead of the source program, written in FORTRAN (or any other programming language). Under instructions from the compiler, the computer reads the source program and translates it into the machine language. The compiler does not just convert one source program statement into one machine-language statement: several minutely detailed machine-language statements are generally generated to create the effect of a single source statement, and the compiler is capable of producing this one-to-many correspondence between the source and the machine languages. In fact, if an elaborately designed compiler is stored in a computer, the source program can be made to look almost like the actual mathematical expressions in the original problem.

A computer may have a library of several different compilers varying in their complexity and efficiency. There are four compilers generally associated with FORTRAN: the E compiler, the G compiler, the H compiler, and the WATFIV compiler. The WATFIV compiler, developed at the University of Waterloo (Ontario), is a truncated compiler, that is, it covers only the elementary

---

* More than 100 programming languages have been developed for communication with computers. Many of these are completely dead; many others have only special applications. FORTRAN's nearest competitors are ALGOL, COBOL, and PL/1 languages. FORTRAN was the first programming language to be standardized through the U.S.A. Standards Institute procedures.

phases of programming; it is used extensively in teaching FORTRAN programming, because it generally requires less time for compilation. Guided by the WATFIV compiler, the computer, in addition to translation, does the following things:

1/ It prints out ("lists") on a sheet of paper, on consecutively numbered lines, all the statements that it reads on the punched cards of the source deck; thus the programmer can examine the printed list and verify the correctness of the card punching from the coded source program.

2/ If a card—and the printout—contains an ungrammatical statement, that is, a statement which violates spelling, punctuation, vocabulary, or syntax rules, the computer prints out, on the next line, a "diagnostic," that is, an error message, which tells the programmer which rule was broken.

3/ If a statement in the program directs the computer to perform an impossible calculation (such as division by zero) or is faulty and therefore untranslatable, the computer prints out the identification of the faulty statement and terminates the execution of the program.

The combination of a language with a compiler for a specific machine is called a "system." Thus the FORTRAN programming system consists of two parts: the FORTRAN language and the FORTRAN compiler. If a computer is equipped with a FORTRAN compiler, the programmer who has learned the FORTRAN language will be able to write programs intelligible to the computer.

The purpose of this textbook is to teach you the FORTRAN language and its use in computer programming. As stated earlier, FORTRAN has had the widest adoption as the programming language, and, as such, is acceptable to most digital computers.

1-5. IBM system/360

Digital computers are being designed and manufactured in many forms and of many capacities. The capacity of a computer is generally measured by the size and quantity of the numbers it can accept and process. The computer system used in writing this book was the IBM System/360. The limitations on numbers indicated throughout the book apply to this system.

questions

1-1/ Define a digital electronic computer.

1-2/ Define data.

1-3/ Define a program.

1-4/ Define an algorithm.

1-5/ What is the basic difference between a digital computer and an analog computer?

1-6/ Define an alphameric character.

1-7/ What is the most popular medium for recording computer programs and data?

1-8/ Distinguish between the source language and the object (machine) language.

1-9/ What is FORTRAN? What is the derivation of the word?

1-10/ What is the alphabet of the machine language?

1-11/ What is a compiler?

1-12/ What is a diagnostic?

1-13/ What does the WATFIV compiler do?

chapter 2

numbers and specifications

2-1. punched card

In Fig. 1-2 we saw a standard card used for entering information into the computer. An identical, but differently punched, card is shown in Fig. 2-1. Let us study the card.

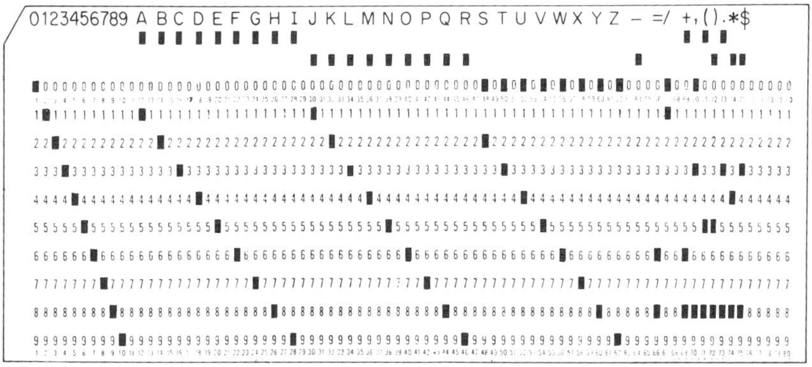

Figure 2-1

This card is alternately called a data card, an IBM card, or a Hollerith card. IBM stands for the International Business Machines Corporation, which has been in the forefront of computer development. Dr. Herman Hollerith, given the task of improving the method of recording information in the 1890 U.S. census, adopted and refined the principle of punching information on paper tape and cards.

A standard data card has 80 columns of ten digits each, the digits running vertically down from 0 to 9. Thus there are ten rows of identical digits, from the first row of 0's down to the tenth row of 9's. The columns are numbered from left to right by small numbers under the rows of 0's and 9's. The blank space above the row of 0's provides space for three additional rows. Of these, the top row is used for the printed characters, as they are transcribed from a single line on the coding sheet. For illustration, the top line of the card shown in Fig. 2-1 shows all the alphameric and special characters used in writing programs and data.

The next two rows in the blank space and the ten rows of digits are reserved for the holes that are punched simultaneously with the printing of the characters in the top row. The upper row in the blank space (below the printed characters) is called Row 12, or + row, and the lower row is called Row 11, or − row; these rows are not numbered.

At the instant a character is printed at the top of the card, a hole or holes are punched in the vertical column below the character. The purpose of the holes is to form openings for electrical contacts at the time the card is read by the computer, and thus to transmit signals identifying the characters into the machine. The holes are punched in accordance with the following code:

a/ A numerical digit is represented by a single hole in that digit's row; that is, 5 at the top of the card is represented by a hole in row 5, in the column below the printed 5.

b/ Letters of the alphabet are represented by two holes: one in Row 12, 11, or 0, the other in rows from 1 to 9; as with the digits, both holes are in the same column below the printed letter; thus letter B is represented by holes in rows 12 and 2.

c/ Special characters are represented by one, two or three holes; thus − (minus) is represented by a single hole in Row 11 (hence its alternate name, − row), = is represented by two holes in Rows 6 and 8, and + is represented by three holes in Rows 6, 8, and 12 (the + row).

It is not necessary to memorize the code relating the characters and the holes. A special electric machine, called a *key punch,* punches coded holes in a card automatically as the characters are printed along the top edge of the card. A key punch is similar to a typewriter. A description of the machine and its operating procedures is given in Appendix A.

2-2. types of numbers

The computer operates with two types of numbers: whole numbers, that is, numbers *without* decimal points, called *integers* or *fixed-point numbers,* and numbers *with* decimal points, called *real numbers* or *floating-point numbers*. At this time we need not concern ourselves with the reasons for this distinction; they will be presented later.

examples

Integers or fixed-point numbers	Real or floating-point numbers
2	2.17
1970	−19.70
0	+0.04
−10	0.
+6	610.5

Commas are not allowed in FORTRAN numbers. Thus 102,678 and 21.618,472 are invalid; they must be written 102678 and 21.618472. The plus sign (+) before positive numbers is optional; the minus sign (−) is, of course, mandatory.

The *real* numbers are further subdivided into two groups: those with the significant digits* close to the decimal point, such as 7.642, and those with the significant digits distant from the decimal point; examples of the latter are the length of a light year, 5,870,000,000,000 miles, or the thickness of an oil film on water, 0.000,000,2 in. The last two numbers can be more concisely and conveniently represented by numbers between 0.1 and 1.0 multiplied by the powers of 10; thus, one light year = 0.587×10^{13} miles, and the oil film thickness = 0.2×10^{-6} in.

A number expressed in this form is said to be *normalized.*

The two groups of real numbers will be discussed in Articles 2-4 and 2-5.

2-3.   integers; data fields; FØRMAT; the I specification

Figure 2-2 shows, on a line of a coding sheet, three integer numbers, +4, 206, and −17. The first two numbers are positive, but only 4 is preceded by the plus sign; as stated earlier, the plus sign is optional.

When the computer scans the card punched from this line and receives electrical signals through the holes, it registers the presence of +4 in columns 2 and 3, of 206 in columns 6, 7, 8, and of −17 in columns 10, 11, 12; at the same time it interprets the absence of signals through the other columns as

---

* A discussion of significant digits appears in Appendix B.

COMM	STATEMENT NUMBER	CONT.	FORTRAN STATEMENT

1	2	3	4	5	6	7	8	9	10	11	12	13	14	15	16	17	18	19	20	21	22	23	24	25	26	27	28	29	30	31	32	33
	+	4				2	0	6		−	1	7																				

Figure 2-2

zeros, even though no zeros are punched in these columns. Thus, the information punched on the card appears to the computer as shown in Fig. 2-3.

0	+	4	0	0	2	0	6	0	−	1	7	0	0	0	.	.	.	.	.	.	.	.
1	2	3	4	5	6	7	8	9	10	11	12	13	14	15	16	17	18	19	20	21	22	23

Figure 2-3

Obviously, it is not clear what numbers the computer has read; if signs are taken as indicators of the beginning of a number, there appear to be two numbers on the card: the first one, +40020600, and the second, −17, followed by zeros to the right edge of the card. This, of course, is not right.

To guide the computer to the correct numbers, we must tell it *where* the numbers are located; using the computer terminology, we must tell it what *data fields* the numbers occupy. Thus, if we tell the computer that the field of the first number covers the first three columns on the card, the field of the second the next five columns, and that of the third the next four columns, the computer will readily identify the numbers as +4, 00206 (or +206), and −17.

The computer is informed of the fields of the numbers by a FØRMAT* statement. A FØRMAT statement consists of the word FØRMAT followed by parentheses containing, for every number on the card, a specification giving the type of the number and the width of its field. A number of the integer type is identified by the *I specification:* the specification consists of the letter I followed by a digit which gives the number of columns reserved for the field of the number.

Thus, the FØRMAT statement identifying the numbers shown in Fig. 2-2 would be coded as shown in Fig. 2-4.

STATEMENT NUMBER	CONT.	FORTRAN STATEMENT

1	2	3	4	5	6	7	8	9	10	11	12	13	14	15	16	17	18	19	20	21	22	23	24	25
			2	0		F	Ø	R	M	A	T	(	I	3	,	I	5	,	I	4	)			

Figure 2-4

---

* The letter Ø (oh) in FØRMAT is slashed to distinguish it from 0 (zero). You are urged to form the habit of slashing all Ø's when encoding programs.

The first specification, I3, identifies the first field of three columns and the integer +4 in it (Fig. 2-5); the second specification, I5, identifies the second field of five columns and the integer 206; and the third specification, I4, identifies the third field of four columns and the integer −17.

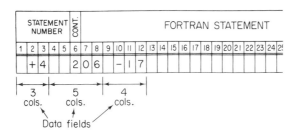

Figure 2-5

The FØRMAT statement is always written on the coding sheet, and punched on the card, starting in the seventh column. The commas separating the specifications are not mandatory, but do help to separate the descriptions of the fields; however, a comma may not appear before the closing parenthesis:

$$(I3, \ I5, \ I3,)$$
NO!

For cross-referencing with other statements in the program, the FØRMAT statement is always identified by some number, such as 20, written anywhere in the field of the first five columns (Fig. 2-4). The FØRMAT statement, though it serves to identify the data, is not a part of the data; it is a part of the program.

Even though an integer may be described by I4, it need not occupy all four columns of its field; it may be a two-digit number, such as 25; but there may not be any other digits or marks in the field of four columns reserved for 25 described by I4, except a + or − sign preceding it; furthermore, the number must be *right-justified* in its field, that is, its rightmost digit must be in the rightmost column of the field; this is because the computer regards all blank spaces as zeros and, therefore, in a field of four columns, would interpret | | |2|5| as 0025, i.e., 25, but | |2|5| | as 0250, i.e., 250. Had the numbers of Fig. 2-2 been encoded as shown in Fig. 2-6, and accompanied by the FØRMAT statement of Fig. 2-4, the computer would assign zeros to the blank spaces between the numbers and the right boundaries of their fields, and would read the numbers as +40, 206, and −170.

STATEMENT NUMBER					CONT.								FORTRAN STATEMENT												
1	2	3	4	5	6	7	8	9	10	11	12	13	14	15	16	17	18	19	20	21	22	23	24	
+	4					2	0	6		−	1	7												

Figure 2-6

The field of a negative number must always have a spare column for the minus sign. An extra column is not necessary for the plus sign of a positive number, although there is no prohibition against it. The sign may appear in any blank column preceding the number, as long as it is within the field.

Note that, in all coded statements so far, every character, be it a letter, a digit, or a comma, occupies a column of its own. Two characters encoded in the same column would call for two punches in the same column on a card; although this is not impossible, this would be a sure way to confuse the computer. On the other hand, a FØRMAT statement need not be as compact as it appears in Fig. 2-4; blank spaces may be left between the word FØRMAT and the first parenthesis and between the individual specifications within the parentheses.

The agreement of the specifications with the data can be checked by adding up the fields in the FØRMAT statement; in Fig. 2-4 the field widths are 3, 5, and 4, and these add up to 12; in Fig. 2-5 the last digit of the data is in Column 12. This check gives some assurance that the specifications and the data match.

2-4.   real numbers; the F specification

As stated in Article 2-2, a real, or floating-point, number has a decimal point. A real number may have an ordinary form, such as 7.24, or it may have a normalized form, that is, it may be written as a product of a decimal, beginning with a nonzero digit, and a power of 10, such as 0.26×10^2.

Real numbers are described to the computer in the same manner as integers, that is, by specifications contained in a FØRMAT statement. An ordinary real number, such as 7.24, is described by an *F specification*, consisting of the letter F (from "floating point") followed by a number containing a decimal point, such as 9.2. Let us assume F9.2 as the specification for 7.24. The meaning of F9.2 is that the number is real (F), that it is located in a field of nine (9) columns, and that it has two (.2) digits to the right of its decimal point.

Consider the set of specifications and the associated numerical data shown below. The specifications are written in the FØRMAT statement 30 (30 is a reference number), and the numbers are punched on a card.

30 FØRMAT (F6.1,F3.0,F7.2)

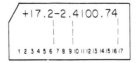

The distinct identities of the numbers may not be immediately obvious to the reader, but the computer recognizes them instantly in the light of the specifications. These specifications inform the computer that all the coded numbers are real (F), that the first number is to be found in the first field of six columns and has one digit to the right of its decimal point (this makes it 17.2), that the second number occupies the next field of three columns and has a decimal point but no digits to the right of it (−2.), and that the third number occupies a field of seven columns and has two digits to the right of its decimal point (4100.74).

It should be noted that the field count includes columns occupied by the sign (if any) and the decimal point.

Right justification is not required for real numbers identified by the F specification. Thus the numbers shown above could be punched on a card and described by the specifications of the FØRMAT statement 40, as shown below:

40 FØRMAT (F7.1,F6.0,F9.2)

The computer would still read, in the first field of seven columns +17.2, in the second field of six columns −2., and in the third field of nine columns 4100.74. Since the length of the decimal portion of a number is controlled by the decimal digit in the specification, the computer does not hang additional decimal zeros on the number to match the blank spaces on the right of the field; thus it stores +17.2, not +17.200.

If a number less than 1.0, say, −0.24, is punched on a card without the zero before the decimal point, that is, as −.24, it is stored with a 0, that is, as −0.24.

Occasionally, by mistake or design, a number punched on a card and the specification for it do not agree with regard to the decimal point. Let us suppose, for example, that four numbers on a data card are described by

50 FØRMAT (F6.2,F6.2,F6.0,F6.2)

and that the numbers are punched as follows:

The computer will scan four 6-column fields. In the first field it will find 43.2, with one decimal digit; though the first specification, F6.2, calls for two decimal digits, the machine will not move the decimal point one space to the left and store 4.32; it will honor the location of the decimal point as shown on the card, but will store 43.20, to satisfy the specification. In the second field the computer will right-justify the number, that is, it will interpret the two blanks between 123 and the right boundary of the field as zeros, will place a decimal point to the left of the two zeros, and will store −123.00. In the third field it will treat the rightmost blank as a zero and, because the third specification, F6.0, calls for a decimal point without decimal digits, it will store −6780.. From the fourth field it will store 6.2386, that is, it will honor the number as shown in the field, and will ignore the specification of two decimal digits. In short, the computer never changes the location of the decimal point shown on a data card.

To save space on a data card, a real number may be punched without the decimal point; thus 7.24, occupying four spaces, may be punched in three spaces, as 724. In the latter case the number must be described by F3.2. Obeying this specification, the computer will pick up the three digits of 724 and will store the number with the decimal point inserted before the last two digits.

2-5. exponential real numbers; the E specification

A real number which consists of a decimal multiplied by a power of 10, such as 0.26×10^2, cannot be punched on a card in a single line, because the exponent 2 of 10 is raised above the line. To make such a number punchable on a card, it is put in the *exponential form:*

$$0.26E+02$$

In this form the letter E (from "exponent") represents the base 10 and +02 represents the exponent of 10, that is, the power to which 10 is raised. Thus, the value of the number appearing in the exponential form is equal to the product of the *real number* preceding E (called *mantissa*) and 10 raised to the power of the *integer* following E (called *characteristic*). Examples of numbers in three forms are given below.

Exponential form	Normalized form	Ordinary form
0.123E+08	0.123×10^8	12300000.
+.212E−02	$+.212 \times 10^{-2}$	+0.00212
−.50E−04	$-.50 \times 10^{-4}$	−0.00005

A real number in ordinary form is written in normalized form in two steps:

1/ The decimal point of the number is moved to the left side of the first (leftmost) significant digit in the number; in the process the point passes n digit positions, and the number becomes a decimal with a significant digit in the first position;

2/ The resulting decimal is multiplied by 10^n if the point was moved to the left and by 10^{-n} if the point was moved to the right.

The exponential form of real numbers is used primarily for coding very large or very small numbers, although a number like 7.24 can also be written 0.724E+01.

Attention is directed again to the fact that, in an exponential number, the mantissa is always real* and the characteristic is always an integer. The maximum characteristic (exponent) possible in the IBM System/360 is 76 (see Appendix C). If a compiler encounters a number that has an exponent with three digits, it will truncate the rightmost digit; thus, it will truncate 0.17E+126 to 0.17E+12.

Like the numbers of the other types, numbers in exponential form are described, in a FØRMAT statement, by specifications of their own, the *E specifications*. An E specification is similar to an F specification, except that the letter E replaces F. Thus, the specification E11.3, identifying the number +.212E−02, means that the number is real and in exponential form (E), that it is located in a field of eleven (11) columns, and that the *mantissa* has three (.3) digits to the right of its decimal point. It should be thoroughly understood that 11 is the total count of the columns in the data field, and that 3 is the count of the digits in the *mantissa only*, to the right of its decimal point. Since +.212E−02 has only nine characters, two columns in the field of eleven will be blank.

A number described by an E specification (or by any other specification) must obviously be punched in the specified field on a card; however, the form of the number is allowed a great deal of flexibility. Table 2-1 shows a number of ways in which a number, such as −12.3 and described by E10.2, may be punched on a data card.

Form 1 is the standard form: the number is shown in the normalized form, with 0 preceding the decimal point, and with E followed by a sign and a two-digit characteristic; this is the form in which E numbers appear on the printout, except that the + sign after E may be omitted; the computer resolves the conflict between the specification E10.2 and the three decimal digits on the data card by ignoring the decimal part of the specification: it stores the number with three decimal digits.

Form 2 shows that the two zeros and the + sign after E may be omitted.

---

* But see Form 10 in Table 2-1.

Form	Columns									
	1	2	3	4	5	6	7	8	9	10
1	−	0	.	1	2	3	E	+	0	2
2				−	.	1	2	3	E	2
3				−	.	1	2	3	+	2
4				−	1	.	2	3	E	1
5				−	1	2	.	3	E	0
6		−	1	2	3	0	.	E	−	2
7						−	1	2	.	3
8			−	1	2	.	3			
9						−	1	2	3	0
10					−	1	2	3	E	1

Table 2-1

Form 3 shows that even E may be omitted, except that, in this case, the + sign must be restored. Forms 4, 5, 6 show that forms other than normalized are permitted. Form 7 shows that the number may be punched in the F form, without E and without the characteristic. Form 8 shows that a number in the F form may be punched anywhere in the field; all other forms must be right-justified. Form 9 shows that a number may be punched in the I form, that is, without a decimal point, but, in this case, the decimal part of the E specification (.2), which is always ignored if the mantissa contains a decimal point, takes effect and causes the number to be stored with a decimal point to the left of its last two digits (12.30). The same thing happens in Form 10: the decimalless mantissa receives a point to the left of its last two digits (1.23).

The forms shown in Table 2-2 are incorrect.

Form	Columns									
	1	2	3	4	5	6	7	8	9	10
11			−	.	1	2	3	E	2	
12	−	1	.	2	3	E	+		0	1
13						−	1	2	3	
14					−	1	2	3		

Table 2-2

In Form 11 the number is not right-justified; some compilers will interpret the blank in the 10th column as zero and will store $-.123 \times 10^{20}$. In Form 12 the characteristic has three digits, since the blank after + may be interpreted as zero; thus the third digit, 1, may be truncated. The number in Form 13 will be stored as −1.23. And the number in Form 14, with three zeros added to right-justify it, will be stored as −1230.00.

Note again that, regardless of the decimal part of an E specification, the computer stores the full value of the mantissa if it is punched with a decimal point.

Given the specifications of the FØRMAT statement 60 and a card punched with three numbers in the exponential form, as shown below:

60 FØRMAT (E10.2,E5.1,E11.0)

the computer will read the following values:

Exponential form	Normalized form	Ordinary form
−0.64E+03	-0.64×10^{3}	−640.
1.5E1	0.15×10^{2}	15.
+241.E−10	$+0.241\times10^{-7}$	+0.0000000241

It should be carefully noted that data numbers such as 1.23−7 and 123−5 are acceptable to the computer only if they are identified by E specifications. At the same time, it should be realized that shorthand notation of such type invites trouble, and that it is only prudent to include E in exponential numbers.

Compilers truncate numbers that are too long: the WATFIV compiler keeps only the first seven significant digits* of a number, and the G compiler the first nine. Thus if 0.012300456789 is punched on a data card, the WATFIV compiler truncates the number to 0.01230045, and the G compiler cuts it to 0.0123004567, even if the specification is F14.12.**

---

* Consecutive digits beginning with the first nonzero digit.
** Asked to print the latter number back, the computer prints 0.0123004578, instead of 0.0123004567. The difference between the input and output is caused by the conversion of the decimal input to the hexadecimal form in storage, the rounding of the stored number, and by still another conversion to the decimal output. These conversions are explained in Appendix C. The example shows that the computer is not always precise.

2-6. printout

The obvious purpose of the computer is to give answers to questions and problems. In many cases, particularly in the case of mathematical and scientific problems, the answers are numbers. Therefore, generally, the computer, as the final step in its operations, reports numbers.

In most cases the numbers are printed in lines on a continuous sheet of paper, which issues from the system printer and automatically folds into 11 x 15-in. pages. The lines are printed across the 15-inch width, and one line accommodates 132 characters. When not printed on paper, the results are punched on cards or recorded on magnetic tapes or disks.

The forms of the numbers on the printout are the same as those that the computer accepts at its receiving end: the computer prints integers (I type), ordinary real numbers (F type), and exponential real numbers (E type). The positions in which the numbers are to be printed on a line are indicated to the computer by a FØRMAT statement, just as the locations of the numbers on a punched card are indicated by a FØRMAT statement.

The computer is more formal in printing numbers than in reading them. It was shown earlier that, although integers punched on a card must always be right-justified, real numbers may appear anywhere in their field. Not so on the printout. The computer, in printing out numbers, strictly adheres to the following rules:

1/ It begins the field of the first number in the first space in which a character may be printed. This first space is not marked on the paper, but, if the WATFIV compiler is used, the first space is indicated by the letter C in the phrase **CORE USAGE,** which concludes the printout.

example 2-1. The number 0.24E 01, described by a FØRMAT specification E8.2, will be printed as follows:

```
0.24E 0I
123456789  ←——
CORE USAGE
```
These numbers do not appear on the printed sheet; they are shown here only to help count spaces.

2/ It right-justifies all numbers in their fields.

example 2-2. Numbers 21, 6.204, 0.15E−02, accompanied by a FØRMAT statement (I5,F7.3,E9.2), will be printed out as follows:

```
 21  6.204 0.15E-02
 1 2 3 4 5 6 7  8 9 10 11 12 13 14 15 16 17 18 19 20 21 22
```

Note that the sum of the fields, $5 + 7 + 9 = 21$, gives the position of the last printed digit.

3/ In exponential numbers with a positive exponent it follows the letter E, depending on the compiler, either with the plus sign or with a blank.

> **example 2-3.** Numbers +672, +0.232E+04, −5.3, associated with (I4,E10.3,F5.1), will be printed:

```
        672 0.232E+04 -5.3
    or  672 0.232E 04 -5.3
        1 2 3 4 5 6 7 8 9 10 11 12 13 14 15 16 17 18 19
```

4/ It never abbreviates exponential numbers, that is, it always prints E, followed by a sign (or a blank for the plus sign) and *two* digits of the characteristic.

> **example 2.4.** Numbers +0.74E−2 and −0.612+5, accompanied by (E10.2,E10.3), will be printed:

```
        0.74E-02-0.612E+05
    or  0.74E-02-0.612E 05
        1 2 3 4 5 6 7 8 9 10 11 12 13 14 15 16 17 18 19 20 21
```

5/ If the numbers (quantities) of the decimal digits in the number and the specification do not agree, the computer will (a) continue with zeros in the decimal part of the number if the specification is excessive, (b) truncate the rightmost decimal digits of the number if the specification is deficient.

> **example 2-5.** Numbers −6.17 and +0.2413E−07, accompanied by (F8.4,E12.2), will be printed:

```
        -6.1700      0.24E-07
        1 2 3 4 5 6 7 8 9 10 11 12 13 14 15 16 17 18 19 20
```

6/ If the truncated decimals begin with a 5 or a higher digit, the computer generally rounds up (increases by 1) the last remaining digit.

> **example 2-6.** Number 6.87, described by F5.1, will be printed:

6.9

1 2 3 4 5 6

7/   The computer always normalizes an exponential number and usually prints 0 (zero) before the decimal point.

NAME		Integer or fixed–point	Real or floating–point	
FORM			Ordinary	Exponential
DESCRIPTION		Whole; no frac–tion; no decimal point	Whole and/or frac–tion; decimal point	Mantissa: whole and/or fraction, decimal point Letter E (optional) Characteristic: integer
SIGNS	+		Optional	(If E is omitted, + is mandatory before the characteristic)
	−		Mandatory	
COMMA		Comma is not allowed in any of the numbers		
MAXIMUM VALUE		$\pm(2^{31}-1) =$ $\pm 2,147,483,647$	$\pm 0.7237 \times 10^{76}$	
MAXIMUM NUMBER OF SIGNIFICANT DIGITS		10	COMPILER $7 \longleftarrow$ WATFIV $\longrightarrow 7$ $9 \longleftarrow$ G $\longrightarrow 9$ } Mantissa 2 Characteristic	
EXAMPLES	CORRECT	576 ; +576 ; −20 ; 0 ; 2000000000	576. ; +576.0 ; −198.45 ; 0. ; 0.0001234567 (leading zeros are not considered to be significant digits)	0.21E+03 ; +.4256738E−2 ; −12.3+4
	INCORRECT	672. (decimal point) ; 10,568 (comma); 12000000000 (too large)	6 (no decimal point); −11.234,56 (comma) ; 0.12300456789 (too long)	5.E+85 (characteristic too large); E+2 (no mantissa) 0.67E2.5 (characteristic real)
SPECIFICATION		I	F	E
FIELD		Column count includes columns with signs, digits, decimal point, E, and blank after E		
RIGHT JUSTIFICATION IN FIELD		Mandatory	Optional	Mandatory
PRINTOUT		Plus signs may be omitted; Numbers are right justified; Numbers with insufficient field specifications may be truncated or printed as a series of asterisks		Numbers are normalized; Characteristic has 2 digits; A plus sign may be replaced by a blank before a positive characteristic

Table 2-3.   Summary of Numbers in IBM System/360

example 2-7. Number 342.1E−2, associated with (E10.4), will be printed:

$$0.3421E\ 01$$
1 2 3 4 5 6 7 8 9 10 11

Some compilers omit the initial 0, if the specification lacks one space. Thus 342.1E−2, described by (E9.4), may be printed:

$$.3421E\ 01$$
1 2 3 4 5 6 7 8 9 10

8/ If the length of the number (including the negative sign) exceeds the length of the field in the specification—the case known as *FØRMAT overflow*—the computer, unable to print the entire number, prints asterisks in the specified field.

example 2-8. Number −641.3, accompanied by (F6.2), will be printed ******, because the computer cannot print −641.30 in six spaces; changing the specification to F6.1 will result in a printout of −641.3.

A summary of the computer numbers and their characteristics appears in Table 2-3.

2-7. the X specification

Consider a card punched with two numbers, 74 and 16.42, as shown below:

```
7 4     16 .4 2
   |             |
1 2 3 4 5 6 7 8 9 10 11 12
```

A description of the two numbers and of their locations on the card can be conveyed to the computer by

$$1\ FØRMAT(I4,F7.2)$$

which would indicate that the first 4 columns on the card contain an integer number (I), and the next 7 columns contain a real number (F) with two decimal digits.

Let us now suppose that we wish the computer to read and store only the second of the two numbers, namely, 16.42. We cannot write

2 FØRMAT(F7.2)

because the computer, scanning the first 7 columns on the card, would find 74001 (interpreting blank spaces as zeros), would insert the decimal point to the left of the last two digits (as required by the specification), and would store 740.01. Neither can we write

3 FØRMAT(F11.2)

because then the computer would store 740016.42 (or 740016.40 with the WAT-FIV compiler).

The means to attain our objective is found in the X specification. This specification blanks out spaces in both the input and output records. In FOR-TRAN, the letter X, besides its alphabetic purpose, denotes a *blank space;* thus, 7X means 7 consecutive blank spaces on the record. Therefore, to steer the computer to 16.42 on the card above, we would write

4 FØRMAT(4X,F7.2)

or

5 FØRMAT(5X,F6.2)

or

6 FØRMAT(6X,F5.2)

Either one of these sets of specifications would make the computer overlook 74 in the first group of columns and pick up 16.42 in the following group of columns.

If the first number, 74, were not on the card, we could still make the computer store 16.42 by any one of the specifications above, or by

7 FØRMAT(2X,F9.2)

or

8 FØRMAT(F11.2)

On the output, the computer, directed by the X specification, leaves blank spaces in the printout in the same manner as it bypasses columns to be ignored on a punched card. However, *every FØRMAT statement containing specifications for a printout must always begin with a description of the carriage control character,* that is, the character which serves as a signal for the forward (vertical) movement of the sheet in the printer (such as is produced by turning the roller in a typewriter). In Chapter 4 we shall learn that there are several carriage control characters. At this point, however, we shall mention only one, namely 1X, a single blank, because it belongs in the family of X specifications. When it appears *first* among the specifications for a printout, 1X causes the printed sheet to move up one line before the printer begins printing.

When the printer, ordered to print a number such as 32.4, encounters the statement

20 FØRMAT(1X,F6.1)

it does the following things: (1) it interprets 1X, the symbol for a single blank, as a signal to move the printed sheet up one line, and moves it, and (2) it prints 32.4, right-justified, in the first field of six spaces, as shown below:

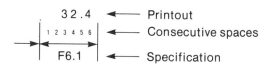

If the FØRMAT for printing 32.4 were

21 FØRMAT(4X,F6.1)

the printer would divide 4X into 1X and 3X, would interpret 1X as the signal to move the sheet one line, and would produce the following printout:

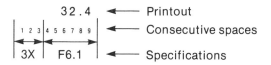

On the other hand, if the FØRMAT were

22 FØRMAT(F6.1)

the compiler, seeking a carriage control signal for the printer, would examine the field of 6 spaces occupied in storage by the number to be printed and would regard the first character it finds in that field as the carriage control signal; generally it interprets it as 1X and advances the sheet one line. The loss of one space for the signal would reduce the field to 5 spaces, and the printout would appear as follows:

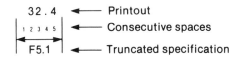

Finally, were the FØRMAT for printing 32.4 written in the following form:

23 FØRMAT(F4.1)

the compiler would still requisition the first space from the field of 4 for the advance signal. This time the four characters of 32.4 would not fit into the remaining three spaces—a case of FØRMAT overflow—but the printer, rather than print three asterisks, would truncate the leftmost digit of the number. Thus the printout would be

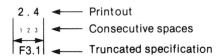

The preceding discussion makes it clear that it is essential to write 1X (or another carriage control character) *first* in the FØRMAT for a printout, both to serve as a signal to advance the sheet and to protect the adjacent data field.

2-8. mistakes in specifications

It was shown in the preceding article that FØRMAT specifications may be written with a certain amount of flexibility. However, flexibility is not synonymous with sloppiness. Incorrectly written specifications do not always stop the computer; occasionally it will blithely operate with wrong numbers to which it is led by wrong specifications, as we have seen in Articles 2-4 and 2-7. Wrong numbers, of course, produce wrong results.* And, unthinkingly and unwittingly, a programmer or a proponent may accept wrong results as valid.

To illustrate the point, let us study the data card shown in Fig. 2-7. Vertical

---

* Programmers put it less delicately: "Garbage In-Garbage Out" (GIGO).

lines drawn on the card help to distinguish the fields occupied by the several numbers (shown at the top of the card) and the fields of blanks (shown in Row 11 as 2X, 2X, 3X).

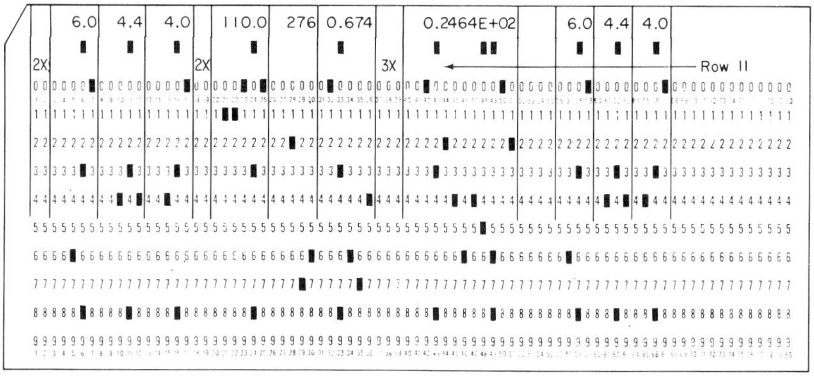

Figure 2-7

If we wish the computer to store all the numbers shown on the card, we can describe them as follows:

2 FØRMAT(2X,3F5.1,2X,F6.1,I5,F6.3,3X,E12.4,4X,3F4.1)*

If we wish to store only 6.0, 4.4, and 4.0, we can do it with either one of the following sets of specifications:

3 FØRMAT(2X,3F5.1)

or

4 FØRMAT(55X,3F4.1)

As shown in Article 2-4, the punched data will override some mistakes in specifications. If the FØRMAT #3 above were written as shown below:

5 FØRMAT(2X,3F5.0)

that is, with a specification stating that data numbers have no decimal digits, the card reader, scanning the proper fields, would still pick up the entire numbers and store them as 6.0, 4.4, and 4.0, and not as 6., 4., and 4..

---

* 3F5.1 is an abbreviation of F5.1,F5.1,F5.1 (see Article 3-4).

But if the FØRMAT statement for storing 6.0, 4.4, and 4.0 were miscoded or mispunched, as shown below:

6 FØRMAT(7X,3F6.1)

the computer would divide the data fields of Fig. 2-7 as follows:

6.0   4.4   4.0   110.0

| 7 | 6 | 6 | 6 |◄────── Number of spaces

and would store 4.4, 4.0, and 110.0, instead of 6.0, 4.4, and 4.0.

On output, the printer is quite strict. We have already seen, in the preceding article, that a correctly stored number may be printed out incorrectly, due to a faulty specification; thus we saw that an omission of 1X in a FØRMAT statement associated with a printout may cause 32.4 to be printed out as 2.4.

Again, if we asked the computer to write out 0.674 and 0.2464E+02 with the FØRMAT shown below:

7 FØRMAT(1X,F6.1,E12.2)

that is, with reduced numbers of decimal digits in the specifications, the printout would be:

0 . 7   0 . 25E 02 ◄──── Printout

1 2 3 4 5 6 7 8 9 10 11 12 13 14 15 16 17 18 19 ◄──── Consecutive spaces

Both numbers would lose the two rightmost digits, but in both of them the last remaining digit would be increased by 1 to compensate for the loss of the part which begins with a 5 or a higher digit.

Key punch operators make mistakes in punching cards most often when characters on the coding sheet are illegible or when similar looking characters are written without some distinguishing marks. The characters that give most trouble, and the recommended ways of representing them to avoid confusion, are tabulated below:

Digit	Letter	Special
0	Ø	
1	I	/ or '
2	Z	
5	S	

A slash (/) should be long enough and have enough slope to make it look different from 1 (one), I, or the apostrophe(').

In coding a program, a pencil is always preferable to a pen; penciled entries, if incorrect or illegible, can be erased, and the coding sheet made neat and easy to punch cards from. Inked entries cannot be erased, superimposed corrections may be difficult to read, and blotted-out characters waste space and mar the sheet.

questions and problems

2-1/   What are the three common names for a punched card?

2-2/   How many hole locations are there on a card?

2-3/   Print-punch on a card (1) your family name, your given name and initial, beginning in the first column; (2) your birthday, month (as a word), and year, beginning in the 31st column; (3) your social security number in parentheses, beginning in the 51st column. Duplicate the card.

2-4/   Name and describe two groups of numbers on which the computer operates.

2-5/   Name two forms of a real number acceptable to the computer, and give an example of a number in both forms.

2-6/   What is a normalized number? Can a normalized number be punched on a card? If not, why not?

2-7/   What is a data field?

2-8/   What specifications are used to describe numbers to the computer? Give an example of each and explain the component parts of each.

2-9/   What is a FØRMAT statement? Where on a coding sheet or a punched card does it begin? Where is its reference number shown?

2-10/   Tabulate the following numbers in three groups under the headings "Integer," "Real," and "Invalid," and, in the last case, state why invalid.

(a)	.5	(f)	7,650.3	(k)	00400
(b)	$52.45	(g)	7	(l)	3456.7E10
(c)	16,000	(h)	2−20	(m)	23.45+6
(d)	5678.901	(i)	00.4	(n)	5^2
(e)	5.4E−.5	(j)	8.2E+85	(o)	26E−04

2-11/   In numbered columns (as on a coding sheet) write, in one line, three numbers, one an integer, the second an ordinary real number, and the third an exponential real number, and, in the next line, a complete FØRMAT statement containing a specification for each.

2-12/   Which of the following pairs of numbers are identical?

         (a)   .00042   4.2E+04
         (b)   24.75   +0024.75
         (c)   1900.   1.9E3
         (d)   12.78E+01   .001278E+04
         (e)   4.0   4.
         (f)   .0078   78.0E−04

2-13/   The distance from the earth to the sun is approximately 93,000,000 miles. Express this distance as an exponential number.

         Write an E specification that will provide a field for this number preceded by the plus sign.

2-14/   What printouts will result from the following combinations of numbers and specifications? Assume that a carriage control signal is present.

         (a)   61;   +341.2   ;   −0.123E2
                (I4 ,   F7.2   , E11.3)
         (b)   +123   ;   1124.62   ;   −12.3E−1
                (I3 ,   F6.2 ,   E12.2)
         (c)   −6425   ;   212.32   ;   −0.646−2
                (I4   ,   E11.5 ,   F9.5)
         (d)   −15   ;   +6.173   ;   0.1234E−3
                (I5 ,   F4.2 ,   E11.3)

2-15/   What does 6X represent when it appears

         (a)   In a FØRMAT statement on input?
         (b)   In the beginning of a FØRMAT statement on output?
         (c)   Anywhere but in the beginning of a FØRMAT statement on output?

2-16/   Given the card of Fig. 2-7 and the following FØRMAT:

                        FØRMAT(25X,I5)

         what value will the computer store upon reading the card?

chapter 3

computer components – FORTRAN statements

3-1. components of a computer

In Article 1-1 and Fig. 1-3 you were shown a three-line program and one line of data which, submitted to the computer on four punched cards, were to cause the computer to compute and report the value of $Y = (P + Q)/(P - R)$.

In detail the computer was expected to

1/ Read information on all four cards.

2/ Store—memorize—the read information, associating the names P, Q, R with the numbers on the data card.

3/ Compute $(P + Q)/(P - R)$, replacing P, Q, R in the formula by the numbers taken from the memory, and store the result, assigning to it the name Y.

4/ Fetch the computed value of Y from the memory and print it.

5/ Coordinate the operations described in the first four steps.

This five-point breakdown gives us an insight into the makeup of the computer. The computer has five components, one for each of the functions described above. These components are

1/ The *input*, or reading, unit.

2/ The *memory*, or storage, unit.

3/ The *arithmetic-logic*, or computing, unit.

4/ The *output*, or reporting, unit.

5/ The *control*, or coordinating, unit.

These five units are shown schematically in Fig. 3-1.

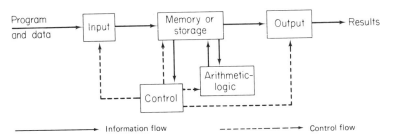

Figure 3-1

The *input unit* is the component of the computer that reads the information submitted to it on punched cards or tape or on magnetized tape or disks. Electrical pulses transmitted through the holes or from the magnetized spots send information from the cards, etc., into the memory of the machine.

The *memory unit* is a bank of *storage locations* or *memory locations*. Each location consists of a row of tiny magnetic iron rings (called cores), each of which lies at an intersection of two energizing wires.* Pulses sent simultaneously along any two intersecting wires affect the magnetization of the core at their intersection only, as shown in Fig. 3-2; no other core on these two wires is affected.

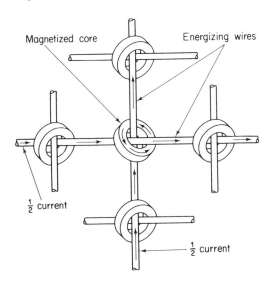

Figure 3-2

The magnetization of the ring expresses itself in the form of the circular magnetic lines of force pointing in one direction, say clockwise. If pulses are

---

* Research is producing new storage cells other than iron rings.

sent along the same two wires in the opposite directions to the first, the magnetic lines of force in the ring reverse and point in the counterclockwise direction.

Since the cores are always magnetized in one or the other direction, it follows that a memory location can store a number or an instruction only in terms of the clockwise- or counterclockwise-magnetized cores. If a clockwise-magnetized core is called 1 and a counterclockwise-magnetized core 0, it follows that only 1's and 0's can be stored in a memory location and that a number or any other item of information can be stored in a memory location only if it is expressed in terms of 1 and 0. In sum, 1 and 0 form the only alphabet available to the computer. The 1's and 0's stored in the cores are called *binary digits*, or *bits*. By association, the cores themselves are often referred to as bits.*

The number of magnetic cores (or other physical devices for storing information) in a memory location varies from computer to computer; it may be as low as 12 or as high as 64, usually in multiples of 6 or 8. The sequence of bits (or digits) stored in a location is called a *word*. A location of an IBM System/ 360 computer is composed of 32 magnetic cores: therefore, its word consists of 32 bits. This word is subdivided into four modules, called *bytes,* of 8 bits each, or eight half modules, *half-bytes,* of 4 bits each.

The *arithmetic-logic unit* is the component that performs mathematical computations (such as adding two numbers) and logical operations (such as comparing two numbers). The numbers to be manipulated in this unit arrive from the memory, and the result of the manipulation is sent back to the memory.

The *output unit* is the reverse of the input unit. It fetches the results of the computations from the memory and reports them in one of several ways:

---

* In the table below, Line 1 shows the ascending powers of 2, from right to left. In the *binary* system of numbers, explained in Articles C-3, 10, and 11, in Appendix C, the *integer* decimal numbers are expressed as the sums of the ascending powers of 2; thus

Line						
1	Powers of 2	2^4	2^3	2^2	2^1	2^0
2	Cores					
3	Decimal 6	0	0	1	1	0
4	Decimal 11	0	1	0	1	1

the decimal $1 = 2^0$, the decimal $2 = 2^1$, the decimal $6 = 2^2 + 2^1$, the decimal $11 = 2^3 + 2^1 + 2^0$, and so on. The cores of a storage location, shown in Line 2 of the table, correspond to the ascending powers of 2. The presence of a power of 2 in a decimal number is indicated by magnetizing the corresponding core 1, the absence of a power of 2 by magnetizing the core 0. Thus to store the decimal 6, the cores are magnetized as shown in Line 3; to store the decimal 11, the cores are magnetized as shown in Line 4.

as a printout on a sheet, as holes punched on cards, or as magnetized spots on a tape or a disk.

The fifth and last, but not least, component is the *control unit.* This unit coordinates the operations of the other four units. The processing of the program and data begins with a signal from the control unit to the input unit to read the program and to transmit it to the memory. When the program has been stored, the control unit begins to send out a series of alternate *fetch* and *execute* signals. A *fetch* signal, sent to a memory location, causes a program instruction stored there to be delivered to the control unit, which interprets it and establishes the circuits between the computer units involved in implementing the instruction; then an *execute* signal causes the instruction to be performed and the machine to advance to the next fetch-execute sequence. Program instructions are normally fetched from sequential storage locations, but occasionally a "jump" instruction received by the control unit causes it to break the sequential pattern and send the next fetch signal (for the next instruction) to a memory location that is not located sequentially. Eventually—and normally—a fetch signal brings an instruction that says STØP, and the execution of this instruction causes the computer to stop.

As a consequence of their processing operations, the control unit and the arithmetic-logic unit are commonly referred to as the *central processing unit,* or *CPU,* of the system. The memory unit, which is housed together with the control and arithmetic-logic units, is sometimes thought of as a part of the CPU; strictly speaking, though, the memory is not a processing unit.

The flow of information within the computer is shown in Fig. 3-1 by solid lines; broken lines represent the flow of control signals.

3-2. FORTRAN statements

As may be seen from the heading above the coding sheet grid in Fig. 1-1, all one-line statements on the sheet are called FORTRAN statements. They are called so because they are written in the FORTRAN language, which the FORTRAN compiler, stored in the machine, can translate into the machine language.

A FORTRAN program consists of a sequence of FORTRAN statements. These statements instruct and inform the computer. Conforming to these two "instruct and inform" functions, FORTRAN statements belong to one or the other of two classes: *executable statements* and *nonexecutable statements.* Executable statements direct the computer to perform some operation; nonexecutable statements are descriptive or informative and require no action.

The executable statements are divided into three groups:

1/ *Input* and *output*—to transmit information between the computer's memory and its input and output units.

2/ *Arithmetic assignment*—to assign a constant value or a computed value to a variable.

3/ *Transfer*—to alter the sequence in which other executable statements are performed.

The nonexecutable statements are divided into two groups:

1/ *Specification*—to describe the type and arrangement of the input and output data (Example: FØRMAT).

2/ *Subprogram*—to describe subordinate programs required for repetitive computations within the main program.

The computer executes the statements of the program sequentially, except when the order of execution is altered by a transfer, or jump, statement.

Rules of FØRTRAN statements

1/ A statement may not begin before the 7th column and may not extend beyond the 72nd column; a statement need not begin in the 7th column.

2/ A statement may or may not be numbered, depending on whether it is referred to elsewhere in the program; its number may be any integer between 1 and 99999 (without a comma) placed anywhere in columns 1-5 in line with the statement.

3/ Statement numbers need not maintain any order; they may be numbered 1, 2, 3, . . . ; or they may be numbered 10, 20, 30, . . . , providing an opportunity for assigning an intermediate number to a statement inserted in between to satisfy the demands of the program.

4/ Long statements (those that tend to go beyond column 72) may be continued on additional (continuation) lines, not to exceed nineteen additional lines. The continuation lines must be identified in column 6 by some arbitrary mark, such as an asterisk, or by consecutive digits; column 6 of the first line of the statement may remain blank or may be marked 0. Continuation lines may be indented to give (to a person) an additional indication that the statement is continued.

5/ Columns 73-80 may be used for numbering all program statements (and cards) consecutively; occasionally a card deck is dropped, and the cards become mixed; the consecutive numbers make it simple to put the cards back in order. Numbers in columns 73-80 are ignored by the compiler.

6/ Data may appear anywhere in columns 1-80; data in excess of 80 spaces must be punched on additional cards, but these extra cards may not be marked as continuations of the first data card; the rule for reading continuation cards is presented in Article 5-1.

3-3.   input/output statements

An input statement commands the computer (1) to read an item of information and (2) to store it in an identifiable location in its memory.

To enable the computer to execute such a command, the input statement must (1) inform the computer what input unit it should use for receiving the information, for example, a card reader, or a magnetic tape reader, and (2) provide a list of names for the memory locations in which the items of information shall be stored; these items can be subsequently retrieved from the memory by calling the names of the locations (like dialing a unique telephone number for time information).

A typical input statement has the following form:

READ (5,10)A,B

This statement is shown again in Fig. 3-3, followed by a FØRMAT statement and a data statement.

COMM.	STATEMENT NUMBER				CONT.	FORTRAN STATEMENT																								
1	2	3	4	5	6	7	8	9	10	11	12	13	14	15	16	17	18	19	20	21	22	23	24	25	26	27	28	29	30
						R	E	A	D	(	5	,	1	0	)	A	,	B											
			1	0		F	Ø	R	M	A	T	(	F	6	.	2	,	F	6	.	2	)							
		4	.	1	7			0	.	2	2																		

Figure 3-3

The integer 5 in the parenthetical expression (5,10) is a code symbol which identifies the card reading component of the input system of the computer; needless to say, this component reads only the information punched on cards. However, 5 alone is not enough to activate the card reader; the combination of signals that will cause the execution of the command must come from a set of holes corresponding to the characters READ 5; PERUSE 5 or SEE 5 will not do.

If the information were recorded on a magnetic tape to be read by the magnetic tape reader #2, the parenthetical expression would be written (2,10).

The integer 10 in the parenthetical expression is the number of the

FØRMAT statement that describes the type and location on the data card of the information which the card reader is to read and send into storage. We know, from Article 2-4, that the FØRMAT statement in Fig. 3-3 describes two real numbers in ordinary form (F), each occupying a field of six columns and each having two decimal digits.

The letters A and B in the READ statement are the names arbitrarily assigned to the two memory locations in which the two numbers, 4.17 and 0.22, found with the aid of the FØRMAT statement, will be stored. If, later on, a mathematical operation involving 4.17 and 0.22 needs to be performed, these two numbers will be called from storage by their names A and B.

To summarize, the effect of the instructions and data punched on three cards from Fig. 3-3 will be to cause the computer (1) to utilize its card reader to read 4.17 and 0.22 on the data card and (2) to store these two numbers, under labels A and B, in the memory.

An output statement is similar to the input statement; its typical form is

WRITE (6,20) A,B

Figure 3-4 shows this statement, followed by a FØRMAT statement, on a coding sheet.

\multicolumn{30}{c}{FORTRAN STATEMENT}
1	2	3	4	5	6	7	8	9	10	11	12	13	14	15	16	17	18	19	20	21	22	23	24	25	26	27	28	29	30
						W	R	I	T	E	(	6	,	2	0	)	A	,	B										
		2	0			F	Ø	R	M	A	T	(	1	X	,	F	I	0	.	3	,	F	I	0	.	3	)		

Figure 3-4

The integer 6 in (6,20), combined with the signals from WRITE, causes the printing component of the output system to print the values of A and B on a sheet of paper. The values of A and B are delivered to the printer from the memory locations A and B.

The integer 20 identifies the FØRMAT statement that holds the specifications for the printout. The first specification, 1X (as has already been explained in Article 2-7), is a special signal to the printer which causes it to advance the page on which the values are to be printed one line vertically. The next two specifications inform the printer that the two numbers are to be printed, each in a field of ten columns, and each with three decimal digits.

Combining all the statements which appeared in this article, we can write a complete program (Fig. 3-5) that will demonstrate the input/output functions of the computer.

1	2	3	4	5	6	7	8	9	10	11	12	13	14	15	16	17	18	19	20	21	22	23	24	25	26	27	28
						R	E	A	D	(	5	,	1	0	)	A	,	B									
			1	0		F	Ø	R	M	A	T	(	F	6	.	2	,	F	6	.	2	)					
						W	R	I	T	E	(	6	,	2	0	)	A	,	B								
			2	0		F	Ø	R	M	A	T	(	1	X	,	F	1	0	.	3	,	F	1	0	.	3	)
						S	T	Ø	P																		
						E	N	D																			
			4	.	1	7			0	.	2	2															

Figure 3-5

The printout resulting from this program will be

```
    4.170        0.220    ←———— Printout
1 2 3 4 5 6 7 8 9 10 11 12 13 14 15 16 17 18 19 20 21  ←———— Consecutive spaces
```

The last two statements in the program

> STØP
> END

are generally mandatory in every program. More about these two statements will come later in the book.

The writing of the input/output statements is governed by the following rules:

1/ The first word of a statement must be READ for input and WRITE for output.

2/ READ/WRITE must be followed by a parenthetical expression containing two integers, the first a symbol for the input/output unit, the second the number of the associated FØRMAT statement; the two integers must be separated by a comma.

3/ The parenthetical expression is normally followed by a list of names of the memory locations in which the data values are to be stored or are stored; the names must be separated by commas.

4/ No commas may appear after READ/WRITE, after the parenthetical expression, and after the last name in the list.

3-4. condensed specifications

You may have observed in the FØRMAT specifications above that there is in them a certain amount of repetition of identical field and type specifications, such as F6.2, F6.2 or F10.3, F10.3. FØRTRAN provides a writing shortcut for such repetition, by permitting grouping of identical specifications in the algebraic fashion, that is, by prefixing the repeating specification by an *integer repetition number,* that is, a constant which gives the number of repetitions. Thus F6.2, F6.2 may be condensed to 2F6.2; similarly, E9.2, E9.2, E9.2, E9.2 may be shortened to 4E9.2.

Furthermore, if certain specifications repeat in identical groups, such as those shown underlined in the following FØRMAT statement,

FØRMAT(F6.2,I3,F4.1,I3,F4.1,I3,F4.1)

the statement can be condensed by enclosing the repeating group within an inner pair of parentheses and prefixing the parenthetical expression by the repetition number, as follows:

FØRMAT(F6.2,3(I3,F4.1))

Note that the parentheses are balanced: there are two facing right (open) and two facing left (closed). This balance must be maintained at all times. An odd number of parentheses will always stop the computer.

3-5. control cards

A computer is a delicate and expensive machine. Only experienced personnel are allowed to operate it. Therefore students learning to program do not normally have access to the computer. They write their programs on coding sheets and submit the sheets to the computer organization for punching on cards and processing through the computer; or they punch the cards themselves and feed them into an automatic card reader. Eventually they receive printed sheets listing their programs and the results (if any).

To make the work of the computer system as automatic as possible and to keep accurate accounts of the operation of the system, the computer organization requires computer users to include in their program/data decks a number of control cards. Instructors should inform their students what these cards are, how they should be punched, and where some of them may be obtained. The complete deck consisting of the program, the data, and the control cards is called a *job.*

A job is required to have the following cards, in the order indicated:

1/ A colored job card which separates one student's job from another's. This card usually shows the authorized budget and project numbers and the name of the programmer, and an arbitrarily selected name of the job.

example:

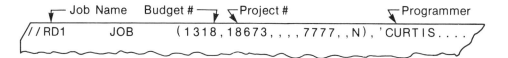

Job Name   Budget #   Project #   Programmer

//RD1   JOB   (1318,18673,,,,7777,,N),'CURTIS....

2/   One or two additional control cards, depending on the compiler.

example:

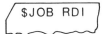

$JOB RDI

3/   The first *comment* card. This card begins with the letter C (for 'comment') punched in the first column. The C is followed, with arbitrary spacing, by the name of the student, the name or number of the program, and any other information of interest to the student and the instructor. The computer stores the comment statement, ignores it in the execution of the program, and passes it on to the printer for printing on the sheet.

example:

C CURTIS, JACK   INPUT/OUTPUT   PROGRAM 1

4/   The deck of program cards. The program deck may contain any number of explanatory comment cards, all of which must begin with a C.

5/   One or more control cards, depending on the compiler and the mode of processing the job.

example:

$ENTRY

6/   Data card or cards.

7/ One or two final control cards, depending on the compiler.

All cards in the job deck, except the first, are normally white.

A typical job deck, invoking the WATFIV compiler for processing the program of Fig. 3-5 is shown in Fig. 3-6. It has five control cards which begin with // or $; these cards are marked by asterisks on the left of the figure.

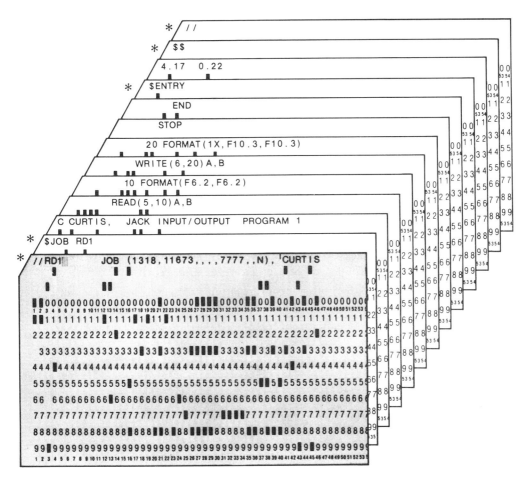

Figure 3-6

3-6. batch processing

Batch processing is a manner of operating a computer system in which a number of jobs, each consisting of the program and data decks with control cards, are deposited sequentially by a card reader on a magnetic tape or disk to form an *input batch.* This batch is transmitted from the tape (or disk) to the central processing unit (CPU), which processes the jobs in sequence, and transmits the jobs and the results of processing to another magnetic tape or disk to form an *output batch.* The information recorded in the output batch is conveyed to the printer which prints it on paper.

The reason for batching jobs is that direct communication between the card reader and the CPU, and between the CPU and the printer, is slow compared to the speed of processing. Therefore, to free the CPU for other tasks, mainly processing, the card reader forms an input batch by transferring a series of jobs, relatively slowly, from the cards to the magnetic tape. Whenever a break occurs in the many activities of the CPU, the input batch is thrust into it from the magnetic tape, the CPU processes the batch, and flings out the output batch— jobs and results—onto another tape, all at a much greater speed. The printer, again more slowly, transfers the output batch from the tape to the paper.

questions and problems

3-1/ Name and describe the five functional components of a digital electronic computer. Draw a diagram showing the flow of the information and control signals.

3-2/ Describe a memory location. How does it function? How many digits can a single cell of a memory location represent?

3-3/ What two distinct types of information are stored in the memory of a computer?

3-4/ Name the four media used for recording the data to be processed by a computer.

3-5/ How is the information transmitted from a punched card into the memory?

3-6/ Name the two classes of FORTRAN statements. What is the difference between them?
Name and describe all the groups of statements within the classes above.

3-7/ In what class and group do the following statements belong?

(a) READ   (b) WRITE   (c) FØRMAT

3-8/ Write a program that will

(a) Store numbers 6.0, 4.2, 0.1714 in the memory locations labeled D, E, F.

(b) Store numbers 505, 21, 4 in the memory locations labeled J, K, L.

(c)   Store numbers 1.46E+02, 17.3E−1, 0.23+3 in the memory locations P, Q, R.

(d)   Print all these numbers in one line.

3-9/   What character is punched first on a comment card and where?

3-10/   In what columns do you write (a) a FORTRAN statement; (b) a statement number; (c) data; (d) a continuation of a FORTRAN statement; (e) a mark for a continuation?

chapter 4

H (Hollerith), P, and G specifications- carriage control

4-1. the H (Hollerith) specification

The F, E, and I field specifications in FØRMAT statements provide for the reading and writing of *numbers only*. Quite often it is desirable to accompany the numerical information with some descriptive information, such as titles (IN-VENTØRY), column headings (NAME PAY,$), or units (INCHES). This can be done by using the *Hollerith* or *H specification*.

An example of a Hollerith specification is

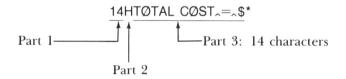

As shown in the example, a Hollerith specification consists of three parts. Proceeding from right to left, Part 3 contains the descriptive information that is to be printed: TØTAL CØST∧=∧$; Part 2 is the letter H; and Part 1 is an integer number equal to the total number of alphameric and special characters (including blanks) that form Part 3. There are no blanks on either side of the

---

* In Article 1-1 it was stated that, in the text of this book, the symbol ∧ shall be used to represent a blank space. However, on a program card or a data card a blank must be shown simply as a blank; do not attempt to punch ∧ on a card: it is not on the keyboard, anyway. Remember that a blank is a character.

letter H; if, say, three blanks had been inserted accidentally between H and TØTAL, as follows:

$$14H_{\wedge\wedge\wedge}TØTAL_{\wedge}CØST_{\wedge}=_{\wedge}\$$$

the computer would include *them* in the count of characters in Part 3, and, limited by the integer 14 in Part 1, would drop the three rightmost characters, $=_{\wedge}\$$, in Part 3. However, if the three blanks, as shown above, are desired in the printed output, Part 1 should be changed from 14 to 17.

A complete command to the computer to produce a printout of

$$TØTAL_{\wedge}CØST_{\wedge}=_{\wedge}\$$$

may be written as follows:

```
      WRITE(6,10)
10    FØRMAT(1X,14HTØTAL.CØST.=.$)
```

Note that the WRITE statement contains no list of variable names because there are no corresponding data to be fetched from the memory; the information to be printed is all contained in the H specification of the FØRMAT statement. Thus the carriage control signal 1X will advance the sheet one line, and the printer will print the 14 characters and blank spaces of

$$TØTAL_{\wedge}CØST_{\wedge}=_{\wedge}\$$$

If it is desired to follow the $ sign with a figure of, say, 145.67, the program may be modified as follows:

```
      C = 145.67
      WRITE(6,11)C
11    FØRMAT(1X,14HTØTAL.CØST.=.$,F6.2)
```

whereupon the computer will print

$$TØTAL_{\wedge}CØST_{\wedge}=_{\wedge}\$145.67$$

It can be seen that Hollerith and other specifications may be mixed in a FØRMAT statement. As with other specifications, commas help to set specifications apart, but are not mandatory.

A minor inconvenience of the Hollerith specification is the necessity of counting exactly all the characters and blanks in Part 3 to the right of H. With FORTRAN IV compilers of the IBM System/360 this counting may be eliminated by enclosing all the characters of Part 3 within two quotation marks, or apostrophes, and dropping the H and preceding integer number altogether. Thus, either specification,

6HRADIUS   or   'RADIUS'

will produce RADIUS in the printout.

Examples of the use of the Hollerith specification are presented below.

example 4-1.

1	2	3	4	5	6		7	8	9	10	11	12	13	14	15	16	17	18	19	20	21	22	23	24	25	26	27	28	29	30	31	32	33	34	35	36	37	38
							W	R	I	T	E	(	6	,	1	)																						
				1			F	Ø	R	M	A	T	(	1	X	,	1	7	H	F	E	B	R	U	A	R	Y		2	7	,		1	9	7	9	)

Figure 4-1

The carriage control signal 1X will advance the sheet one line, and the printer, beginning at the left edge of the sheet, will print the 17 characters and blank spaces of

FEBRUARY‿27,‿1979

example 4-2. The program of Fig. 4-1 can also be written as shown in Fig. 4-2.

1	2	3	4	5	6		7	8	9	10	11	12	13	14	15	16	17	18	19	20	21	22	23	24	25	26	27	28	29	30	31	32	33	34	35	36	37	38
							W	R	I	T	E	(	6	,	2	)																						
				2			F	Ø	R	M	A	T	(	1	X	,	'	F	E	B	R	U	A	R	Y		2	7	,		1	9	7	9	'	)	

Figure 4-2

The printout will be the same as in Example 4-1.

example 4-3. Assume the following values to be in storage locations R (for radius) and A (for area):

Storage location	R	A
Value	5.0	78.5

To obtain a printout of these values in one line, with their titles and units, we may write the program shown in Fig. 4-3.

```
FORTRAN STATEMENT
  1 2 3 4 5 6 7 8 9 10 11 12 13 14 15 16 17 18 19 20 21 22 23 24 25 26 27 28 29 30 31 32 33 34 35 36 37 38 39 40
            W R I T E ( 6 , 3 ) R , A
        3   F Ø R M A T ( 1 X , 9 H R A D I U S   =   , F 3 . 1 , 5 H   I N . ,

 41 42 43 44 45 46 47 48 49 50 51 52 53 54 55 56 57 58 59 60 61 62 63 64 65 66 67 68 69 70
  , 3 X , 7 H A R E A   =   , F 4 . 1 , 7 H   S Q . I N . )
```

Figure 4-3

1X will advance the sheet one line; then the printer will print, in succession, the 9 characters |RADIUS∧=∧|, the value of R in 3 spaces, the 5 characters |∧IN.,|, 3 blanks, the 7 characters |AREA∧=∧|, the value of A in 4 spaces, and the 7 characters |∧SQ.IN.|, as shown below:

```
RADIUS∧=∧5.0∧IN.,∧∧∧AREA∧=∧78.5∧SQ.IN.  ←——— Printout
   9H      F3.1  5H  3X    7H    F4.1    7H  ←——— Specifications
```

Note the blank spaces preceding IN. and SQ. IN.; these spaces separate the values from the units that follow them.

The Hollerith specification may also be used on input. Let us suppose that a printout of a monthly inventory of goods must begin with the title

INVENTØRY∧FØR

followed by the name of the month to the right of the title.

We could write a command to print the title for the month of January in one of two ways:

```
WRITE(6,4)
4 FØRMAT(1X,21HINVENTØRY∧FØR∧JANUARY)
```

or

```
WRITE(6,5)
5 FØRMAT(1X,'INVENTØRY˄FØR˄JANUARY')
```

But doing it this way, we would need twelve different programs, one for each month in the year, because of the difference in the FØRMAT statement. We can get by with a single program if, instead of writing a particular specification (such as 21HINVENTØRY˄FØR˄JANUARY), we make the machine READ the name of a month together with the inventory records for that month. We accomplish the reading and storing of the particular name by combining a READ statement (without a list), a *dummy* Hollerith specification in the associated FØR-MAT statement, and a data card punched with the particular name, as shown below:

```
READ(5,7)
7 FØRMAT(1X,23HDDDDDDDDDDDDDDDDDDDDDDD)
```

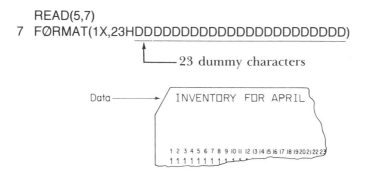

Obeying the READ command, the machine will read the data card in conjunction with FØRMAT 7: the first specification, 1X, will make it ignore the first column on the card; the second specification, 23HDD . . . , will make it replace the 23 dummy characters DD . . . in the specification by the 19 characters of the title it finds in columns 2-20 on the data card (INVENTØRY FØR APRIL) and the following four blanks in columns 21-24 (to satisfy the demand for a total of 23 characters). As a result, Statement 7 will change from

```
7 FØRMAT(1X,23HDDDDDDDDDDDDDDDDDDDDDDD)
```

to

```
7 FØRMAT(1X,23HINVENTØRY˄FØR˄APRIL˄˄˄˄)
```

We have used 23 characters in the dummy specification because the longest name of a month is SEPTEMBER; therefore, the longest possible title is

INVENTØRYˬFØRˬSEPTEMBER

which has 23 characters, including blanks. To match this—and other—titles, there must be 23 dummy characters in the Hollerith specification; the dummy characters may be anything, even blanks, because eventually they will be replaced by the characters of a particular title.

Now, if we continue the program segment above with the statement

WRITE(6,7)

the computer, executing this command in accordance with the *changed* FØRMAT statement 7, will advance the sheet one line (since 1X, or blank, appearing first, is a carriage control signal), and will print, in spaces 1-19:

INVENTØRYˬFØRˬAPRIL

If the data card associated with the READ statement above had a 0 (zero) in the first column, as shown below,

and FØRMAT 7 remained in its original form, 1X would cause the machine to ignore the 0 in the first column, the dummy characters would be replaced as previously, and the printer would single-space and print in the same manner as for a card with a blank in the first column. But if FØRMAT 7 were changed to

FØRMAT(24HDDDDDDDDDDDDDDDDDDDDDDDD)
⌐24 D's

the machine would store the 0 together with the title, and would *double-space* the sheet before printing the title; we shall see in the next article that 0 is the carriage control signal for double-spacing the sheet.

The data card with the title for April should be placed in the data deck with, and ahead of, the inventory information for the month of April.

As stated earlier, the characters of the dummy specification may be anything. Thus FØRMAT 7 may be written

7   FØRMAT(1X,23H _____)
                      └─23 blanks

or

7   FØRMAT(1X,'ABCDEFGHIJKLMNOPQRSTUVW')
                   └─any 23 letters

Thus a single program, with each month's inventory data deck preceded by a corresponding title card, may be used to process and print inventory information throughout the year.

It may be added, as a warning, that if the program segment for reading and printing the title is written without 1X in the beginning of the FØRMAT statement, that is, as follows:

READ(5,8)

8   FØRMAT(23H _____)
                   └─23 spaces

WRITE(6,8)

and the title on the data card begins in the first column, as shown below,

the machine will store the title, but, in printing, will convert its first character, I, into a signal for single-spacing the sheet, will advance the sheet one line, and will print NVENTØRY˄FØR˄APRIL beginning at the left edge of the sheet.

For most compilers, the number of characters in a Hollerith specification may not exceed the number of characters which the printer can print on one line, namely, 132. If a Hollerith statement contains more than 132 characters, it should be broken up into units of 132 characters or less, each unit enclosed between apostrophes, and the units separated by slashes, followed by carriage control characters, as shown in the following program segment:

```
     WRITE(6,1)
   1 FØRMAT(1HO,'ALL MEN BY NATURE HAVE A DESIRE TØ KNØW.  A SIGN ØF TH
   1 IS IS THE JØY WE TAKE IN ØUR SENSES, FØR QUITE APART FRØM THEIR US
   2 EFULNESS WE '/1HO,'LØVE THEM FØR THEIR ØWN SAKE, AND THE SENSE ØF
   3 SIGHT ABØVE ALL.  FØR NØT ØNLY AS A HELP IN ACTIØN BUT ALSØ WHEN W
   4 E HAVE NØ INTENTIØN'/1HO,'  ØF ACTING WE VALUE ØUR SIGHT ABØVE ALMØ
   5 ST EVERYTHING ELSE.  THE REASØN FØR THIS IS THAT ØF ALL  THE SENSES
   6  SIGHT MAKES KNØWLEDGE MØS'/1HO,'T PØSSIBLE FØR US AND SHØWS US TH
   7 E MANY DIFFERENCES BETWEEN THINGS.'/1HO,75X,'ARISTØTLE')
```

The quotation above, containing 463 characters, will be printed on four double-spaced lines, the first three lines 132 characters long. The name of the author will appear on the fifth line, beginning in the 76th space.

natural apostrophes

If an alphameric statement that we wish to print contains natural apostrophes, we can write the specification for it in the H form, in the usual way:

$$21H'IT'S_\wedge TØM'S,'_\wedge HE_\wedge SAID$$

including every apostrophe and blank in the count of 21.

But if we try to enclose the statement in the Hollerith apostrophes, we must distinguish the natural apostrophes from the enclosing apostrophes; we accomplish this by doubling the natural apostrophes, as shown below:

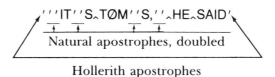

Natural apostrophes, doubled

Hollerith apostrophes

The doubled apostrophes are regarded as single characters, even though they occupy two spaces.

Either specification above, associated with a WRITE statement, will produce the same printout, namely:

$$'IT'S_\wedge TØM'S,'_\wedge HE_\wedge SAID$$

4-2   carriage control characters

As mentioned earlier, the printer always expects to receive a signal that will make it advance the sheet one or more lines. In Article 2-7 it was shown that

1X is a symbol for a blank space and that, coincidentally, 1X (that is, a "blank" character) is a signal for advancing the sheet one line, if 1X begins the Format statement for a printout. If 4X appears at the beginning of a FØRMAT statement, the printer divides it into 1X and 3X and treats 1X as the signal to advance the sheet one line; then, obeying 3X, it advances horizontally three spaces before printing on the line.

There are other signals that control the movement of the sheet in the printer. The characters that represent these signals, the effects of these signals, and the manner in which these signals are coded in FØRMAT statements, are tabulated below.

Carriage control character	Effect on carriage before printing	Format coding
∧*	Advances sheet one line	1X or 1H∧† or '∧'
0	Advances sheet two lines	1H0 or '0'
—	Advances sheet three lines	1H— or '—'
1	Advances sheet to next page	1H1 or '1'
+	Does not advance sheet	1H+ or '+'

It can be seen in the last column of the table that all control characters are written in a Hollerith form: the control character, in every case, is either preceded by 1H or enclosed in apostrophes; 1X is an equivalent representation of the blank specification 1H∧ or '∧'.

The effects of control characters are illustrated in the following examples.

example 4-4.   Assume that values 17.2, −6.4, and 10.3 are stored in locations A, B, C. To obtain a printout of A and B two lines below the last preceding line on the sheet and that of C on the next line and below B, we write the program shown in Fig. 4-4.

```
      WRITE(6,2)A,B
    2 FØRMAT(1H0,F6.2,3X,F6.2)
      WRITE(6,3)C
    3 FØRMAT(1H ,9X,F6.2)     or ( 10X,F6.2)
```

Figure 4-4

The printer will print

---

* See the footnote in Article 4-1.

(Last preceding line)

```
17.20       -6.40
            10.30
1 2 3 4 5 6 7 8 9 10 11 12 13 14 15
```

example 4-5. Assume that a value of D = −20.4 is to be printed on the same line with 10.30 above, in spaces 19-24; we write the program shown in Fig. 4-5.

						FORTRAN STATEMENT																						
1	2	3	4	5	6	7	8	9	10	11	12	13	14	15	16	17	18	19	20	21	22	23	24	25	26	27	28	29
						W	R	I	T	E	(	6	,	4	)	D												
				4		F	Ø	R	M	A	T	(	1	H	+	,	1	8	X	,	F	6	.	2	)			

Figure 4-5

The printout will be

```
10.30       -20.40
10 11 12 13 14 15 16 17 18 19 20 21 22 23 24
```

A carriage control specification is never shown at the beginning of a FØRMAT statement associated with a READ statement; if one is placed there, its effect will be the same as that of 1X, that is, it will make the card reader ignore (skip) the first space on a data card.

4-3. a complete program

To tie all the loose ends together, we shall write a complete program that will

1/ Present to the computer three data cards, each card punched with a student's number, his height in inches, and his weight in pounds.

2/ Command the computer to store the data for each student in memory locations N, H, W; these three locations will be used for every student, because storing the new data erases the old data.

3/ Print the information on each student in the table arranged as shown below.

(Last preceding line)

	↓ *Col. 12*	
	STUDENT STATISTICS	
↓ *Col. 1*	↓ *Col. 13*	↓ *Col. 30*
NUMBER	HEIGHT, IN.	WEIGHT, LB.
1	66.5	150.0
2	70.0	172.5
3	. . . .	. . . . .

To obtain a well-centered and balanced table in the printout it is always necessary to make a preliminary layout of the table on a coding sheet or a sheet of square-ruled paper and to establish accurately in which column each title or heading should begin and in which column the decimal points should be aligned. The results of such planning are shown in the table above: arrows pointing at the initial letters of the headings tell in which columns the headings should be started to obtain a well-balanced printout.

The program that will produce the printout of the student statistics appears in Fig. 4-6. Shown scattered through the program are control cards and *comment cards*. Comment cards are inserted into the program by the programmer to explain to a reader (and often to himself in the future) the various steps in his algorithm. Comment cards may and should be used liberally. A comment statement must always begin with the letter C in the first column; the computer, spotting that C, will ignore that statement in the execution of the program, but will list it in the printout.

Comment cards may not be included with the data cards; that is, no comment card may follow the $ENTRY control card. The word DATA must not appear on the data cards.

As can be seen from the program, the same FØRMAT statement may be used with several input/output statements, if the data on several cards are punched in identical fields. Also, all FØRMAT statements may be grouped together in the beginning or toward the end (before END) of the program. If the program of Fig. 4-6 is stripped of all control and comment cards, and if all its FØRMAT statements are placed in the beginning, it will take the form shown in Fig. 4-7.

The program of Fig. 4-6 and the program of Fig. 4-7 (if the latter is accompanied by the control and data cards shown in Fig. 4-6) will produce the same printout, as follows:

FORTRAN STATEMENT

```
$JOB            RD1     'WATFIV'                                    Second control card*
C   BOGUSLAVSKY   STUDENT STATISTICS*
C   PRINT TITLES
      WRITE(6,1)
    1 FORMAT(1HO,-'STUDENT STATISTICS')
      WRITE(6,2)
    2 FORMAT(1HO,-'NUMBER',-'6X,'HEIGHT,IN.',-6X,'WEIGHT,LB.')
C   STORE DATA    FIRST CARD
      STORE DATA
    3 FORMAT(I5,F6.-)
C   FIELDS ABOVE MUST MATCH THOSE ON DATA CARD/NOW PRINT STORED DATA
      WRITE(6,4)
    4 FORMAT(1HO,3X,F5.-,2X,F5.-,F5.-)  FROM DATA CARD/RE-USE FORMAT 3
C   FIRST LINE PRINTED ONLY IN CARRIAGE CONTROL/STORE SECOND CARD
      READ(5,5)
    5 FORMAT(4X,I1,-,I1,-,F5.-)  DIFFER IN STORE CARD 3
C   FORMATS 4 AND 5 STORE CARD 3
      READ(5,3)
      WRITE(6,5)
      STOP
      END
$ENTRY                                                             Control card
1     66.5     50.0                                        ⎫
2     70.0     72.5                                        ⎬ Data cards
3     71.5     81.5                                        ⎭
```

* See Figure 3-6

Figure 4-6

58

FORTRAN STATEMENT

```
    1  FØRMAT(1HØ,1X,'STUDENT STATISTICS')
    2  FØRMAT(1HØ,'NUMBER',6X,'HEIGHT, IN.',6X,'WEIGHT, LB.')
    3  FØRMAT(I5,2(3X,F6.1))
    4  FØRMAT(1HØ,3X,'1',1X,F5.1,2X,F5.1)
    5  FØRMAT(4X,I1,1X,F5.1,2X,F5.1)
       WRITE(6,1)
       WRITE(6,2)
       READ(5,3)N,H,W
       WRITE(6,4)N,H,W
       READ(5,3)N,H,W
       WRITE(6,5)N,H,W
       READ(5,3)N,H,W
       WRITE(6,5)N,H,W
       STØP
       END
```

Figure 4-7

59

$ENTRY		
STUDENT STATISTICS		
NUMBER	HEIGHT, IN.	WEIGHT, LB.
1	66.5	150.0
2	70.0	172.5
3	71.5	181.5

As shown in Fig. 4-6, the execution of a READ statement causes the data card read during the execution to be removed, and the next data card to be exposed, ready for the execution of the next READ statement.

You must have observed that the programs of Figs. 4-6 and 4-7 are filled with repetitions of READ and WRITE statements, a pair of them for every data card. This may have led you to conclude that a similar program for 100— or 15,000—students would be of monstrous size. You would be eminently correct if we wrote the program for 15,000 students in the same manner as we wrote it for three students. The glory of the computer is that it is designed to handle any number of identical operations—millions of them—with programs that are not any longer—if not shorter—than the program of Fig. 4-7. We shall learn how to write such programs later in the book.

4-4. debugging

We have now studied one complete program and have probably submitted one or two programs to the computer. In all likelihood your programs have returned to you neatly *listed*—that is, printed out—but without any results following the program on the sheet, or with results liberally sprinkled with ***** or UUUUU. This would mean that your programs had not run. In such cases a printout would display, in addition to your program, one or more diagnostics—error messages—pointing out to you the sins that you had committed in writing the program.

If your instructor sees your printout before you do, he may use his red pen to point out to you where you have made the errors and to suggest corrections. On the other hand, he may prefer to let *you* find your errors. You will remember your mistakes better—and avoid them in the future—if you find them yourself. So, if you are on your own, study the diagnostics and, with their help, try to find the errors in your program and then correct them.

The procedure of finding and correcting errors is called *debugging* the program. Having debugged the program to your satisfaction, proceed to the nearest keypunch, and punch new cards to replace the ones that have errors (a punched card cannot be corrected). Throw away the bad cards, insert the newly punched cards, and submit the repaired deck to the card reader for another run.

To get credit for a program, you must run and rerun it, until the desired results appear in the printout below the program.

The printout never shows the data submitted with the program. This does not mean that data cards have no errors; on the contrary, the trouble is often there, often due to the mismatching of the FØRMAT specifications and the data fields.

A sure way to successful programs or, at least, to fewer errors and the correspondingly reduced annoyance of debugging, is to use logic, common sense, and care in writing a program. After every statement you write, ask yourself whether the computer can decipher it or execute it. For example, do not ask the computer to find A = B + C, if you have not given it the values of B and C. Do not ask the computer to READ B, if you have not got a data card with the value of B on it. Execute your statements with a pencil and paper as you write them, and discover whether *you* can execute them, and, if you can, whether the result of your execution makes sense.

4-5. the P, or scale, specification

Occasionally it may be desired that the data punched on a card in grams (262.2), be stored in the memory in kilograms (0.262); or that a stored fractional value (0.17) be printed out in percent (17.); or that a number stored in the exponential form, that is, as a fraction between 0.0 and 1.0 times a power of 10 (0.123E+02), be printed out in *scientific notation*, that is, as a number between 1.0 and 10.0 times a power of 10 (1.23E+01).

The first two transformations described above involve real numbers in the F form; in the first example the transformation is effected by dividing 262.2 by 10^3; in the second, by multiplying 0.17 by 10^2. The third example has to do with a real number in the E form; in this example the number changes its form but not its magnitude.

The mathematical relationship between the external values (data or printed output) and the internal (stored) values of F numbers is given by equation (4-1):

$$\text{EXTERNAL VALUE} = \text{INTERNAL VALUE} * 10.0^s \qquad (4\text{-}1)$$

where   EXTERNAL VALUE is a value punched on a data card or printed on a sheet,
INTERNAL VALUE is a value stored in the memory of the computer,
10^s is the scale factor which transforms the internal value into the external value, or vice versa.

In FORTRAN the transformation of an F number is accomplished by writing a *P*, or *scale*, specification in front of the F specification which describes the number to be stored or printed. The general form of a P specification is:

$$sP$$

where s is the exponent of the scale factor 10.0^s in Equation (4-1) and P is the letter identifying the P specification. If the internal value is smaller than the external value, s is positive.

example 4-6. The number 145.1 is punched in the first five spaces on a data card. It is desired (1) to store 145.1 as 1.451 and (2) to obtain the following printout:

ʌ1.451ʌ14.51ʌ14.51ʌ0.01451ʌ1.451

The desired results will be produced by the following program:

```
        READ(5,1) A
    1   FØRMAT (2PF5.1)
        WRITE(6,2) A,A,A,A,A
    2   FØRMAT (1H0,F6.3,1P2F6.2,−2PF8.5,0PF6.3)
        STØP
```

Note that storing 145.1 at A as 1.451 requires sP = 2P in front of F5.1 in the first FØRMAT; also that, on output, the first A, which is to be printed as 1.451, requires no P specification in front of F6.3; that the next two A's, both of which are to appear as 14.51 and which are described by 2F6.2, require 1P (not P) in front of the specification; that the fourth A, to be printed as 0.01451, has its specification F8.5 preceded by −2P; and that the fifth A, which, like the first A, is to be printed 1.451, requires 0P in front of F6.3: 0P is necessary because a P specification attached to an F specification applies automatically to all succeeding F (and E) specifications, until it is abrogated by a subsequent P specification.

With E numbers the P specification works only on output; it is inoperative on input.

When an sP specification is written in front of an E specification which describes an E number to be printed, the mantissa (decimal fraction) of the stored number is multiplied by 10^s and, simultaneously, its characteristic (exponent) is reduced by s; this changes the appearance of the number but leaves its magnitude unchanged.

As with F numbers, a P specification written in front of an E specification applies automatically to succeeding E specifications. Moreover, if an output FØRMAT statement contains a mixture of F and E specifications, a P specification in front of any one of these specifications applies automatically to all succeeding F and E specifications until it is abrogated by a new P specification. If an input

FØRMAT statement contains a mixture of F and E specifications, a P specification affects only the succeeding F specifications, until it is abrogated by another P specification; the E specifications are not affected.

The P specification may not be used with the I specifications.

example 4-7. The numbers 145.1 and −0.987E−03 are punched on a data card. It is required that 145.1 be stored as 1.451 and that the following printout be produced:

∧1.451∧−0.987E−03∧14.51∧−0.00987E−01∧0.01451∧−987.E−06

The following program and data will do it.

```
        READ(5,1) A,B
    1   FØRMAT(2PF5.1,E11.3)
        WRITE(6,2) A,B,A,B,A,B
    2   FØRMAT(1H0,F6.3,E11.3,1PF6.2,−2PE13.5,F8.5,3PE10.0)
        STØP
145.1∧−0.987E−03   ← Data
```

Note that in FØRMAT 1 the specification 2P will not affect the specification E11.3; however, in FØRMAT 2 the specification −2P will affect both E13.5 and the following F8.5; also note that in the specifications −2PE13.5 and 3PE10.0 the fields have changed, reflecting the changes in the mantissas; similarly, in Examples 4-6 and 4-7, the F fields have changed to fit the decimal digits.

4-6. the G specification

The G specification is a generalized specification that makes it possible to store and print real and integer values without regard for their type. The form of the specification is Gw.d, where G describes the type and w is the width of the field of the value; on input, .d is the number of digits to the right of the decimal point: if the value is an integer, the .d is ignored; on output, .d is the number of digits in the printed value. In many ways, the G specification is like the E specification.

The .d in the G specification should normally be made at least equal to the number of significant digits in the value, and the w should at least be equal to d + 7. For example, the G specification for -17.25 should be G11.4, because it may be printed as -0.1725E 02. The same specification may be used on input:

it makes no difference whether the value is punched in the F form or E form in the 11-space field.

A special feature of the G specification on output is that it makes a real number appear in the E form if it is less than 0.1 or equal to or greater than 10^d; and in the F form if it is less than 10^d, down to 0.1. A number in the F form is always printed with 4 blanks between it and the right edge of the field; the blanks are intended for the exponent, such as E 02, which is not printed. For example, 11. has two significant digits: therefore it should be described by G9.2; 11. lies between 0.1 and 10^2; therefore it will be printed in the F form, in a field of 9 spaces, with 4 blanks on its right, as follows: ∧∧11.∧∧∧∧.

Now 110. also has two significant digits: therefore it may also be properly described by G9.2. But 110. is greater than 10^2; therefore it will be printed in the E form, as follows: ∧0.11E∧03.

If 11. and 110. are described, on output, by G13.6, so that the range of the F numbers is increased to 10^6, both numbers will be printed in the F form, as follows: 11. as ∧∧11.0000∧∧∧∧ and 110. as ∧∧110.000∧∧∧∧. Note that the .d of 6 makes the printer continue with zeros after the significant digits until the total count of digits is 6.

The integer values are printed right-justified in the specified field without any regard for d in the specification.

Even though the G specification applies indiscriminately to both integer and real values, it is still important for the names selected for the values on a data card to be in the matching mode.

example 4-8. Make the computer use the G specifications to store and print the following four values:

$$9 \qquad .09 \qquad 9. \qquad 90.$$

Show the printout.

Program:

```
      READ(5,1) K,A,B,C
  1   FØRMAT(4G4.2)
      WRITE(6,2) K,A,B,C
  2   FØRMAT(1H0,4G8.1)
      STØP
```

Printout:

∧∧∧∧∧∧∧9∧0.9E-01∧∧9.∧∧∧∧∧0.9E∧02

questions and problems

4-1/ What do the following specifications mean when they begin a FØRMAT statement on output?

(a) |1H1|; (b) |1X|; (c) |1H∧| ; (d) |1H0| ; (e) |1H+|; (f) |1H-|

4-2/ What will the following specification do on the printout?

11X,22HBATØN∧RØUGE,∧LØUISIANA

4-3/ What will the following specification do on the printout?

1H0,5X,'PI∧ = ∧3.1416'

4-4/ Write the statements that will cause the following information to be printed as Hollerith characters on the indicated lines. For each WRITE statement, give two single-line FØRMAT statements, one for each version of the H specification.

(a)	Line 1:	CØMPUTER PRØGRAMMING
(b)	Line 1:	A
	Line 2:	B
	Line 3:	C
(c)	Line 1:	+ 5.26
	Line 2:	− 17.42
	Line 3:	− 12.16

Arrange the decimal points in one vertical column.

4-5/ Write a program that will produce an identical copy of the laboratory tabulation shown below.

(Last preceding line)

	WEIGHT CHANGES, GRAMS		
	SAMPLE A	SAMPLE B	SAMPLE C
TEST 1	5.26	2.17	−1.05
TEST 2	4.17	−0.05	0.62
TEST 3	−2.47	−1.59	1.12

Submit the numerical data to the computer on three data cards.

4-6/ Write a bank statement program that will do the following:

(a) Store positive deposits and negative withdrawals 872.65, −170.22, −416.23, 109.50, −6.54, −12.24, in locations P, Q, R, S, T, U.

(b) Print, on a line two spaces down, two headings, DEPØSITS,ᴧ$, beginning in the 13th column, and WITHDRAWALS,ᴧ$, beginning in the 29th column.

(c) Print, on a line two spaces down, the first deposit and the first withdrawal, with the decimal points in the 18th and 36th columns.

(d) Print, single-spaced, the rest of the deposits and withdrawals.

If different executable statements in the program require the same FØRMAT specifications for their execution, write *one* FØRMAT statement for all these statements and refer to its number in all of them.

4-7/ The following table shows, in the first column, the names of four variables, in the second column, their given values, in the third column, their stored values, and, in the fourth column, their printed values.

Variable	Given value	Stored value	Printed value
P	−12.345	−1234.50	−123450.
N	6	6	6
Q	0.8765	87.65	87.65
R	0.56789E+02	0.56789E+02	567.89E−01

(a) Write the READ and FØRMAT statements which will store the given values in the form shown in the third column of the table.

(b) Write the WRITE and FØRMAT statements which will print the names of the variables, each name followed by the equals sign and the corresponding value shown in the fourth column of the table.

4-8/ Make the computer use the G specifications to store and print the following six values:

0.055   0.55   5.5   55.   550.   55

chapter 5

formats
—T specification
—unformatted input/output

5-1. multiple-record formats

Data processed by a computer consist of records. A *record* is defined as the information on *one* input card, or on *one* output card, or on *one* printed line of the output. As has been shown in the preceding examples, a set of input data is usually punched on more than one card; it is usually necessary to punch output on several cards or to print it on several lines.

We can send the data punched on several input cards into the memory in the usual way by writing, for each card, a READ statement that lists the variables corresponding to the values on the card, and accompanying the READ statement with a FØRMAT statement that describes the types and locations of the values on the card. For example, if we wanted to read and store the values of three variables, A, B, and C, and the values for A and B were punched on one card and the value for C on the second card, we could write the set of statements shown in Fig. 5-1.

1	2	3	4	5	6		7	8	9	10	11	12	13	14	15	16	17	18	19	20	21	22	23	24	25	26	27	28
							R	E	A	D	(	5	,	3	)	A	,	B										
							R	E	A	D	(	5	,	4	)	C												
		3					F	Ø	R	M	A	T	(	F	4	.	0	,	F	6	.	2	)					
		4					F	Ø	R	M	A	T	(	F	5	.	2	)										

The header row above the column numbers reads: FORTRAN STATEMENT

Figure 5-1

But it can be seen that this method of reading-in multiple records is cumbersome; it involves repetition of the READ and FØRMAT statements. The input operation can be reduced to a single READ statement, accompanied by a single FØRMAT statement, by the use of a *slash* (/) in the FØRMAT statement. Thus the three variables of the example above can be read into the memory by the pair of statements shown in Fig. 5-2.

1	2	3	4	5	6	7	8	9	10	11	12	13	14	15	16	17	18	19	20	21	22	23	24	25	26	27	28
																			FORTRAN STATEMENT								
						R	E	A	D	(	5	,	7	)	A	,	B	,	C								
					7	F	Ø	R	M	A	T	(	F	4	.	0	,	F	6	.	2	/	F	5	.	2	)

Figure 5-2

The function of the slash is (a) to indicate the end of the specifications applicable to the numbers punched on the first record, that is, on the first data card, (b) to produce a signal that removes the first card, and (c) to instruct the card scanner to go to the left end of the next card. Let us assume that the two data cards submitted with the program sequence in the example above are each punched with five numbers; specifications F4.0 and F6.2 will instruct the card reader to take the values of A and B from columns 1-4 and 5-10 on the first card; the slash will cause the reader to disregard the remaining three numbers on the card and to return to the left end of the card deck, while the first card is being removed; and the specification F5.2 will make the reader take the value of C from columns 1-5 on the second card. The closing parenthesis of the FØRMAT statement will act as a slash, causing the second card, with the four remaining numbers, to be removed and the reader to return to its leftmost reading position.

The preceding explanation takes care of the data that exceed the 80-space capacity of a single data card, that is, of the data that require continuation cards. For every continuation data card there must be a slash in the FØRMAT statement. Such slashes divide the specifications into groups, each group describing the values on the corresponding single card in the data deck.

In the example above, specifications precede and follow the slash; this is the usual case. Occasionally, however, slashes appear next to the opening or closing parenthesis, or follow one another, without intervening specifications. The effects of such slashes are explained in the next paragraph.

A READ operation involves two parallel processes: the computer reads the FØRMAT statement, and the card reader, instructed by the computer, reads cards in the data deck. In general, as the computer passes through a FØRMAT statement, it encounters one or more slashes (or no slashes) and eventually the closing parenthesis, which it regards as a slash. The data deck must have a card for every slash, including the closing parenthesis. If the computer finds

N specifications before a slash, it instructs the card reader to read N values on the card corresponding to the slash, to remove the card, and to reset to the left end of the next card. If the computer finds no specifications before a slash, it instructs the card reader to remove the corresponding card without reading it. Thus if the computer encounters K slashes (including the closing parenthesis) in a FØRMAT statement, the card reader inspects and removes K data cards, but reads values only on the cards corresponding to the slashes preceded by specifications.

If a FØRMAT statement contains a slash next to the closing parenthesis, the data deck must have a card for the last slash and *a card for the closing parenthesis,* even though the computer will instruct the card reader to ignore the last card for which there are no specifications between the last slash and the closing parenthesis. If the card reader does not find the card that it wants to ignore, it makes the computer declare an error.† To prevent the error message the programmer must include the necessary card—even a blank card—in the data deck or, more simply, should not put a slash before the closing parenthesis, unless the FØRMAT statement is to be reused in executing the READ command (see Article 5-2).

Consider the following example:

```
   READ(5,8) A, B, C
 8 FØRMAT(/F4.0/F3.0///3X,F6.1)
```

Encountering the first slash (the one next to the left parenthesis), the reader ignores the first card in the data deck; the card is removed, and the reader remains at the left edge, ready to scan the second card. On the second card it reads the value of A in columns 1-4. The second slash stops further reading, removes the second card, and resets the reader to the left edge of the third card. On the third card the reader picks up the value of B in columns 1-3. The third slash removes the third card and resets the reader to scan the fourth card. The fourth and fifth slashes, without specifications preceding them, cause the reader to ignore the fourth and fifth cards, and these cards are removed, the reader remaining at the left edge. Scanning the sixth card, the reader skips the first three columns (3X) and reads the value of C in columns 4-9. The closing parenthesis removes the sixth card and sends the reader to its leftmost position.

To summarize, the reader expects to see a data card for every slash (and the closing parenthesis) in a FØRMAT statement, but ignores every card for which there are no specifications before the corresponding slash.

Just as slashes can make the card reader skip data cards, they can also

---

† If it operates with the G compiler. The WATFIV compiler does not generate an error message and prints the results, but on a *new* page.

make the output unit punch results on separate cards, or print them on separate lines on a sheet, or skip cards and lines. The principle is the same as on the input: a slash without a preceding specification causes the output unit (puncher or printer) to remain in its leftmost position and a card to be skipped (which is removed unpunched) or the printout sheet to advance one line.

The manner in which slashes function in output statements is illustrated in the following example. In this example, the symbol 1X, which precedes every group of specifications, is a carriage control signal that causes the printed sheet to advance one line, as explained in Article 2-7, before the values corresponding to the specifications are printed.

Assume that the following values are stored in the memory:

$$A = 5.22 \qquad B = 4.15 \qquad K = 15 \qquad L = 200$$

$$\text{WRITE(6,9) K, A, L, B}$$
$$9 \quad \text{FØRMAT(/1X,I5,F6.2///1X,I5/1X,F8.3/)}$$

The printer, encountering the first slash, remains at the left edge of the sheet and advances the sheet one line, thus causing the first line of the printout to remain blank. The first signal 1X causes the sheet to advance another line, and the printer prints on the second line 15 (= K) in spaces 4-5 (two characters, right-justified, in a field of five spaces) and 5.22 (= A) in spaces 8-11 (four characters, right-justified, in a field of six spaces). The second slash causes the printer to stop and return to the left edge of the sheet. The third and fourth slashes advance the sheet two lines, leaving the third and fourth lines blank. The second 1X advances the sheet to the fifth line, and the printer prints on it 200 (= L) in spaces 3-5. The fifth slash returns the printer to the left edge. The last 1X brings up the sixth line, and the printer prints 4.150 (= B) in spaces 4-8. The sixth (last) slash returns the printer to the left end. The closing parenthesis, acting as a slash without a specification (in effect, acting as the seventh slash), advances the sheet one line and places the seventh line before the printer.† If the FØRMAT of the next WRITE statement begins with 1X, the seventh line will remain blank.

We may summarize the rules for slashes on output as follows:

1/ Every slash makes the printer stop printing on a line and return to the left edge of the sheet; the closing parenthesis acts as a slash.

2/ A slash that stops printing on a line *does not make the sheet advance one line.*

3/ A slash makes the sheet advance one line if it follows an opening

---

† Ending a WRITE FØRMAT statement with a slash before the closing parenthesis does not generate an error message similar to the one generated by the slash next to the closing parenthesis in a READ FØRMAT statement, because, on a printout, there is always the next line.

parenthesis or another slash, *without a specification between them,* as shown
in the three examples below:

Example 1	Example 2	Example 3

$$(_\uparrow \overset{*}{/}CCS, \ldots F4.1 \qquad /_\uparrow \overset{*}{/}_\uparrow \overset{*}{/}CCS, \ldots F4.1/_\uparrow^{*})$$

in which arrows point to the specificationless spaces between a slash
and a parenthesis or between slashes, and the asterisks mark the
slashes and the parenthesis that make the sheet advance one line.
The sheet moves one line because a slash (or the closing parenthesis)
without a preceding specification serves notice that the line which it
terminates is to remain blank. Since the signal that causes the sheet
to advance one line is 1X, one may better understand the operation
of the specificationless slash (or the closing parenthesis) if, in the
examples above, one imagines 1X inserted at every arrow.

4/   As shown in the examples above, *a carriage control specification (CCS)
     must follow every slash, unless the slash is followed by another slash or the
     closing parenthesis; in the latter cases the computer fills the void between the
     slashes with 1X.*

Several consecutive slashes, say 5, may be shown in a Format statement
in the explicit form:

FØRMAT (/////1X,F5.2)

or in a condensed form:

FØRMAT (5 (/),1X,F5.2)

In the condensed form, a single slash, enclosed in parentheses, is preceded
by the repetition number.

As stated in Article 2-3, a comma before the closing parenthesis is forbidden. A comma before the slash next to the closing parenthesis has no effect,
but is superfluous.

5-2.   limited and extended formats

Format specifications enable the computer to guide an input/output unit
to the correct locations of the values on the records: for instance, they guide
the card reader to the right cards and to the right locations of the data on

the cards, or they show the printer where to print results on the printout sheet.

We have learned in the preceding article that an input/output unit works on a record (a card or a line of printout) until the computer, scanning a Format statement, encounters either a slash or the final closing parenthesis; when either event occurs, the input/output unit stops working on the record and returns to its leftmost position.

In the examples of the preceding article there was exact correspondence between the variables and the specifications: for every variable in the READ/ WRITE list there was a matching specification in the associated FØRMAT statement. Cases arise, however, when specifications outnumber variables; and vice versa. What then?

In the former case, the answer is simple: the computer ignores superfluous specifications, just as the card reader ignores superfluous data. But in the latter case, the case of an insufficient or *limited FØRMAT*, the action is much more complex; the computer does not ignore the excessive variables: it *extends* the limited FØRMAT statement by rescanning a part, or all, of it until it obtains a specification for every variable in the list. The specifications picked up on rescanning apply to the variables *on new records*, because the rescanning begins only after the computer has gone through the closing parenthesis of the FØRMAT statement and has thereby sent the input/output unit to a new record.

The following paragraphs describe how the computer extends a limited FØRMAT statement and to what new records it sends the input/output unit.

When the number of variables in a READ/WRITE statement exceeds the number of field specifications in the associated FØRMAT statement, the computer, having made one pass through the available specifications, returns for additional specifications to the beginning of the FØRMAT statement, that is, to the opening parenthesis at the left end of the statement, *unless the statement contains within it pairs of inner parentheses.* In the latter case, the computer returns to the *rightmost opening* parenthesis in the statement. If an opening parenthesis is preceded by a repeat constant, e.g., 2 (I2,I3), the condensed specification is expanded, *within the parentheses,* e.g., (I2,I3,I2,I3); the computer returns to the opening parenthesis of this expansion only if it happens to be rightmost in the statement. The computer keeps on returning to the rightmost opening parenthesis (from the right end of the FØRMAT statement) until all the variables in the READ/WRITE statement have been matched with the specifications *in number and type. On its first pass* through the FØRMAT statement the computer makes a note of the opening parenthesis to which it must return, but otherwise ignores it.

If the computer encounters a slash between field specifications in a limited FØRMAT statement, it sends the input/output unit to its leftmost position; the computer continues to scan the post-slash specifications; as the input/output unit receives them, it resets to a new record and applies the post-slash specifications to the new record.

As stated earlier, FØRMAT specifications for input differ from those for output in one respect: WRITE FØRMAT statements always begin with a carriage control specification (CCS) that regulates the vertical movement of the printed sheet; in addition, if the statement contains an inner opening parenthesis to which the computer returns for additional specifications, this inner opening parenthesis must be followed by a CCS, and a slash must precede the CCS, on either side of the return parenthesis (the position of the slash will, naturally, affect the printout). The CCS at the point of return is necessary because the printer, having reset to its leftmost position, is ready to type a new line and needs a control signal to determine its location. The absence of a slash would make the computer, on its first pass through the statement, interpret the inner CCS as a Hollerith character to be printed and not as a carriage control specification.

The travels of the computer in search of specifications are shown diagrammatically in Fig. 5-3.

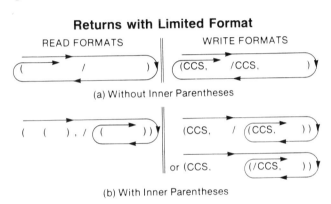

Returns with Limited Format

READ FORMATS   WRITE FORMATS

(a) Without Inner Parentheses

(b) With Inner Parentheses

Figure 5-3.

Examples of returns and equivalent extended FØRMAT statements are given below.

READ FØRMATS:

(a)   (F6.2,I3,I5)   Limited

     Return to

= (F6.2,I3,I5/F6.2,I3,I5/F6.2, . . .)   Extended

     Match

(b)   (F6.2, (I3,I5))   Limited

     Return to

= (F6.2,I3,I5/I3,I5/I3,I5. . . .)   Extended

(c)   ((F6.2, (I3,I5))) = (F6.2,I3,I5)   Same as (a)

Match (arrow from F6.2 into (I3,I5)); Return to

(d)   (F6.2,2(I3,I5))   Limited

= (F6.2, (I3,I5,I3,I5))   Expanded

Match; Return to

= (F6.2,I3,I5,I3,I5/I3,I5,I3,I5/I3, . . .)   Extended

(e)   ((F6.2,2(I3,I5)))   Limited

= ((F6.2, (I3,I5,I3,I5)))   Expanded

Match; Return to

= (F6.2,I3,I5,I3,I5/F6.2,I3,I5,I3, . . .)   Extended

WRITE FØRMATS:

(f)   ((1H0,F6.2,2(I3,I5)))   Limited

= ((1H0,F6.2, (I3,I5,I3,I5)))   Expanded

Match; Return to

= (1H0,F6.2,I3,I5,I3,I5/1H0,F6.2,I3, . . .)   Extended

(g)   (1H0,F6.2,2(I3,I5)/(1H0,2(I3,I5)))

= (1H0,F6.2, (I3,I5,I3,I5)/(1H0, (I3,I5,I3,I5)))   Expanded

Match; Return to

= (1H0,F6.2,I3,I5,I3,I5/1H0,I3,I5,I3,I5/1H0,I3,I5, . . .) Extended

An incorrect way to write a WRITE FØRMAT statement is:

$$\begin{array}{c} \overline{|\text{Match}/} \\ \downarrow \\ (1\text{H}0,\text{F}6.2,2(\text{I}3, \ \text{I}5)) \\ \Big/ \overline{\text{Return to}} \end{array}$$

because there is no control character at the point of return; the computer will convert the first space of I3 into a single-space carriage control character and will print the value corresponding to I3 in the two-space field.

The following WRITE FØRMAT:

(2 (1H0,F6.2,I3))

is also in error, because it is equivalent to

((1H0,F6.2,I3,1H0,F6.2,I3))

and the second 1H0, not preceded by a slash, will be interpreted as a Hollerith specification for printing 0 (zero) and not as a control signal.

Thus we can formulate the following rules for the limited FØRMAT statements:

READ FØRMAT Statements: When the computer, on reading a limited FØRMAT statement, encounters a slash or the final closing parenthesis, it causes the card reader to stop reading a card, to remove it, and to return to its leftmost position. Reading statements with slashes, the computer goes through the slashes to supply the specifications for each new card exposed by a slash. Having encountered the closing parenthesis, the computer rescans the FØRMAT statement from the return point established as described above. If a statement has a slash immediately before the closing parenthesis, the computer, finding no specifications after the last slash, instructs the card reader to ignore the data card corresponding to the missing specifications; *the card must be in the deck for the card reader to ignore,* otherwise the computer declares an error. When the computer rescans a FØRMAT statement without slashes, it applies each set of the rescanned specifications to a new card.

WRITE FØRMAT Statements: When the computer, on reading a limited FØRMAT statement, encounters a slash or the final closing parenthesis, it sends the printer to its leftmost position. The computer always completes scanning the FØRMAT statement before it returns to a point established as described above. The first specification after every slash must be a carriage control specification; if a control character is not present, the computer will convert the first space of the first specification after the slash into 1X, and the printer will advance the sheet one line and print the value corresponding to the abbreviated specification in the shortened field, occasionally truncating the leftmost digit of the value.

The printout sheet may be advanced, without printing, by the following simple sequences:

ADVANCE	SEQUENCE
One line	WRITE (6,1) 1　FØRMAT (1X) or (1H⌃)
Two lines	WRITE (6,2) 2　FØRMAT (1H0) or (/)
Three lines	WRITE (6,3) 3　FØRMAT (1H–) or (//)
To the new page	WRITE (6,4) 4　FØRMAT (1H1)

The following sequence is invalid:

WRITE (6,5)
5　FØRMAT ( )

The effects of FØRMATS with limited specifications and slashes on the card reader and the printer are illustrated in the following examples.

example 5-1.

READ (5,1) A, B, C
1　FØRMAT (F6.2)

Only one field specification is shown for the three variables in the list; therefore, the computer passes through this specification three times, making the card reader read the values of the variables A, B, C from three consecutive cards. Thus the value of A is read from the first card in F6.2 format; then the closing parenthesis on the right terminates the reading of the card and resets the reader to read the second card; it also returns the computer to the left parenthesis (the only one there is) to find the specification for the second variable, and the value of B is read from the second card in the same F6.2 format; once again the closing parenthesis resets the card reader to the third card and the computer to the left parenthesis of the FØRMAT statement, and the value of C is read from the third card in F6.2 format.

example 5-2.

```
READ (5,2) I, J, K, L, M
2 FØRMAT(I2, I3/)
```

There are here five variables and two specifications. The values of I and J are read from the first card in formats I2 and I3. The slash terminates the reading of the first card, and the absence of specifications between the slash and the closing parenthesis causes the card reader to ignore the second card, remove it, and reset to the left end of the third card; the closing parenthesis sends the computer to the opening parenthesis to rescan the specifications; K and L are read from the third card in formats I2 and I3; the slash and the closing parenthesis cause the fourth card to be ignored; and M is read from the fifth card in format I2.

On the third pass the computer does not reach the slash (it completes the execution of the READ command by matching M with I2), and therefore the card reader does not expect to find the sixth data card (which it would if the READ list had a sixth variable N).

example 5-3.

```
READ (5,3) C, I, J, K, L, M, N
3 FØRMAT (F6.2, (I3, I5))
```

The card reader reads C, I, J on the first card in the consecutive fields of 6, 3, and 5 spaces, corresponding to F6.2, I3, and I5. The computer returns to I3 and the card reader reads K and L on the second card in the fields of 3 and 5 spaces. Again the computer returns to I3 and the card reader reads M and N on the third card in the fields of 3 and 5 spaces.

example 5-4.

```
WRITE (6,4) C, I, J, K, L, M, N
4 FØRMAT (1X, E11.4, 2(I3, I5))
```

This is an example of how *not to write* a FØRMAT statement.

On the first pass through the FØRMAT statement, the printer, instructed by 1X, advances the sheet one line and then prints the values of C, I, J, K, L in one line in formats E11.4, I3, I5, I3, I5. The closing parenthesis stops printing on the first line, but, since there are two variables M and N left to be printed, the computer returns to the opening parenthesis of the inner pair of parentheses, including the repeat constant, that is, to 2(I3, I5), interpreting it as (I3, I5, I3, I5). However, there being no control character in front of the first I3, the computer converts one space of the field I3 into 1X, causing the printer to advance the sheet one line; then the printer prints the value of M in the two-space field; if M is 25, no harm is done; but if M is 462, the first digit 4 is truncated, and the result appears as 62.

One correct way to write the FØRMAT statement above is

4   FØRMAT (1X,E11.4,2(I3,I5)/1X,I3,I5)

The slash stops the printer after it has printed the first five variables on the first line, the second 1X causes the sheet to advance one line, and the values of M and N are printed on the second line in formats I3 and I5. The computer passes through the FØRMAT statement only once.

example 5-5.

WRITE (6,5) E, I, J, K, L, M
5   FØRMAT (1H0,F6.2,I3,I5/(1H0,I4,I6))

The specification 1H0 causes the sheet to advance two lines, and the printer, stationed at the left side of the sheet, prints the values of E, I, and J in formats F6.2, I3, I5. The slash terminates printing on the first line and sends the printer back to the left side of the sheet. The second 1H0 causes the sheet to advance two lines, and the printer prints the values of K and L in formats I4 and I6. The rightmost parenthesis stops printing on the second line and returns the printer to the left side of the sheet. The specification for the third line begins at the rightmost opening parenthesis, that is, at the second 1H0. Thus the sheet advances two lines, and M is printed on the third line in format I4.

example 5-6.   The following program illustrates a complete process of reading in a set of data and its printout in two forms.

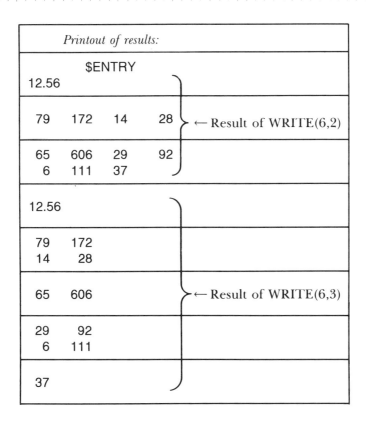

example 5-7.

    READ (5,1) A,B
  1 FØRMAT (2F4.1)
    WRITE (6,2) A,A,A,B,B,B
  2 FØRMAT (1H0,'A',F4.1/2(1H0,1X,F4.1/)†1H0,'B',F4.1/
    *2(1H0,1X,F4.1/))
    STØP

Data card:

In this example the computer stores the values of A and B and prints each value three times, preceded by an identifying letter, as shown on the right. If the FØRMAT statement were expanded, it would read:

```
PRINTOUT:

A 1.2
  1.2
  1.2
B 3.4
  3.4
  3.4
```

    (1H0,'A',F4.1/1H0,1X,F4.1/1H0,1X,F4.1/†1H0,'B',F4.1/
    *1H0,1X,F4.1/1H0,1X,F4.1/)

where the comma marked by the dagger appears to be superfluous. The WATFIV compiler does not require this comma in the condensed FØRMAT statement, but the G compiler declares an error if it is omitted.

5-3. the T specification

A T specification gives the number of the column that begins the field of the value described by the specification following the T specification. The form of the T specification is Tn, where T indicates that the specification is of the T type, and n is the number of the column. The following combination means that the field of the integer number described by I4 begins in column 7. A T specification may be used both on input and output.

Let us assume the following sequence:

READ(5,1) A,K,B

1   FØRMAT(T3,F4.1,T15,I3,T9,F3.0)

Data card:

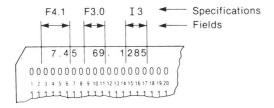

The machine will store 7.4 at A, 285 at K, and 69. at B.

Note that the values on the data card may be punched anywhere and in any order, as long as the beginnings of their fields are correctly described by T specifications.

The following sequence:

WRITE (6,2) A,K,B
2   FØRMAT (1H0,T2,F3.1,T11,I3,T6,F3.0)

will produce the following printout:

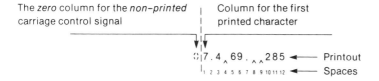

Note that, on output, a T specification makes the computer begin the column count with the *zero* column which is assumed to contain the *non-printed* carriage control character, such as 0 or −; the zero column precedes Column 1 in which printing begins. Thus, in the previous example, T11 means that the field of K (= 285) begins in Column 11, counting from the zero column, or in Column 10, counting from Column 1 of the actual printout.

On input, there is no zero column; the T count always begins with space 1 on the data card.

A useful property of the T specification is that it enables the computer to assign to different variables values from a single field (or overlapping fields). Consider the following sequence:

> READ (5,1) H,I,P
>
> 1   FØRMAT (T3,F5.1,T4,I2,T3,F2.1)
>
> WRITE (6,2) H,I,P
>
> 2   FØRMAT (1H0,T4,F5.1,T15,I3,T11,F3.1)

Data card:

```
     652.7
  ∧ ∧
```

The computer will store 652.7 at H, 52 at I, and 6.5 at P. The printout will be:

```
Carriage control,       |
or zero, column ──┐      |
                  ▼|  ∧ ∧ 6 5 2 . 7 ∧ ∧ 6 . 5 ∧ ∧ 5 2
                   | 1  2  3  4  5  6  7  8  9 10 11 12 13 14 15 16
                   |
```

The T specification can also be used with the Hollerith specifications, as shown below:

> K = 1978
>
> WRITE (6,1) K
>
> 1   FØRMAT (1H0,T5,'JUNE',T10,I4)

The printout will be:

```
Carriage control,    |
or zero, column ──┐   |
                  ▼|  ∧ ∧ ∧ J U N E ∧ 1 9 7 8
                   | 1  2  3  4  5  6  7  8  9 10 11 12
                   |
```

5-4.   unformatted (format-free) input/output

One can readily see that writing correct FØRMAT specifications requires thought, planning, knowledge of detail, concentration, and attention.

Occasionally a programmer wishes to obtain a quick result of the manipulation of some numerical data, without planning the punching of the data, without regard for the form of the result, and without captions that normally accompany the result in a formal printout. Since these cosmetic effects are produced by the specifications listed in FØRMAT statements, it is easy to see that omitting FØRMAT statements should remove a considerable drag on the writing of a program. A programmer in a hurry *can* omit FØRMAT statements, provided he substitutes statements that inform the compiler that the input/output are to be in the unformatted form. These substitute statements, and their effects, are different for the WATFIV compiler on the one hand and the G and H compilers on the other. Therefore they are presented below in separate subsections.

the WATFIV compiler

numerical data

Example 5-8 illustrates, in parallel, the formatted and unformatted (format-free) methods of input of the numerical data.

example 5-8.   Store -2.5, 6, 6, and 46.0 at A, J, K, and B.

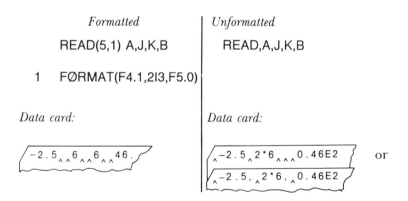

	Formatted	*Unformatted*
	READ(5,1) A,J,K,B	READ,A,J,K,B
1	FØRMAT(F4.1,2I3,F5.0)	

Rules for the unformatted input of numerical data:

1/   An unformatted input command must be in the form:

$$\text{READ, list}$$

where the word **READ** is followed by a comma and by a list of variables separated by commas;

2/   The numbers on the data card must agree in order and mode with the listed variables; they may be separated from one another by one or more blanks, or by commas, or by both; the real numbers may be in the F or E form; consecutive identical values may be written in groups consisting of the repetition number, the multiplication sign, and one value of the repeating number;

3/ The data may be punched on several cards; the computer reads the successive cards until it finds the values for all listed variables; if it does not find all the values, it declares an error; it ignores values in excess of those required by the list; thus the computer will store the same values as in Example 5-8 from the data deck shown on the right;

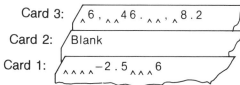

4/ A number may not continue from one data card to another;

5/ A new READ statement begins the reading of a new data card, that is, the card following the last data card read by the preceding READ statement.

Example 5-9 illustrates the formatted and unformatted methods of output of numbers.

example 5-9. Print the values stored in Example 5-8.

Formatted

```
     WRITE (6,2) A,J,K,B
2    FØRMAT (1H0,F5.1,2I3,F7.2)
```

Printout:

$ENTRY	*Line 0*
ˏ−2.5ˏˏ6ˏˏ6ˏˏ46.00	*Line 2*

1 2 3 4 5 6 7 8 9 10 11 12 13 14 15 16 17 18

Unformatted

```
PRINT, A,J,K,B
```

Printout:

$ENTRY   *Line 0*
ˏˏ−0.2500000Eˏ01 ˏˏˏˏˏˏˏˏˏˏˏˏˏ6 ˏˏˏˏˏˏˏˏˏˏˏˏˏ6ˏˏˏˏ0.4600000Eˏ02   *Line 1*
1 2 3 4 5 6 7 8 9 10111213141516171819202122232425262728293031323334353637383940414243444546474849505152535455565758 59

Rules for the unformatted output of numbers:

1/   An unformatted output command must be in the form:

PRINT,   list

where the word PRINT (not WRITE) is followed by a comma and by a list of variables separated by commas;

2/   The printout begins on the first line after $ENTRY;

3/   All real numbers are printed in the E form, right-justified in 17-space fields and with seven decimals, in accordance with the E17.7 specification; all integers are printed right-justified in 13-space fields, in accordance with the I13 specification; the first field begins in the zero column (see Article 5-3);

4/   Numbers that do not fit in the 132 spaces available on a line are printed on the successive single-spaced lines; fields are not split between two lines;

5/   A blank line will not be produced on the sheet by writing the command:

PRINT   or   PRINT,

alphameric data

Example 5-10 illustrates the formatted and unformatted methods of input of the alphameric data.

example 5-10.   Store the two expressions:

$$A/(3.14*R**2) \qquad \text{and} \qquad SQRT(X)$$

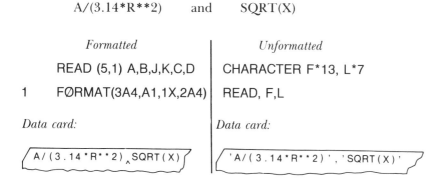

Formatted	*Unformatted*
READ (5,1) A,B,J,K,C,D	CHARACTER F*13, L*7
1 FØRMAT(3A4,A1,1X,2A4)	READ, F,L

Data card: *Data card:*

A/(3.14*R**2)ₐSQRT(X)   'A/(3.14*R**2)','SQRT(X)'

Rules for the unformatted input of alphameric data:

1/   A single variable, of either mode, may be assigned a string of as many as 78 alphameric characters; such a variable is said to be of the CHARACTER type;

2/ A variable of the CHARACTER type must be identified at the beginning of the program as to its type and size, that is, as to the number of characters in the string assigned to it. Thus if 13 characters are to be stored at F, the program must begin with

CHARACTER F*13

3/ The alphameric data are stored by the same READ command that stores the numerical data;

4/ A string of alphameric characters to be stored by a READ command must be punched on a data card between apostrophes. If several strings are punched on a card, the strings, in apostrophes, must be separated by commas, or one or more blank spaces, or both;

5/ A string may not continue from one data card to another; but if strings corresponding to several variables are punched on several cards, the computer will read the cards until it has found a string for each variable;

6/ If strings of equal size, say of eight characters each, are to be assigned to the variables A, B, C, the CHARACTER declaration statement may be written in full:

CHARACTER A*8, B*8, C*8

with commas between the variables, or it may be condensed to:

CHARACTER*8 A, B, C

where commas, again, appear only between the variables.

Example 5-11 illustrates the formatted and unformatted methods of output of the alphameric data acceptable to the WATFIV compiler.

example 5-11. Print the values stored in Example 5-10.

Formatted	Unformatted
WRITE(6,2) A,B,J,K,C,D	PRINT, F,L
2 FØRMAT(1H⌃,3A4,A1,3X,2A4)	

Printout: | *Printout:*

```
         $ENTRY                    $ENTRY
A/(3.14*R**2)⌃⌃⌃SQRT(X)   A/(3.14*R**2)⌃SQRT(X)
```

Rules for the unformatted output of alphameric data:

1/ The alphameric values are printed by the same PRINT command that prints the numerical data;

2/ The alphameric values are printed, one after the other, on single-spaced lines, each value in a field as wide as the number declared for the corresponding variable in the CHARACTER statement; each value is preceded by a single blank in the first column of the field; the blank of the first field is in the zero column;

3/ To make individual values appear on separate lines, each corresponding variable should be given a dimension between 67 and 132 in the CHARACTER statement.

direct *PRINT* commands

The numerical and alphameric values need not be stored by a READ command in order to be printed. The list of a PRINT command may contain not only variables, but also values, both numerical and alphameric, and even expressions. The alphameric values must be enclosed in apostrophes. The computer will evaluate the expressions and print the results. Expressions may not begin with the left (opening) parenthesis, as in (2 + 3)*K; they are acceptable, however, if a + sign is placed before the expression, as in +(2 + 3)*K; without the + sign, the compiler attempts to treat the parenthetical expression as an *implied DØ* (explained in Chapter 10). The fields of the printout begin in the zero column. If the first value to be printed is alphameric, (which is enclosed in apostrophes in the PRINT list), its first character (but second after the apostrophe) is printed in Column 1 on the sheet.

A direct PRINT command is illustrated in Example 5-12.

example 5-12.

```
    PRINT,'AREA OF THE CIRCLE 2 FT. IN DIAMETER =',
*3.14*2.**2/4.,' SQ. FT.'
```

Printout:

```
     $ENTRY
AREA OF THE CIRCLE 2 FT. IN DIAMETER =     0.3140000E 01  SQ. FT.
1 2 3  4  5  6  7  8   9 10 11 12 13 14 15 16 17 18 19 20 21 22 23 24 25 26 27 28 29 30 31 32 33 34 35 36 37 38 39 40 41 42 43 44 45 46 47 48 49 50 51 52 53 54 55 56 57 58 59 60 61 62 63 64
```

In Example 5-8 we saw that the expression 2*6 on a data card means two integer 6's, to be stored at, say, J and K; in the list of a direct PRINT command 2*6 is an expression which the computer evaluates and prints as 12.

Since only 132 characters can be printed on one line on a sheet, an alphameric string in a direct PRINT command may not have more than 132 characters between apostrophes; a string of this length must be—and may be—punched on continuation cards, since a single card has only 66 spaces for characters (columns 7 through 72). A natural apostrophe within a string must be shown as two consecutive apostrophes (see Article 4-1). This doubled apostrophe will be printed out as one apostrophe, but it will be counted as two characters in the string.

In punching long strings of characters one must not forget the opening and closing apostrophes of each string, particularly when they are on different cards; nor the continuation mark in column 6; nor the commas after PRINT and between strings. One must also be sure not to exceed 132 characters between the apostrophes. A smaller number of characters is, of course, acceptable and even advisable, to avoid splitting a word at the end of a line. If, however, each string is to appear on a separate line, the number of characters in a string should not be less than 67, otherwise the computer will crowd two strings on the same line.

Example 5-13 shows a direct command to print a portion of a poem by Wordsworth and the resulting printout.

example 5-13.

```
   PRINT, 'SHE WAS A PHANTOM OF DELIGHT
 *                                                        ',
 * 'WHEN FIRST SHE GLEAMED UPON MY SIGHT,
 *                                                        ',
 * 'A LOVELY APPARITION, SENT
 *                                                        ',
 * 'TO BE A MOMENT' 'S ORNAMENT.
 *                                                        ',
 * '                          WORDSWORTH'
   STOP
```

Printout:

```
        $ENTRY
SHE WAS A PHANTOM OF DELIGHT
WHEN FIRST SHE GLEAMED UPON MY SIGHT,
A LOVELY APPARTION, SENT
TO BE A MOMENT'S ORNAMENT.
                          WORDSWORTH
```

the G and H compilers—NAMELIST

The G and H compilers are made to accept data and generate output, without FØRMAT specifications, by the nonexecutable statement NAMELIST.

We know that, to store A = 1.2 and K = 7 from a data card, we must punch the two values on a card, as follows:

and then write in the program

```
        READ(5,1) A,K
   1    FØRMAT(F4.1,I3)
```

To produce an output of the values, we write:

```
        WRITE(6,2) A,K
   2    FØRMAT(1H0,F6.1,I4)
```

Making use of NAMELIST, we punch the data card as follows:

and write in the program:

```
        NAMELIST /NL/ A,K
        READ(5,NL)
        WRITE(6,NL)
```

The information on the data card consists of three parts, of which the middle part is the *list* of the variables and their values: A=1.2,K=7. This list is given an arbitrary name, such as NL, of not more than 6 alphameric characters, beginning with a letter; it must be different from the names of variables or arrays (arrays are presented in Chapter 10). The name, preceded by &, is punched ahead of the list, beginning in space 2, thus: ∧&NL. The list is followed by the third part, &END. The list must be separated from &NL and &END by one or more blanks. Blanks may also be embedded in the list: we may write A∧=∧1.2,∧∧K∧∧=∧7. Each variable and its value must be separated from the next variable by a comma. A comma may also be punched between the last item in the list and &END.

A glance at the program above shows that the name of the list, NL, is written on all three lines, first, in the NAMELIST statement, between slashes, followed by the variables in the list, separated by commas; second, in the **READ** statement where it replaces the FØRMAT number between the parentheses; and third, similarly, in the **WRITE** statement. The NAMELIST statement must precede all executable statements.

The output of the program is printed, beginning at the left edge of the sheet, on three single-spaced lines, as follows:

```
&NL
A=ʌʌ1.19999981ʌʌʌʌ,K=ʌʌʌʌʌʌʌʌʌʌ7
&END
```

†An array K of five different values (say, 1,2,3,4,5) may be stored and printed by the following sequence:

```
DIMENSIØN K(5)
NAMELIST /KAY/ K
READ(5,KAY)
WRITE(6,KAY)
```

Data card:

```
/ ʌ&KAYʌK=1,2,3,4,5ʌ&END /
```

Printout:

```
&KAY
K=ʌʌʌʌʌʌʌʌʌʌ1,ʌʌʌʌʌʌʌʌʌʌ2,ʌʌʌʌʌʌʌʌʌʌ3,ʌʌʌʌʌʌʌʌʌʌ4,ʌʌʌʌʌʌʌʌʌʌ5
&END
```

Note that K is dimensioned ahead of its appearance in the list of the NAMELIST statement. Also note that, on the data card, the name of the array, K, appears once, without subscripts, and is followed by the equals sign and the values of the elements, separated by commas.

If the elements of K are all the same, say 7, the data card may be punched:

```
/ ʌ&KAYʌK=5*7ʌ&END /
```

where 5*7 must be punched without embedded blanks.

---

† Read the rest of the article after studying arrays.

The following sequence:

```
DIMENSIØN B(3)
NAMELIST /BEE/ B
READ(5,BEE)
WRITE(6,BEE)
```

Data card:

```
/ ^&BEE^B=3*9.87^&END /
```

will print:

```
&BEE
B=^^9.86999989^^^^,9.86999989^^^^,9.86999989
&END
```

An array of many elements may be continued on several data cards, in all and any spaces but the first; it must be followed, on the last card, by &END, after at least one blank or a comma. The printout of the elements may appear on several lines.

A variable or array name may appear in different lists. The following sequence:

```
NAMELIST /EL/ L /EN/ L,N
READ(5,EL)
N = L**2
WRITE(6,EN)
```

Data card:

```
/ &EL ^L=6 ^&END /
```

will produce:

```
&EN
L=^^^^^^^^^^6,N=^^^^^^^^^^36
&END
```

NAMELIST may not be used to store and print alphameric values.

5-5. list-directed input/output

Another type of unformatted input/output which is acceptable to the G and H compilers is called the *list-directed* input/output.

Typical forms of the list-directed READ and WRITE statements are:

> READ(5,*) A,B,K,L
> WRITE(6,*) A,B,K,L

where the asterisks replace the numbers of the FØRMAT statements, because the FØRMAT statements are not used.

A data card for a READ(5,*) statement may be punched with numeric and alphameric values. Each value on the card must be separated from the others by at least one *separator,* which may be a blank or a comma. Alphamerics must be divided into groups of not more than four characters, and each group must be enclosed in apostrophes; blanks within the apostrophes do not act as separators. Identical consecutive values on the card, say 5, 5, 5, may be combined by multiplying a repetition factor by one value: 3*5.

A WRITE(6,*) statement does not write the alphameric data, even if the data were stored by a READ(5,*) statement; therefore for an output of the alphameric data a recourse must be had to a normal WRITE command, with an associated FØRMAT statement.

Example 5-15 illustrates the list-directed input/output of numerical values.

example 5-15.

> READ(5,*) A,B,K,L
> WRITE(6,*) A,B,K,L
> STØP

Data card:

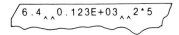

6 . 4 ⌄⌄ 0 . 1 2 3 E + 0 3 ⌄⌄ 2 * 5

Printout:

⌄⌄6.39999962⌄⌄⌄⌄⌄⌄⌄123.000000⌄⌄⌄⌄⌄⌄⌄⌄⌄⌄⌄⌄⌄⌄⌄5⌄⌄⌄⌄⌄⌄⌄⌄⌄⌄⌄⌄5

Note that the real numbers are printed in the F form. Also note that on the data card the second number is punched 0.123E+03. Had it been punched

0.123E∧03, the computer would interpret the blank in the number as a separator and would store 0.123 at B and 3 at K, instead of 5 at both K and L.

Example 5-16 illustrates the list-directed input of the alphameric values and their output with the normal WRITE and FØRMAT statements.

example 5-16.

```
      READ(5,*) A,B,C
      WRITE(6,2) A,B,C
  2   FØRMAT(1H0,3A4)
      STØP
```

Data card:

```
/ 'BATØ'∧∧'N∧RØ'∧∧'UGE∧' \
```

Printout:

∧BATØN∧RØUGE

The WATFIV compiler accepts the READ(5,*) and WRITE(6,*) statements, but only for numerical values; it does not store or print list-directed alphameric values. It prints real numerical values in the E form.

5-6. repeated characters

If it is desired that the computer print any one character, say X, in several consecutive spaces on a line, or on several lines, one may employ a combination of a Hollerith specification, a slash, and a repetition number. Thus to obtain the following printout:

```
                    XXXXX
                    XXXXX
                    XXXXX
```

one may write:

```
        WRITE(6,1)
  1    FØRMAT(3(1X,'XXXXX'/))
```

If the number of characters to be printed on a line is large, punching them on a card is time consuming and subject to error. In such cases one may resort to a shortcut consisting of the character to be printed enclosed in apostrophes, the apostrophes themselves enclosed in parentheses, and the opening parenthesis preceded by the repetition number of the character. Thus FØRMAT 1 above may be shortened to:

```
  1    FØRMAT(3(1X,5('X')/))
```

questions and problems

5-1/ How many data cards will be read by each of the following sets of statements?

(a)   READ(5,1) A, B, C, I
  1   FØRMAT(F6.1,F7.3/E10.4/I5)
(b)   READ(5,2) D, E, F
  2   FØRMAT(/F5.1//F6.2/F7.2)
(c)   READ(5,3) P, Q, R, S
  3   FØRMAT(F5.1/F5.1//F5.1///F5.1)

5-2/ Given the following sets of statements, in which lines will the results be printed?

(a)   WRITE(6,1) I, A, K, B, C, E
  1   FØRMAT(1X, 2(I3, F6.2)/1X, F6.2, F7.3)
(b)   WRITE(6,2) A, L, B
  2   FØRMAT(/1X, F10.2/1X, I4, F8.2)
(c)   WRITE(6,3) A, B, I
  3   FØRMAT(1X, F5.2/1X, F5.2, I5/)

5-3/ Given the following sets of statements, in what lines and in which spaces will the results be printed?

(a)   WRITE(6,1) A, K, L, M, N
  1   FØRMAT(1X, F6.2, (I3, I6))

(b)   WRITE(6,2) A, K, L, M, N
    2 FØRMAT(1X, F6.2, 2(I3,I6))
(c)   WRITE(6,3) B, I1,I2,I3,I4,I5,I6,I7,I8,I9,I10
    3 FØRMAT(1H0,F6.2,2(I3,I5)/(1H0, 2(I3,I5)))

5-4/   A data card is punched as follows:

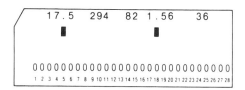

Make the computer store, first, the integer numbers and, second, the real numbers. Then make the computer print, first, the real numbers on one line and, second, the integer numbers on another line, both lines double spaced. Each number is to begin in a column divisible by 5, the count of columns beginning with the first column that may contain a printed character.

5-5/   Given the numbers:

$$X = 5.23, \quad Y = 10.45, \quad I = 12345$$

(a)   Write a program with unformatted commands which will make the computer store the numbers from a data card and print them.
(b)   Write a program to print the numbers with a direct PRINT command.

5-6/   Write a program with unformatted commands which will make the computer store the following group of numbers:

$$A = 92.6, \quad B = 897.0, \quad J = 762$$

and then print the group four times on one or more lines.

5-7/   Given the two sets of numbers:

	X	Y	N
Set 1	3.	.09	2
Set 2	65.	40.6	1

make the computer evaluate the expression

$$W = X**N + Y**N$$

for each set.

Use the unformatted commands for input and output.

5-8/ Submit the poem of Example 5-12 on data cards and write an unformatted program to print each line of the poem on a separate line.

5-9/ Write a program with a direct PRINT command that will print, across the entire width of the sheet, the following passage:

> Once upon a sunny morning a man who sat in a breakfast nook looked up from his scrambled eggs to see a white unicorn with a golden horn quietly cropping roses in the garden. The man went up to the bedroom where his wife was still asleep and woke her. "There's a unicorn in the garden," he said. "Eating roses." She opened one unfriendly eye and looked at him. "The unicorn is a mythical beast," she said, and turned her back on him.
>
> Thurber, The Unicorn in the Garden

5-10/ Rewrite the programs of Problem 5-5(a) for processing with the G compiler.

5-11/ Write a program with list-directed commands that will store and print the following numbers:

A = 2.5, B = 2.5, C = 2.5, D = 0.456E4, K = 4, L = −105

5-12/ Write a program that will print the character A, twenty times to a line, on four triple-spaced lines.

chapter 6

arithmetic operations, expressions, and statements

6-1.   constants and variables

Consider the following program statement:

$$A = B*H/2.$$

(In FORTRAN, the asterisk, *, is the multiplication sign.) In this statement we observe two types of quantities that are used in the arithmetic operations of the computer. Quantities A, B, and H are called *variables;* the quantity 2. is a *constant.*

A constant is a fixed number, integer or real, like 2.0, 3.1416, −5.0, 100, which is included in the program and retains its value throughout the program. For example, in the statement above—which defines the area A of a triangle from its base B and height H—A, B, and H may assume and acquire various values, but 2.0 remains fixed; it is a constant. Numbers punched on cards as data, and varying from card to card, are not considered to be in the category of constants; only the numbers included in the program which remain fixed are designated as such.

Letters A, B, and H are symbolic names given to quantities that may change in value during a program. For example, in the program statement above, B and H may take on different values, assigned to them by the data cards, and the computer will calculate and report the corresponding values of A. As stated earlier, in all these computations 2. will remain constant.

Symbolic names in FORTRAN need not necessarily be single letters. They can be any combination of six or fewer letters or digits, beginning with a letter, particularly if the mnemonic character of such a combination helps the programmer to visualize the relationship expressed by the arithmetic statement. For example, instead of writing A = B*H/2., the programmer may write AREA = BASE*HEIGHT/2..

Symbolic names serve two purposes: first, they identify the variables that occur in a problem and that are incorporated in a computer program, if the problem is to be solved by the computer; second, they identify the locations in the memory in which the numerical values corresponding to the variables are stored.

Thus, when the computer sees the statement

READ (5,1) BASE, HEIGHT

it affixes the names BASE and HEIGHT to two locations in its memory, and then stores in those locations the two numerical values that it finds on the data card associated with the READ statement.

If the READ (5,1) BASE, HEIGHT statement is repeated in the program, the computer reads the second data card, and stores the values from that card in the same BASE/HEIGHT locations, erasing the values received from the first card; and so on.

In the computer terminology, the names of the memory locations, such as BASE and HEIGHT above, are called *addresses*. The memory locations may be compared to a bank of mail boxes in an apartment building, each with a name on it; the data may be compared to the letters, bearing the corresponding names, deposited in the mail boxes.

• Because the input data may contain two types of numbers, integer and real, to be eventually assigned to the variables in the program, the variables themselves are divided into integer and real variables. The two classes of variables are distinguished by the letter that denotes the variable or begins the name representing the variable.

Integer variables are always represented by the six letters I, J, K, L, M, and N, or by names beginning with one of those letters. Examples of names of integer variables are

I, JØB, KØUNT, L8, MARK, NAME

Real variables are represented by the remaining twenty letters of the alphabet or by names beginning with those letters. Examples of names of real variables are

A, CØUNT, HEIGHT, P7, VØLUME

Special characters, such as +, *,), are not permitted in variable names; the only exception occurs in the names of array elements, such as AREA(K,L): these will be treated later in the book.

Examples of incorrectly written *integer* variables are

> D1 (D is reserved for real variables)
> I.2 (. is a special character)
> 2NN (begins with a digit)
> LØGARITHM (nine letters)

Examples of incorrectly written *real* variables are

> PRØDUCT (seven letters)
> LENGTH (L is reserved for integers)
> A*B2 (* is a special character)
> 6AX (begins with a digit)

Words existing in the FORTRAN language itself, such as FØRMAT, STØP, READ, should not be used to identify variables.

6-2. integers and real numbers

In Article 2-2 it was shown that a computer operates on numbers of two types or *modes: integer* and *real.* To review: integer numbers are *whole* numbers, without a decimal point; real numbers have a decimal point and may have a fractional part.

The computer performs arithmetic operations on the numbers in the two modes in two different ways. Real numbers are handled in the ordinary manner of arithmetic, and their decimal portions, limited only by the capacity of the memory locations, are included in all calculations. Examples of operations on real numbers are

		Stored real result
$5.2 + 6.17$	$=$	11.37
$0.217 - 2.6454$	$=$	-2.4284
$1./30.$	$=$	0.03333333
$-1./30.$	$=$	-0.03333333

Integer numbers, which may not have fractional parts, cannot keep fractional parts that result from the operation of division. Thus, if the computer divides one integer by another, and the quotient tends to have a fractional part, the computer *truncates* the fraction, that is, drops it, and stores only the whole part of the quotient. The following examples illustrate the effect of truncation:

Stored integer result

3/2	=	1
10/3	=	3
2/3	=	0

It is obvious, if accurate results are desired, that integer numbers may not be used in arithmetic operations involving division. Even though no harm results from the use of integers in the operations of addition, subtraction, and multiplication, these three operations can seldom be divorced from the operation of division; therefore, all arithmetic operations are customarily carried out in the mode of real numbers. In that mode the computer preserves the fractional parts and always puts the decimal point in the right place.

The question may be asked: Why integer numbers? The answer is that the machine manipulations of integer numbers are much simpler than those of the real numbers and therefore take less computer time. Consequently, integer numbers are used in all situations where there is no chance of an arithmetic error.

Such situations present themselves principally in all cases of counting. Integer numbers are used to count quantities and operations. Computers would not be practical if problems occurred singly, or if only individual solutions were required. But where identical operations must be repeated a great many times, as in finding the squares of all numbers from 1 to 1000, computers provide a service that cannot be surpassed, except by more efficient computers. It is in the cases of repetitive operations, which must be counted, that the integer numbers find their greatest and most useful application. In addition, integers are used to identify statement numbers (such as the number of a FØRMAT statement), as signals for operational devices (5 for card reader), and as subscripts of elements in arrays or series (which we shall study later).

The truncation of the decimal part that occurs during the division of one integer by another provides a method for testing the exact divisibility of one number by another. Let us suppose that it is desired to find out whether 19 is exactly divisible by 5. Let I = 19, J = 5. We ask the computer to calculate K = I/J; the computer gets K = 19/5 = 3. Now we ask the computer to calculate L = K*J; the computer gets L = 3*5 = 15. Since L is not equal to I, 19 is not divisible by 5.

In contrast with integers, real numbers are used in all cases where they represent measurements or quantities that employ a decimal point: 26.4 in. and $4.98 are examples.

Aside from the decimal point, there is another difference between integer numbers and real numbers. As mentioned earlier in this article, memory locations have a limited capacity. Therefore, a division of a whole real number by another whole real number may produce an approximate fraction; for example, 1./3. = 0.3333333; multiplying 0.3333333 back by 3. gives 0.9999999 and not 1.. Also, it is shown in Appendix C that most fractions cannot be represented exactly in the binary system, the system on which the operation of most computers is based. Thus, the computer may store—and print—0.03 as 0.0300000012. In contrast, an integer number, being a whole number, always has an exact binary counterpart.

Both integer and real numbers may be positive or negative. The writing of the plus sign is optional.

6-3. arithmetic operators

FORTRAN has five operational symbols or *operators* for performing arithmetic operations. The operations, the corresponding symbols, and examples are shown in the following table.

Operation	Symbol	Example
Addition	+	A + B
Subtraction	−	A − B
Multiplication	*	A * B
Division	/	A / B
Exponentiation	**	A ** B

The asterisk * is used as the multiplication symbol because the small "x" does not exist on the FORTRAN keyboard, and the large "X" is used as a blank symbol or a variable. The symbol for exponentiation, **, is written in two columns, but is considered to be a single symbol; the meaning of A**B is A^B; in FORTRAN everything is written in one line.

There are no symbols in FORTRAN such as $\sqrt{}$ or $\int$. Operations corresponding to these symbols are carried out through the medium of the five basic operations above.

6-4. arithmetic expressions and operations

A FORTRAN *arithmetic expression* consists of one or several variables and/or constants (called collectively *operands*) connected by arithmetical operators, which indicate the operations (if any) to be performed on the operands. Six examples of arithmetic expressions are shown in the box below:

D	J + K	D / 3.
3	L * I 2	B ** 2. − 4. * A * C

Simple expressions, such as the preceding ones, may be enclosed in parentheses and combined by means of operators into more complex expressions, like the two shown here:

| (J + K) * L * I 2 | (B - (B ** 2 . - 4 . * A * C) ** . 5) / (2 . * A) |

In FORTRAN, arithmetic expressions are written and processed in accordance with a number of inflexible rules.

rule 1. All characters and symbols must be written in one line.

rule 2. Two operators may not appear next to each other. If one of the operands is negative, it and its sign must be enclosed within parentheses. Thus, A*—D is incorrect; the correct form is A*(—D).

rule 3. hierarchy. If an expression has no parentheses, the computer carries out the operations in accordance with the rules of hierarchy, or priority, which are as follows:

Exponentiation (indicated by two asterisks, **) is performed first.

Multiplication (one asterisk, *) and *division* (slash or solidus, /) are performed next.

Addition (+) and *subtraction* (−) are performed last.

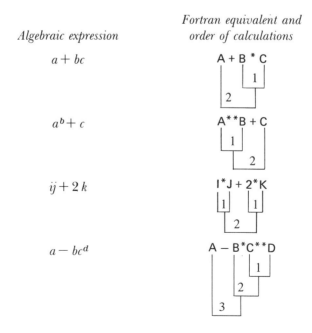

rule 4. equal rank. When an expression contains operators of equal rank, the order of execution is from left to right.

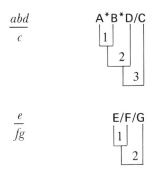

A frequent mistake is to write the second expression as E/F*G; to the computer this means $(e/f)g = eg/f$.

While the sequence of the operands is not of significance in the case of the *real* quantities, in the *integer* mode the sequence of the operands is important, because in the latter mode the computer truncates fractions. This is illustrated in the following examples:

Real mode:

7./5.*4.	=	1.4*4.	=	5.6
7.*4./5.	=	28./5.	=	5.6

Integer mode:

7/5*4	=	1*4	=	4
7*4/5	=	28/5	=	5

rule 5. parentheses. Expressions enclosed in parentheses are evaluated before the execution of the operations outside the parentheses. Within the parentheses, Rule 3 of hierarchy applies. When there are nested parentheses, that is, when one set of parentheses contains another set of parentheses, the innermost set of parentheses has priority, and the calculations proceed from the innermost set to the outermost set.

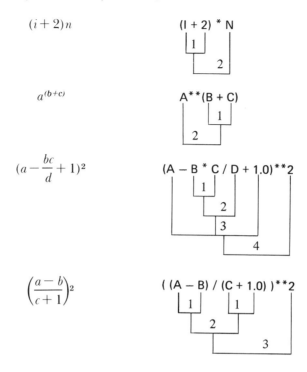

rule 6. exponentiation.   Expressions of the form A**B**C seem to be ambiguous; it is not clear whether $(A^B)^C$ or $A^{(B^C)}$ is meant. However, the expression A**B**C is not ambiguous to the computer; it accepts it and computes it, but, contrary to Rule 4, *from right to left,* that is, it raises B to the power C, and then raises A to the power B^C; in other words, it yields the value $A^{(B^C)}$.

To avoid ambiguity and mistakes, it is always safest to enclose the first desired exponentiation in parentheses, as shown below:

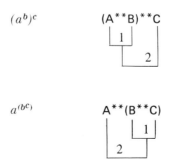

A negative quantity may not be raised to the power of a *real number;* thus, $(-5.)^{2.}$ is illegal. The reason for this is that raising to a real power is done by logarithms, and a negative quantity has no logarithm. However, if the power is an *integer* number, raising to the power is performed by multiplication, and the operation is legal; thus, $(-5.)^2 = (-5.)*(-5.) = 25..$

rule 7. mode.   As shown in Article 6-2, variables and constants exist in integer and real modes. These two modes may be mixed in arithmetic expressions; however, one is advised to avoid mixed modes, unless one has thoroughly learned the ways in which the machine treats mixed expressions.

Generally speaking, the machine treats all quantities in a mixed expression as *real,* and operates on them to produce a *real* result. In the following examples, let:

$$A = 5.6, \qquad B = 1.2, \qquad I = 4, \qquad J = 5$$

Then:

$$B - I = 1.2 - 4 = -2.8$$
$$A * I = 5.6* 4 = 22.4$$
$$A / J = 5.6 / 5 = 1.12$$
$$I ** B = 4 ** 1.2 = 5.278$$
$$A*I + I**B = 22.4 + 5.278 = 27.678$$

But if one writes

$$A * (J/I) + I - B$$

the computer, first of all, evaluates the expression within the parentheses, which happens to be a ratio of two integers, 5/4; though the normally expected result is 1.25, the computer truncates it to 1 and then proceeds to calculate the mixed product of A (= 5.6) and 1, and stores it as 5.6 (and not as 1.25*5.6 = 7.0). The expression is now reduced numerically to

$$5.6 + 4 - 1.2$$

and the computer evaluates it as 8.4. This result may or may not be wrong, depending on whether one has foreseen and taken into account the effect of the truncation.

In conclusion it should be noted that, although the results of operations on arithmetic expressions in mixed mode are always real, the real results may be transformed into truncated integers if they are stored under integer names. This is explained further on in the chapter.

reminders

1/ Never omit the multiplication symbol *; AD is a variable name; it does not mean A*D. Also, (A+B)(C−D) is wrong; it should be written (A+B)*(C−D).

2/ Do not allow two operators to be next to each other: A/−D should be written A/(−D).

3/ Never forget to pair parentheses; there should be as many parentheses facing left as facing right; count them.

4/ Feel free to use parentheses when the order of operations is not clear.

5/ Do not write B**(1/4), unless you do want the result to be B**0 = 1; otherwise, write B**0.25 or B**(1./4.).

6/ Do not mistake B**3./2. for $B^{1.5}$: it is $B^3/2$.

7/ B/A*C is BC/A, not B/AC.

8/ Watch out for terms in which one integer is divided by another.

9/ It is always safe to raise any integer or real number to an integer power.

6-5. arithmetic statements

An *arithmetic statement,* or *arithmetic assignment statement,* is an executable statement that orders the computer to calculate the value of an arithmetic expression and to assign the computed value to a variable. The statement always has the form of an equation, with the name of the variable on the left and the arithmetic expression on the right of the equals sign. Consider the arithmetic statement

$$A = B * H / 2.$$

In FORTRAN, this statement does not have the inert meaning of mathematics, namely, that A is equal to BH/2. Rather, it is a command calling for action: it orders the computer to *copy* the numbers stored at B and H into its internal calculator, to calculate in it the value of BH/2, and then to store the result at A. Storing the result at A erases whatever value may have been stored at A earlier, just as recording on a tape erases the earlier recording. However, *copying* into the calculator from B and H does not destroy the values stored at B and H.

One perhaps startling illustration of the difference between a mathematical equation and an arithmetic statement is provided by the following statement:

$$X = X + 2.$$

As an equation in mathematics, this expression is meaningless. But as an arithmetic statement, it orders the computer to copy the number stored at X (say 7.), to increase it by 2. (making it 9.), and to store the new value (9.) at X, destroying the original value of X (7.).

6-6.   rules for writing arithmetic statements

1/ The name of the variable to which the value of the arithmetic expression is assigned must be on the left side of the equals sign.

2/ The name on the left side must be a single name, such as A, X, JØB, RØØT, etc. No mathematical operators may appear on the left side; M − L on the left side is illegal.

3/ The expression on the right side may be any arithmetic expression described in Article 6-4; it may be a single constant, such as 2., or an involved expression combining variables, constants, and operators.

4/ As explained in Article 6-4, Rule 7, the arithmetic expression on the right side of the equals sign may be in mixed mode; that is, some factors in it may be integer and others real. The computer operates on such an expression to produce a *real* result. What happens to this result depends on the variable to which the result is assigned. If the variable is real, say X, the result is stored at the address X intact, with the decimal point and the fraction; but if the variable is integer, say K, the fractional part of the result is truncated and the remaining whole part, without the decimal point, is stored at the address K. Thus,

$$\overset{6.155}{} \qquad \overset{5.278}{}$$
$$X = 5. * 1.231 - 2 + 4 ** 1.2$$

sends 9.433 into storage at X, and

$$K = 5 * 1.231 - 2. + 4. ** 1.2$$

sends 9 into storage at K.

If the expression is entirely in the integer mode, the result, generally, is a truncated integer. This integer is stored, depending on the variable to which it is assigned, with or without the decimal point. Thus

$$T = 7 / 2 * 5 / 4 \qquad (=3)$$

stores 3. at T, and

$$L = 7 / 2 * 5 / 4$$

stores 3 at L.

5/ The values of the variables appearing in the expression on the right side must be *defined*, that is, present in the computer's memory; otherwise, the expression cannot be evaluated.

The following examples will illustrate the operations of the arithmetic statements.

Assume that the memory addresses shown below contain in them the following values:

Address:	A	C	I	J	RATE	TAX
Value:	4.	6.4	2	7	600.	75.

If these values are used in the arithmetic statements shown in the table below, we shall obtain the results shown on the right side of the table.

ARITHMETIC STATEMENT	COMPUTATION	RESULT	
		VALUE	STORED AT
F = A**I + J	$(4.)^2 + 7 = 23.$	23.	F
PAY=RATE-TAX	600. - 75. = 525.	525.	PAY
K = J/I	7/2 = 3	3	K
C = C + J*A	6.4+(7)(4.)= 34.4	34.4	C (original 6.4 at C is destroyed)

summary

If an arithmetic statement has the name of a real variable on the left and an integer expression on the right, the expression will be evaluated in the integer mode (with all fractions truncated), and the result will be assigned to the real variable on the left side as a real number (with the decimal point).

If the name of the variable on the left is in integer mode, and the expression on the right is real, the expression will be evaluated in the real mode, its fraction (if any) and the decimal point will be truncated, and the remaining whole number will be assigned to the integer variable on the left.

Finally, if the expression on the right is in mixed mode, the result (with possible truncations during the computation) will be real and will be assigned to the variable on the left intact or truncated, depending on whether the variable is respectively real or integer.

6-7. FLØAT and INT functions

The current acceptance by the compilers of the mixed mode in expressions has put into relative disuse two functions, FLØAT and INT, which were in more frequent use when the mixed mode was prohibited. FLØAT and INT are still accepted by all compilers: FLØAT converts an integer into a real number, and INT converts a real number into an integer, as shown in the four examples below.

	Earlier practice	*Current practice*
Example 1.	X = FLØAT(N) Example: X = FLØAT(3) 3. is stored at X	X = N Example: X = 3 3. is stored at X
Example 2.	J = INT(R) Example: J = INT(5.4) 5 is stored at J	J = R Example: J = 5.4 5 is stored at J
Example 3.	K = INT(R*FLØAT(N)) Example: K = INT(5.4*FLØAT(3)) = INT(5.4*3.) = INT(16.2) 16 is stored at K	K = R*N Example: K = 5.4*3 = 16.2 16 is stored at K
Example 4.	L = INT(R)*N Example: L = INT(5.4)*3 = 5*3 15 is stored at L	I = R L = I*N Example: I = 5.4 = 5 L = 5*3 = 15 15 is stored at L

In Example 4 note that, in order to duplicate the result of the earlier practice, it is first necessary to convert R into the integer I and then multiply I by N; without the conversion, the result would be 16, as in Example 3.

6-8. mathematical or library functions

A *function* is a variable whose value depends on another variable or *argument.* For example, sin θ is a function of the argument θ because, when θ changes, sin θ changes; or $\sqrt{x}$ is a function of the argument x, because when x changes, $\sqrt{x}$ changes.

A programmer who wishes to include the sine of 27 degrees or the square root of 5 in his arithmetic statements does not have to look up the corresponding values in trigonometric tables or tables of square roots; he can write the arguments (27 or 5) directly in his statements, provided he precedes them by the names of the prewritten and prestored programs that generate the requisite functions. When the compiler spots the names of such programs during translation, it incorporates into the object program instructions that cause the prewritten programs to become operative during the execution of the program.

Prewritten programs are available for a number of the more common mathematical functions. These functions are listed in Table 6-1 with their FORTRAN names, examples, and restrictions.

Table 6-1. Mathematical Functions

Function	Fortran name	Example	Remarks
Sine of θ	SIN	SIN(THETA)	θ in radians †
Cosine of θ	CØS	CØS(THETA)	
Tangent of θ	TAN	TAN(THETA)	
Arc sine X	ARSIN	ARSIN(X)	Result in radians, between $+\frac{\pi}{2}$ and $-\frac{\pi}{2}$
Arc cosine X	ARCØS	ARCØS(X)	
Arc tangent X	ATAN	ATAN(X)	
Hyperbolic tangent X	TANH	TANH(X)	
Absolute value of X	ABS	ABS(X)	
Square root of X	SQRT	SQRT(X)	$X \geq 0$
Exponential: e^X	EXP	EXP(X)	
Natural logarithm of X	ALØG	ALØG(X)	$X > 0$
Common logarithm of X	ALØGIO	ALØGIO(X)	

† If you want the sine of 27°, do not write SIN(27.): Write SIN(27./57.3); trigonometric arguments must be in radians.

The argument of a mathematical function must always be real (not integer) and *must always be enclosed in parentheses.*

The simple form of a mathematical function conceals the complicated calculation which the computer performs to supply the needed value. For instance, if SIN(A) were not available to the programmer as a FORTRAN function, the expression that he would have to write instead is

$$A - \frac{A^3}{3!} + \frac{A^5}{5!} - \frac{A^7}{7!} + \ldots$$

or, in FORTRAN,

A − A**3/(3.*2.) + A**5/(5.*4.*3.*2.) − A**7/(7.*6.*5.*4.*3.*2.) + . . .

Fortunately, the programs needed to evaluate many mathematical functions form a library resident in the computer; for this reason they are also known as the *library functions.*

6-9. STØP and END statements

In Article 1-4 it was shown that when a source program, that is, the program written in FORTRAN by the programmer, is submitted to the computer, it must first be compiled, that is, translated into the machine language, before it can be executed by the computer. Thus a source program is processed through the machine twice: once to be translated, the second time to be executed. Each of these two processes has a terminal point: the translating operation is terminated by the statement END, the very last statement in every program; the execution process is terminated by the statement STØP, usually just ahead of the END statement. The word STØP stops the execution but not the translation; the compiler translates the program through the STØP statement until it receives the signal END, which indicates to it that the program has reached its end. Then the compilation stops, and the execution begins and continues until the STØP statement is reached.

Thus the sequence of the two statements

STØP
END

causes the compiler to translate the program through STØP, to stop compiling when it sees END, and to turn the translated program over to the computer for execution through STØP.

Although it is not infrequent for STØP to precede END at the end of a source program, occasionally a STØP, and even several STØPs, may appear at other points in the program. For instance, the program may instruct the computer to check the data for consistency (it may be told that students' grades may not exceed 100) and to STØP if it detects an inconsistency; the early STØP prevents the computer from executing the rest of the program and processing the erroneous data (e.g., computing the grade average).

questions and problems

6-1/ What letters are reserved to identify integer variables?

6-2/ In the following list of names, identify the names acceptable for integer variables and real variables and the names unacceptable for either type.

(a)	J6	(e)	DEVICES	(h)	W1234
(b)	BØEING	(f)	A	(i)	2AB
(c)	BØEING 747	(g)	NUMBER	(j)	INTEGER
(d)	X/Y				

6-3/ What are the principal uses of integer numbers and real numbers?

6-4/ Give the results of the following operations performed with integers:

(a)	$4+6$	(d)	$2 : 5$	(f)	$(7 : 3)(2 \times 3)$
(b)	$4-6$	(e)	6×4	(g)	$(9 : 3)(4 : 6)$
(c)	$5 : 2$				

6-5/ Write an equivalent FORTRAN expression for each of the following algebraic expressions:

(a) $a + b^2$

(b) $b + \dfrac{c-d}{a}$

(c) $\dfrac{a+b}{c+d}$

(d) a^{-b}

(e) $(i^2 + k^2)^2 + 2jk + j$

(f) $1 + a + \dfrac{a^2}{2!} + \dfrac{a^3}{3!}$

(g) $\dfrac{ab}{c+2}$

(h) $\left(\dfrac{a}{b}\right)^{c-1}$

(i) $2\pi r^2$

(j) $k^3 + \left(\dfrac{mn}{2i}\right)^{2k}$

6-6/ Write an equivalent algebraic expression for each of the following FORTRAN expressions:

(a)   A + B/(C + D)   (b)   A + B/C**2 − D
(c)   I + 2*J − N**2   (d)   ((A + B)/(C + D))**2 + E**2
(e)   − A − A * A   (f)   2.*A/(B + C**D)
(g)   I/K*L**3   (h)   D − E/1.5 + 6.7/A/X
(i)   A+X*(B+X*(C+D*X))
(j)   6.4*A**4−2.3*B**3+1.8*C*C+3.2

6.7/   Write an equivalent FORTRAN expression for each of the following expressions:

(a) $\dfrac{1 + \cos Y}{1 - \cos Y}$ (b) $-\dfrac{1}{2A} + \sin\left(\dfrac{A}{2}\right)$

(c) $(2\pi)^{1/2} D^{D+1} e^{-D}$ (d) $\log_{10}\left(\dfrac{A - B}{C + D}\right) - F$

(e) $\log_e (e^{F+G} + \sqrt{\cos X})$

(f) $X \log_{10}\left| \arctan\dfrac{X}{2} \right|$

6-8/   Write an equivalent algebraic expression for each of the following
FORTRAN expressions:

(a)   CØS(X) + Y*SIN(X)
(b)   EXP(X/Y**3)
(c)   ALØG(A + B)
(d)   A/(B**2−4.5)−ALØG10(C*2.5)
(e)   B+EXP(C+D)+SQRT(SIN(B))
(f)   ALØG10(ABS((1.0+CØS(Y))/(1.0−CØS(Y))))

6-9/   Given the following variables:

B, J, HAT, MØNTH, A5, L2N

and the following data:

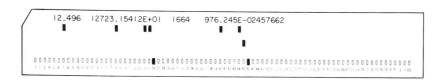

write a program that will:

(a) Order the computer to READ the numbers on the data card and to store them consecutively at the addresses of the variables above in accordance with the specifications

F10.3, I5, E12.5, I6, E14.3, I6

(b) Order the computer to print, two lines down, the values of the variables in the same order and in accordance with the same specifications as above.

(c) Order the computer to print, two lines down, the values of the following variables:

HAT, L2N, J, A5, B, MØNTH, B, J

in accordance with the specifications

F10.7, I8, I5, F10.6, F10.6, I12, E10.3, I10

(d) Order the computer to print, two lines down, all the integers in accordance with the specification I12 repeated as often as necessary.

(e) Order the computer to print, two lines down, all the real numbers in accordance with the specification F12.5 repeated as often as necessary.

Guided by the specifications above, the machine will fail to print one number. Why?

6-10/ If the following statements are executed, what values will be assigned to each of the variables?

(a) $A = 2./8.*20.$ (b) $D = 123 + 305$
(c) $J = 19/2 + 6/4$ (d) $E = 19/2 + 6/4$
(e) $K = 19./2 + 6/4.$ (f) $M = 50.E1 + 699.9$

6-11/ Given the following values:

A	B	C	D	K	L
2.5	2.	3.2	8.	3	2

compute the values of the variables on the left side of the equals sign.

(a) $I = L/K$ (b) $J = K/L + A$
(c) $X = B - C/D + A$ (d) $T = B**K/C*(B*C)$
(e) $N = (D + 2.*B)**L$ (f) $F = .2E1*.314E1*5.$
(g) $AREA = B*D/2.$ (h) $P = (D/B)**(K - 1)$

6-12/   Write a program that will command the computer to

(a)   Store the following data:

$$a = 6.0; \quad b = 2.0; \quad c = 4.0; \quad x = 25.0;$$
$$y = 4.50; \quad z = 2500.; \quad g = 70.05; \quad i = 15$$

(b)   Calculate the values of

Result, Answer, Root, h, and *j*

as given by the expressions below:

$$Result = \frac{2a^2 + 16b}{c}; \quad Answer = x^{.17} + e^y + \log_e z; \quad h = g^{.16} + i^2 + gi;$$

$$Root = Answer^{0.5}; \quad j = i \cos g + gi + \sqrt{gi}$$

(c)   Write out the values of

a, b, c, Result
x, y, z, Answer, Root
g, i, h, j

on three double-spaced lines.

Notes on the program:

You may write the data on one or several lines on the coding sheet or punch them on one or several cards.

Choose your own FØRMAT specifications for the data and the printout. Be sure that the READ specifications will enable the computer to find the data, and the WRITE specifications will produce a neatly arranged table of ñumbers.

6-13/   Write a program that will

(a)   Read in the values of X, Y, A, B, and I from three data cards.
(b)   Calculate the value of

$$SØLN = AX + BY + I$$

(c)   Make both the data and the result appear in the printout.
        Write *single* FØRMAT statements for both the input and the output.

Punch the data as follows:

Card 1:	100.0	70.0	(values of X and Y)
Card 2:	5.0	2.0	(values of A and B)
Card 3:	250		(value of I)

Make the printout appear in the form shown within the frame below:

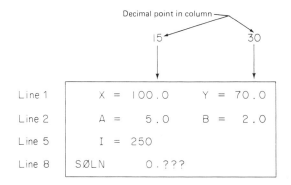

Use the following specifications: real numbers, F6.2; integers, I4; SØLN, E15.6.

chapter 7

the GØ TØ statement
—the DUMP

7-1.   the unconditional GØ TØ statement

Let us suppose that we have three data cards, each punched with two numbers, and that we wish to obtain, for every card, a printout of the two numbers on the card and of their sum. To accomplish this we may write the following program:

```
1    FØRMAT(2F6.2)
2    FØRMAT (1X,2F6.2,5X,F7.2)
     READ(5,1) A, B
     SUM = A + B
     WRITE(6,2) A, B, SUM
     READ (5,1) A, B
     SUM = A + B
     WRITE (6,2) A, B, SUM
     READ(5,1) A, B
     SUM = A + B
     WRITE (6,2) A, B, SUM
     STØP
     END
```

The computer will execute this program in the sequential order, reading the values of A and B on the first card, storing them, adding them up, and printing out the result, reading the second card, storing a new pair of values under A and B, and adding them up, and so on, until all three results have been printed out and the STØP statement has been reached.

117

It should be obvious that, even with three data cards, the program is repetitious, and its writing is tedious. The situation would be calamitous if we had 1000 cards. Thus a definite need exists for a statement in the program that would tell the computer to repeat the READ, SUM, WRITE sequence as long as there are cards to be read. FØRTRAN provides such a statement: It is the UNCØNDITIØNAL GØ TØ statement, or, simply, the GØ TØ statement. Its use, in application to the program above, is illustrated below.

```
1   FØRMAT(2F6.2)
2   FØRMAT(1X, 2F6.2, 5X, F7.2)
3   READ (5,1) A, B
    SUM = A + B
    WRITE (6,2) A, B, SUM
    GØ TØ 3
    END
```

The function of the GØ TØ statement is to send the computer back to statement 3 in the program after it has finished the first READ, SUM, WRITE sequence, and thus to make it go again through the same cycle or *loop*. This looping from GØ TØ 3 to READ continues as long as the computer finds cards to read. When the computer fails to find a card and cannot execute the READ statement, a message is generated that stops the execution automatically; thus there is no need for the STØP statement. However, the END statement is still mandatory, because it serves to terminate the compilation of the program, not its execution. In the program above, each executed loop produces one record, that is, one line of print with the values of A, B, and SUM.

Making the computer stop by denying it a card to read is not considered an elegant way to terminate a program; it is almost like inviting a man to dinner and then seating him to an empty table. The computer, like the offended guest, makes its exit (out of the program), but not without venting its feelings in a sort of protest: it concludes the printout with a message of error. Ways to prevent such a message will be described later.

The following points in connection with the GØ TØ statement must be noted. The general form of the statement is

$$\text{GØ TØ } n$$

where n is an integer number of the statement to which the computer is directed to go. This is another case of the need for statement numbers, similar to that existing between the READ and FØRMAT statements.

We may not write in a program

$$I = 5$$
$$\text{GØ TØ } I$$

and expect the computer to substitute 5 for I when it attempts to execute the GØ TØ statement; it will not. There are no commas in the GØ TØ statement.

The GØ TØ statement is called the unconditional *transfer of control* statement because, when this statement is reached, the control does not descend sequentially to the next statement in the program but is transferred unconditionally (that is, without any IFs, such as we shall encounter later) to the statement numbered *n*, which may be situated either before or after the GØ TØ statement.

GØ TØ may not transfer control to the END statement, which is never numbered.

7-2. initialization

Another illustration of the GØ TØ statement is presented in the following program:

```
        SUM = 0.
        A = 1.
    10  SUM = SUM + A
        A = A + 1.
        GØ TØ 10
        END
```


This program will make the machine compute the sum of all integers from 1 to infinity—or, at least, of all the numbers whose sum does not exceed the capacity of a memory location.

The program begins with two *initializations:* The statement SUM = 0. tells the machine to attach the name (address) SUM to a location in the memory and to store 0. in that location; this automatically clears the location of any other number that may have been stored there from a previous program. The statement A = 1. attaches the address A to another location and puts 1. into it, simultaneously clearing it of any other number. Thus the summation in Statement 10, which should begin with the SUM of 0. and A of 1., will have the right start. This concept of initialization should be clearly understood. Initialization is automatically taken care of in the case of a READ statement, which clears memory locations before storing new values in them.

The statement SUM = SUM + A begins the summation: The machine adds 0. and 1. and replaces 0. in SUM with 1.. The statement A = A + 1. adds 1. to the initial 1. in A and replaces the initial 1. in A by 2.. The statement GØ TØ 10 sends the computer through the second cycle of summation: the machine adds 1. from SUM and 2. from A, gets 3. and stores it in SUM. Next, A is increased to 2. + 1. = 3., the machine goes into the third cycle, SUM becomes 3. + 3. = 6., and so on.

It can be seen that this program will cause the machine to operate in a closed, or never-ending, loop, increasing A and SUM to infinity; such runaway cycling is prevented by setting, within the program, an upper limit on the value of A, or by controlling the time of processing or the number of sheets of the printout. Since no WRITE statement is included, no record of the summation will be printed. It should also be noted that no READ statement is shown: the values needed for the computation are introduced by the initialization statements.

7-3. the flow chart

The loop of the GØ TØ program provides us with an opportunity to introduce the concept of the *flow chart*. A flow chart is a graphical representation of the flow of operations that are to be performed by the computer. The chart consists of rectangles and other geometric figures (each shape having its symbolism) connected by lines with arrows to indicate the sequence of operations. Figure 7-1 shows the flow chart that parallels the program of Article 7-2.

The oval with the word START is the shape used for the terminal points of the program, START and STØP; there is no STØP oval in Fig. 7-1 because, theoretically, the calculation is in an endless loop.

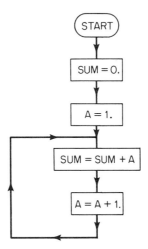

Figure 7-1

A variable is said to be *defined* when a value is assigned to it. The rectangles are used for all processing operations that define variables and store the assigned values in the memory locations named after the variables. A variable may be defined directly, as in SUM = 0., where 0. is assigned to SUM and stored in the location SUM without any calculation; or a variable may be defined after a calculation, as in A = A + 1., where the value stored in the location A is copied into the calculator, increased there by 1., and the resulting sum A + 1. is sent into the location A to replace the value that had just been copied from it.

The GØ TØ statement itself is not enclosed in any geometric figure; its effect is represented by the line with arrowheads which leads from A = A + 1. back to SUM = SUM + A. This line, together with the two rectangles it connects, forms the closed loop of the program.

A flow chart furnishes a visual representation of the step-by-step execution of the program and therefore is often of great help in planning the writing of the program, especially a lengthy and complex program. Except in simple cases, the programmer is urged to sketch a flow chart *before* writing the program; this preliminary action can be compared to consulting a map before driving through a strange territory. Furthermore, a flow chart, like a picture that is worth a thousand words, reveals quickly the intent of the program to any person who may find it necessary to study the program.

7-4.   the CØMPUTED GØ TØ statement

The unconditional GØ TØ statement is limited in its usefulness, because it can transfer control to a single statement in the program and therefore limits the computer to the repetition of a single loop. The CØMPUTED GØ TØ statement is a variant of the GØ TØ statement, which can send the computer along one of several paths, each of which is designed to produce a result corresponding to a specified condition. The destinations to which the computer travels to get results are usually different arithmetic statements, which are given random numbers M, K, J, L, etc.; the conditions that dictate along which paths the computer is to travel are given code numbers, which are represented by the index I. The two sets of numbers are cross-referenced in the CØMPUTED GØ TØ statement in the following manner:

$$\text{GØ TØ (M, K, J, L, ...),I}$$

The meaning of the statement is as follows: if I has a value of *1*, the computer transfers control to the *first* statement *M* in the list; if I has a value of *3*, control is transferred to the *third* statement *J* in the list; and so on. The value of I must be established earlier in the program; it may be supplied as part of the input data, or it may be computed in the course of the program.

Note carefully the format of the statement: all the variables in the list are separated by commas and are enclosed in parentheses, and there is a comma between the closing parenthesis and the index I.

The operation of the CØMPUTED GØ TØ statement is illustrated in the following example.

example 7-1.   A bank pays interest in accordance with a graduated scale, as shown in the following table:

Amount on deposit, $	Class	Rate of interest, %
0.01-10,000.00	1	5
10,000.01-50,000.00	2	6
50,000.01 and up	3	7

The depositors' cards are punched with their account number (NØACCT), the amount of their deposit (AMØUNT), and their class number (KLASS).

The following program will calculate the amount of interest (RETURN) on each individual account and the cumulative total of interest owed to depositors (SUM), and will print, for each account, the number of the account, the interest, and the cumulative total.

```
  1   FØRMAT(I6, 5X, F10.2, 5X, I1)
  2   FØRMAT(1X, I6, 4X, F7.2, 20X, F7.2)
      SUM = 0.
  3   READ(5,1) NØACCT, AMØUNT, KLASS
      GØ TØ (10,20,30), KLASS
 10   RETURN = AMØUNT*5./100.
      GØ TØ 7
 20   RETURN = AMØUNT*6./100.
      GØ TØ 7
 30   RETURN = AMØUNT*7./100.
  7   SUM = SUM + RETURN
      WRITE(6,2) NØACCT, RETURN, SUM
      GØ TØ 3
      END
```

SAMPLE DATA:

NØACCT	AMØUNT	KLASS
100	6000.00	1
200	60000.00	3
300	20000.00	2

The flow of the execution is illustrated by the flow chart in Fig. 7-2, and the calculations for one loop of the program, based on the sample data above, are described in detail below.

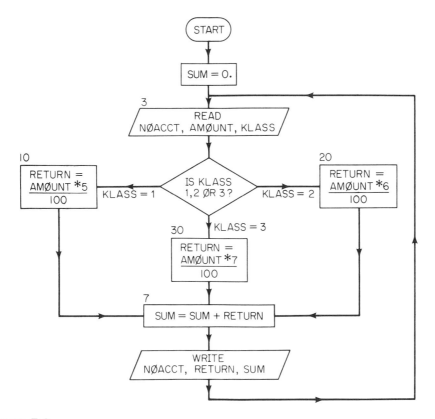

Figure 7-2

The oval at the head of the diagram announces the START of the program. The rectangle that follows it initializes SUM to 0.. The next figure is a slanted parallelogram. This figure is used for input/output operations; accordingly, it contains the instruction to the computer to READ the first data card and to store 100, 6000.00, and 1 at the addresses NØACCT, AMØUNT, and KLASS. The GØ TØ statement puts the machine at the branching of the ways; it has to travel along one of three paths leading to Statements 10, 20, or 30, and its decision depends on the value of KLASS. The branching point is marked in the flow chart by a diamond, the geometric figure selected for statements involving decisions. The value of KLASS on the first data card is 1; therefore, the machine selects the path corresponding to the *first* number in the list of the GØ TØ statement, namely, 10; accordingly, the machine travels to Statement 10 and executes it, causing the calculation of

$$\text{RETURN} = \frac{6000.*5.}{100.} = 300.$$

The next consecutive statement of the program, GØ TØ 7, causes the computer to jump to Statement 7 and to perform the calculation of the cumulative SUM = 0. + 300. = 300.. The WRITE statement produces the printout of 100 (NØACCT), 300. (RETURN), and 300. (SUM); since this is an output operation, it is shown in a slanted parallelogram. Finally, GØ TØ 3 returns the computer to Statement 3, READ, to begin the second cycle.

Upon reading the second card the computer discovers that the deposit belongs in KLASS 3 and therefore travels the KLASS 3, namely, GØ TØ 30, route; otherwise, the procedure is the same as before. The loop is traversed until the program has been executed for all available cards. When the READ statement finds no card to read, the machine stops.

Note that a statement GØ TØ 7 is shown in the program after Statement 10; this is necessary to keep the computer from executing the program in the sequential order and computing the 5%, 6%, and 7% returns on the same deposit. For the same reason a GØ TØ 7 appears after Statement 20. But it is not shown after Statement 30, because Statement 7 follows Statement 30, and therefore control descends directly from 30 to 7.

7-5. the DUMP

If a program has not run, its debugging can be speeded up by examining the values held in the computer memory after any or every executable step in the program. To make the examination possible, the computer is asked, at one or several points in the program, to *dump* certain contents of its memory on the paper. Consider the following program:

```
   READ (5,1) I,J,K
 1 FØRMAT (3I3)
   DUMP I, K
   N = I + J + K
   DUMP N
   WRITE (6,2) N
 2 FØRMAT(1H0,I4)
   STØP
   END
```

In this example, the two DUMP commands are written informally: their acceptable FORTRAN forms are given in the following paragraphs.

Data card:

Depending on the compiler invoked to translate the program into the machine language, the first DUMP command will produce the values of either I and K or of I, J, and K; the second DUMP command will produce the value of N. The WRITE command will produce another value of N. The order in which these values will appear depends on the compiler. The WATFIV, the G, and the H compilers all possess the DUMP capability.

the WATFIV compiler

The WATFIV compiler causes the computer to dump information only if the program contains machine-hindering or machine-stopping errors. In the absence of such errors the DUMP commands are ignored. Some of the errors that produce dumps are: (1) an assignment of an undefined variable, such as L = M, where M is undefined, and (2) a mismatching of an input/output operation and of the code integer of an input/output unit, for example, writing WRITE(5,1) instead of WRITE(6,1). Such errors, while triggering a dump, generally produce a defective printout, because L cannot be evaluated and is dumped as UUUUU . . . , and the command WRITE(5,1) cannot be executed.

One error which induces the WATFIV compiler to produce both a dump and a complete printout is the omission of the STØP statement from the program.

The general form of the DUMP command to be used with the WATFIV compiler is:

DUMPLIST/NAME1/A,K, . . . P/NAME2/ARRAY,B, . . . J

where

/NAME1/, /NAME2/ are the arbitrary names, between slashes, of the lists of the variables to be dumped
A,K, . . . P, ARRAY,B, . . . J are the single or array† variables forming the lists that follow each name.

Substituting the formal expressions for the informal DUMP commands in the program above, and omitting the STØP statement, we obtain the following program:

READ (5,1) I,J,K

1   FØRMAT (3I3)

---

† Arrays are presented in Chapter 10.

> DUMPLIST/LIST1/I,K
>
> N = I + J + K
>
> DUMPLIST/LIST2/N
>
> WRITE (6,2) N
>
> 2   FØRMAT (1H0,I4)
>
> END

where LIST1 is the name arbitrarily selected for the list I,K, and LIST2 is the name selected for the list containing only N.

The execution of this problem produces the following printout (after the program):

```
**WARNING** END STATEMENT NOT PRECEDED BY A TRANSFER
─────────────────────────────────────────────────────────────────
          $ENTRY
──㉑───────────────────────────────────────────────────────────────
***ERROR*** AN END STATEMENT WAS USED TO TERMINATE EXECUTION
─────────────────────────────────────────────────────────────────
          PROGRAM WAS EXECUTING LINE     8 IN ROUTINE M/PROG WHEN TERMINATION OCCURRED
─────────────────────────────────────────────────────────────────
****DUMPLIST FOR ROUTINE M/PROG FOLLOWS****
&LIST2───────────────────────────────────────────────────────────
N=        ㉑ , &END
&LIST1───────────────────────────────────────────────────────────
I=        ⑦ K=        ⑩ , &END
```

The printout shows the WARNING and ERROR diagnostics caused by the absence of the STØP statement and, in circles, four values: the value of N produced by the WRITE command; the value of N, again, produced by the DUMP of LIST2, and the values of I and K produced by the DUMP of LIST1. The values are printed in the reverse order from that in which the corresponding lists appear in the program. The values are preceded by the *list name* which begins with an & (for example, &LIST2), and each set of values closes, after a comma, with &END.

The general form of the DUMPLIST statement shows that the two DUMPLIST statements of the preceding program could have been combined into a single statement, as follows:

> DUMPLIST/LIST1/I,K/LIST2/N

It makes no difference whether the DUMPLIST statements are written separately or in combination: the printout is the same in both cases.

Shown below is the printout of a program operating on real numbers and of the resulting answers and dumps.

```
      READ (5,1) A,B,C,D
   1  FORMAT (4F4.1)
      DUMPLIST/LIST1/A,B,C
      P = A + B
      Q = C*D
      DUMPLIST/LIST2/P,Q
      R = A+B+C+D
      DUMPLIST/LIST3/P,R
      WRITE (6,2) P,Q,R
   2  FORMAT (1H0,3F5.1)
      END
```

Data card:

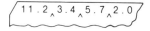

```
**WARNING** END STATEMENT NOT PRECEDED BY A TRANSFER

          $ENTRY
14.6 11.4 22.3
***ERROR*** AN END STATEMENT WAS USED TO TERMINATE EXECUTION

          PROGRAM WAS EXECUTING LINE    11 IN ROUTINE M/PROG WHEN TERMINATION OCCURRED

****DUMPLIST FOR ROUTINE M/PROG FOLLOWS****
&LIST3
P=   0.1460000E 02,R=   0.2229999E 02,&END
&LIST2
P=   0.1460000E 02,Q=   0.1140000E 02,&END
&LIST1
A=   0.1120000E 02,B=   0.3400000E 01,C=   0.5700000E 01,&END
```

It must be clearly understood that errors in mathematics, logic, or data do not belong in the class of the machine-hindering or machine-stopping errors. If a programmer, intending to write C − 5. or GØ TØ 2 in a program, writes mistakenly C + 5. or GØ TØ 5, the compiler and the computer will readily process the erroneous information and, just as readily, will print the wrong results, but will not print the error-revealing dump.

Another category of errors which produces no dump consists of the violations of the syntax, that is, of the rules of writing FORTRAN statements. The compiler intercepts defective expressions with unmatched parentheses, such as C* (D, or with consecutive operators, such as A/−B, and omissions of statement numbers referred to in other statements, and forthwith cancels the execution of the program.

the G and H compilers

If the compiler to be invoked is the G or the H compiler, the DUMP command must be in one of the following general forms:

CALL   DUMP (A$_1$,B$_1$,F$_1$, ... A$_N$,B$_N$,F$_N$)
CALL PDUMP (A$_1$,B$_1$,F$_1$, ... A$_N$,B$_N$,F$_N$)

where A and B are the variables that indicate the limits of the list to be dumped and F is an integer code number that indicates the mode of the dump. The code is 4 for integer numbers and 5 for real numbers. The execution of a program is terminated after CALL DUMP; CALL PDUMP allows the execution to continue. Thus the program written above for the WATFIV compiler is modified for the G or H compiler and for continued execution as follows:

```
         READ (5,1) I,J,K

  1      FØRMAT (3I3)

         CALL PDUMP (I,I,4,K,K,4)

         N = I + J + K

         CALL PDUMP (N,N,4)

         WRITE (6,2) N

  2      FØRMAT (1H0,I4)

         STØP

         END
```

A single variable to be dumped, such as I, is repeated in the list twice, because each such variable constitutes the beginning and the end, that is, the limits, of the list required by the CALL.

The G and H compilers make the computer dump the contents of its memory regardless of whether it has completed the execution of the program or not. At the end of the program shown above the computer would print:

0639BC	7
0639C4	10
0639C8	21
21	

where the first three numbers—on the right—are the dumped values of I, K, and N, and the final 21 is the value of N produced by the command WRITE.

The three numbers on the left (0639BC, etc.) are the hexadecimal† addresses of the memory locations from which the dumps were made; we need not concern ourselves with these addresses.

If the WRITE command in the program were mistakenly written WRITE(5,2) N, the computer would produce the same dump as above but would omit the final 21.

To obtain the dump of the entire list I, J, K in the program, the first CALL statement would be written:

```
CALL PDUMP (I,K,4)
```

Shown below is a program that processes and dumps real numbers.

```
      READ (5,1) A,B,C,D
  1   FØRMAT (4F4.1)
      CALL PDUMP (A,D,5)
      Q = A + B
      CALL PDUMP (Q,Q,5)
      R = A+B+C+D
      S = C*D
      T = Q/D
      CALL PDUMP (R,T,5)
      WRITE (6,2) Q,R,S,T
  2   FØRMAT (1H0,4F6.2)
      STØP
      END
```

Data card:

```
11.2  3.4  5.7  2.0
    ^    ^    ^
```

The program generates the following dumps and results:

038154   0.111999998E+02   0.339999962E+01   0.569999981E+01
                                              0.200000000E+01

038164   0.145999994E+02

———————

† The hexadecimal system of numbers is explained in Appendix C.

038168   0.222999878E+02   0.113999996E+02   0.729999924E+01

14.60   22.30   11.40   7.30

questions and problems

7-1/   What is the difference between the UNCØNDITIØNAL GØ TØ and the CØMPUTED GØ TØ statements?

7-2/   What are the punctuation requirements of the CØMPUTED GØ TØ statement?

7-3/   Which of the following statements are invalid and why?

(a)   GØ TØ K
(b)   GØ TØ 8642
(c)   GØ TØ (6,101,5)4
(d)   GØ TØ (7,6,5,4),A
(e)   GØ TØ (1,2,3,4),IT12

7-4/   The memory has the following values in storage:

$$I = 3 \qquad J = 2$$

Which statements will be executed after each of the following statements?

(a)   GØ TØ 1234   (b)   GØ TØ (2,3,4,5),J
(c)   GØ TØ (1,3,5,7),I

7-5/   Draw a flow chart and write a program with an UNCØNDITIØNAL GØ TØ statement that will make the computer find the sum of the four numbers given on each of the five data cards below and will print out the four numbers and the sum, with headings, as shown in the printout below the data.

Card	Data			
1	7.60	18.010	100.2	.20
2	99.	16.05	954.263	7.15
3	1.123	4.06	0.002	79.12
4	1000.0	822.6	6.32	240.56
5	600.45	7.236	11.11	199.42

Arrange the printout to appear with two blank lines above the headings and double-spaced thereafter.

Printout:

```
     CARD*              NUMBERS              *    SUM


      1  *    7.600   18.010   100.200   0.200  *   126.010
      ↑  ↑      ↑        ↑         ↑        ↑     ↑     ↑
Col.  5  8     15       25        35       45    51    58
```

Write one pair of WRITE/FØRMAT statements for the headings and one pair for one line of the numerical table printout; the second pair of statements will be used repeatedly in the GØ TØ loop.

Use the F8.3 specification for all real numbers.

7-6/ A company with a payroll of 5000 employees has decided to pay a bonus based on the employee's length of service. The length of service is divided into four groups, as follows:

Group mark	1	2	3	4
Years of service	0-10	11-20	21-30	Over 30
Bonus, $	200	500	1000	1500

Employees' records, punched on cards, show, among other things, their NUMBER, their regular PAY, and their length of service MARK (from 1 to 4).

Draw a flow chart and write a program with a CØMPUTED GØ TØ statement that will compute, for the first eight employees, the TØTAL amount of their pay check (including the bonus), and will print out their NUMBER, the regular PAY, the service MARK, and the TØTAL amount to be shown on the pay check.

Data:

Employee Number	Pay, $	Service mark
1	650.50	3
2	1010.67	4
3	420.20	1
4	470.65	1
5	1850.00	4

Employee Number	Pay, $	Service mark
6	817.20	3
7	540.65	2
8	820.60	2

Make the printout appear in the following form:

Employee number	**Pay, $**	**Service mark**	**Paycheck**
1	650.50	3	
↑	↑	↑	↑
Col. 15	Col. 30	Col. 42	Col. 56

Double-space all the lines.
Fields: F8.2 for real numbers; I5 for integers.

7-7/   A firm makes wholesale sales to stores and retail sales to the public. Retail customers get no discount, while stores get a 40 per cent discount.

A record of a sale shows

(1)   The catalog number of the item sold.
(2)   The quantity of the items sold.
(3)   The unit price of the item.
(4)   The type of the customer: 1 for wholesale and 2 for retail.

Assume the following set of records:

Item no.	Quantity	Unit price	Customer
321	80	2.75	1
17	2	4.98	2
1124	4	1.19	2
10927	150	0.90	1
415	1	9.98	2
17	1	4.98	2
282	10	0.78	2

Write a program, including a CØMPUTED GØ TØ statement, which will generate, for every sale, a line of printout showing the item catalog number, the gross price of the items sold, the discount granted (if any), and the net price. Leave a blank line below the titles (suggested below), and single-space the sales records.

Item no.   **Gross price**   **Discount**   **Net price**

7-8/   Write a program, invoking the WATFIV compiler,

(1)   To store five integer numbers:

7   2   5   6   4

and five real numbers:

10.2   44.7   51.0   9.2   14.7

(2)   To find the sum and the product of the integer numbers and the sum of the real numbers.
(3)   To print the two sums and the product.
(4)   To dump
    (a)   The second integer number
    (b)   All real numbers
    (c)   The integer sum and product and the real sum
    (d)   The two sums.

Repeat the program invoking the G compiler. You will need special control cards; learn what they are from the instructor or the computer organization.

the IF statements
—the A specification

8-1. the arithmetic IF statement

Let us suppose that we have a discontinuous graph, such as shown in Fig. 8-1, and that we want the computer to calculate the ordinates y on this graph corresponding to the various abscissas x. We can see from the graph that, if x is less than 0, the values of y are given by the equation

$$y = 3x + 2$$

Also that, if x is greater than 0, the values of y are given by the equation

$$y = x + 2$$

and, finally, that, if x is equal to 0,

$$y = +2$$

A little reflection will show that we cannot give the computer a value of x (say, -2) and ask it to compute the corresponding value of y without telling the machine which expression for y it should use in the computation. The machine has three expressions to choose from, and therefore it needs guidance to make the right decision in the choice of the expression to use. This guidance is furnished by the *arithmetic IF* statement, which has the following general form:

IF (REX) M, J, K

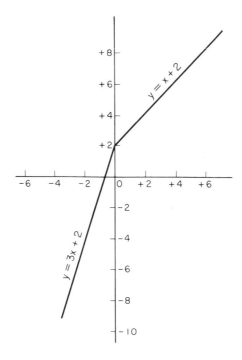

Figure 8-1

in which the argument REX† is any arithmetic expression in real or integer mode, such as described in Article 6-4, and M, J, K are the numbers of any three statements preceding or following the IF statement.

The meaning of the statement is as follows: if the argument REX is known—or computed—to be less than 0, the machine will go to Statement M (the *first* statement in the list) and execute that statement and then the statements that follow it in sequence; if REX is equal to 0, the computer will execute Statement J (the *second* statement in the list) and the statements that follow it; and if REX is greater than 0, the machine will execute Statement K (the *last* listed statement) and the statements that follow it.

Written in an explicit form, the IF statement would appear like this:

$$\text{IF} \quad \begin{cases} (\text{REX} < 0) & \text{G}\varnothing \text{ T}\varnothing \text{ M} \\ (\text{REX} = 0) & \text{G}\varnothing \text{ T}\varnothing \text{ J} \\ (\text{REX} > 0) & \text{G}\varnothing \text{ T}\varnothing \text{ K} \end{cases}$$

Note that in the general form of the IF statement the argument REX is enclosed in parentheses and the three statement numbers in the list, M, J, and K, are separated by two commas.

---

† Coined from 'R' ('rithmetic) and 'EX' (expression).

The following discussion explains the application of the IF statement to the problem shown in Fig. 8-1. Let us assume that we wish to obtain the values of y corresponding to the values of x varying from -2.4 to $+1.2$ by increments of $+0.1$. First, we draw a flow chart, as shown in Fig. 8-2, then parallel it with the program shown below, cross-referencing the two with statement numbers.

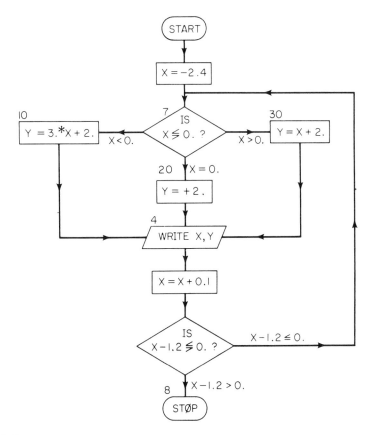

Figure 8-2

Program:

```
      X = −2.4
  7   IF(X) 10,20,30
 10   Y = 3.*X + 2.
      GØ TØ 4
 20   Y = +2.
      GØ TØ 4
 30   Y = X + 2.
  4   WRITE(6,1) X, Y
```

```
1  FØRMAT(1X, 2F6.1)
   X = X + 0.1
   IF(X − 1.2) 7,7,8
8  STØP
   END
```

There are no data cards to be read. The first statement initializes X to −2.4, the value of the leftmost abscissa. Next, executing the IF statement, the computer notes that X, which is −2.4, is less than 0., and transfers control to Statement 10, which computes Y = 3.*(−2.4) + 2. = −5.2. Statement GØ TØ 4 transfers control to WRITE, which prints out −2.4, −5.2. Statement X = X + 0.1 increases the value of X to −2.4 + 0.1 = −2.3. Now the sequential order brings us to the second IF statement of the program, which compares the present value of X with the maximum value of +1.2, with which we have decided to terminate the program.

This second IF statement examines not X but the difference X − 1.2; if X is less than 1.2, the upper limit of X decided upon, that is, if X − 1.2<0., or if X is equal to 1.2, that is, if X − 1.2 = 0., the value of X must be used in the computation of Y; therefore, in *both cases* the second IF statement sends the computer back to Statement 7, the first IF statement, which determines along which route X should travel to find the right expression for Y; but if X is greater than 1.2, that is, if X − 1.2 > 0., the value of X is not needed, and the machine is ordered to go to Statement 8, STØP.

The IF statement described above is called the arithmetic IF statement because it examines arithmetic expressions, such as

$$X − 1.2, \text{ or } Q + 2.*R, \text{ or, simply, } P,$$

to determine whether they are less than, equal to, or greater than 0..

A review of the preceding program will reveal that Statement 20 is not really necessary: if X = 0., the value of Y may be obtained from either Statement 10 or Statement 30; therefore, the sequence of statements from 7 to 4 may be rewritten in either one of the following two ways and produce the same result:

```
 7  IF(X) 10,10,30      or       7  IF(X) 10,30,30
10  Y = 3.*X + 2.                10  Y = 3.*X + 2.
    GØ TØ 4                          GØ TØ 4
30  Y = X + 2.                   30  Y = X + 2.
 4  WRITE(6,1) X,Y                4  WRITE(6,1) X,Y
```

The printout that results from either version of the program is shown in Fig. 8-3(a).

X	Y		X	Y
-2.4	-5.2		-2.400000	-5.199999
-2.3	-4.9		-2.299999	-4.899998
-2.2	-4.6		-2.199999	-4.599997
-2.1	-4.3		-2.099998	-4.299995
-2.0	-4.0		-1.999998	-3.999994
-1.9	-3.7		-1.899998	-3.699993
-1.8	-3.4		-1.799997	-3.399992
-1.7	-3.1		-1.699997	-3.099991
-1.6	-2.8		-1.599997	-2.799990
-1.5	-2.5		-1.499996	-2.499989
-1.4	-2.2		-1.399996	-2.199987
-1.3	-1.9		-1.299995	-1.899986
-1.2	-1.6		-1.199995	-1.599985
-1.1	-1.3		-1.099995	-1.299984
-1.0	-1.0		-0.999995	-0.999984
-0.9	-0.7		-0.899995	-0.699984
-0.8	-0.4		-0.799995	-0.399983
-0.7	-0.1		-0.699995	-0.099983
-0.6	0.2		-0.599995	0.200017
-0.5	0.5		-0.499995	0.500017
-0.4	0.8		-0.399994	0.800017
-0.3	1.1		-0.299994	1.100017
-0.2	1.4		-0.199994	1.400016
-0.1	1.7		-0.099994	1.700016
0.0	2.0		0.000006	2.000005
0.1	2.1		0.100006	2.100005
0.2	2.2		0.200006	2.200006
0.3	2.3		0.300006	2.300005
0.4	2.4		0.400006	2.400005
0.5	2.5		0.500006	2.500006
0.6	2.6		0.600006	2.600005
0.7	2.7		0.700006	2.700006
0.8	2.8		0.800006	2.800005
0.9	2.9		0.900006	2.900005
1.0	3.0		1.000006	3.000006
1.1	3.1		1.100005	3.100005

(a)   (b)

Figure 8-3

An observant reader will notice that the printout does not display the terminal value of X, namely, 1.2, and the corresponding value of Y. Something has caused the computer, after it had examined the final difference X − 1.2, that is, 1.2 − 1.2, to STØP rather than return to Statement 7 for the final pass through the program and the computation of the final Y.

The answer to the mystery is found in the binary system on which most computers operate. It is shown in Appendix C that many fractional numbers

X	Y
−2.4	−5.2
−2.3	−4.9
−2.2	−4.6
−2.1	−4.3
−2.0	−4.0
−1.9	−3.7
−1.8	−3.4
−1.7	−3.1
−1.6	−2.8
−1.5	−2.5
−1.4	−2.2
−1.3	−1.9
−1.2	−1.6
−1.1	−1.3
−1.0	−1.0
−0.9	−0.7
−0.8	−0.4
−0.7	−0.1
−0.6	0.2
−0.5	0.5
−0.4	0.8
−0.3	1.1
−0.2	1.4
−0.1	1.7
0.0	2.0
0.1	2.1
0.2	2.2
0.3	2.3
0.4	2.4
0.5	2.5
0.6	2.6
0.7	2.7
0.8	2.8
0.9	2.9
1.0	3.0
1.1	3.1
1.2	3.2

Figure 8-4

in the decimal system cannot be represented exactly in the binary system; for instance, the fraction 0.1 is stored in the computer as 0.099999905. Continuous additions of this approximate value of 0.1 to the initial value of X (performed in the devious ways of the machine and the binary system) produce a series of values of X that are almost never equal to the expected simple values. This can be seen in Fig. 8-3(b), which shows the printout of the values of X and Y carried out to the sixth decimal place. This table makes it clear that when the computer makes the last incrementation, the value of X increases from 1.100005 to a probable 1.200005; testing this value against 1.2, the computer obtains a positive difference and stops, instead of returning to Statement 7 for the final pass through the program and the evaluation of Y.

A scheme for guarding against losses of results is to compare the accumulated X with a value between the specified final value (1.2) and the next incremented value (1.3); for example, changing the statement IF(X − 1.2)7,7,8 to IF(X − 1.25)7,7,8 will make the computer compare 1.200005 with 1.25 and return to Statement 7; then, at the end of the next pass, compare 1.300005 with 1.25 and stop.

The printout resulting from this substitution is shown in Fig. 8-4 on facing page.

8-2. logical expressions

In Article 8-1 we saw that a segment of a program may have several variants, some shorter than others. The first variant of the original program read like this:

```
 7  IF(X) 10,10,30
10  Y = 3.*X + 2.
    GØ TØ 4
30  Y = X + 2.
 4  WRITE(6,1) X, Y
```

The substance of this segment was as follows: If X was less than or equal to 0, the computer was to go to Statement 10, compute Y = 3.*X + 2., and then go to Statement 4, WRITE X,Y. If, on the other hand, X was greater than 0, the computer was to go to Statement 30, compute Y = X + 2., and then move sequentially to WRITE X,Y.

These operations, which required five statements of the program (or seven statements in the original version), may be summarized in the following three statements:

```
IF (X≤0):          Y = 3.*X + 2.
IF (X>0):          Y = X + 2.
WRITE X,Y
```

The intent of these statements is as follows: Upon reading the first IF statement above, the computer is to examine X to see whether it is smaller than or equal to 0; if it is TRUE, the computer is to calculate Y = 3.*X + 2. Obviously, if the first IF statement is true, the second IF statement (X > 0) is FALSE; consequently, the computer is to bypass the calculation Y = X + 2. and to move on to the third statement, WRITE X,Y, where Y is obtained from Y = 3.*X + 2.

If, on the other hand, the computer, upon reading the first statement, discovers that X is not less than or equal to 0, that is, that X $\leqslant$ 0 is FALSE, it ignores Y = 3.*X + 2. and moves to the second statement, which is TRUE, and executes Y = X + 2.; then it writes the corresponding X,Y.

The preceding discussion has led us to a new FORTRAN statement: the *logical IF* statement. Directed by this statement, the computer examines an expression of the type (X $\leqslant$ 0) or (X > 0), called a *logical expression*, or *LEX* for short, to which the answer is not a calculated number but a word: TRUE or FALSE; depending on the answer, it executes, or does not execute, the command or the assignment associated with the LEX in the logical IF statement.

Since a logical expression forms the argument, or the core, of the logical IF statement, let us first study the core, that is, the logical expression.

In its simpler form a logical expression (LEX) is a comparison of two arithmetic expressions (REXes); both REXes must be in the same mode. The two REXes are compared by means of *relational operators*. The general form of a logical expression is

$$\text{LEX} = (\text{REX1 . RELATIØNAL ØPERATØR . REX2})$$

where the three members of the expression are separated by two periods.

The preceding discussion will be brought into better focus by the following table which shows the six basic logical expressions available in FORTRAN, accompanied by examples, their mathematical meaning, and the logical results. Note that the differences between the logical expressions are due entirely to their relational operators, which are .LT. (less than), .EQ. (equal to), .GT. (greater than), .NE. (not equal to), .LE. (less than or equal to), and .GE. (greater than or equal to). The periods before and after a relational operator are necessary to keep the computer from mistaking a logical argument, such as S.LE.D (S $\leqslant$ D), for a real variable, SLED. Note that in the last line of the table a real constant 1. before the relational operator causes two periods to occur in succession. Also note that the relational operators .LE. and .GE., which impose two conditions, require that only one condition be satisfied for the logical expression to be true.

Logical expression Relational operator ↓	Example	Mathematical meaning	If X = 2. and Y = 3.
REX1.LT.REX2	2.+X.LT.Y	$(2 + X) < Y$	LEX is FALSE
REX3.EQ.REX4	3.*Y.EQ.X+7.	$3Y = (X + 7)$	LEX is TRUE
REX3.GT.REX4	3.*Y.GT.X+7.	$3Y > (X + 7)$	LEX is FALSE
REX5.NE.REX2	X.NE.Y	$X \neq Y$	LEX is TRUE
REX2.LE.REX6	Y.LE.X**2	$Y \leqslant X^2$	LEX is TRUE
REX7.GE.REX6	Y+1..GE.X**2	$(Y + 1) \geqslant X^2$	LEX is TRUE

A logical expression that is TRUE at one time during the execution of the program may become FALSE at a later time (and vice versa), if the values of one or both of the arithmetic expressions that make it up undergo a change in the course of the program. Thus, if some program operation changes the Y in the preceding table from 3. to 7., the first and the third LEXes will become TRUE, the second and the fifth FALSE, and the fourth and the sixth will remain TRUE.

The logical expressions can be expanded by connecting two or more of them by *logical operators* .AND. and .OR. . The operator .AND. connects two or more LEXes and requires all of them to be TRUE for the combined LEX to be TRUE; if at least one LEX is FALSE, the combined LEX is FALSE. The operator .OR. makes the combined LEX TRUE if at least one of the component LEXes is TRUE; if all the component LEXes are FALSE, the combined LEX is FALSE.

The operator .AND. has a precedence over the operator .ØR. . Evaluating the logical expression

P.ØR.Q.AND.R

the computer first assigns a logical value S to Q.AND.R; if both Q and R are TRUE, S is TRUE; otherwise S is FALSE. Then the computer determines the logical value V of P.ØR.S; if both P and S are FALSE, V is FALSE; otherwise V is TRUE.

The order of evaluation can be controlled or reversed by means of parentheses: expressions within the parentheses are evaluated first. Given the expression

(P.ØR.Q).AND.R

the computer first finds the logical value G of P.ØR. Q. G is FALSE only if both P and Q are FALSE. Then it finds the logical value H of G and R; H is TRUE only if both G and R are TRUE.

While the relational operators may not compare arithmetic expressions (REXes) in different modes, the logical operators may connect logical expressions (LEXes) in different modes.

Examples of the use of the logical operators are presented in the table on page 144.

The final logical operator is .NØT. . This operator precedes a logical expression and negates it; the expression to which .NØT. applies must be enclosed in parentheses to avoid ambiguity. The application of .NØT. is illustrated below.

Logical expression	*Example*	*If X = 2. and Y = 3.*
.NØT.(LEX)	.NØT.(X.GT.Y)	NOT FALSE; LEX is TRUE

Logical expression	Example	If $X=2.$, $Y=3.$, $Z=4.$, $I=3$, $J=1$
LEX1.AND.LEX2	X.GT.Y.AND.3.*X.LT.Z	FALSE and FALSE; LEX is FALSE
LEX3.OR.LEX4.OR.LEX5	J.EQ.1.OR.J.EQ.4.OR.J.EQ.5	TRUE or FALSE or FALSE; LEX is TRUE
LEX6.OR.LEX4	J.EQ.2.OR.J.EQ.4	FALSE or FALSE; LEX is FALSE
LEX7.AND.LEX8	3.*X.EQ.2.*Y.AND.I.EQ.3*J	TRUE and TRUE; LEX is TRUE

In the discussion of Fig. 8-3 we pointed out the possibility of errors in the cases of differences such as $1.200005 - 1.2$, which the computer interprets as being greater than 0., rather than being equal to 0. . A similar pitfall exists in the case of the logical expressions involving numbers with fractions. Consider, for example, a logical expression X + Y.GT.3.0. If X = 1.9 and Y = 1.1, X + Y = 3.0, and therefore X + Y.GT.3.0 is FALSE; but the computer may have stored under X 1.900002 and under Y 1.100001, and thus obtain X + Y = 3.000003; as a consequence, it would interpret the logical expression as TRUE. Therefore, in writing logical expressions precautions should always be taken to avoid comparing numbers whose differences may approach 0.; the error in the case above may be prevented by writing X + Y.GT.3.0005.

8-3. the logical IF statement

Now that we are acquainted with the nature of the logical expression, we can advance to the study of the *logical IF* statement, whose operation is controlled by the TRUE/FALSE value of the logical expression which forms its argument.

The general form of the logical IF statement is

IF (LEX) V = REX

where V = variable name

or

IF (LEX) GØ TØ

or

IF (LEX) IF (REX)

and its operation is as follows:

1/ LEX is evaluated.

2/ If LEX is TRUE, the statement to its right is executed:
  (a) If that statement is of the form V = REX, i.e., an arithmetic statement, the value of V is computed and stored, and control passes sequentially to the next statement in the program.
  (b) If the statement on the right is a GØ TØ (unconditional or computed) or IF(REX) (the arithmetic IF), control is transferred to the statement indicated by the GØ TØ or by the IF(REX).

3/ If LEX is FALSE, the statement on its right is ignored, and control passes sequentially to the next statement.

example 8-1. The following program segment and two sets of data show the operation of the logical IF statement with a V = REX.

```
Line 1    READ, A, B, C
     2    P = 3.*A + B
     3    IF(A.LE.B) P = A + 4.*C
     4    R = C + P
```

	A	B	C
Data 1	2.0	5.0	3.0
Data 2	10.0	5.0	3.0

Analysis:

DATA 1: Line
2: P is computed to be 11.0
3: LEX is TRUE; P is recomputed to be 14.0
4: R = 3.0 + 14.0 = 17.0

DATA 2: Line
2: P is computed to be 35.0
3: LEX is FALSE; P is not recomputed
4: R = 3.0 + 35.0 = 38.0

example 8-2. Rectangular and triangular pieces, illustrated in Fig. 8-5, are to be cut out of plywood. For each piece, data cards give a shape MARK, 1 for a rectangle and 2 for a triangle, and dimensions BASE and HEIGHT, in feet.

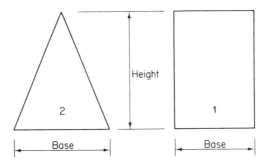

Figure 8-5

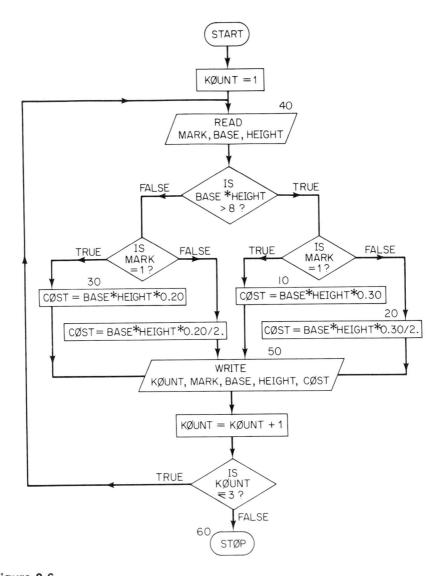

Figure 8-6

If BASE*HEIGHT exceeds 8 sq ft, the cost of plywood is $0.30 per sq ft; if not, the cost is $0.20 per sq ft.

A flow chart of the steps required to compute and print the costs of the individual pieces is shown in Fig. 8-6. To shorten the problem, the number of the pieces and of the corresponding data cards is limited to three.

The chart initializes the KOUNT of the pieces at 1. The three items of the data on the first card are read. The data are analyzed: Is BASE*HEIGHT greater than 8? If TRUE, the computer will assign a higher unit price to the piece. However, before computing the cost of the piece, the computer has to settle another question: Is the piece rectangular or not? That is, is the MARK of the piece 1 or not? Depending on the two answers to each of the two questions, the chart shows four paths leading to four different computations of the cost. The computation made, the results are printed, and the KOUNT is increased by 1. The computer is faced with a new decision: Does KOUNT exceed the number of data cards, that is, 3? If FALSE, the computer returns to read the next (second) card and retraces the steps in the chart; if TRUE (KOUNT = 4), the computer stops.

A program paralleling the flow chart of Fig. 8-6 is shown in Fig. 8-7. The statements in the program are numbered in correspondence with the steps in the flow chart. The lines of the program are numbered consecutively for cross-referencing with the actual steps of the program execution shown after Fig. 8-7.

```
       70  FØRMAT(II,2F2.0)
       80  FØRMAT(1HØ,2I5,2F10.0,F10.2)
 1         KØUNT=1
 2     40  READ(5,70)MARK,BASE,HEIGHT
 3         IF(BASE*HEIGHT.GT.8.)GØTØ(10,20),MARK
 4         IF(MARK.EQ.1)GØTØ30
 5         CØST=BASE*HEIGHT*0.20/2.
 6         GØTØ50
 7     30  CØST=BASE*HEIGHT*0.20
 8         GØTØ50
 9     10  CØST=BASE*HEIGHT*0.30
10         GØTØ50
11     20  CØST=BASE*HEIGHT*0.30/2.
12     50  WRITE(6,80)KØUNT,MARK,BASE,HEIGHT,CØST
13         KØUNT=KØUNT+1
14         IF(KØUNT.LE.3)GØTØ40
15     60  STØP
           END
   13.4.  ⎫
   22.3.  ⎬ DATA
   15.1.  ⎭
```

Figure 8-7

```
Line  1    KØUNT = 1
      2    READ:  1.,   3.,     4.
      3    LEX is TRUE; GØ TØ 10
      9    CØST = 3.60
     10    GØ TØ 50
     12    WRITE:    1,    1,    3.,    4.,    3.60
     13    KØUNT = 2
     14    LEX is TRUE; GØ TØ 40
      2    READ:    2,    2.,    3.
      3    LEX is FALSE; GØ TØ ignored
      4    LEX is FALSE; GØ TØ ignored
      5    CØST = 0.60
      6    GØ TØ 50
     12    WRITE:    2,    2,    2.,    3.,    0.60
     13    KØUNT = 3
     14    LEX is TRUE; GØ TØ 40
      2    READ:    1,    5.,    1.
      3    LEX is FALSE; GØ TØ ignored
      4    LEX is TRUE; GØ TØ 30
      7    CØST = 1.00
      8    GØ TØ 50
     12    WRITE:    3,    1,    5.,    1.,    1.00
     13    KØUNT = 4
     14    LEX is FALSE; GØ TØ ignored
     15    STØP
```

example 8-3. In Line 3 of the program in Fig. 8-7 the computed GØ TØ statement may be replaced by the arithmetic IF statement as follows:

$$\text{IF(BASE*HEIGHT.GT.8.)IF(MARK} - 2)10,20,60$$

and the operations and computations which ensue will be the same as in Example 8-2. The student is advised to verify this.

It should be noted that the third alternative of the arithmetic IF, which sends the computer to Statement 60, STØP, cannot ever occur, because MARK cannot exceed 2; but the statement number 60 (or any other number which is used in the program) must be shown to complete the arithmetic IF statement.

Until now, we have relied on the computer to stop the execution of the program when it returned to the READ statement and found no card to read. Although it is an effective way to stop the program, sending the computer to READ a card that is not there amounts to giving it a false instruction, and the computer retaliates by printing out an error message on the sheet.

Line 14 in Fig. 8-7 illustrates a method of averting the error message: After a predetermined number of cards (3) have been read and processed, the computer establishes the fact by means of the logical IF statement and transfers control to STØP instead of READ.

example 8-4. Four real numbers are punched on a data card, in consecutive fields of 5 spaces each, each number with one decimal digit. A program to determine the largest number may be written as follows:

```
        READ (5,1)   A,B,C,D
    1   FØRMAT (4F5.1)
        BIG = A
        IF (B.GT.BIG)   BIG = B
        IF (C.GT.BIG)   BIG = C
        IF (D.GT.BIG)   BIG = D
        WRITE (6,2)   BIG
    2   FØRMAT (1H0,F5.1)
        STØP
```

If the data card is punched:

```
 -25.5ˆ17.2ˆ-0.4ˆ14.5
```

the printed result is:

ˆ17.2

alternate program

The library of mathematical functions has a function AMAX1 which selects the largest real number in a group. The general form of the function is:

$$AMAX1 \quad (R,S,T, \ldots)$$

where the real arguments R, S, T, . . . , enclosed in parentheses and separated by commas, are the values to be compared and AMAX1 is the subprogram which compares them and selects the largest. If AMAX1 is invoked, the program above reduces to:

```
      READ (5,1)   A,B,C,D
  1   FØRMAT (4F5.1)
      BIG = AMAX1 (A,B,C,D)
      WRITE (6,2)   BIG
  2   FØRMAT (1H0,F5.1)
      STØP
```

The corresponding function for integers has the general form:

$$MAX0 \ (I,J,K, \ . \ . \ .)$$

8-4. trailer card

In the program of Fig. 8-7, after the computer has read the last card in the data deck and processed it, it is prevented from returning to the READ statement and attempting to read a nonexistent card by the last IF statement (Line 14), which tells the computer that, if the KØUNT of cards exceeds 3, it must STØP. It was easy to write this IF statement, because we knew that the deck had 3 cards. But what if someone gives us a deck of cards 2 inches thick and asks us to process them? Counting the cards is out of the question; not only is it time-consuming, it may also result in a wrong count.

Fortunately, there is a simple solution: a *trailer card.* A trailer card is a card placed at the end of a data deck with a value on it that does not appear on any card in the deck; it may even be a blank card.

To illustrate, let us place a blank card at the back of the data deck in Fig. 8-7. During the execution, the computer reads the MARK in the first column of all the data cards; this MARK is always 1 or 2. When the computer attempts to read the blank trailer card, it interprets the blank in the first column as zero. Taking advantage of this interpretation, we can bring the execution to a halt by writing

$$IF(MARK.EQ.0) \ STØP$$

immediately after the READ statement on Line 2. This new statement at once makes the STØP statement on Line 15 redundant. Furthermore, no longer dependent on the value of KØUNT for halting the execution, we can reduce Line 14 to

GØ TØ 40

Thus, with a blank trailer card in the data deck, the program and data of Fig. 8-7 will appear, with the resulting printout, as shown below:

PROGRAM

```
70  FØRMAT(I1,2F2.0)
80  FØRMAT(1H0,2I5,2F10.0,F10.2)
    KØUNT = 1
40  READ(5,70)MARK,BASE,HEIGHT
    IF(MARK.EQ.0)STØP
    IF(BASE*HEIGHT.GT.8.) GØ TØ (10,20),MARK
    IF(MARK.EQ.1)GØ TØ 30
    CØST=BASE*HEIGHT*0.20/2.
    GØ TØ 50
30  CØST=BASE*HEIGHT*0.20
    GØ TØ 50
10  CØST=BASE*HEIGHT*0.30
    GØ TØ 50
20  CØST=BASE*HEIGHT*0.30/2.
50  WRITE (6,80)KØUNT,MARK,BASE,HEIGHT,CØST
    KØUNT=KØUNT+1
    GØ TØ 40
    END
```

Data cards:

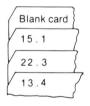

```
Blank card
15 . 1
22 . 3
13 . 4
```

Printout:

```
1    1    3.    4.    3.60
2    2    2.    3.    0.60
3    1    5.    1.    1.00
```

Of course, if we punch 7 in the first column of the trailer card, the IF statement terminating the execution should obviously be

IF(MARK.EQ.7)STØP

The printout that results from the program above shows, in the last line, the total KØUNT of cards in the data deck, namely, 3. This scheme can be used to count cards in any deck of cards, punched or blank.

8-5. "END=L" transfer

The effect of a trailer card at the end of a data deck can be created—without the trailer card—by a job control card that is normally required behind the data deck of the job submitted for processing (see the next to the last card in Fig. 3-6). We know that the trailer card operates by sending to the computer a unique message (for instance, a zero instead of a number) which, interpreted by the IF statement, causes the computer to refrain from executing the READ statement again.

A similarly effective unique signal is transmitted to the computer by the first character on the job control card mentioned above, usually $ or /. However, we cannot incorporate either of these symbols in an IF statement; we cannot write

IF(MARK.EQ.$) STØP

Instead, we tell the computer, in the READ statement itself, to what statement it should transfer control when it receives the $ or / signal from the job control card. This is accomplished by including in the READ statement, together with the processing unit and FØRMAT numbers, the "END=L" transfer command as follows:

READ(5,2,END=3) K

where END=3 (separated by a comma from the preceding FØRMAT number 2) informs the computer that it should transfer control to Statement 3 after it has encountered $ or / on a card, instead of an integer value of K. The operation of "END=L" is illustrated in Example 8-5.

example 8-5. Write a program, containing an "END=L" command, that will make the computer count cards in a given data deck and print their number. (In the example, the deck contains eight blank cards.)

		Program	Comments
Line			
1		K = 0	The count of cards, K, is initialized at zero.
2	1	READ(5,2,END=3) N	The computer is told to read the number
3	2	FØRMAT(I1)	N on the first data card; since the card is blank, the computer stores 0 at N; the purpose of this command is to make the computer read every card until it sees $ or / on a job control card.
4		K = K + 1	K is increased by 1, that is, the card read on Line 2 is counted.
5		GØ TØ 1	The computer is sent back to Line 2 to
6	3	WRITE(6,4) K	read the next data card; when it encoun-
7	4	FØRMAT(1H0,I2)	ters $ or / on a job control card, END=3
8		STØP	transfers control to Statement 3 on Line 6, which orders the computer to print the value of K, the count of blank cards.

Printout:

8

8-6.   the A specification

We have learned in Chapter 2 that the I, F, and E specifications, accompanying variable names, enable the computer to read numbers on data cards and to store those numbers in memory locations bearing the names of the variables as addresses. Thus, given two cards with the following program statements:

```
    READ(5,1) WEIGHT, KLASS
  1 FØRMAT(F5.1,I2)
```

and a card with the following data in the first seven columns:

the computer would store 180.4 under WEIGHT and 3 under KLASS.

So far we have encountered data cards with numerical values only. Now we are going to learn that data may consist of characters other than numeric;

namely, that data may include, in addition to the numerals, all the letters of the alphabet, the special characters

$$+ \quad - \quad * \quad / \quad = \quad , \quad . \quad (\quad) \quad ' \quad \$ \quad {}_\wedge$$

symbol for a blank space

and all combinations of the alphameric (i.e., numeric and alphabetic) and special characters. The alphameric and special characters may be stored under variable names in the same manner as that employed to store numbers, namely, by matching the variable names with the FØRMAT specifications that identify the alphameric type and the fields of the data. The FØRMAT specification employed for this purpose is the *A specification,* which has the general form

$$Aw$$

in which A identifies the data as alphameric and w is an integer that gives the width of the alphameric field, that is, the number of columns occupied by the alphameric characters associated with the variable name. Thus, given two program cards:

```
    READ(5,2) NAME, SEX, AGE
  2 FØRMAT(A4,A4,A4) or (3A4) or (2A4,F4.1)
```

and a data card punched in the first 12 columns:

```
LEE ,MALE42 . 4
```

the computer will store LEE$_\wedge$ under NAME, MALE under SEX, and 42.4 under AGE.

In Article 3-1 it was shown that a memory location of an IBM System/360 computer consists of 32 iron cores, grouped in 4 bytes of 8 bits each. It was also stated that the contents of a memory location are called a *word.* Now the coding system for storing alphameric characters in the computer is such that only one character may be stored in a byte; therefore only four-character, or shorter, alphameric words may be stored in a location. Longer strings of characters must be divided into words of four characters each, and each word stored in a separate location. Blank spaces ($_\wedge$) are regarded and stored as characters.

Storage of the alphameric data is illustrated in the following examples.

example 8-6. The name LEE may be stored in two ways:

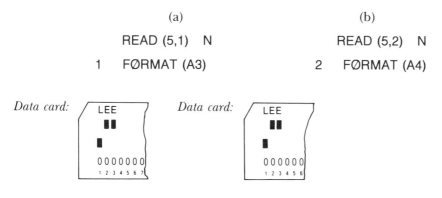

(a)

READ (5,1) N

1   FØRMAT (A3)

Data card:

(b)

READ (5,2) N

2   FØRMAT (A4)

Data card:

In the case (a) the computer stores the three characters of LEE left-justified, that is, it stores them in the first three bytes of the location N, and fills the rightmost byte with a blank; in the case (b) the computer fills the location completely with LEE‸, including the blank space it picks up in the fourth column on the data card. In both cases the contents of the location N are:

N | L | E | E | ‸ |

example 8-7. A person's name, sex, and age may be stored as follows:

READ (5,1) N1,N2,N3,SEX,AGE

1   FØRMAT (4A4,2X,A4)

Data card:

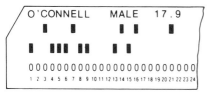

The data are stored as:

N1 | O | ' | C | O |
N2 | N | N | E | L |
N3 | L | ‸ | ‸ | ‸ |
SEX | M | A | L | E |
AGE | 1 | 7 | . | 9 |

example 8-8. An attempt to store in one location more than four characters results in the truncation of the excess characters on the left.

READ (5,1)   N
1   FØRMAT (A5)

Data card:

The datum is stored as: N | M | I | T | H |

Guided by the specification A5, the computer reaches the right edge of the 5-column field with SMITH in it, and *retains only the last four characters it has read,* namely, MITH, which it can store in four bytes; the leftmost S is truncated.

It is often necessary to tabulate names, and names, of course, differ in length. In such cases a field of certain width, say 16 columns, is allocated to names on data cards; then every name in that field is read and stored in four locations, in accordance with the sequence:

READ (5,4)   N1,N2,N3,N4
4   FØRMAT (4A4)

Every name with fewer than 16 characters would have the rightmost remainder of its 16-character storage space filled with blanks.

On output the computer prints the four-character contents of each storage location in the specified field, if the field is A4 or longer. If the field is described by A4, the four characters fill the field; if the field is longer than A4, say A6, the computer leaves the two leftmost spaces in the field blank, and prints the four stored characters in the four rightmost spaces of the field. If the field is shorter than A4, say A2, the computer prints only the two leftmost characters and truncates the two characters on the right. It must be remembered, of course, that, in an output FØRMAT statement, the field specifications are preceded by a carriage control specification. Thus, if Example 8-7 is continued with the following sequence:

```
        WRITE (6,5)   N1,N2,N3,SEX,AGE
     5  FØRMAT (1X,4A4,3X,A4)
```

the printout, single-spaced from the preceding line, will be:

O'CONNELL‸‸‸MALE‸‸‸17.9

Note that the blanks stored in a location are reproduced on the printout; thus the three blanks stored in the location N3 (with the last L of O'CONNELL) appear between O'CONNELL and MALE.

If a single character on a data card, say X, is read in with the specification A1, the computer stores it in the leftmost byte of a storage location, and the

Data card:

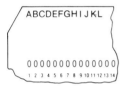

other three bytes remain empty. On output, in response to the specifications A1, A2, A3 or A4, this X may be made to appear as X, X‸, X‸‸ or X‸‸‸.

A datum stored with an A specification must be reported out with an A specification; it would not do to store the age 17.9 with A4 and to order its printout with F4.1.

Also, names and similar data, stored in four-character groups with the specification A4, should be ordered out with the same specification A4, and not with a wider specification, such as A6; in the latter case the four characters of every group into which the data are divided would be printed right-justified in a field of six columns, and a name like HENDERSØN, stored with 3A4 and ordered out with 3A6, would appear as ‸‸HEND‸‸ERSØ‸‸N‸‸‸. The specification that would produce HENDERSØN‸‸‸ is 3A4.

However, a *complete* 4-character word may be ordered out with a wider specification. Thus JANE, stored with A4 and ordered out with A7, would be printed, right-justified, as ‸‸‸JANE. But ordered to print JANE with too short a specification, such as A3, the computer will print only JAN; that is, it will print those characters in storage, beginning on the left, that fit within the specified field; the fourth character, E, that extends beyond the field, is truncated.

The rules for input and output are summarized graphically in Fig. 8-8.

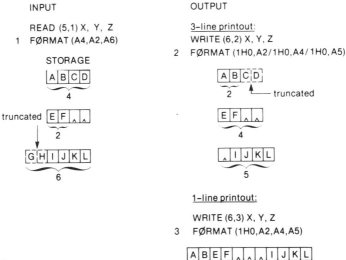

Figure 8-8

To conclude, the data are left-justified and truncated on the left on input, and the four characters in a location are right-justified and truncated on the right on output.

It is not significant whether a variable name associated with an A specification is real or integer: SMITH may be stored under N1, N2 or under A1, A2. However, in logical expressions that involve comparisons by means of operators such as .EQ. or .GT., the mode of the variable names may not be mixed. For example, let us suppose that we wish to determine the names of all the BROWNs in a deck of four cards that contain the following names:

```
CAMPØ^^^^^^^ MICHAEL
BRØWN        BUSTER
BRØWN        BENTØN
GØNZALEZ^^^^CARLØS
```

To obtain the desired result, we precede the four data cards with a single card punched BROWN and then place this combined data deck behind the program deck shown in Fig. 8-9.

On output the computer will print

```
BRØWN^^^^^^^BUSTER
BRØWN        BENTØN
```

| 1 | 2 | 3 | 4 | 5 | 6 | 7 | 8 | 9 |10 |11 |12 |13 |14 |15 |16 |17 |18 |19 |20 |21 |22 |23 |24 |25 |26 |27 |28 |29 |30 |31 |32 |33 |34 |35 |36 |37 |38 |39 |40 |41 |42 |43 |44 |45 |46 |47 |48 |49 |

```
1          READ(5,1)B1,B2,B3         Reads ⟶  [BRØWN∧∧∧∧∧∧∧]
2     1    FØRMAT(5A4)   ⟵ This Format is also used by READ on Line 6
3          K=0
4     2    K=K+1
5          IF(K.GT.4)STØP
6          READ(5,1)A1,A2,A3,A4,A5
7          IF(B1.EQ.A1.AND.B2.EQ.A2.AND.B3.EQ.A3)GØTØ3
8          GØTØ2
9     3    WRITE(6,4)A1,A2,A3,A4,A5
10    4    FØRMAT(1H0,5A4)
11         GØTØ2
12         END
```

Figure 8-9

If in line 1 of the program in Fig. 8-9 we used variable names N1, N2, N3 instead of B1, B2, B3 to read in BRØWN from the first data card, and then compared, in line 7, N1 with A1, etc., the program would fail because of the mixed mode of the variable names. The explanation of the failure is given in Article C-15 in the Appendix. There it is shown that a pattern of magnetization of the bits in a memory location may represent either a real number or an integer number, which are entirely different. Thus, while BRØWN stored under N1 does appear to be equal to BRØWN stored under A1, actually BRØWN at N1 is interpreted as an integer number and BRØWN at A1 as a real number. Since these two numbers are different, the computer treats the two BRØWNs as unequal.

While the alphameric characters can be stored in the memory by means of a READ statement, they, unlike numbers, cannot be stored by means of an assignment statement. Thus the name JACK cannot be stored under K by the statement:

K = JACK

However, the computer *can be* tricked into accepting an alphameric assignment. The roundabout way in which this can be done is shown in the following sequence:

```
      READ (5,1)   L
  1   FØRMAT (A4)
      K = L
```

Data card:

/ JACK /

That is, JACK is first stored under L by a READ statement; then the value of L (= JACK) is assigned to K.

As with comparisons, mixed mode is not allowed in assigning alphameric data. If JACK were READ in under P, the computer would balk at executing the assignment statement:

$$K = P$$

But it would execute:

$$Q = P$$

and store JACK under Q.

Some computer systems fail to produce satisfactory results when the alphameric data are stored under real names. This is because equal quantities, when stored in real mode, may become unequal, if ever so slightly (See Art. 8-1). This slight inequality would be enough to make them fail the equality test. Therefore it is recommended that, as an insurance of good results, the alphameric data be always stored under integer names.

When we store JACK under K we must not lose sight of the fact that JACK is actually stored as a string of 0's and 1's, and that this string may also represent an integer number or a real number. The following program prints the integer number corresponding to JACK.

```
        READ (5,1)   K
    1   FØRMAT (A4)
        WRITE (6,2)   K, K
    2   FØRMAT (1H0,A4,3X,I10)
        STØP
```

Data card:

/ JACK /

Printout:

JACK   −775830574

8-7. the DUMP of alphameric and special values

In Article 7-5 it was shown that the contents of the computer memory may be *dumped* on paper for an inspection. In the examples of Article 7-5 only numbers were used to illustrate the dumping operation. But the values to be dumped may also be made up of alphameric or special characters. The following example illustrates the storage of the first 12 letters of the alphabet in locations X, Y, and Z, their retrieval by means of the WRITE command, and their dump effected by calling DUMP. The program was translated by the G compiler, which dumps the contents in the alphameric form if the third argument in the call for DUMP is made 9.

```
          READ (5,1)   X,Y,Z
     1    FØRMAT (3A4)
          WRITE (6,2)   X,Y,Z
     2    FØRMAT (1H0,A4)
          CALL DUMP (X,Z,9)
          STØP
```

Data card:

```
ABCDEFGHIJKL
```

Printout:

ABCD
EFGH
IJKL

Dump:

03B9CC   ABCDEFGHIJKL

The WATFIV compiler dumps the alphameric contents of the memory in the decimal form only. The conversion from the decimal form to the alphameric form is rather involved, and therefore only the G and H compilers should be generally invoked to dump alphameric values.

questions and problems

8-1/   Which of the following arithmetic IF statements are invalid and why?

(a)   IF (A) 10, 20, 30   (e)   IF (K + L), 7, 8, 9
(b)   IF (J) 10, 10, 30   (f)   IF (C − 2) 10, 11, 12
(c)   IF (K + L) 7, 8   (g)   IF (C = 5.) 5, 6, 7
(d)   IF (K − L) 1, 2, 3   (h)   IF (X) 3, 4, 5,

8-2/   Write arithmetic IF statements for the following conditions:

(a)   If m is less than 0, execute Statement 5; if m is equal to or greater than 0, execute Statement 6.
(b)   If x is greater than 2, execute Statement 1; if x is equal to 2, execute Statement 2; if x is less than 2, execute Statement 3.
(c)   If d is less than or equal to 0, execute Statement 20; if d is greater than 0, execute Statement 30.

8-3/   The values of the variables are as shown below:

$$A = 4. \quad B = 2. \quad C = 3. \quad K = 2 \quad L = 3$$

Give the number of the statement that will be executed next after the following arithmetic IF statements:

(a)   IF (B) 10, 20, 30   (d)   IF (B + C − A) 1, 2, 3
(b)   IF (K − 2) 5, 6, 7   (e)   IF (B**K − A) 7, 8, 9
(c)   IF (K − L) 5, 6, 6   (f)   IF (A/B − C) 4, 5, 6

8-4/   For each of the following programs give the values stored at X and SUM after the STØP statement is executed.

(a)
```
          X = 2.
          SUM = 5.
      1   SUM = SUM + 5.*X
          IF(SUM − 30.) 1,1,2
      2   STØP
```

(b)
```
          X = 4.
          SUM = 0.
      4   SUM = SUM + X**2
          X = X + 2.
          IF(X−10.)4,6,6
      6   STØP
```

(c)   K = 2
          X = 0.
          SUM = 2.
      4   X = X + 2.
          SUM = SUM + 2.*X
          IF (7. − X) 3, 4, 4
      3   K = K + 2
          X = 0.
          IF (6 − K) 5, 5, 4
      5   STØP

8-5/   In a tensile test of a steel specimen observations are made of the unit stress (STRESS) in the specimen and of the corresponding unit deformation (DELTA) of the specimen. The relationship between these two quantities may be approximately represented by the graph shown in Fig. 8-10.

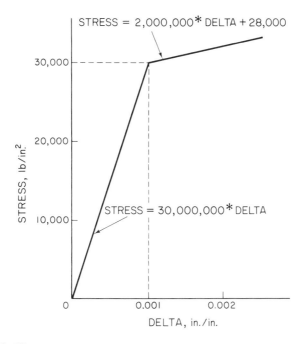

Figure 8-10

Draw a flow chart and write a program that will compute STRESS corresponding to DELTA between 0.0 and 0.002 in./in. at intervals of 0.0001 in./in.

Arrange the results in the following form:

(2 spaces)
DELTA, IN./IN.   STRESS, LB./SQ.IN.
(2 spaces)
  0.0000   00000.
  ↑   ↑
Col. 20   Col. 45

Single-space the tabulated values.
Choose your own fields for STRESS and DELTA.

8-6/   Find the logical values of the following expressions if A = 2., B = 5., C = 10., I = 2, J = 3, K = 6.

(a)   C.EQ.B
(b)   B.LE.A
(c)   K.GT.I**2
(d)   B.GT.A.AND.C.EQ.A*B
(e)   K.NE.I*J.OR.B.GE.A*2.5

8-7/   Write logical expressions for the following conditions.
(a)   A is greater than 2B and is less than 3C.
(b)   D is greater than all of A, B, and C.
(c)   D is greater than at least one of A, B, C.
(d)   A is greater than B and less than 2C.
(e)   A differs from B, and C differs from D and E.

8-8/   Write a complete program for Example 8-1 that will produce a printout of the two values of R without a message of error.

8-9/   In structural mechanics a simple beam loaded as shown in Fig.

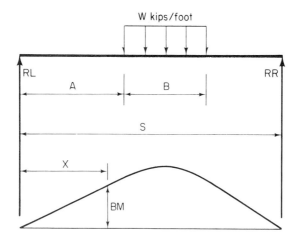

Figure 8-11

8-11 develops reaction forces at both ends and resisting bending moments throughout the length of the beam. The distribution of the bending moments is shown in the lower diagram.

Let
X   = distance to any point from the left end
BM = bending moment at that point
RL = reaction at the left end

From the principles of equilibrium:

$$RL = \frac{WB}{2S}(2(S-A)-B)$$

and

when $X \leqslant A$: $BM = RL(X)$

when $A \leqslant X \leqslant A+B$: $BM = RL(X) - \dfrac{W(X-A)^2}{2}$

when $A+B \leqslant X \leqslant S$: $BM = RL(X) - WB(X-A-\dfrac{B}{2})$

Write a program that will make the computer calculate the bending moments at both ends and at all points between them 0.5 ft apart and print them out.
Use the logical IF and any other statements.
Arrange the printout in the form of a table with the following headings:

X, FEET   MØMENT, KIP-FEET

Data: A = 5. ft, B = 6. ft, S = 15. ft, W = 0.8 k/ft

8-10/   The personal records for students in a university are kept on data cards in the following typical form:

508206038COLEMAN, HOWARD˄˄˄˄˄˄˄˄˄1˄˄20˄˄˄1˄˄˄3˄˄70˄185

The first entry, in a field of 9 spaces, is the social security number, and the second, in a field of 20 spaces, is the student's name. The six numbers, in the 4-space fields following the name, represent, consecutively, in code or actually, the following characteristics:

SEX: Male—1, Female—2
AGE: years
MARITAL STATUS: Single—1, Married—2
CLASS: Freshman—1, Sophomore—2, Junior—3, Senior—4
HEIGHT: inches
WEIGHT: pounds

Given ten data cards, write a program, containing one or more logical IF statements which will produce a printout of the social security numbers and the names of all male seniors 6 feet and taller.

Data cards:

```
435900321BECKHAM,  RICHARD~~~~~~~1~~22~~~2~~~4~~73~180

439828037DAVIS,  ROGER          1  21  1  2  74 182

437789069ROSS,  CLAUDIA         2  24  2  4  66 128

435808561MCMULLAN,  LISA        2  20  2  2  61 106

437829176PENDERGRASS,  JAMES    1  22  1  4  72 168

435846190JENNINGS,  JOHN        1  19  1  1  73 184

433482201BORSKEY,  RONALD       1  21  1  3  69 178

435825304DAVIS,  MICHAEL        1  21  1  3  67 152

439883473COLEMAN,  BEVERLYE     2  20  1  1  63 120

439886528HENDERSON,  MARK       1  23  2  4  74 175
```

8-11/ A sum of $100 is invested for one year. The rate of interest is 6 percent per year, and the interest is compounded every five days.

Write a program which will produce a tabulation of the values of the initial $100 at the end of every 5-day interval throughout the year.

The printout is to appear as follows:

5-DAY INTERVAL	VALUE, $
1	? . ?
2	? . ?
3	? . ?
. . .	. . . . .

notes

1/ *Simple interest* is interest paid on the *original principal only.* Thus, at 6 percent per year, simple interest on \$100 is $100 \times \frac{6}{100} = \$6$ at the end of one year, \$12 at the end of two years, etc.

2/ *Compound interest* is interest paid on the *original principal increased by the previously paid interest.* Thus, at 6 percent per year, compound interest on \$100 at the end of one year is $100 \times \frac{6}{100} = \$6$, increasing the principal to \$106; at the end of the second year, the interest is $106 \times \frac{6}{100} = \$6.36$, increasing the principal to \$112.36; etc.

3/ Interest may be compounded at intervals of less than a year. Then the rate is equal to the annual rate divided by the number of intervals in a year. If the 6 percent interest is compounded twice a year, the rate is $6/2 = 3$ percent per half-year. Thus, at the end of a half-year \$100 increases by $100 \times \frac{3}{100} = \$3$ to \$103, six months later \$103 increases by $103 \times \frac{3}{100} = \$3.09$ to \$106.09; etc.

4/ A general formula for computing the VALUE of a SUM, invested at RATE percent per year, compounded CI times a year, and kept invested for NI compounding intervals, is derived as follows:

$$\text{Rate per compounding interval} = \frac{\text{RATE}}{100 \times \text{CI}}$$

VALUE at the end of the first interval

$$= \text{SUM} + \text{SUM} \times \frac{\text{RATE}}{100 \times \text{CI}} = \text{SUM}(1 + \frac{\text{RATE}}{100 \times \text{CI}})$$

VALUE at the end of the second interval

$$= \text{SUM}(1 + \frac{\text{RATE}}{100 \times \text{CI}}) + \text{SUM}(1 + \frac{\text{RATE}}{100 \times \text{CI}}) \times \frac{\text{RATE}}{100 \times \text{CI}}$$

$$= \text{SUM}(1 + \frac{\text{RATE}}{100 \times \text{CI}})(1 + \frac{\text{RATE}}{100 \times \text{CI}}) = \text{SUM}(1 + \frac{\text{RATE}}{100 \times \text{CI}})^2$$

By extension, at the end of the last interval, NI:

$$\text{VALUE} = \text{SUM}(1 + \frac{\text{RATE}}{100 \times \text{CI}})^{\text{NI}}$$

$$= \text{SUM}(F)^{\text{NI}}$$

where $F = 1 + \dfrac{\text{RATE}}{100 \times \text{CI}}$.

8-12/ Given the variables and their values:

P = 2.   Q = 5.   R = 10.   S = 2.5   T = −4.
U = .FALSE.   V = .TRUE.   I = 2   J = 3   K = −2

compute the logical values of X, Y, and Z in the following statements:

X = U.AND.V.OR..FALSE.
Y = P**I + Q.LE.Q/R + S
Z = R**2+S*T −10.E+02.LE.Q + 2.*R.AND.(X.OR..NOT.Y)

chapter 9

the DØ
statement

9-1. the nature and operation of the DØ statement

In Article 8-1 we studied a program for computing the values of the coordinates on two straight lines shown in Fig. 8-1. To determine the values of Y corresponding to the integer values of X between −5. and 0., we may write the following sequence:

```
         X = −5.
     10  Y = 3.*X + 2.
         WRITE X, Y
     40  X = X + 1.
         IF(X) 10, 10, 8
      8  STØP
```

This sequence represents a loop of operations through which the computer cycles six times (from X = −5. through X = 0.); when X becomes equal to +1. (that is, greater than 0.), the execution of this program segment ends.

FØRTRAN has a compact statement that instructs the computer to go through a *range* of computations a predetermined number of times without an explicit statement for testing the terminal value of X, such as IF(X) 10,10,8. The statement that does this is called the *DØ statement*. Written with a DØ statement, the sequence shown above looks like this:

$$X = -5.$$

Repeating Loop | → DØ 40 I = 1,6,1
10 Y = 3.*X + 2.
4 WRITE X, Y
40 X = X + 1. | Range of the DØ

8 STØP

The explanation of the DØ line above is as follows. The sequence of the program from the first statement following the DØ statement to Statement 40 (the number that follows the word DØ) is called the *range of the DØ statement* or, simply, the *range of the DØ*. The computer is to cycle or pass through this range a number of times. Each cycle, as the computer passes through the range in execution, is identified by an integer number, which is called the *identifier*, or *index*, I, of the cycle. The three numbers on the right of the equals sign are known as the *index parameters* and are, from left to right, the *initial* value of I (the number or index of the first cycle), the *end-test* value of I (the terminal number toward which cycle numbers approach by incrementation), and the *increment* of I (the number by which a cycle number is increased after every passage of the computer through the range). Thus, in the program segment above, the initial I is 1, the end-test I is 6, and the increment of I is 1; as the computer keeps on passing through the range, the successive cycles are identified by numbers 1, 2, 3, 4, 5, and 6.

The computer makes the last pass through the range when (1) the index of the cycle equals the end-test value of I, or (2) the cycle index has a value which, upon the next incrementation, becomes larger than the end-test value of I. In the example above, the index of the last cycle is 6; however, if the index parameters in the example were 1, 6, 2, the cycles would receive index numbers 1, 3, and 5; the next index of 7, being larger than 6, would prevent the computer from executing the DØ sequence again.

While the *range* of the DØ, in the example above, is defined as the sequence *from the first statement following the DØ 40 to Statement 40*, the *repeating loop* includes the DØ 40 statement itself, because it is the DØ statement that contains the mechanism for indexing the cycles of execution. This distinction between the range and the loop applies to all DØ sequences.

The operations that the computer performs in going through a DØ range are shown below; the statements that are marked by asterisks are performed by the computer automatically.

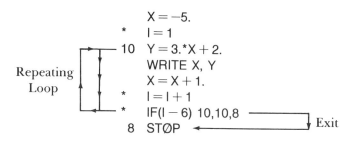

Parts of the corresponding numerical execution are shown below:

$$X = -5.$$
$$I = 1$$

```
10   Y = 3.*(-5.) + 2. = -13.  ┐
     WRITE      -5.,      -13.  │  First
     X = -5. + 1. = -4.         │  Cycle
     I = 1 + 1 = 2              │
     (2 - 6) < 0; GØ TØ 10  ┘
```

```
10   Y = 3.*(-4.) + 2. = -10.  ┐
     WRITE      -4.,      -10.  │  Second
     X = -4. + 1. = -3.         │  Cycle
     I = 2 + 1 = 3              │
     (3 - 6) < 0; GØ TØ 10  ┘
```

. . . .

```
10   Y = 3.*(0.) + 2. = 2.   ┐
     WRITE      0.,      +2.   │  Sixth
     X = 0. + 1. = + 1.       │  Cycle
     I = 6 + 1 = 7            │
     (7 - 6) > 0; GØ TØ 8  ┘
 8   STØP
```

It can be seen that, at the end of the sixth pass, the computer increases I to 7, then discovers that the value of I has exceeded the test value $(7 > 6)$, and forthwith transfers control to STØP. The computer retains in storage the final value of I after its exit from the DØ loop, but this final value varies with the compilers: the G and H compilers store the index of the last cycle (6), while the WATFIV compiler stores the last cycle index plus the increment (7). When in doubt, one may find out by asking the computer to write I after its exit.

Flow charts for the preceding program may be written explicitly, as shown in Fig. 9-1, or implicitly, as shown in Fig. 9-2.

The general form of the DØ statement is

$$DØ \; N \; I = J, K, L$$

where N is the number of the last statement in the range of the DØ.

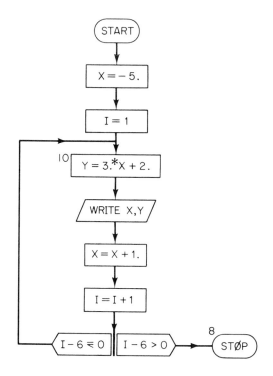

Figure 9-1

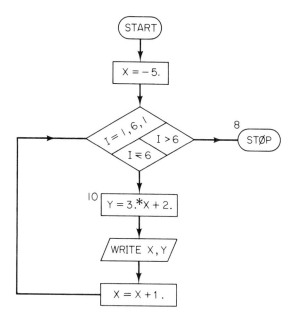

Figure 9-2

172

I is a variable name in integer mode which defines (numerically) the current cycle of execution.

J, K, L are either variables or constants in integer mode that define, respectively, the initial value of I, the end-test value of I, and the arithmetic increment of I; if J, K, L appear in the DØ statement in the variable form, they must be defined numerically earlier in the program in order to make the DØ statement executable; values of J, K, L must be positive; they may not be zero.

Consider, for example, the following sequence:

```
      READ J, L
      K = 2*J + L
      DØ 8 M = J, K, 2    (M is used as the cycle index here,
      READ A, B            instead of I; any integer letter or
      P = A + B            name is acceptable)
  8   WRITE A, B, P
      STØP
```

The machine will read the card with values of J and L, say 3 and 5; it will compute K = 2*3 + 5 = 11 and will transform the DØ statement into

$$DØ \ 8 \ M = 3, \ 11, \ 2$$

then it will cycle down to Statement 8 five times, reading in the process five cards with values of A and B and performing the subsequent operations, and defining the cycle index M as 3, 5, 7, 9, 11, and 13; the index of the last cycle is 11; when M becomes 13, control passes to STØP.

In the general form of the DØ statement, *the index I becomes incremented only if the computer returns to the DØ statement from the last statement in the range;* if the computer is sent to the DØ by a transfer-of-control statement within the range, say by a GØ TØ, the index I will be initialized to J (the initial parameter); this destroys the effect of incrementation and, as a result, I cannot reach the end-test value, and the computer may never get out of the DØ loop.

The question may be asked: Why do cycle numbers in the preceding example begin with 3 and jump by 2, instead of having a consecutive pattern of 1, 2, 3, . . . , such as was used in the first example of this article?

One answer is that the index I of the DØ statement may be made a component part of the computation, and, when this is the case, it may be desired to exclude certain values of I from the computation.

For example, let us suppose that we wish to find the sum of all two-digit odd numbers. The first such number is 11, the last is 99, and the odd numbers differ by 2. Therefore, we write the following program to find the required sum:

```
      ISUM = 0
      DØ 10 J = 11,99,2
  10  ISUM = ISUM + J
      WRITE ISUM
```

In the first line the sum is denoted by ISUM to maintain the integer mode throughout the program, and ISUM is initialized at 0. The computer will cycle through the two-statement loop 45 times, adding to the consecutive ISUMs the consecutive values of the index J, 11, 13, . . . 99. After the last addition, the computer will increment J to 101 and, upon comparing it with the test value of 99, will transfer control to WRITE, producing a printout of 2475.

For another example of how the index may be made part of the computation and at the same time shorten the program, we may return to the program for finding the coordinates of a straight line, which was discussed in the beginning of this article. An examination of that program will reveal the following correspondence between the values of X and I:

$$
\begin{array}{ccccccc}
\text{X:} & -5 & -4 & -3 & -2 & -1 & 0 \\
\text{I:} & 1 & 2 & 3 & 4 & 5 & 6
\end{array}
$$

We can express the relationship between X and I by the following statement:

$$X = I - 6$$

This statement is acceptable in FORTRAN: $I - 6$ is computed in the integer mode and is stored in the real mode under X. Thus, we can write the program segment for calculating the coordinates of the line as follows:

```
      DØ 4 I = 1, 6, 1
      X = I - 6
      Y = 3.*X + 2.
  4   WRITE X, Y
      STØP
```

It can be seen that, by incorporating I in the computation by means of $X = I - 6$, we have dispensed with the initialization and the incrementation of X, that is, with statements X = − 5. and X = X + 1.

The increment L in the general form of the DØ statement may be omitted if it is equal to 1; that is, the statement

$$DØ \ N \ I = J, \ K, \ 1$$

may be written

$$DØ \ N \ I = J, \ K$$

In the execution of the latter statement, J will be increased by 1 until the total becomes equal to K + 1, at which time control will pass out of the DØ loop.

As has been shown in the explicit form of the program segment (given on page 171), the computer, upon encountering a DØ statement, initializes the index I (that is, sets it equal to J in the general form of the DØ statement) and then makes a complete pass through the range of the DØ *before* comparing the increased value of the index with the test value (K in the general statement). Thus, given the following program segment:

```
   DØ 4 I = 5, 4, 1
   X = I − 6
   Y = 3.*X + 2.
 4 WRITE X, Y
   STØP
```

the computer will initialize I at 5 and will make one pass through the range, printing out X and Y as −1. and −1.; but immediately thereafter I, incremented from 5 to 6, will be compared with 4, and the execution will stop.

9-2. rules of the DØ statement

rule 1. In the general form of the DØ statement,

$$DØ \ N \ I = J, \ K, \ L$$

the statement number N must be an integer constant, the index I an integer variable, and the *indexing parameters* J, K, L integer constants (e.g., 2, 100) or integer variables (e.g., J, MAX); the variables must be defined numerically earlier in the program; parameters with arithmetic operations (e.g., I + 2) are forbidden; negative and zero parameters are forbidden: the parameters must be separated by commas.

rule 2. The cycle index I may not be redefined within the loop. For example, a statement such as

$$I = I + 2$$

may not appear within the loop, because it would cause one cycle to have two index numbers.

rule 3.   The last statement in the range of a DØ may not be a transfer-of-control statement, that is, it may not be a statement that would prevent the computer from returning to the DØ statement.

The following transfer-of-control statements are forbidden at the end of the range:

Any GØ TØ
Arithmetic IF
DØ
STØP

These statements are forbidden because they defeat the purpose of the DØ in one of two ways: If control passes to a statement ahead of the DØ or to the DØ itself, the index I is initialized every time the DØ is executed, that is, I is set equal to its first value J; this, of course, makes the incrementing parameter L inactive and cycle indexing impossible. If, on the other hand, control passes downward from the last statement in the DØ range, the DØ loop is executed only once, which, again, does not accomplish what the loop had been set up for.

rule 4.   The last statement in the range of the DØ must be executable. This means that statements like FØRMAT and END may not appear at the end of the range. However, aside from this restriction, a FØRMAT statement may appear anywhere in the program, either within or outside the range of the DØ.

Transfer from an executable statement at the end of the range to the DØ statement causes the index I to be incremented.

rule 5.   With so many statements barred from occupying the last position in the DØ range, the programmer would find it difficult to write a satisfactory DØ sequence. However, relief is provided by the statement

N CØNTINUE

which is placed on the last line of the DØ range and is given the reference number N of the DØ N I . . . statement. The CØNTINUE statement is called a dummy statement because it generates no instructions; it is, however, an executable statement that receives control from a statement in the range and returns it to the DØ statement. To put it another way, CØNTINUE is a name given to the number N which is needed to terminate the range of the DØ but may not be placed in front of the statements prohibited by Rules 3 and 4.

To illustrate the use of CØNTINUE, consider the problem of determining the number of men in a coeducational student body of 18,000. Men are identified on punched cards by 1 and women by 2. Let us denote the sex of the students by the variable K.

If we ignored the rules of the DØ statement, we might write the program—*incorrectly*—as follows:

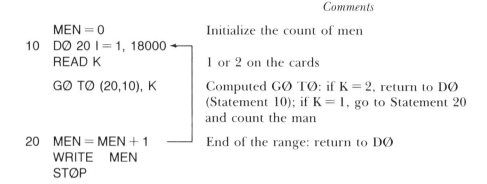

Comments

MEN = 0 — Initialize the count of men

10 DØ 20 I = 1, 18000

READ K — 1 or 2 on the cards

GØ TØ (20,10), K — Computed GØ TØ: if K = 2, return to DØ (Statement 10); if K = 1, go to Statement 20 and count the man

20 MEN = MEN + 1 — End of the range: return to DØ

WRITE MEN

STØP

The program above is incorrect in several ways. Statement 20 is intended to be the last statement in the range, but the computer reaches this statement only when K = 1 (man), and therefore the program fails to satisfy the requirement that the computer always reach the last statement in the range before the incrementation of the index can take place. When K = 2 (woman), GØ TØ returns control to the DØ and causes the index I to be initialized at 1, instead of incrementing the preceding value of I by 1. Thus the test value of 18000 cannot be reached; however, the computer keeps on reading cards; having read the last data card, it finds a control card and stops; and the count of MEN is not printed.

To make the computer traverse the range of the DØ every time, we simply add CØNTINUE after MEN = MEN + 1, take the number 10 from the DØ and give it to CØNTINUE, and change the reference number 20 in the DØ statement to 10; thus we get the following program:

MEN = 0

DØ 10 I = 1, 18000

READ K

GØ TØ (20,10), K

20 MEN = MEN + 1

10 CØNTINUE

WRITE MEN

STØP

Now the computer will execute Statement 20 when K = 1, but it will also reach the end of the range at CØNTINUE every time, regardless of whether K is 1 or 2, and will increment I after every passage of the range; when I hits 18001, the computer will print out the number of MEN.

Since the CØNTINUE statement generates no instructions and is simply the turnaround point at the end of the DØ range, its use to terminate all DØ sequences is recommended.

rule 6.   A logical IF statement is permitted at the end of a DØ range. If LEX in the IF statement is FALSE, the statement is not executed, and control is returned to the DØ; if LEX is TRUE and is followed by V = REX, V = REX is executed and control returns to the DØ; control is not transferred to the DØ only if a TRUE LEX is followed by a GØ TØ or by an IF(REX).

rule 7.   While a transfer-of-control statement is not permitted at the end of the DØ range, it is permitted within the DØ range, as can be seen from the illustration of CØNTINUE under Rule 5. Control may be transferred to a statement *within* the range or *outside* the range. A transfer *may not* be made to the DØ statement which initiates (and precedes) the range; this would initialize the index. A transfer outside the range results in the premature and permanent escape of the computer from the loop.

An illustration of such an escape may be seen in the following calculation of the value of *e* as the sum of a series of terms:

$$e = 1 + \frac{1}{1!} + \frac{1}{2!} + \frac{1}{3!} + \frac{1}{4!} + \ldots$$

Since the terms of the series diminish rapidly toward the right, we wish to impose two arbitrary restrictions on the calculation, which, otherwise, would tend to run to an infinite number of terms: (1) stop the calculation when the number of terms equals 20, or (2) stop the calculation when the value of a term becomes less than 0.00001.

Before we begin writing the program, let us take a look at the series. We see that, beginning with the second term, all the terms contain factorials that increase in the arithmetic progression, 1, 2, 3, . . . ; this corresponds conveniently with the simplest count of the DØ cycles. The first term of the series, 1, does not fit the factorial pattern,† so we set it apart and use it to initialize the SUM of the terms. *Beginning the count with the second term of the series,* we notice that

---

† The first term, 1, can be written as

$$\frac{1}{0!}$$

since 0! = 1; however, Rule 1 prohibits starting the cycle count with 0.

$$\text{the Nth term} = \frac{preceding\ term}{N}$$

for example, the third term, $\frac{1}{3!} = \frac{1}{2!*3}$.

To permit the repeated use of this formula within the DØ loop, we establish the *first preceding TERM*, $\left(\frac{1}{1!}\right)$, ahead of the loop by writing TERM = 1.0; then, in successive cycles, the formula produces the consecutive factorial terms of the series, and the DØ sequence accumulates their sum.

Now we are ready for the program shown in Fig. 9-3.

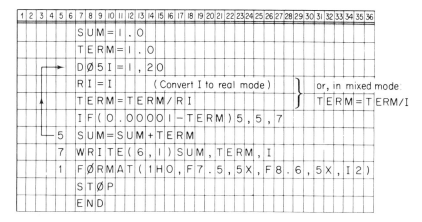

Figure 9-3

The resulting printout is

2.71828   0.000003   9

We can see from the program that as long as (0.00001 − TERM) is less than or equal to zero, that is, TERM is greater than or equal to 0.00001, TERM will be added to SUM, and the computer will return to the DØ statement to pass through another cycle. But if and when TERM becomes less than 0.00001, the IF statement will make the computer jump out of the DØ loop and go to Statement 7 to WRITE the SUM accumulated during the preceding cycle. The printout of SUM, TERM, and I tells us which condition caused the end of the execution.

If the computer completes the execution of the DØ assignment without jumping out of the loop prematurely, it is said that the DØ has been *satisfied* and that the computer has made a *normal* exit from the loop; in the case of a normal exit, control is transferred to the statement following the last statement in the DØ range. If, on the other hand, the computer jumps out of the loop prematurely, its exit is said to be *special;* in this case control may be transferred to the statement following the last statement in the range of the DØ, as in the example above, or to any other statement, as directed by the transfer-of-control statement that caused the jump.

rule 8. Control may not be transferred from a statement outside the DØ loop to a statement within the loop. A sequence, such as the following, is prohibited:

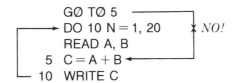

```
      GØ TØ 5
      DO 10 N = 1, 20        NO!
      READ A, B
   5  C = A + B
  10  WRITE C
```

However, some compilers—though not WATFIV—permit a violation of this rule, provided the transfer into the loop is *preceded* by a transfer out of the same loop for the purpose of executing some statements that do not affect the index of the cycle. Thus some compilers permit the following sequence:

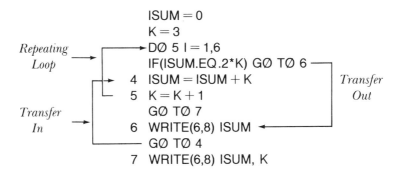

```
                  ISUM = 0
                  K = 3
Repeating         DO 5 I = 1,6
 Loop             IF(ISUM.EQ.2*K) GØ TØ 6
               4  ISUM = ISUM + K              Transfer
               5  K = K + 1                      Out
Transfer          GØ TØ 7
  In           6  WRITE(6,8) ISUM
                  GØ TØ 4
               7  WRITE(6,8) ISUM, K
```

rule 9. When a DØ is satisfied, and the computer makes a normal exit from the loop, it stores a last value of the index I which varies with compilers; with the G and H compilers it is the index of the last cycle; with the WATFIV compiler it is the index of the last cycle plus the increment. If we take the top program on page 174 and include in it a request for the value of the index J, as shown below:

```
        ISUM = 0
        DØ 10 J = 11,99,2
  10    ISUM = ISUM + J
        WRITE    ISUM, J
```

the computer that invokes the G compiler will print:

(ISUM)   2475   (J)   99

while the WATFIV compiler will produce:

(ISUM)   2475   (J)   101

rule 10. If the computer makes a special exit from the loop, it saves the *current* value of the index I. This value will be printed if one writes in the program:

WRITE   I

after the statement to which the exit had been made.

9-3. nested DØs

A DØ loop may contain within it another DØ loop. The former is called the *outer* loop and the latter the *inner* loop. An outer loop may contain several inner loops. DØ loops contained within other DØ loops form an arrangement known as the *nested DØs.*

A restriction imposed on an inner loop is that its range may not extend beyond the range of the outer loop; however, both ranges may end at the same statement.

To illustrate the structure and the operation of a nested DØ, let us suppose that we wish the computer to print all the quarter-hour times during a halfday, as shown in Col. 1 on the right. Before writing a program that will do this, let us first write a program that will print only the hours, as shown in Col. 2. This program is given below:

(1)		(2)	(3)
1	0	1	0
1	15	2	15
1	30	3	30
1	45	.	45
2	0	11	
2	15	12	
. . .	. . .		
11	45		
12	0		
12	15		
12	30		
12	45		

```
        DØ 1 LHØUR = 1,12
   1    WRITE (6,2)  LHØUR
   2    FØRMAT (1X,I2)
        STØP
```

In the program the index has been given the mnemonic integer name LHØUR. This index shall vary from 1 to 12. The range ends on the second line, WRITE. Every time the WRITE command is executed, the printer prints the current value of LHØUR, producing the printout shown in Col. 2.

Now let us write a similar program for the quarter hours within an hour, those shown in Col. 3. The following program will do this.

```
      DØ 1 J = 15,60,15
      MINUTE = J − 15
  1   WRITE (6,3)  MINUTE
  3   FØRMAT (1X,I6)
      STØP
```

In this program the index J shall receive the consecutive values of 15, 30, 45, 60 and will make the variable MINUTE receive the values of 0, 15, 30, 45. We cannot give the name MINUTE to the index, because the initial parameter of a DØ may not be 0. The command WRITE MINUTE on the third line ends the range; four cycles through this range produce the printout shown in Col. 3.

We know that the four quarter-hours occur in every hour. Therefore we can include the DØ for the quarter-hours within the DØ for the hours; that is, every time LHØUR in the first program assumes a value, say 4, MINUTE in the second program will cycle through its four values of 0, 15, 30, 45, producing the combined times of 4 0, 4 15, 4 30, 4 45. The combined times, from 1 o'clock to 12 45, are produced by the following program:

```
      DØ 1 LHØUR = 1,12
      DØ 1 J = 15, 60, 15
      MINUTE = J − 15
  1   WRITE (6,4)  LHØUR,MINUTE
  4   FØRMAT (1X,I2,I4)
      STØP
```

In executing this program, the computer, entering the first (outer) DØ for the first time, assigns the value of 1 to LHØUR; then it enters the second (inner) DØ and cycles 4 times through the range of that DØ (through WRITE), generating and printing the times 1 0, 1 15, 1 30 and 1 45. WRITE is the last line for both the inner DØ and the outer DØ. Therefore the computer, having satisfied the inner DØ, returns from the last WRITE of the inner DØ to the first line of the outer DØ (and of the program). Starting on the second cycle of the outer DØ, it increases the index LHØUR to 2, then enters the inner DØ for the second time, and produces the second set of times, 2 0, 2 15, 2

30, 2 45. This process, repeated 12 times, results in the printout shown in Col. 1 on page 181.

This scheme of nesting one DØ within another may be compared to a small merry-go-round on board of a large one. If the small merry-go-round makes four spins for every spin of the large one, the passenger riding the small one gets 48 small spins within 12 large ones.

For an example from mathematics, consider the problem of finding prime

PROGRAM TO FIND PRIME NUMBERS		PRIME NUMBERS	
PROGRAM	COMMENTS	5	229
		7	233
DØ 4 I = 3,501, 2	Outer loop; I denotes dividends differing by 2	11	239
		13	241
RI = I	I is changed to real mode for extracting square root	17	251
		19	257
M = SQRT(RI)	Root extracted and truncated to integer mode	23	263
		29	269
DØ 5 J = 3,M,2	Inner loop; J denotes divisors differing by 2	31	271
		37	277
K = I/J	If I/J does not divide exactly, K will be truncated	41	281
		43	283
IF(I.EQ.K*J)GØ TØ 4	If LEX is TRUE, K lost nothing in truncation, the division was exact, and the number is not prime: therefor GØ TØ 4, i.e., go out of the inner loop and into the outer loop to test the next dividend. If LEX is FALSE, go to the next statement, 5 CØNTINUE	47	293
		53	307
		59	311
		61	313
		67	317
		71	331
		73	337
		79	347
		83	349
		89	353
		97	359
		101	367
		103	373
5 CØNTINUE	Pass through the inner DØ to test the next divisor	107	379
		109	383
		113	389
WRITE (6,1) I	If the computer makes a normal exit from the inner loop, the number is prime and is printed	127	397
		131	401
		137	409
		139	419
1 FØRMAT(1X, I5)		149	421
4 CØNTINUE	Pass through the outer DØ to test the next dividend	151	431
		157	433
		163	439
		167	443
STØP	The computer makes a normal exit from the outer loop to STØP	173	449
		179	457
		181	461
		191	463
END		193	467
		197	479
		199	487
		211	491
		223	499
		227	

Figure 9-4

numbers, that is, numbers divisible only by 1 and by themselves, between 3 and 501. We know that, with the exception of 2, no even number is a prime number; therefore, we can eliminate even numbers from our consideration. We can also omit 1, to save the division by 1 later in the program.

One way to discover prime numbers is to divide every number under consideration by 3, 5, 7, . . . , and to discard every number that divides exactly, that is, without a fraction. The stopping point for divisors is the largest whole odd number preceding the square root of the number being examined; for example, the square root of 331 is 18.19: therefore, it should be tested by odd divisors from 3 through 17. It should be clear that 17×17 is too small and 19×19 is too large; if 17×19 is equal to 331, it can be quickly discovered by dividing 331 by 17. There is no point in testing 331 against 19, 23, etc., since these divisions would produce quotients that must have already been tested as divisors. In this connection it may also be useful to learn (or recall) that the product of two numbers differing by 2 is always 1 less than the square of the number between them ($6*8 = 7*7 - 1$).

Accordingly, we set up a program (Fig. 9-4) with two DØ loops, the outer loop containing the dividends to be tested by division, that is, all the odd numbers from 3 to 501, and the inner loop containing all the divisors, that is, all the numbers from 3 to the largest odd number preceding the square root of the dividend. For every dividend in the outer loop, the inner loop will cycle enough times to test the dividend by division over the entire inner range and to print out only those numbers that fail to divide by any number exactly.

The results, printed out by the machine in a single column, are shown in two columns to the right of Fig. 9-4; 3 is not shown, because it was divided exactly by the first divisor 3.

9-4. rules of the nested DØs

The rules of the nested DØs are illustrated in Fig. 9-5 and are stated below. Transfers referred to in the rules are shown in circles. Prohibited transfers are marked by crosses.

rule 1. Control is transferred automatically from the last statement in any DØ range to the DØ statement beginning that range, as shown by transfers 1, 2, and 3.

rule 2. When two DØ ranges end with the same statement, control is transferred to the DØ of the inner range until that DØ is satisfied; then control passes to the DØ of the outer range. Thus transfer 2 must be completed before transfer 3 is begun.

rule 3. Control may be transferred between any two statements within a DØ loop, as shown by transfer 4.

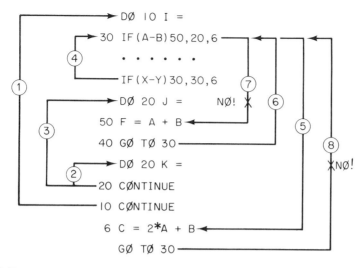

Figure 9-5

rule 4. Control may be transferred from a statement within a DØ loop to a statement outside the loop, as shown by transfers 5 and 6.

rule 5. Control may not be transferred from a statement outside a DØ loop to a statement inside the loop, as shown by transfers 7 and 8; for an exception to this rule, see Rule 8 of the single DØs.

9-5. simultaneous equations

Nested DØs play an important part in the solution of simultaneous equations. A system of m linear equations with n unknowns has the general form

$$
\begin{aligned}
a_{11}x_1 + a_{12}x_2 + \ldots + a_{1n}x_n &= b_1 \\
a_{21}x_1 + a_{22}x_2 + \ldots + a_{2n}x_n &= b_2 \\
\ldots\ldots\ldots\ldots\ldots\ldots\ldots\ldots\ldots\ldots \\
a_{m1}x_1 + a_{m2}x_2 + \ldots + a_{mn}x_n &= b_m
\end{aligned}
\tag{1}
$$

where $x_1, x_2, \ldots, x_n$ are the unknowns or variables,

$a_{11}, a_{22}, \ldots, a_{mn}$ are the known coefficients of the x's,

and $b_1, b_2, \ldots, b_m$ are the known constants of the equations.

An example of a system is

$$
\begin{aligned}
2x_1 + 3x_2 + 4x_3 &= 33 \\
-2x_1 - 2x_2 + 3x_3 &= -2
\end{aligned}
\tag{2}
$$

A system is said to have a solution when a set of values of x_1, x_2, . . . , x_n satisfies simultaneously all the equations in the system. A system may have no solution, in which case it is called *inconsistent*, or it may have one or many solutions, in which case it is called *consistent*. System (2) above is an example of a consistent system with many solutions. If we add its two equations together, we obtain

$$x_2 + 7x_3 = 31 \qquad (3)$$

If we set $x_2 = 3$, $x_3 = \dfrac{31-3}{7} = 4$, and, by substituting into the first equation of system (2), $x_1 = \dfrac{33-9-16}{2} = 4$. Again, if we set $x_2 = 17$, $x_3 = \dfrac{31-17}{7} = 2$, and $x_1 = \dfrac{33-51-8}{2} = -13$; and so on, ad infinitum.

An example of an inconsistent set is

$$\begin{aligned} x_1 + x_2 &= 4 \\ x_1 + x_2 &= 5 \end{aligned} \qquad (4)$$

The two equations are contradictory, because no sum of any two given values can be equal to 4 and 5 at the same time.

A system of equations has a *unique* solution, that is, a *single* set of values for the *x*'s of the system, when, generally, the number of the equations, *m*, is equal to the number of the unknown variables, *n*. The system, of course, may not include contradictory equations, such as the ones that make up system (4), or redundant equations, that is, equations derived from the other equations in the system. Thus Equation (3), derived from system (2), is redundant to system (2); adding it to that system does not endow the system with a unique solution.

In any system of equations, some of the coefficients, *a*, and some or all of the constants, *b*, may be equal to zero.

Consider the following system of equations:

$$\begin{aligned} 3x_1 + x_2 - 2x_3 + x_4 &= 13 \\ 4x_1 - 2x_2 + x_3 + 4x_4 &= 33 \\ 4x_2 - 2x_3 - 3x_4 &= -16 \\ -2x_1 - 4x_2 + 2x_3 \quad\quad &= 0 \end{aligned} \qquad (5)$$

System (5) has four equations and four unknowns. Some coefficients and constants in the system are zero. A cursory inspection reveals no contradiction or redundancy among the equations. Therefore the system may be presumed to have a unique solution.

To solve system (5) with the aid of a computer we must select a method which is readily programmable. One such method is known as the *Gauss†-Jordan††* *method of elimination or reduction.* This method reduces the equations of system (5) to the following form:

$$
\begin{aligned}
1x_1 + 0x_2 + 0x_3 + 0x_4 &= 5 \\
0x_1 + 1x_2 + 0x_3 + 0x_4 &= -2 \\
0x_1 + 0x_2 + 1x_3 + 0x_4 &= 1 \\
0x_1 + 0x_2 + 0x_3 + 1x_4 &= 2
\end{aligned}
\tag{6}
$$

In this form the four variables x, each with the coefficient of 1, appear in a stairlike arrangement on what is known as the *principal diagonal* of the square (4×4) *coefficient matrix,* and the coefficients of all the other variables in each equation are zero. Disregarding the terms with the zero coefficients, we obtain immediately the solution of the system:

$$
\begin{aligned}
x_1 &= 5 \\
x_2 &= -2 \\
x_3 &= 1 \\
x_4 &= 2
\end{aligned}
$$

The procedure which reduces system (5) to system (6) consists of the following steps:

(1) The equation with the largest absolute coefficient of x_1 is exchanged with the equation in the top row of the system (unless it is there already). This largest coefficient is called the *pivot* of the ensuing operation. The selection of the largest coefficient as the pivot prevents a zero coefficient from occupying the pivot position and, at the same time, increases the accuracy of the computations.

(2) The coefficients and constant of the pivot (top) equation are divided by the value of the pivot, reducing the coefficient of x_1 to 1.

(3) The reduced pivot equation is multiplied throughout by the coefficient of x_1 (with the reversed sign) in the second equation of the system and is added to that equation; this step is repeated with every other nonpivot equation (unless it has no x_1 term); as a result, the system is reduced so that x_1 appears with the coefficient of 1 in the pivot row and zero coefficients in all the other rows.

To reduce to 1 the coefficients of x_2, x_3, and x_4, the three steps above are repeated, consecutively, with the matrices of three, two, and one rows, which remain after the pivot rows of the preceding operations have all been excluded.

In this connection it should be understood that multiplying an equation by a constant, or adding one equation to another, changes the form of the equations but does not alter the solution of the system.

We shall use System (5) to illustrate the reducing operation. To simplify

---

† Karl Friedrich Gauss, 1777-1855, a great German mathematician.
†† Camille Jordan, 1838-1922, a French mathematician.

the work of computation, only the coefficients and the constants of the system are written down, resulting in what is known as the *augmented matrix* of the system; the augmented matrix includes the *constants* of the equations; without the constants the matrix is called the *coefficient matrix.*

step 1. The numbers of the *second* equation of System (5) (which has the largest coefficient of x_1, 4) are exchanged with the numbers of the first equation; the new top row of numbers becomes the pivot row.

Pivot Row 1	4	−2	1	4	33
Row 2	3	1	−2	1	13
Row 3	0	4	−2	−3	−16
Row 4	−2	−4	2	0	0

step 2. The pivot is 4; therefore the pivot row is divided by 4; the other equations remain unchanged.

New Pivot Row 1 | 1   −0.5   0.25   1   8.25

step 3. The new pivot row is multiplied by the coefficient 3 of x_1 in the second row (with its sign reversed) and is added to the second row; this is repeated with every non-pivot row, using the coefficient of x_1 in that row as the multiplier.

Pivot Row 1	1	−0.5	0.25	1	8.25
Row 2	3	1	−2	1	13
Pivot Row x (−3)	−3	1.5	−0.75	−3	−24.75
New Row 2	0	2.5	−2.75	−2	−11.75
Row 3	0	4	−2	−3	−16 (no change)
Row 4	−2	−4	2	0	0
Pivot Row x (2)	2	−1	0.5	2	16.5
New Row 4	0	−5	2.5	2	16.5

Tidied up, the matrix looks as follows:

Row 1	1	−0.5	0.25	1	8.25
Row 2	0	2.5	−2.75	−2	−11.75
Row 3	0	4	−2	−3	−16
Row 4	0	−5	2.5	2	16.5

The three steps of the elimination procedure are now repeated with the reduced matrix of the coefficients of x_2, x_3, and x_4, which appears to the right and below the heavy line drawn across the complete matrix above. Where the procedure referred to x_1, we must now substitute x_2 (and, later, x_3 and x_4) in selecting the pivot of the operation. Step 3 must be executed with *every* non-pivot row, even the pivot rows of the preceding operations, unless they have no terms containing the x under consideration.

step 1.   The fourth row (containing -5 of x_2) is exchanged with the top row of the *reduced matrix* (that is, with Row 2).

Row 1	1	-0.5	0.25	1	8.25
Pivot Row 2	0	-5	2.5	2	16.5
Row 3	0	4	-2	-3	-16
Row 4	0	2.5	-2.75	-2	-11.75

step 2.   The pivot is -5; the pivot row is divided by -5.

New Pivot Row 2| 0   1 -0.5 -0.4 -3.3

step 3.   The pivot row is multiplied by the respective coefficients and added to *all* the other rows.

Row 1	1	-0.5	0.25	1	8.25
Pivot Row x (0.5)	0	0.5	-0.25	-0.2	-1.65
New Row 1	1	0	0	0.8	6.6
Pivot Row 2	0	1	-0.5	-0.4	-3.3
Row 3	0	4	-2	-3	-16
Pivot Row x (-4)	0	-4	2	1.6	13.2
New Row 3	0	0	0	-1.4	-2.8
Row 4	0	2.5	-2.75	-2	-11.75
Pivot Row x (-2.5)	0	-2.5	1.25	1	8.25
New Row 4	0	0	-1.5	-1	-3.5

The matrix, after the second reduction, is:

Row 1	1	0	0	0.8	6.6
Row 2	0	1	-0.5	-0.4	-3.3
Row 3	0	0	0	-1.4	-2.8
Row 4	0	0	-1.5	-1	-3.5

It can be seen that the third row is in the form which yields the value of $x_4 = \dfrac{-2.8}{-1.4} = 2$. However, to be consistent, we shall carry on with the procedure.

step 1.   The third and the fourth rows are exchanged.

$$
\begin{array}{r|ccccc}
\text{Row 1} & 1 & 0 & 0 & 0.8 & 6.6 \\
\text{Row 2} & 0 & 1 & -0.5 & -0.4 & -3.3 \\
\hline
\text{Pivot Row 3} & 0 & 0 & -1.5 & -1 & -3.5 \\
\text{Row 4} & 0 & 0 & 0 & -1.4 & -2.8 \\
\end{array}
$$

step 2.   The pivot is -1.5; Row 3 is divided by -1.5.

$$\text{New Pivot Row 3} \mid 0 \quad 0 \quad 1 \quad 0.667 \quad 2.333$$

step 3.   The pivot row is multiplied by the respective coefficients and added to all the other rows.

$$
\begin{array}{r|ccccc}
\text{Row 1} & 1 & 0 & 0 & 0.8 & 6.6 & \text{(no change)} \\
 & & & & & & \\
\text{Row 2} & 0 & 1 & -0.5 & -0.4 & -3.3 \\
\text{Pivot Row x (0.5)} & 0 & 0 & 0.5 & 0.333 & 1.167 \\
\hline
\text{New Row 2} & 0 & 1 & 0 & -0.067 & -2.133 \\
\text{Pivot Row 3} & 0 & 0 & 1 & 0.667 & 2.333 \\
\text{Row 4} & 0 & 0 & 0 & -1.4 & -2.8 & \text{(no change)} \\
\end{array}
$$

After the third reduction, the matrix is:

$$
\begin{array}{r|ccccc}
\text{Row 1} & 1 & 0 & 0 & 0.8 & 6.6 \\
\text{Row 2} & 0 & 1 & 0 & -0.067 & -2.133 \\
\text{Row 3} & 0 & 0 & 1 & 0.667 & 2.333 \\
\text{Row 4} & 0 & 0 & 0 & -1.4 & -2.8 \\
\end{array}
$$

Repeat the elimination procedure for the last time.

step 1.   Omit, since Row 4 is the last row.

step 2.   Divide Row 4 by -1.4.

$$\text{Pivot Row 4} \mid 0 \quad 0 \quad 0 \quad 1 \quad 2$$

step 3. Multiply by the coefficients and add.

Row 1	1	0	0	0.8	6.6
Pivot Row x (−0.8)	0	0	0	−0.8	−1.6
New Row 1	1	0	0	0	5

Row 2	0	1	0	−0.067	−2.133
Pivot Row x (0.067)	0	0	0	0.067	0.133
New Row 2	0	1	0	0	−2

Row 3	0	0	1	0.667	2.333
Pivot Row x (−0.667)	0	0	0	−0.667	−1.333
New Row 3	0	0	1	0	1
Pivot Row 4	0	0	0	1	2

The completely reduced matrix is:

Row 1	1	0	0	0	5
Row 2	0	1	0	0	−2
Row 3	0	0	1	0	1
Row 4	0	0	0	1	2

from which, clearly:

$$x_1 = 5$$
$$x_2 = -2$$
$$x_3 = 1$$
$$x_4 = 2$$

It should be noted that the pivots of the successive matrices occupy positions on the principal diagonal of the original matrix, always in the upper left-hand corner of the matrix; thus the subscripts of the pivot element are always equal, (1,1), (2,2), etc.

The preceding discussion will enable us now to draw a flow chart (Fig. 9-6) for the program which will solve four simultaneous equations by the Gauss-Jordan elimination.

The program which parallels this flow chart is shown in Fig. 9-7, together with the data and the resulting printout.

Obviously enough, the program of Fig. 9-7 has a narrow application, because it can be used to solve only a system of *four* simultaneous equations.

A FLOW CHART FOR FOUR SIMULTANEOUS EQUATIONS

In the notes below, "top" refers to the top row of the *remaining* matrix; in the beginning, of course, it is the top row of the original matrix.

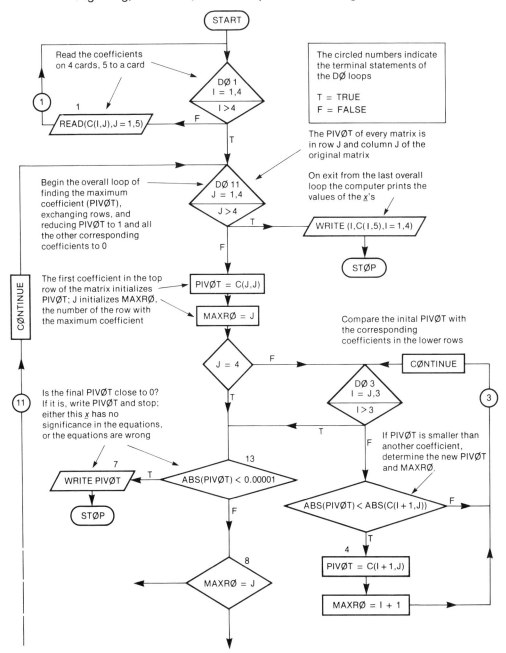

Figure 9-6

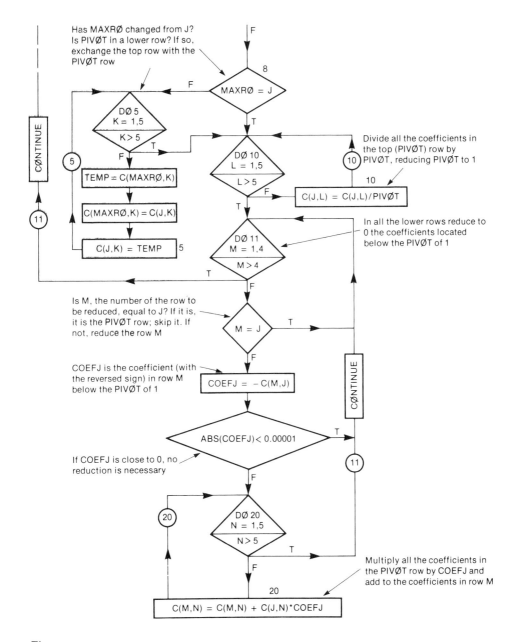

Figure 9-6 (continued)

```
C                              FOUR SIMULTANEOUS EQUATIONS
        DIMENSION C (4.5)
        DO 1 I = 1,4
  1     READ (5,2) (C(I,J),J = 1,5)
  2     FORMAT(5F5.1)
        DO 11 J = 1,4
        PIVOT = C(J,J)
        MAXRO = J
        IF(J.EQ.4) GO TO 13
        DO 3 I = J,3
        IF(ABS(PIVOT) − ABS(C(I + 1,J))) 4,3,3
  4     PIVOT = C(I + 1,J)
        MAXRO = I + 1
  3     CONTINUE
 13     IF(ABS(PIVOT) − 0.00001) 7,8,8
  7     WRITE(6,9) PIVOT
  9     FORMAT(1H0,'PIVOT = ',E10.3,', TOO SMALL/CHECK EQUATIONS')
        STOP
  8     IF (MAXRO.EQ.J) GO TO 6
        DO 5 K = 1,5
        TEMP = C(MAXRO,K)
        C(MAXRO,K) = C(J,K)
  5     C(J,K) = TEMP
  6     DO 10 L = 1,5
 10     C(J,L) = C(J,L)/PIVOT
        DO 11 M = 1,4
        IF(M.EQ.J) GO TO 11
        COEFJ = −C(M,J)
        IF(ABS(COEFJ).LT.0.00001) GO TO 11
        DO 20 N = 1,5
 20     C(M,N) = C(M,N) + C(J,N)*COEFJ
 11     CONTINUE
        WRITE(6,12)(I,C(I,5),I = 1,4)
 12     FORMAT(1H0, 'X(',I2,') = ',E10.3)
        STOP
        END
```

Data cards:

$$
\begin{pmatrix}
3.0 & 1.0 & -2.0 & 1.0 & 13.0 \\
4.0 & -2.0 & 1.0 & 4.0 & 33.0 \\
 & 4.0 & -2.0 & -3.0 & -16.0 \\
-2.0 & -4.0 & 2.0 & & 0.0
\end{pmatrix}
$$

Printout:

```
X( 1) =  0.500E+01
X( 2) = -0.200E+01
X( 3) =  0.100E+01
X( 4) =  0.200E+01
```

Figure 9-7

```
      DIMENSION C(10,11)
      READ(5,21) NN
21    FORMAT(I 2)
      LL = NN + 1
      DO 1 I = 1,NN
1     READ(5,2) (C(I,J),J = 1,LL)
2     FORMAT(11F5.1)
      DO 11 J = 1,NN
      PIVOT = C(J,J)
      MAXRO = J
      IF(J.EQ.NN) GO TO 13
      MM = NN − 1
      DO 3 I = J,MM
      IF(ABS(PIVOT) − ABS(C(I + 1,J))) 4,3,3
4     PIVOT = C(I + 1,J)
      MAXRO = I + 1
3     CONTINUE
13    IF(ABS(PIVOT) − 0.00001) 7,8,8
7     WRITE(6,9) PIVOT
9     FORMAT(1H0,'PIVOT =',E10.3,', TOO SMALL/CHECK EQUATIONS')
      STOP
8     IF(MAXRO.EQ.J) GO TO 6
      DO 5 K = 1,LL
      TEMP = C(MAXRO,K)
      C(MAXRO,K) = C(J,K)
5     C(J,K) = TEMP
6     DO 10 L = 1,LL
10    C(J,L) = C(J,L)/PIVOT
      DO 11 M = 1,NN
      IF(M.EQ.J) GO TO 11
      COEFJ = −C(M,J)
      IF(ABS(COEFJ).LT.0.00001) GO TO 11
      DO 20 N = 1,LL
20    C(M,N) = C(M,N) + C(J,N)*COEFJ
11    CONTINUE
      WRITE(6,12)(I,C(I,LL),I = 1,NN)
12    FORMAT(1H0,'X(',I2,') = ',E10.3)
      STOP
      END
```

Data cards:

```
4
  3.0     2.0    −1.4     0.6    −4.6
 −1.6     4.5     2.5            24.1
          3.5     2.0     4.2    12.1
  4.8    −5.5             0.2   −15.9
```

Printout:

```
X( 1) = −0.500E+00
X( 2) =  0.240E+01
X( 3) =  0.500E+01
X( 4) = −0.150E+01
```

Figure 9-8

However, a few modifications can make the program suitable for the solution of a system with any number of equations. These modifications are:

1/ The specific number of equations, 4, wherever it occurs, is replaced by a general variable NN.

2/ Correspondingly, the number of non-pivot equations, 3 ($= 4 - 1$), is changed to MM $=$ NN $- 1$, and the number of coefficients and constants in an equation, 5 ($= 4 + 1$), is changed to LL $=$ NN $+ 1$.

3/ The computer is informed of the number NN of equations to be solved by a pair of statements in the beginning of the program:

```
          READ (5,21)  NN
     21   FØRMAT (I2)
```

A data card containing the value of NN must precede data cards containing the values of the equation coefficients.

4/ Since the variables NN and LL cannot be used in the DIMENSIØN statement, the numerical dimensions of the coefficient array are made large enough to accommodate the largest system that is likely to be encountered; a parallel change is also made in FØRMAT 2.

Fig. 9-8 shows the program of Fig. 9-7 modified to solve a system of ten or fewer simultaneous equations. The program is followed by the data, showing the values of NN and the array coefficients, and the resulting printout.

A word of caution is in order. If the equation coefficients differ in form from the description F5.1 of FØRMAT 2, change the description to suit the form.

9-6. sorting

Sorting is arranging an array of random numbers in ascending or descending order, that is, from the smallest to the largest or vice versa. If the array includes negative numbers, the largest negative number is the smallest one in the array.

To develop a program for sorting an array of numbers into an ascending sequence, consider the array K shown below and coded A1 on the right:

$$
\begin{array}{cccccc}
8 & -5 & 12 & 50 & -20 & 40 \\
K(1) & K(2) & K(3) & K(4) & K(5) & K(6)
\end{array}
\tag{A1}
$$

The six elements of K are stored in the locations K(1) through K(6), as shown above.

Sorting begins by comparing the numbers in K(1) and K(2). If the number in K(1) is larger than that in K(2), the two numbers are interchanged. If the number in K(1) is smaller than that in K(2), the numbers are left where they are; in A1 above, 8 and −5 trade places. Next the numbers in K(2) and K(3) are compared. If K(2) is larger than K(3), the numbers are interchanged; otherwise there is no interchange. In A1 8 is compared with 12, and both remain in their places. The next comparison is between K(3) and K(4); 12 and 50 remain where they are. After the fourth comparison, 50 and −20 trade places, and, after the fifth, 50 changes places with 40. Thus the largest number, 50, arrives at the last location, K(6), and A1 is transformed into A2:

$$-5 \qquad 8 \qquad 12 \qquad -20 \qquad 40 \qquad 50 \qquad\qquad \text{(A2)}$$

The sequence that performs the switches is shown below:

```
      DØ 1 I = 1,5
      IF (K(I) .LE.K(I+1))   GØ TØ 1
      KEEP = K(I)
      K (I) = K(I + 1)
      K (I + 1) = KEEP
    1 CØNTINUE
```

KEEP is an auxiliary storage location into which the number originally stored in K(I) is copied before that number is erased by the number copied into K(I) from K(I+1); then the number in K(I+1) is erased by copying into K(I+1) the contents of KEEP.

With the largest number, 50, in location K(6), the sorting operation is repeated, but only on the first five elements of A2. The necessary sequence is:

```
      DØ 2 I = 1,4
      IF (K(I) .LE.K(I+1))   GØ TØ 2
      KEEP = K (I)
      K (I) = K(I + 1)
      K (I + 1) = KEEP
    2 CØNTINUE
```

The array will assume the form A3:

$$-5 \qquad 8 \qquad -20 \qquad 12 \qquad 40 \qquad 50 \qquad\qquad \text{(A3)}$$

It can be seen that the two program sequences above are identical except for the maximum value of the index I: it is 5 in the first sequence and $5 - 1 = 4$ in the second. The statement numbers 1 and 2 in the two DØs simply distinguish the two sequences. It can also be deduced that five such DØs are needed to sort the array: the first DØ fills the sixth location, the second the fifth, the third the fourth, the fourth the third, and the fifth the second. Therefore we can combine the five DØs into a single nested DØ as follows:

```
        N = 6
        L = N − 1
        DØ 1 J = 1,L
        M = N − J
        DØ 1 I = 1,M
        IF (K(I) .LE.K(I+1))   GO TO 1
        KEEP = K(I)
        K (I) = K(I+1)
        K (I+1) = KEEP
   1    CØNTINUE
```

where N is the number of elements to be sorted, L is the number of the consecutive arrays, such as A1, A2, A3, . . . , to be examined, and M is the number of comparisons to be made in each array. The program sequence above, beginning with the second statement, is general for an array of any length.

A weakness of the program above is that it makes the computer go on sorting the arrays A2, A3, . . . even if the original array A1 is in perfect ascending order; this is wasteful of the computer time. Given an array such as:

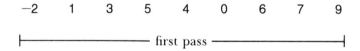

the computer should be made aware, after the first pass and two interchanges resulting in

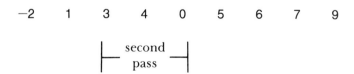

that the first three elements in the original array and the last four elements in the resulting array are in the ascending order and that the second pass should begin with the element *preceding* the first element to move down and end with the last element to move down; that is, the second pass should embrace only the subarray 3 4 0, producing

$$-2 \quad 1 \quad 3 \quad 0 \quad 4 \quad 5 \quad 6 \quad 7 \quad 9$$

| third |
| pass |

The second pass results in only one interchange. The only element to move down is 0; therefore it is the first and the last. Since 0 is preceded by 3, the third pass is limited to the subarray 3 0, producing

$$-2 \quad 1 \quad 0 \quad 3 \quad 4 \quad 5 \quad 6 \quad 7 \quad 9$$

| fourth |
| pass |

The third pass has made 0 move down again, next to 1; therefore there must be the fourth pass, to check the subarray 1 0. It produces the ordered array

$$-2 \quad 0 \quad 1 \quad 3 \quad 4 \quad 5 \quad 6 \quad 7 \quad 9$$

| fifth |
| pass |

The movement of 0 next to −2 calls for the fifth pass, which produces no interchange. Therefore the array is finally in order.

This example supplies the clues for spotting IFIRST and ILAST, the first and the last elements of the subarrays to be checked for interchanges. Since K(I) is always compared with K(I+1) on any pass, the *first* interchange of K(I) with K(I+1) makes IFIRST = I − 1 for the next pass. This IFIRST must be saved, lest it be changed by the subsequent interchanges during the pass; ILAST = I, in which I acquires the values of the subscripts of the lower elements involved in consecutive interchanges. The largest I becomes the value of ILAST for the next pass.

The preceding discussion points up two things: (1) the limits of the DØ vary with every pass, and (2) the number of passes is unknown. Passing must continue until a pass produces no interchange. Not knowing the number of passes, we abandon the idea of a nested DØ and incorporate the variables IFIRST and ILAST to mark the limits of the subarrays to be processed. The redesigned program is shown below, with comments on the right.

200 the DØ statement

Sorting program	*Comments*
DIMENSIØN K(6)	
READ(5,6) K	N is the number of elements.
6 FØRMAT(6I4)	
N = 6	The parameters of the DØ are written in
L = N − 1	the variable form, J,L, because their values
4 J = 1	alter with every pass. On the first pass, the
2 ILAST = 0	entire array will be sorted; therefore J is
DØ 1 I = J,L	initialized at 1 and L at N-1.
IF (K(I) .LE.K(I+1)) GØ TØ 1	
KEEP = K(I)	ILAST is initialized at 0; if ILAST remains
K(I) = K(I + 1)	0 after the pass, the array is in order; if
K(I + 1) = KEEP	0 changes to I, the next pass will stop at
	K(I).
IF(ILAST.EQ.0) ISTART=I−1	After the *first* interchange, ISTART stores
ILAST = I	I−1 and ILAST stores I; sorting on the
	next pass will begin with J = ISTART; the
	change in ILAST from 0 to I insures that
	ISTART will not be altered by the next
	interchange during the pass; ILAST, how-
	ever, will increase with every interchange
	during the pass.
1 CØNTINUE	
IF (ILAST.EQ.0) GØ TØ 3	If there has been no interchange during
	the pass, and ILAST remained 0, the array
	is in order and may be printed out.
L = ILAST	The parameter L of the DØ for the next
	pass is changed to ILAST, the point of the
	last interchange during the current pass.
IF (ISTART.EQ.0) GØ TØ 4	The next pass should begin with J =
J = ISTART	ISTART; however, if the first interchange
GØ TØ 2	during the current pass involved the first
3 WRITE(6,5) K	element, the statement ISTART = I − 1
5 FØRMAT (1H0,6I4)	has made ISTART = 0; since J may not
STØP	be 0, a return is made to J = 1.

Data card:

Printout

ʌ−20ʌʌ−5ʌʌʌ8ʌʌ12ʌʌ40ʌʌ50

questions and problems

9-1/ Which of the following DØ statements are invalid and why?

   (a)   DØ 10 I = K, L, M
   (b)   DØ 20 J = 4, 3
   (c)   DØ 30 N12 = 1, K
   (d)   DØ 40 A = 7, 11, 2
   (e)   DØ 50 J = 1, 100
   (f)   DØ 60 I = K,I+7
   (g)   DØ 70 L = 1, 6.5
   (h)   DØ N I = 1, 11

9-2/ Identify one or more errors in the program segments below; ignore the absence of FØRMAT statements and input unit identification.

   (a)

```
         DØ 20,I = 7, 11
         READ C, K, J
         D = K + J*C
      20 DØ30 J = 1, 5
      30 D = K + J
         STØP
```

   (b)

```
       6 DØ 40 J = − 2, 10, + 2
         READ D, F, I
         B = D + F**I
         CØNTINUE
      40 IF (D + B) 6, 8, 8
       8 STØP
```

   (c)

```
         DØ 50 K = 1, J, 2
         READ A, B
         C = A + B
         K = K + 2
      50 CØNTINUE
         STØP
```

9-3/ Given the following program sequence, answer the questions on p. 202.

```
10   K = 2
20   L = 3
30   DØ 90 I = K, 8, L
40   READ A, B
50   C = A*B
60   IF (A − B) 80, 70, 80
70   GØ TØ 90
80   D = A + B
90   CØNTINUE
100  STØP
```

Data on Cards:	4.0	5.0
	6.0	6.0
	7.0	2.0
	2.0	7.0
	5.0	3.0

. . . .

(a) After control passes from 20 to 30, what is the value of I?

(b) If I = 2, what is the value of C?

(c) If I = 2, what three statements will be executed next after Statement 60?

(d) If I = 5, what three statements will be executed next after Statement 60?

(e) How many cards will have been read by the computer upon its normal exit?

(f) If I = 8 and Statement 80 has been executed, what is the value of D? What three statements will be executed next?

(g) When the normal exit occurs, which statement will be executed next? What is the value of I?

9-4/ Rewrite the first program of Article 8-1 using DØ statements.

9-5/ A number of students took tests, and their consecutive numbers (NØ) and corresponding scores (SCØ) were punched on cards.

You are given a deck of these cards and are told that the deck contains fewer than 100 cards.

Using a DØ statement, write a program that will count the cards, add up the scores, and calculate the average score.

Analysis. If you do not know the number of cards, you cannot specify the middle index parameter, namely, the end-test value of the index I; if you specify a safe value, say 500, in excess of the probable number of cards, the computer will declare an error when it discovers that there are not 500 cards in the deck. You *may* specify 500, but you must keep the computer from arriving at the *no card* condition. To do this, add a trailer card at the back of the deck with a student number in excess of the probable number of students, say 399, and include the following statement within the DØ loop:

IF (NØ.EQ.399) GØ TØ 50

where Statement 50 should be outside the loop and should begin a program sequence designed to compute the average score. When the computer reaches the trailer card, with 399 signaling the end of the data deck, the IF statement will send the computer out of the DØ loop.

If the index parameters are set at 1, 500, 1, the special exit will freeze the value of I at the total number of cards in the deck, *including* the trailer card.

Show on the coding form the data for eight students only, as shown below, but assume, in writing the program, that you do not know the number of cards.

Student number	Score
1	76
2	80
3	54
4	65
5	72
6	91
7	87
8	63

In this program, as in most other programs and examples in this text, the data records are short and simple to reduce the amount of writing and to permit a quick check of the results by a long-hand computation. The use of the computer is justified in cases where longhand checks are not feasible: if you had to average scores on 5000 cards, you would not want to count 5000 cards; even if you did, it is more than likely that you would not get the total count right.

9-6/ A standard piano keyboard, shown in Fig. 9-9, has a total of 88 white and black keys. The keys are arranged in seven repeating groups of 12, with four additional keys at the right end; keys 1 to 12 in Fig. 9-9 form a typical group. The seven white keys in every group are named A, B, C, D, E, F, and G, from left to right; thus keys 1, 13, 25, etc. are the A keys.[†]

[†] The interval between two consecutive keys with the same name (A and A, D and D) is called an *octave*.

Figure 9-9

The purpose of a key is to activate a hammer inside the piano which strikes a string and makes it vibrate and produce a tone. The tone pitch (its highness or lowness) depends on the number of vibrations of the string, expressed in cycles per second, or CPS; the greater the number of cycles, the higher the pitch.

The first A key (key 1) produces 27.5 CPS in its string; the number of CPS produced by the other A keys, proceeding from left to right, is doubled consecutively; for example, key 13 produces 55 CPS, key 25 110 CPS, etc.

Since any two A keys are separated by 12 equal tonal steps, and since the number of cycles is doubled between the two A keys, the CPS produced by any one key is equal to the CPS produced by the preceding key multiplied by $\sqrt[12]{2}$ (the twelfth root of 2).[†]

Write a program, involving nested DØs, which will result in a printout (with titles) of the CPS produced by every key on a standard piano keyboard.

9-7/ Use or modify the program of Fig. 9-8 to solve the following six simultaneous equations:

$$
\begin{aligned}
-2a - 7b + \quad c - 2d - \quad e + 2f &= -29.6 \\
a - \quad b + \quad c - \quad d + \quad e - \quad f &= 6.4 \\
a + \quad b + \quad c + \quad d + \quad e + \quad f &= 5.4 \\
3c + 2d + \quad e \quad\quad &= 5.7 \\
-8b + 6.4c - 3d - 2.5e + 2f &= -55.0 \\
3a - 4b - \quad 2c \quad\quad + \quad e - 2f &= 21.8
\end{aligned}
$$

9-8/ (a) Write a program which will produce a printout of the factorials of the first 12 integers;

(b) Repeat for the first 13 integers.

Is the factorial of 13 correct? Remember that the computer cannot store integers greater than 2147483647 (see Table 2-1).

[†] The division of the octave into twelve equal tonal steps, called *equal temperament*, was proposed by Mersenne (a monk and a physicist) about 1635. Fifty years later Johann Sebastian Bach (a musician, but no monk, not with twenty children) tuned his clavichord (an ancestor of the piano) in equal temperament and composed the famous "48 Preludes and Fugues for the Well Tempered Clavichord" to demonstrate that the scheme is sound.

9-9/   Given the array

$$-2 \quad 6 \quad 4 \quad 1 \quad 7 \quad -1 \quad 9 \quad 3 \quad 4 \quad 5$$

write a program which will make the computer
(1)   Store the array and print it in the original order;
(2)   Arrange the array in ascending order and print the ascending array;
(3)   Arrange the array in descending order and print the descending array.

chapter 10

arrays-the DATA statement

10-1. one-dimensional arrays and subscripted variables

An *array* is a group of *elements* or quantities of the same type. If a group of elements is arranged in a single row, it is called a *one-dimensional array.* If the elements form a matrix, that is, a table of several rows and columns, the group is called a *two-dimensional array.* Two-dimensional arrays will be considered later in the chapter.

An example of a one-dimensional array is a series of examination scores, such as 75, 64, 89, ... These scores could be assigned names, such as A, B, C, . . . , and entered into the memory from the punched cards by a statement such as

READ (5,1) A, B, C . . .

The more usual—and efficient—way of naming varying quantities of the same type is to assign to them a single name with varying subscripts. For example, the scores in the array above can be given one generic name S, and the individual scores identified by small numerical subscripts 1, 2, 3, . . . ; thus the first score of 75 would be named S_1, the second of 64 S_2, etc. A name, such as S, used with subscripts, is called a *subscripted variable.*

In FORTRAN notation, which requires all characters to appear in a line, that is, without subscripts or superscripts, the subscripts are shown as full-sized numerals enclosed in parentheses, following the generic name. Thus S_1 becomes S(1), S_2 becomes S(2), etc. Adopting this notation, we can read in the values of an array by a statement such as

READ (5,1) S(1), S(2), S(3), . . . S(I), . . . S(N)

In the statement above, S(N) represents the last, the Nth, element of the array, and S(I) represents the Ith element of the array, where the integer I may have any value from 1 to N.

Even with a subscripted variable it would be cumbersome to write a READ statement, such as the one above, for an array of many elements, say 100, since we would have to write out S(1), S(2), . . . 100 times. Fortunately, FORTRAN provides us with a shorthand method of describing the entire array. For example, an array of 100 test scores may be entered into the memory by the following simple statement

$$\text{READ (5,1) (S(I), I = 1, 100)} \tag{10-1}$$

or even by a yet simpler statement

$$\text{READ (5,1) S} \tag{10-2}$$

if either of the two statements is accompanied by an indication to the computer of the length of the array, that is, of the number of elements in the array; this is done by a DIMENSIØN statement explained in Article 10-2.

The notation in the first shorthand statement (10-1) is called the *indexing* of the list, or of the array. S(I) denotes any element in the array; I is the integer *index* or *subscript of an element of S;* and the statement I = 1,100 means that the subscript I of S varies, by increments of 1, from 1 to 100. Actually, statement (10-1) is a shorthand way of writing

$$\text{READ (5,1) S(1), S(2), ... S(99), S(100)}$$

The index need not be called I; it may have any integer name.

In statement (10-1) note carefully the disposition of the parentheses and the commas. Obeying this statement, the computer will store 100 test scores in its memory at addresses $S_1, S_2, . . . S_{100}$.

The indexing concept of the subscripted variables is similar to that of the DØ statement. The index of a subscripted variable identifies an element; the index of a DØ statement identifies a cycle of execution. In statement (10-1) indexing identifies 100 elements of the array S, from the first to the last; if the initial and incremental parameters of a DØ statement are both 1, the cycles are identified (and, in effect, counted) from the first to the last. If the initial and incrementing parameters of a DØ statement have values other than 1, the cycles are still executed consecutively, but the index values assigned to them depend on the values of the parameters; in the same manner, a notation such as

$$(S(I), I = 1,100,2)$$

indicates, or refers to, all the elements with *odd* subscripts.

The input of an array by means of the two statements

$$READ\ (5,1)\ (S(I), I = 1,100)$$
$$1\quad FØRMAT\ (1X, F5.2)$$

is said to be effected through the operation of the *implied DØ*, because the machine assigns subscripts to the elements in the same order and manner in which it assigns indices to the cycles of a DØ.

The data for the READ statement above must appear on 100 cards, each card punched with a single number in columns 2-6; the reason for this lies in the limited format, as explained in Article 5-2, and, further on, in Article 10-4.

10-2. the DIMENSIØN statement

The two shorthand statements of Article 10-1, namely,

	READ (5,1) (S(I), I = 1,100)	(10-1)
and	READ (5,1) S	(10-2)

each of which introduces an array into the program, must be always preceded by a DIMENSIØN statement, as follows:

$$DIMENSIØN\ S(100)$$
$$READ\ (5,1)\ (S(I), I = 1,100)$$

or

$$DIMENSIØN\ S(100)$$
$$READ\ (5,1)\ S$$

The DIMENSIØN statement is a nonexecutable statement that informs the compiler that it should reserve 100 locations in the memory of the computer for the 100 elements of the array S; either of the two READ statements above,

(10-1) or (10-2), will cause the computer to store the *entire* array of 100 elements in those locations.

The DIMENSIØN statement belongs with the FØRMAT and END statements in the category of the statements that inform but do not command.

The following four rules apply to the DIMENSIØN statements for one-dimensional arrays:

rule 1. A DIMENSIØN statement *must* appear in the program involving arrays; the statement is usually placed at the beginning of the program.†

rule 2. A subscripted variable must appear in the DIMENSIØN statement before it is used in the program, for example, DIMENSIØN $S(20)$.

rule 3. The statement must give the *maximum* dimension of the array, even if a particular set of data has fewer elements than what the array is dimensioned for.

rule 4. The dimension given in the DIMENSIØN statement must be *numeric;* a statement like DIMENSIØN S(I) is invalid; it must be, for example, DIMENSIØN S(12).

10-3. allowable subscripts

In Articles 10-1 and 10-2 we saw and used two types of subscripts: integer constants, such as 2 or 3, and integer variables, such as I or J. In addition to these two types, we may also combine integer constants and variables into arithmetic expressions that may also be used as subscripts. The table below gives a list of the allowable subscripts, with examples; in this table K and K′ denote any two integer constants, and I denotes any integer variable; the value of a defined (evaluated) subscript must always be positive.

Allowable subscript	Examples Subscript	Element
K	2	S(2)
I	J	S(J)
I±K	$\begin{cases} J+2 \\ I-3 \end{cases}$	$\left. \begin{matrix} T(J+2) \\ T(I-3) \end{matrix} \right\}$
K*I	3*J	S(3*J)
K*I±K′	4*L−3	A(4*L−3)

---

† It will be shown later in the book that the DIMENSIØN statement may be omitted if the dimensions of the array are shown in the CØMMØN statement (Article 11-11) or in a TYPE statement (Article 12-2).

It is important to note the order of the terms in the arithmetic expressions used as subscripts: I+K and K*I are allowed, but K+I and I*K are not; in other words, the positions of the constants and variables are not interchangeable. Some compilers permit the interchange, but, unless the compiler is checked out on this point, it is safest to adhere to the forms above, which are acceptable to all compilers.

10-4. operations with one-dimensional arrays

Like all the data heretofore, arrays are input and output through the medium of READ and WRITE statements accompanied by FØRMAT statements. Because the arrays are usually referred to by a single generic name, such as S, while the elements of the array are punched on cards or printed on a sheet either singly or in groups (say, five to a card or a line), it is important to be scrupulously correct in writing the field specifications in the FØRMAT statements, in order that correct numbers may be either stored or reported out in response to the READ or WRITE commands. In this connection, a review of the behavior of the computer in the case of a limited format, as presented in Article 5-2, will be helpful.

Let us consider an array B of five elements:

$$10.2 \quad 20.1 \quad 3.6 \quad 1.7 \quad 11.2$$

These elements can be entered into the memory in several ways (preceded each time by DIMENSIØN B(5)):

a/ All elements can be punched on a single card, each element in a field of six columns, beginning at the left edge of the card. The following pair of statements will store the array:

```
  READ(5, 1) B      or  (B(I), I = 1,5)
1 FØRMAT (5F6.1)
```

The READ statement, conforming to the DIMENSIØN B(5) statement, calls for the storing of five elements, and the FØRMAT statement specifies five fields, which can be found on the card; therefore, only one card is necessary and only one card will be read. If the fields on the card are not filled with numbers, zeros will be stored.

b/ Individual elements can be punched on separate cards, five cards in all, each element in the first six columns. Then we must write

```
  READ (5,1) B      or   (B(I), I = 1,5)
1 FØRMAT (F6.1)
```

The READ command calls for the reading of five values, but the short FØRMAT furnishes only one field; therefore, as soon as the specification is exhausted, the system resets to the left parenthesis of the specification and *to a new record,* and the specification is reapplied to the new record; thus five cards are needed and will be read.

c/ Another program with five data cards may be written

```
      DØ 2 I = 1,5
   2  READ(5,1) B(I)
   1  FØRMAT(F6.1)
```

The READ statement now calls for the reading of *one* element in each DØ cycle, and the FØRMAT specifies the necessary field; five cards are needed.

d/ The storing of five values from three cards, the first two cards with two values each and the third card with one, may be programmed as follows:

```
      READ(5,1) B      or   (B(I), I = 1,5)
   1  FØRMAT(2F6.2)
```

B(1) and B(2) will be read from the first card, B(3) and B(4) from the second, and B(5) from the third; since no reading of B(6) is called for, the extra field specification will be ignored in reading the third card.

e/ Another program for three cards may be written as follows:

```
      DØ 2 I = 1, 5, 2
   2  READ(5,1) B(I), B(I + 1)
   1  FØRMAT(2F6.2)
```

The computer will cycle three times, reading from the first card B(1) and B(2), from the second B(3) and B(4), and from the third B(5) *and B(6).* If there is no sixth value on the third card, the computer will store 0.0.

In this last case the program must be preceded by

```
                 DIMENSIØN B(6)
```

even though the sixth value does not exist; dimensioning for five values only will bring forth an error message.

The principles described above in connection with the READ statement apply to the input of data; the same principles apply with equal force to the output of data through the medium of the WRITE statement; the examples above will remain valid if we substitute WRITE for READ, *lines of printout* for *data cards,* and assume that a carriage control character begins the FØRMAT specifications.

If the number of spaces occupied by the data on a card is greater than the number of spaces to be scanned as indicated by the FØRMAT statement, the computer reads and stores only that portion of the data which corresponds to the specification, and disregards the rest.

For example, let us assume that the names of 100 students and their test scores are punched on 100 separate cards, the names in columns 1-20 and the scores in columns 21-25, and that it is desired to find the average of the scores. Since the names are not needed in the calculation, a segment of the program to store the scores is written as follows:

```
        DIMENSIØN S(100)
        READ (5,1) S
      1 FØRMAT (20X, F5.0)
```

The computer, on examining the first card, will ignore the first 20 spaces and will store the score punched in columns 21-25, corresponding to F5.0. Stopped immediately thereafter by the right parenthesis of the FØRMAT specification, it will reset to the left parenthesis and to the second card. This process will be repeated 100 times for 100 cards.

If, on the other hand, the scores, without names, are punched in groups of five per card, and the program reads

```
        DIMENSIØN S(100)
        READ (5,2) S
      2 FØRMAT (5F5.0)
```

the computer will read the first five scores S_1 through S_5 from the first 25 columns on the first card, the next five scores from the 25 columns on the second card, and so on; only 20 cards will be read, but 100 scores will be stored.

To print an array S of 100 scores we can write

```
        DIMENSIØN S(100)
        WRITE (6,3) S
      3 FØRMAT (1X, 4F5.0)
```

and the scores will be printed out, four values per line, on 25 single-spaced lines. The DIMENSIØN statement above may be omitted if it has appeared earlier in the program.

If the statements are written

WRITE (6,4) S

4   FØRMAT (1X, F5.0)

the scores will be printed, one per line, on 100 single-spaced lines.

Any FØRTRAN operation may be performed with the elements of an array in the same manner as it is performed with the constants, variables, or arithmetic expressions composed of constants and variables. Examples of such operations follow.

example 10-1. A card is punched with five values of a one-dimensional array in the 5F6.2 format. The values are

20.44 42.16 16.05 5.42 0.17

It is required to write a program to find the sum of these values.

a/   If the array concept is not used, a program may be written as follows:

```
    READ(5,1) A,B,C,D,E          A different name for
                                 each element
1   FØRMAT(5F6.2)
    SUM = A + B + C + D + E
    WRITE(6,2) SUM
2   FØRMAT (1X, F7.2)
```

b/   Employing the array concept and denoting the array by A, we may write

```
    DIMENSIØN A(5)
    READ(5,1) A                  The entire array will be
                                 stored
1   FØRMAT(5F6.2)
    SUM = A(1) + A(2) + A(3) + A(4) + A(5)
    WRITE (6,2) SUM
2   FØRMAT(1X, F7.2)
```

c/   Combining the array concept with a DØ statement, we may write:

```
      DIMENSIØN A(5)
      READ(5,1) A
   1  FØRMAT(5F6.2)
      SUM = 0.00
      DØ 3 I = 1,5
   3  SUM = SUM + A(I)
      WRITE(6,2) SUM
   2  FØRMAT (1X, F7.2)
```

In this last program, as the computer cycles five times through the DØ range, A(I) becomes successively A(1), A(2), . . . , and the corresponding values of the elements are brought from storage and added to SUM.

In all three cases above the printout is 84.24.

The last program, obviously, is the only acceptable one in the case of a long array consisting of 100 or 1000 elements.

example 10-2. Eight elements of a one-dimensional array are punched on two cards, four per card, in the 4F6.1 format. The elements are

$$_{\wedge\wedge}-6.7_\wedge+11.2_\wedge+66.7_{\wedge\wedge}+4.1$$
$$_\wedge+82.6_\wedge-61.7_\wedge-40.3_{\wedge\wedge}+3.2$$

Write a program that will find the sum of the positive numbers Program. Denote the array by P.

```
      DIMENSIØN P(8)
      READ(5,1) P
   1  FØRMAT(4F6.1)
```
The entire array will be stored; after reading the four elements on the first card in accordance with the given format, the computer will go to the second card for the remaining four elements; it knows there are eight from the DIMENSIØN statement.

```
      SUM = 0.0
      DØ 3 I = 1,8
      IF(P(I).LT.0.0)GØTØ3
      SUM = SUM + P(I)
   3  CØNTINUE
      WRITE(6,2) SUM
   2  FØRMAT (1X, F7.1)
      STØP
```
This will bypass negative numbers.

Having inspected the eight elements, the computer makes the normal exit and prints the result.

The printout is 167.8.

example 10-3.   In Example 8-4 the largest of four values was found, in the first program, by direct comparison and, in the second, by invoking the function AMAX1. The second program, of course, is the one to use when the number of values is large. But, even in the more efficient second program of Example 8-4, it is necessary to write the list of the variables A, B, C, D, a chore in the case of a large number of values. The concept of the array eliminates this chore, as shown in the following two variants of the second program of Example 8-4. In these variants the four variables A, B, C, D are replaced by the elements $X(1)$, $X(2)$, $X(3)$, $X(4)$ of the array X.

Variant 1.

```
      DIMENSIØN X(4)
      READ (5,1)   X
   1  FØRMAT (4F5.1)
      BIG = AMAX1 (X(1),X(2),X(3),X(4))
      WRITE (6,2)   BIG
   2  FØRMAT (1H0,F5.1)
```

In Variant 1 the list of variables has been eliminated from the READ statement but not from the BIG = AMAX1 $(X(1), \ldots)$ statement. The latter list can be done away with by incorporating in the program the DØ statement, as shown in Variant 2.

Variant 2.

```
      DIMENSIØN X(4)
      READ (5,1)   X
   1  FØRMAT (4F5.1)
      BIG = X(1)
      DØ 3 I = 2,4
   3  BIG = AMAX1 (BIG,X(I))
      WRITE (6,2)   BIG
   2  FØRMAT (1H0,F5.1)
```

AMAX1, MAX0, and similar functions always require *at least two* arguments within the parentheses. Thus, while it is correct to make the computer pick up the entire array X by writing READ(5,1) X, it would be incorrect to write in Variant 2

$$BIG = AMAX1 (X)$$

and expect AMAX1 to compare the four elements of X. Equally unacceptable to AMAX1 and MAX0 is an implied DØ within the argument:

$$\text{BIG} = \text{AMAX1 } (\text{X(I), I} = 1,4) \quad \leftarrow \text{NO!}$$

example 10-4. This example illustrates the effects of FØRMAT on the output of a one-dimensional array, mainly on the spacing of the lines of the printout.

Twenty elements of a one-dimensional array I are punched on four cards, as shown:

1	2	3	4	5
6	7	8	9	10
11	12	13	14	15
16	17	18	19	20

The following program describes the input of this array and its output in accordance with different FØRMATs. The effects of the various specifications are explained under Comments.

Program	*Comments*
DIMENSION I (20)	20 storage locations are reserved for the elements of I.
READ (5,1) I 1 FØRMAT (5I5)	The limited Format is used 4 times to store the array from 4 cards, each card punched with 5 elements.
WRITE (6,2) I 2 FØRMAT (1H0,10I5/1H0,10I5)	The printer double spaces and prints the first 10 elements on the line; the slash sends it to the left edge of the sheet; the printer double spaces again and prints the remaining 10 elements.
WRITE (6,3) I 3 FØRMAT (1H0,10I5)	The printer duplicates the preceding printout by reusing the limited FØRMAT.
WRITE (6,4) I 4 FØRMAT (2 (1H0,10I5/))	The FØRMAT is equivalent to (1H0,10I5/ 1H0,10I5/); therefore the printout is the same as before, but the second slash makes the sheet advance one line beyond the second printed line (See Art. 5-1).

WRITE (6,3)   I

This command and the corresponding printout are duplicated to show the blank line produced by the preceding command.

WRITE (6,5)   I
5   FØRMAT (2 (1H0,10I5/),1H+)

This FØRMAT is equivalent to (1H0,10I5/ 1H0,10I5/1H+); therefore the printout is the same as before, but 1H+ keeps the sheet from advancing after the second slash has sent the printer to the left edge of the sheet.

WRITE (6,3)   I
STØP

This command is issued again to show the effect of 1 H+.

Printout:

$ENTRY

```
~~~~1~~~~2~~~~3~~~~4~~~~5~~~~6~~~~7~~~~8~~~~9~~~10  ⎤
                                                   ⎥ 1st WRITE
    11   12   13   14   15   16   17   18   19   20 ⎦

     1    2    3    4    5    6    7    8    9   10  ⎤
                                                   ⎥ 2nd WRITE
    11   12   13   14   15   16   17   18   19   20 ⎦

     1    2    3    4    5    6    7    8    9   10  ⎤
                                                   ⎥ 3rd WRITE
    11   12   13   14   15   16   17   18   19   20 ⎦




     1    2    3    4    5    6    7    8    9   10  ⎤
                                                   ⎥ 4th WRITE
    11   12   13   14   15   16   17   18   19   20 ⎦

     1    2    3    4    5    6    7    8    9   10  ⎤
                                                   ⎥ 5th WRITE
    11   12   13   14   15   16   17   18   19   20 ⎦

     1    2    3    4    5    6    7    8    9   10  ⎤
                                                   ⎥ 6th WRITE
    11   12   13   14   15   16   17   18   19   20 ⎦
```

example 10-5. Parts (a) and (b) of this example illustrate the use of the index of the implied DØ to identify the elements of an array.

(a)   *Program*   *Comments*

```
      DIMENSION A(3)
      READ (5,1)   A
  1   FØRMAT (3F4.1)
      WRITE (6,2) (I,A(I),I=1,3)
  2   FØRMAT (/(1X,'A(',I1,')∧=',F4.1))


      STØP
```

The slash and 1X advance the sheet two lines, and the printer prints the values of I and the corresponding A(I), in pairs, on three consecutive lines

Data card:

```
  ∧1 . 2 ∧3 . 4 ∧5 . 6
```

Printout:

```
              $ENTRY


  A ( 1 ) ∧=∧1 . 2
  A ( 2 ) ∧=∧3 . 4
  A ( 3 ) ∧=∧5 . 6
```

(b)   *Program*   *Comments*

```
      DIMENSIØN A(3)
      READ (5,1)   A
  1   FØRMAT (3F4.1)
      WRITE (6,2) (I,I=1,3),(A(I),I=1,3)
  2   FØRMAT (1H0,'I',3I5/1H0,'A∧',3F5.1)




      STØP
```

The sheet advances to the second line, and the printer prints "I" and its 3 values on the line; the sheet advances to the fourth line, and the printer prints "A" and its 3 values

Data card:

```
  ∧1 . 2 ∧3 . 4 ∧5 . 6
```

Printout:

$ENTRY

I∿∿∿1∿∿∿2∿∿∿3

A   1.2 3.4 5.6

If an array is overdimensioned, that is, if the number of reserved storage locations exceeds the number of elements to be processed, the computer must not be allowed to fill the superfluous reserved locations with improper data or zeros; nor must it be asked to supply information from the superfluous locations.

Improper storage may occur if an implied DØ is not used in a READ statement to describe an array that is shorter than the dimension assigned to it in the beginning of the program. For example, if an array J has three elements, punched on a single card, and the computer encounters the following sequence:

```
        DIMENSIØN J (5)
        READ (5,1)   J
   1    FØRMAT (3I5)
```

the machine will store the three elements from the data card, and then it will look for the remaining two elements (to satisfy the dimension of 5) on the next card, which may or may not be a part of the data deck; if the next card is blank, it will store zeros at J(4) and J(5); if the next card is a control card, the machine will write a diagnostic to the effect that the data are improper.

Errors and diagnostics may be prevented by including in the READ statement an implied DØ that defines the limits of the array, as illustrated in Example 10-6.

example 10-6.

```
        DIMENSIØN J (5),K(5)
        READ(5,1)    (J(I),I=1,3),(K(1),I=1,3)
   1    FØRMAT (3I3,3I2)
        WRITE(6,2)    (J(I),I=1,3),(K(1),I=1,3)
   2    FØRMAT (1H0,3I3/1H0,3I3)
        STØP
```

Data card:

/ ˄10˄11˄12˄5˄6˄7 /

Printout:

˄10˄11˄12

˄˄5˄˄6˄˄7

Example 10-6 illustrates the use of the implied DØ in both the READ and the WRITE statements. However, if the WRITE statement were written:

WRITE(6,2)   J,K

the machine would reuse FØRMAT 2 in an attempt to find five values of both J and K in storage and, failing in that, would print:

˄10˄11˄12

UUUUUU˄˄5

˄˄6˄˄7UUU

UUU

using the UUU's to point out the absence of values in locations J(4), J(5), K(4), and K(5).

In Article 9-3, to illustrate the operation of a nested DØ, we presented a program that found prime numbers and printed them, one at a time, in a column. Now that we are familiar with arrays, we can write a program to find prime numbers as the elements of an array, store them as an array, and print the entire array with a single command, in any desired pattern.

Such a program is shown in Example 10-7. In this program the prime numbers are assumed to form an array K, arbitrarily dimensioned for 100 elements. The first three elements are established by assignment. All the subsequent odd numbers, identified by N and beginning with 5, are tested for primeness. N is tested by dividing it consecutively by K(3), K(4), . . . , K(J), . . . K(J) need not exceed M = SQRT (R), where R = N; for example, if N = 109, M = SQRT(109.) = 10, and therefore 109 is tested by dividing it by the primes 3, 5, and 7. It should be observed that the number of divisors of 109, 3, is smaller than M (= 10), the value which the last divisor should not exceed; this observation will be made use of in the program. After every division of N by K(J), the quotient L is multiplied back by K(J); if the product is equal to N, N is not a prime; if no product is equal to N, N is a prime number.

example 10-7. Write a program to find the first 100 prime numbers, considering the numbers as an array K.

Program	Comments
DIMENSIØN K (100)	100 locations are reserved for the first 100 prime numbers.
K (1) = 1 K (2) = 2 K (3) = 3	The first three prime numbers are stored by assignment.
N = 3	N, the number to be tested for primeness, is initialized at 3.
DØ 4 I = 4,100	I is the subscript of K; this begins the search for all prime numbers from K(4) to K(100).
2 N = N + 2	N is incremented (from 3 to 5 in the first cycle).
R = N	N is converted to real R for the purpose of extracting the square root.
M = SQRT (R)	M is the fractionless square root of N and the upper limit of divisors for N.
DØ 3 J = 3,M	This begins the testing of N; J's are the successive subscripts of the K's used as the divisors of N; the last J is unknown, because it grows with N; however, as noted in the discussion above, the number of divisors cannot exceed M; therefore M is a safe end-test value for J.
IF (K(J).GT.M) GØ TØ 4	If the divisor K(J) is smaller than M, N must be tested by the sequence of statements which follow; if the testing has reached the point where K(J) is greater than M, the computer goes to 4 to make N an element in the array.

L = N/K(J)	L is the quotient in the division test.
IF (N.EQ.L*K(J)) GØ TØ 2	If the LEX is TRUE, N is not a prime; the computer goes back to increase N.
3 CØNTINUE	
4 K (I) = N	N is made an element in the array with the subscript equal to the I of the cycle.
WRITE (6,5) K	The entire array of 100 prime numbers is printed on 10 double-spaced lines, 10 elements to a line.
5 FØRMAT (1H0,10I4) STØP	

Printout:

```
       $ENTRY
^^^1^^^2^^^3^^^5^^^7^^11^^13^^17^^19^^23
  29  31  37  41  43  47  53  59  61  67
  71  73  79  83  89  97 101 103 107 109
 113 127 131 137 139 149 151 157 163 167
 173 179 181 191 193 197 199 211 223 227
 229 233 239 241 251 257 263 269 271 277
 281 283 293 307 311 313 317 331 337 347
 349 353 359 367 373 379 383 389 397 401
 409 419 421 431 433 439 443 449 457 461
 463 467 479 487 491 499 503 509 521 523
```

10-5. two-dimensional arrays

A *two-dimensional array* is a group of quantities arranged as a matrix, that is, in rows and columns, as shown below:

	Column 1	Column 2	Column 3
Row 1	67.50	59.40	52.75
Row 2	48.20	36.18	45.25

This array may represent the sales of three different brands (shown in the three columns) in two stores (shown in the two rows).

Since the quantities in the table are all of the same type, they, like the quantities in a one-dimensional array, can be given one generic name, say T; and, like the quantities in a one-dimensional array, they can be distinguished from one another by means of subscripts.

An element in a two-dimensional array receives two subscripts, the *first* one for the *row* it is in, the *second* for the *column* it is in, counting the rows downward and the columns from left to right. The two subscripts are enclosed in parentheses and are separated by a comma. Thus the name of the first element in the table above, 67.50, would be T(1,1); the name of the element 52.75 would be T(1,3), and that of 48.20, T(2,1).

Just as with one-dimensional arrays, a two-dimensional array must be DIMENSIØNED, but its DIMENSIØN statement must indicate the extent of the array in two directions, both its depth and its length. Thus the DIMENSIØN statement for the array above would be

DIMENSIØN T(2,3)

The first subscript, 2, indicates the total number of *rows;* the second, 3, the total number of *columns.* The product of the two dimensions, 6, is equal to the number of elements; an occasional element may have a 0. value, as, for instance, when a store reports no sale of a brand or does not report it at all.

Encountering the DIMENSIØN statement, the computer reserves 6 sequential locations for the elements of the array and assigns to them addresses *by columns,* as shown in the diagram on the right; that is, it reserves the first two locations for the elements in rows 1 and 2 in the first column of the matrix, the next two locations for the elements in rows 1 and 2 in the second column, and so on. Note that the order of addressing the locations is such that the first subscript varies (with the rows), while the second one remains constant until all the elements in the column have been taken care of.

Address	*Location*
T(1,1)	
T(2,1)	
T(1,2)	
T(2,2)	
T(1,3)	
T(2,3)	

If now the computer receives the command:

READ (5,1) T   (10-3)

it will read numbers on the data card (or cards), one number after the other, and store them, in order, in the locations shown above. Since the order of the addresses is T(1,1), T(2,1), T(1,2), etc., it is of paramount importance that the order of the elements on the data card be identical with that of the addresses: that is, the elements must be punched on the data card by columns, element T(1,1), 67.50, first, element T(2,1), 48.20, second, element T(1,2), 59.40, third, and so on.[†] Thus a data card punched as shown below:

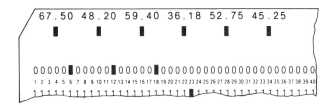

will cause the storage locations reserved for the array T to be filled as shown on the right.

The FØRMAT statement that properly connects the READ command with the data card above is:

1   FØRMAT (6F6.2)

If the FØRMAT statement were in the limited form:

Address	Location
T(1,1)	67.50
T(2,1)	48.20
T(1,2)	59.40
T(2,2)	36.18
T(1,3)	52.75
T(2,3)	45.25

FØRMAT (F6.2)

the elements would have to be punched, by columns, on six cards.

As in the case of the one-dimensional arrays, the subscripts of the elements of two-dimensional arrays need not be numbers; they may be letters and arithmetical expressions involving letters, numbers, and operational symbols. For example, T(I+1,J) represents an element in a two-dimensional array T in row I+1 and column J. (It is customary, though not mandatory, to indicate the row number by I and the column number by J.) In this general form a subscripted variable name T is not restricted to a single element of the array but may be used to refer to any element in the array. It may be that, in a program, the variable names I and J are used to count certain quantities and operations. If, during the execution of the program, I becomes 1 and J becomes 3, and then it becomes necessary to define the element T(I+1,J), a substitution of the constants would produce T(1+1,3), that is, T(2,3); this description, applied to the sales array above, would define the element as 45.25.

[†] Further on it will be shown that the order of the elements on a data card need not always be by columns. We shall get to that—and the relevant modifications—in due time.

10-6. operations with two-dimensional arrays

In Article 10-1 we were shown an *indexed* READ statement (also called a READ with an implied DØ):

$$\text{READ (5,1)(S(I),I=1,100)} \tag{10-1}$$

which meant that the computer would vary the index I of S(I), by increments of 1, from 1 to 100 and in this manner store 100 elements of the array S.

In the same manner we can write an indexed READ statement for a two-dimensional array:

```
    DIMENSIØN T(2,3)
    READ (5,2) ((T(I,J),I=1,2), J=1,3)          (10-4)
  2 FØRMAT (6F7.2)
```

In the operation dictated by this notation the outer variable (J) receives the first value (1) in its range (from 1 to 3), and the inner variable (I) cycles through its range (from 1 to 2); then the outer variable receives the next value (2), and the inner variable cycles again through its range (from 1 to 2), and so on. In detail, the operation goes through the following steps:

1/ The outer subscript J (next to the rightmost parenthesis) receives the value of 1, and this 1 is substituted for J in the innermost set of parentheses, forming T(I,1).

2/ Within the second (middle) set of parentheses, I of T(I,1) assumes, in succession, a value of 1 and then a value of 2 (as indicated by the range I = 1,2), resulting in the storage of T(1,1) and T(2,1).

3/ With the range of I corresponding to J = 1 exhausted, J receives the next value in its range, 2, resulting in T(I,2).

4/ As in Step 2, I cycles again from 1 to 2, resulting in the storage of T(1,2) and T(2,2).

5/ Finally, J becomes 3, producing T(I,3).

6/ I cycles again between 1 and 2, resulting in the storage of T(1,3) and T(2,3).

To summarize, the elements are stored in the following sequence:

T(1,1), T(2,1), T(1,2), T(2,2), T(1,3), T(2,3),

in agreement with the sequence by columns shown at the beginning of Article 10-5.

It should require no great stretch of imagination to see that the cycling of values through I and J is similar to the cycling of the index values during the execution of the nested DØ statements; thus the term "implied DØ" applies to two-dimensional arrays as well as to one-dimensional arrays.

It must be clearly understood that a row and a column of an array need not be identified exclusively by the indices I and J; any two integer variables, such as M and L, or KRØW and KØLUMN, will serve the same purpose; moreover, if I and J were reversed in position, that is, if the variable T were subscripted T(J,I), the computer would automatically interpret J, the *first* subscript, as the index of a *row*, and I, the *second* subscript, as the index of a *column*. The important rule to remember is that the range of a subscript in the READ statement must agree with its range in the DIMENSIØN statement. For example, in the two statements

DIMENSIØN T(2,3)
READ(5,2) ((T(J,I),I=1,3),J=1,2)   (10-5)

the range of J, the first subscript in T(J,I), and therefore representing rows, should be 1,2, in agreement with the first DIMENSIØN 2 (the number of rows).

Note carefully the difference between the two indexed READ statements (10-4) and (10-5). The READ statement (10-4) has the inner loop of rows within the outer loop of columns, that is, a column is held constant and the rows are varied; this sequence is in agreement with the normal sequence of storing which the computer employs when the command to store is made by an unindexed READ statement. But the READ statement (10-5) has the rows (J) in the outer loop and the columns (I) in the inner loop; that is, a row is held constant while the columns are varied. Consequently, the matrix values will be stored in the following order:

T(1,1), T(1,2), T(1,3), T(2,1), T(2,2), T(2,3)

Thus if the READ statement (10-5) is used to store the array T shown at the beginning of Article 10-5, its elements must be punched, on a card or several cards, not by columns but by rows, in the following order:

67.50   59.40   52.75   48.20   36.18   45.25

Any other order would result in the jumbling of the matrix. Equally chaotic would be the result of matching the data above with the READ statement (10-4); one effect of such combination would be to store 59.40 under T(2,1).

The rules and regulations that govern the input of arrays apply with equal force to the output of arrays. In response to the command

$$\text{WRITE}(6,3) \text{ T}$$
$$3 \quad \text{FØRMAT (1X, 6F7.2)}$$

the computer would print out the values in one line, by the customary columns:

T(1,1)	T(2,1)	T(1,2)	T(2,2)	T(1,3)	T(2,3)
67.50	48.20	59.40	36.18	52.75	45.25

To make the computer print out the values in the form of the original matrix, that is, by rows, we would copy the command of the READ statement (10-5) and accompany it with a short FØRMAT:

$$\text{WRITE}(6,4) ((T(J,I),I = 1,3), J = 1,2)$$
$$4 \quad \text{FØRMAT (1X, 3F7.2)}$$

obtaining

T(1,1)	T(1,2)	T(1,3)
67.50	59.40	52.75

T(2,1)	T(2,2)	T(2,3)
48.20	36.18	45.25

But were we to command with an unsubscripted statement

$$\text{WRITE}(6,4)\text{T}$$
$$4 \quad \text{FØRMAT(1X, 3F7.2)}$$

the computer would proceed in the column order and would print out, in two lines,

T(1,1)	T(2,1)	T(1,2)
67.50	48.20	59.40

T(2,2)	T(1,3)	T(2,3)
36.18	52.75	45.25

which is not the original matrix at all.

An interesting implied DØ is:

WRITE(6,1)   (I,I = 2,60,2)

1   FØRMAT (1H0,10I4)

This command, without a DIMENSIØN statement, makes the computer print all the even integers from 2 to 60 in three rows:

2	4	6	8	10	12	14	16	18	20
22	24	26	28	30	32	34	36	38	40
42	44	46	48	50	52	54	56	58	60

Caution must be exercised in writing WRITE statements for arrays. In commanding the computer to print out an entire array, we must not say WRITE (6,4) T (I, J) instead of WRITE (6,4) T; in other words, we must not subscript T. T (I, J) refers to a single element; if I and J are defined earlier in the program as, say, 1 and 3, the computer would print only the value of $T(1,3)$. To produce a printout of the entire array, $T(I,J)$ must be bracketed together with two ranges such as I = 1,3 and J = 1,2, to form an implied DØ.

Another precaution concerns the combination of a DØ statement with an implied DØ and an excessive FØRMAT to write out an array. Consider the following program:

```
      DIMENSIØN K (2,3)
      READ (5,1) K
   1  FØRMAT (6I2)
      DØ 2 I = 1,2
   2  WRITE (6,3) (K(I,J),J = 1,3)
   3  FØRMAT (1X, 4I3)
      STØP
```

Data card:

/ 1 4 2 5 3 6 /

The machine will enter the DØ range with I = 1, and cycle through the three values of J, printing *only three* values of K, regardless of the four-field specification; it will then return to the DØ statement, set I = 2, and print the second set of three values of K. The computer processes only three values on each pass through the range.

Printout:

```
      . . . . . . .
˄˄1˄˄2˄˄3
˄˄4˄˄5˄˄6
```

An interesting operation that can be performed on a matrix is to turn it clockwise through 90 degrees, that is, to stand it on its right end. This operation can be performed by spelling out the individual elements in the WRITE statement and accompanying it with the appropriate FØRMAT, as shown below:

```
    WRITE(6,5) T(2,1), T(1,1), T(2,2), T(1,2), T(2,3), T(1,3)
  5 FØRMAT (1X, 2F7.2)
```

The resulting printout for the matrix of Article 10-5 will be

```
    48.20      67.50
    36.18      59.40
    45.25      52.75
```

The WRITE statement above can be written more concisely with an implied DØ. The procedure is described below.

Original matrix				Rotated matrix (with original subscripts)	
T(1,1)	T(1,2)	T(1,3)		T(2,1)	T(1,1)
T(2,1)	T(2,2)	T(2,3)		T(2,2)	T(1,2)
				T(2,3)	T(1,3)

Study the rotated matrix. The second subscript varies downward normally, that is, 1, 2, 3. But the first subscript is 2 in the first column and 1 in the second column. This is just the opposite of what we would get in response to the statements

```
    WRITE (6,2) ((T(I,J),I = 1,2), J = 1,3)
  2 FØRMAT (1X, 2F7.2)
```

because the printer would print

```
        T(1,1)      T(2,1)
        T(1,2)      T(2,2)
        T(1,3)      T(2,3)
```

that is, the columns would be reversed. But now, if we change the subscript I of $T(I,J)$ to 3-I, in order to make the first subscript vary from 2 to 1, as I varies from 1 to 2, and write the statements

```
        WRITE (6,2) ((T(3-I,J),I = 1,2), J = 1,3)
    2   FØRMAT (1X, 2F7.2)
```

the machine will compute the subscript 3-I as the index I cycles between 1 and 2, and will print out

```
        T(2,1)      T(1,1)
        T(2,2)      T(1,2)
        T(2,3)      T(1,3)
```

Do not become confused by the fact that the printed result has 3 rows and 2 columns, while J, the second subscript, which denotes columns, cycles through 1, 2, 3. We are not writing a new matrix with new dimensions. We are only tricking the computer into writing the old matrix in a new form, using a combination of a doctored-up subscript and a format limited to two specifications.

One cannot be too careful with Format statements that contain Hollerith headings and rely on a total or partial reuse of the specifications. If we wish to obtain a printout of the array T in the following form:

```
    THE ARRAY T
^^^67.50^^^59.40^^^52.75

    48.20   36.18   45.25
```

we should not write:

```
        WRITE (6,1) ((T(J,I),I = 1,3),J = 1,2)
    1   FØRMAT (1H0,9X,'THE ARRAY T'/1H0,3F8.2)
```

because the computer will use the limited format twice to print:

```
        THE ARRAY T
67.50    59.40    52.75
        THE ARRAY T
48.20    36.18    45.25
```

Again, FØRMAT 1 should not be in the following form:

```
1 FØRMAT (1H0,9X,'THE ARRAY T'/2 (1H0,3F8.2))
```

because the computer will expand the expression within the inner parentheses to 1H0,3F8.2,1H0,3F8.2, will treat the last 1H0 as a Hollerith 0 (and not as a carriage control signal), and will print the six elements on one line, as follows:

```
        THE ARRAY T
67.50    59.40    52.750    48.20    36.18    45.25
```

with the Hollerith 0 on the end of the third element.

The FØRMAT statement which will produce the right printout is:

```
1 FØRMAT (1H0,9X,'THE ARRAY T',2 (/1H0,3F8.2))
```

example 10-8. Given the following matrix:

```
 - 5.5      6.6      10.2       8.7
   4.2      8.4     - 2.7      14.5
  20.4     -2.5      11.6       6.4
 - 6.5      6.9       5.2     - 5.0
```

write a program that will:

1/ Enter the matrix into storage from four data cards, each card punched with a row of elements.

2/ Find the sum of the elements on the diagonal between −5.5 and −5.0.

3/ Find the product of the same elements.

The program, with comment cards, is shown in Fig. 10-1.

```
C DENØTE ARRAY ELEMENTS BY E
      DIMENSIØN E(4,4)
C ENTER ARRAY BY RØWS-KEEP I CØNSTANT-VARY J
      READ(5,1)(((E(I,J),J=1,4),I=1,4)
C ELEMENTS IN 5-SPACE FIELDS ØN DATA CARDS
    1 FØRMAT(4F5.1)
C CALL DIAGØNAL SUM DSUM-INITIALIZE AT 0.
      DSUM=0.
C BØTH SUBSCRIPTS ØF DIAGØNAL ELEMENT ARE
C SAME,E.G.(1,1),(2,2)-THERE ARE 4 ELEMENTS
      DØ2I=1,4
    2 DSUM=DSUM+E(I,I)
      WRITE(6,4)DSUM
C CALL DIAGØNAL PRØDUCT DPRØD-INITIALIZEAT 1.
      DPRØD=1.
      DØ3I=1,4
    3 DPRØD=DPRØD*E(I,I)
      WRITE(6,4)DPRØD
    4 FØRMAT(1HO,E13.6)
      STØP
      END
-5.5    6.6   10.2    8.7  ⎫
 4.2    8.4   -2.7   14.5  ⎬  Data
20.4   -2.5   11.6    6.4  ⎪
-6.5    6.9    5.2   -5.0  ⎭
```

Figure 10-1

The resulting printout is

⌃0.950000E 01

⌃0.267960E 04

Arrays can be conveniently stored by an *unformatted* READ statement. For instance, the array K

1 2 3 4 5 6 7 8

may be punched on the cards as shown on the right, that is, anywhere on the cards, and with any number of blank cards in between, and the two statements

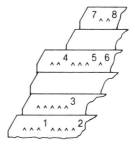

```
DIMENSIØN  K (8)
READ,  K
```

will make the computer search the cards until it finds and stores all eight K's. The two statements

```
DIMENSIØN  K (4,2)
READ,  K
```

will make the computer store the eight numbers as a two-dimensional array

```
            1      5
            2      6
            3      7
            4      8
```

As stated in Article 5-4, the unformatted method of storing requires the services of the WATFIV compiler.

10-7. the array DUMP

In Art. 7-5 it was shown that the computer, if asked, dumps the values of the variables which it has in storage at any instant during the execution of the program.

The dumping capability of the computer extends to the arrays, since arrays, after all, are groups of values: the only difference between the individual values and the array values is that the latter are identified by subscripted names instead of individual names. Thus the individual variables A, B, C, D, if grouped in an array P(4), are referred to as P(1), P(2), P(3), P(4).

With the WATFIV compiler, a command to dump A,B,C,D is written:

```
DUMPLIST/LIST1/ A,B,C,D
```

and a command to dump the array P is written:

```
DUMPLIST/LIST2/ P
```

The WATFIV compiler cannot dump individual elements of an array, such as P(3). A dump of this element can be obtained only if it is identified individually, say, as C.

With the G compiler, a command to dump A,B,C,D may be written:

    CALL DUMP (A,D,5)

where 5 is the code for a dump of *real* numbers, and a command to dump the array P is written:

    CALL DUMP (P(1),P(4),5)

Unlike the WATFIV compiler, the G compiler accepts commands to dump individual elements of an array; for example, P (3) will be dumped by the command:

    CALL DUMP (P(3),P(3),5)

A dump of a two-dimensional array reproduces the elements in the order in which they appear on the data card. For instance, if the array N:

1	2	3
4	5	6

is punched on the data card:

and is read in by the statement:

    READ (5,1)   N
  1 FØRMAT (6I2)

the dump will appear as follows:

         1   4   2   5   3   6

Shown below are two printouts of the programs, results, and dumps produced by the WATFIV and G compilers, corresponding to the following data:

ARRAY DUMP   <u>WATFIV COMPILER</u>

```
1          DIMENSION J(4),C(2,3)
2          READ(5,1)   J,C
3        1 FORMAT(4I3,6F5.1)
4          DUMPLIST/L1/J/L2/C
5          WRITE(6,2)   J,((C(I,K),K=1,3),I=1,2)
6        2 FORMAT(1H0,4I3/(1H0,3F5.1))
7          END
```
WARNING   END STATEMENT NOT PRECEDED BY A TRANSFER

$ENTRY

```
 2    4   6    8

11.1  22.2  33.3

44.4  55.5  66.6
```
ERROR   AN END STATEMENT WAS USED TO TERMINATE EXECU-
TION

PROGRAM WAS EXECUTING LINE   7 IN ROUTINE M/
PROG WHEN TERMINATION OCCURRED

****   DUMPLIST FOR ROUTINE M/PROG FOLLOWS   ****

```
&L2
C=     0.1110000E  02,     0.4439999E  02,     0.2220000E  02,
       0.5550000E  02,     0.3330000E  02,     0.6660001E  02,&END
&L1
J=            2,          4,          6,          8,&END
```

ARRAY DUMP   <u>G COMPILER</u>

```
           DIMENSION J(4),C (2,3)
           READ(5,1) J,C
         1 FORMAT(4I3,6F5.1)
           CALL PDUMP(J(1),J(4),4,J(2),J(2),4,C(1,1),
                                    C(2,3),5,C(1,3),C(1,3),*5)
           WRITE(6,2) J,((C(I,K),K=1,3),I=1,2)
         2 FORMAT(1H0,4I3/(1H0,3F5.1))
           STOP
           END
```

```
034908              2          4          6          8

03490C              4

034918     0.111000004E+02   0.443999939E+02   0.221999969E+02
           0.555000000E+02   0.333000031E+02   0.666000061E+02
```

034928   0.333000031E+02

2   4   6   8

11.1   22.2   33.3

44.4   55.5   66.6

10-8. the DATA statement

We have learned so far two ways of storing information in the memory of a computer, and yet there is still another. The two we know are the *assignment statement*, such as

$$A = 2.5$$

and the *READ statement*, such as

$$READ(5,1)\ A$$

the latter accompanied by a FØRMAT statement 1 and a data card punched with the value of A.

The third method we are to learn now is the *DATA statement.* For comparison, the three methods of storing the values of K and L are presented in the three programs shown across the page below. Included in each program are identical manipulations of K and L to obtain a value of M. Not shown are the data card for the READ program, punched with 2 and 3 in the first two 2-column fields, and the printout of the value of M, which, of course, is 5 in every case.

Assignment Program	*READ Program*	*DATA Program*
K = 2	READ(5,1) K,L	DATA K,L/2,3/
L = 3	1 FØRMAT(2I2)	M = K + L
M = K + L	M = K + L	WRITE(6,2) M
WRITE(6,2) M	WRITE(6,2) M	2 FØRMAT (1H0,I2)
2 FØRMAT(1H0,I2)	2 FØRMAT(1H0,I2)	STØP
STØP	STØP	

It can be seen, in the DATA program, that a DATA statement consists of three parts:

1/ The word DATA.

2/ A list of variables, separated by commas, which are to be defined by an assignment of values.

3/ The values, placed between slashes and separated by commas, which are to be assigned, in order, to the variables in the list.

The effect of the DATA statement is to place the values that appear between the slashes into the memory locations assigned to the listed variables, and to *do it before the execution of the program begins.* This is the principal difference between the DATA statement and the other two methods, and we shall explain it by referring to the three programs above.

The compiler, as it translates the program with the DATA statement, lodges the values 2 and 3 in the K and L locations during the compilation, so that these values are immediately available for the computation of M when the execution begins. On the other hand, during the compilation of the program with the assignment statement, the compiler labels two locations with the names K and L, but stores 2 and 3 in two other locations; it is the execution of the assignment statements, K = 2 and L = 3, that causes 2 and 3 to be transferred into the K and L locations. Finally, in the program with the READ statement, it is the execution of the READ command that brings the values 2 and 3 from the punched data card into the K and L locations.

It follows that the DATA statement is not an executable statement; the computer does not have to execute it, because the values necessary for the execution of the program are *loaded*—together with the program—into the proper memory locations by the compiler.

It can be seen, from the examples and the discussion above, that a DATA statement reduces both the length of the program and the time of its execution. Of course, computer programs are not written for the manipulation of constant quantities, such as K = 2 and L = 3 above; they are written principally to process quantities that vary, such as ages, incomes, and inventories, and these are usually submitted on punched cards. But many a program contains a constant, such as π (pi), or g, or 144., and the proper way to load it into a program is via the DATA statement.

Another advantage of the DATA statement is that it can load alphameric quantities into the memory, a feat that an assignment statement cannot do. We may not write

$$A = B\emptyset\emptyset K$$

and yet we may write

$$DATA\ A/4HB\emptyset\emptyset K/$$

or $$DATA\ A/'B\emptyset\emptyset K'/$$

and the word BØØK will wind up in the location reserved for A.

If a word has more than four characters, it should be divided into four-character modules, or *words* (see Article 8-6), and each word loaded separately. Thus

DATA A, B, C/'SEPT','EMBE','R'/

will put SEPTEMBER in the three locations A, B, and C.

On the output, SEPTEMBER will be printed out if we write

WRITE(6,4) A, B, C
4   FØRMAT(2A4,A1)

The list of variables in a DATA statement may contain arrays and subscripted variables; the WATFIV compiler also accepts implied DØs, provided the parameters of the DØ are numeric and not alphabetic. Thus the three modules of SEPTEMBER in the example above may be treated as the three elements of the array MØNTH:

DIMENSIØN MØNTH (3)

DATA MØNTH/'SEPT','EMBE','R'/

An example of subscripted variables in a DATA statement is:

DIMENSIØN K(10)

DATA K(3),K(7)/5,10/

This sequence will assign 5 to the third element of K and 10 to the seventh.

The WATFIV compiler accepts an implied DØ in a DATA statement, if the DØ is written as shown in the following example:

DIMENSIØN K(3,4)

DATA ((K(I,J),J=,4),I=1,3)/1,2,3,4,5,6,7,8,9,10,11,12/

If the literal data contain natural apostrophes, as in the following sentence (see end of Article 4-1),

'IT'S TØM'S,' HE SAID

the sentence must be divided into four-character modules, each module placed between two Hollerith apostrophes, and each natural apostrophe punched double (though considered a single character). This creates a multiplicity of apostrophes, as can be seen in the broken up sentence below:

DIMENSION A(6)

Hollerith apostrophes

DATA A/' '˭IT˭' ','S˄TØ','M˭'S,',' '˭˄HE',' ˄SAI',' D˄˄˄ '/

Natural apostrophes

Much confusion· can be avoided if the Hollerith apostrophes on each side of a module are replaced by 4H in front of the module, because, in the latter case, the natural apostrophes are punched in their normal, single, form:

DATA A/4H'IT',4HS˄TØ,4HM'S,,4H'˄HE,4H˄SAI,4HD˄˄˄/

If we wish to assign a constant value, say, 7.2, to four different variables, A, B, C, D, we may either write:

DATA A,B,C,D/7.2,7.2,7.2,7.2/

or condense the list of values, using the repetition number:

DATA A,B,C,D/4*7.2/

If the constants appear in groups, such as:

DATA A,B,C,D/7.2,2.5,7.2,2.5/

it is not correct to condense the statement to:

DATA A,B,C,D/2*(7.2,2.5)/   ◄——✕——   NO!

because parentheses are not permitted between the slashes, except when they occur within the apostrophes.
But we can write:

DATA A,C,B,D/2*7.2,2*2.5/

The rules concerning the repetition number apply to the alphameric data. It is correct to write:

DATA A,B/'P','P'/

or   DATA A,B/2*'P'/

It is also correct to write:

DATA A,B,C,D/'P','Q','P','Q'/

but it is incorrect to apply a repetition number to groups:

DATA A,B,C,D/2*('P','Q')/   ←——✗———   NO!

Finally, 13 asterisks may be stored as an array T by the sequence:

DIMENSIØN T (13)
DATA T /13*'*'/

Values loaded into the memory via a DATA statement may be redefined later in the program, usually by an assignment statement, but *never* by another DATA statement.

A DATA statement may not be used to load values into storage that is CØMMØN to a main program and a subprogram (see Article 11-9).

If a value assigned to the variable K by a DATA statement is literal, and K appears later in the program on the right side of an assignment statement, the variable on the left side must be in the same mode as K, that is, integer. It is correct to write:

L = K

but   A = K

is invalid.

Example 10-9 illustrates the use of the DATA statement in a longer program.

example 10-9. Write a program to compute the weights of spheres, 1, 2, and 3 inches in diameter, made of aluminum, copper, lead, and gold. The unit weights of the materials, in pounds per cubic foot, are: aluminum, 169; copper, 555; lead, 708; gold, 1205.

Use the DATA statement to load all the given data.

Program

```
   DIMENSIØN NAME(6), DENSTY(4), WEIGHT(3,4)
   DATA NAME, DENSITY,PI/'ALUM','INUM','CØPP','ER','LEAD','GØLD',
 *169.,555.,708.,1205.,3.1416/
   DØ 7 J=1,4
   DØ 7 I=1,3
   D=I
 7 WEIGHT(I,J)=PI*D**3/6.*DENSTY(J)/1728.
   WRITE(6,2)NAME,(I,(WEIGHT(I,J),J=1,4),I=1,3)
 2 FØRMAT(1H0,'DIAMETER,',10X,'WEIGHT ØF A SPHERE, LB.'/1H0,
 *3X,'IN.',5X,2A4,3X,A4,A2,5X,A4,6X,A4/(1H0,4X,I1,2X,4F10.2))
   STØP
```

Printout

DIAMETER,	WEIGHT ØF A SPHERE, LB.			
IN.	ALUMINUM	CØPPER	LEAD	GØLD
1	0.05	0.17	0.21	0.37
2	0.41	1.35	1.72	2.92
3	1.38	4.54	5.79	9.86

10-9.   FØRMAT as data

In the preceding article we have learned that data can be loaded into the memory as part of the program. Now we are going to learn a reverse technique, namely, that of removing a FØRMAT statement from a program and reading it in as data, during the execution of the program; the technique is known as the *object-time FØRMAT*. Why do it? Because a fixed FØRMAT requires all the data to be in a fixed form, in perfect agreement with the specifications of the FØRMAT statement. For example, if a program sequence reads

```
3  READ(5,4) K,L,M
4  FØRMAT (3I4)
```

then all the cards in the data deck must be punched as shown in Fig. 10-2, with all the numbers in consecutive fields of four spaces. The computer, reading the first card, will store 17 at K, 102 at L, and 4 at M.

But if a user of the program above, unaware of the FØRMAT statement

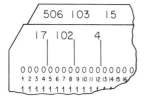

Figure 10-2

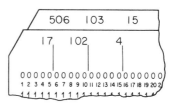

Figure 10-3

4, submits data cards with numbers punched in five-space fields, as shown in Fig. 10-3, the machine, guided by Format 4, will assign 1 to K, 7001 to L, and 200 to M. To read the second deck correctly, the FØRMAT specifications must be changed from (3I4) to (3I5); but this means that the entire program must be recompiled.

To avoid the necessity of recompiling a program for every new deck of data that comes along, we may remove the straitjacketing FØRMAT statement from the program, and precede each data deck by a *data* card, describing the FØRMAT that governed the punching of the data. This would enable the computer to read in the specifications appropriate to the data that follow them, and thus make no mistakes in storing them. The mechanics of this operation are explained below.

To store the data shown in Fig. 10-2 and the appropriate FØRMAT, that is, (3I4), we need in the program two READ statements, the first to read the FØRMAT specifications (let us call them Q) *that are submitted with the data,* the second to read the data. The first READ statement must be accompanied, *in the program,* by a FØRMAT statement whose specifications (call them P) describe the specifications Q; that is, specifications P must describe (3I4), and specifications Q must describe the data ⌄⌄17⌄102⌄⌄⌄4. The execution of the second READ statement, guided by the specifications Q, stores 17, 102, and 4 at K, L, and M. But where does the execution of the first READ statement, guided by the specifications P, put (3I4)? It can only be in another set of memory locations. Now, (3I4) is a string of five alphameric characters (including the parentheses in the count): therefore, the specifications P must be the A specifications. Since a location in the IBM System/360 can store a word of not more than four characters, at least two locations are needed to store the five characters of (3I4): (3I4, described by the specification A4, can go into the first location, and the remaining), described by A1, into the second.

What addresses are to be given to these two locations? We want to be able to describe, and call for, (3I4) by a single name. We can do this if we regard the two locations as the consecutive storage locations of an array, and assign to them, and to the array in them, one name. Let this name be F (for FØRMAT). Then, (3I4 is stored in location F(1) and) in location F(2). Calling for the array F, we get (3I4). The array, naturally, must be dimensioned.

The preceding discussion is summarized in the program/data sequence shown in Fig. 10-4.

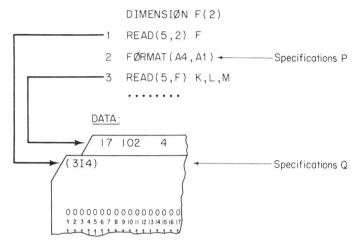

Figure 10-4

When the machine executes

1   READ(5,2) F

it stores, as the two elements of the array F, the contents of the first data card, namely, (3I4); these contents are the specifications Q, which describe the numerical data on the cards which follow. Next, the machine executes

3   READ(5,F) K, L, M

This being the second READ statement, the machine reads the second card, containing the first set of the numerical data. Note that, in the parentheses, the second digit has been replaced by F, the name of the array that holds the specifications for the numerical data. Guided by (3I4) of the array F, the machine correctly sorts out the three numbers on the card and stores them under K, L, and M.

Note that the array F is identical with the specifications of the FØRMAT statement 4 in the beginning of this article. Observe, however, that neither 4 nor FØRMAT appears with (3I4) on the data card; indeed, (3I4) begins in the very first column of the card, exactly where the computer, guided by A4 of FØRMAT 2, would start looking for it. The parentheses of the specifications belong with them; they may not be left out.

The principle of reading-in FØRMAT specifications for input can also be applied to the output; all we have to do is add an array FT for storing the output specifications, and use FT in the parentheses of the WRITE statement. This is shown in the modified program/data of Fig. 10-5.

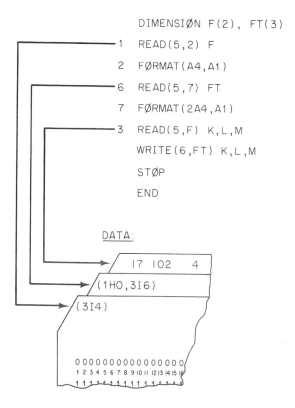

Figure 10-5

The array FT (for the output specifications) has three elements, because the addition of the carriage control specification 1H0 has increased the number of characters in the specifications to nine. The printout will show three numbers in six-space fields.

It should be noted that the two READ statements 1 and 6, the two FØRMAT statements 2 and 7, and the two data cards with the specifications could be combined on single cards, as shown in Fig. 10-6.

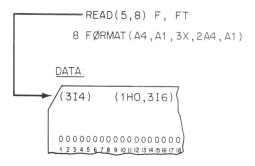

Figure 10-6

In the preceding illustration, numbers on the consecutive data cards were assumed to occupy fixed positions; therefore, the array F describing them remained constant. Similarly, the constant array FT would produce a regular table of printed numbers.

In the next example we shall show that arrays, such as F or FT, may change in the course of the execution of the program, depending on the data and the results obtained from them.

Consider an inventory record kept in a store:

Item No.	Quantity on hand	Order received for	Balance
7	200	150	50
13	100	200	−100?

For the purpose of restocking the inventory, the computer is programmed to produce a printout of the balance of supplies on hand, which is determined by subtracting orders from the quantity on hand. Obviously, a balance cannot be a negative number, as shown in the second line above, for Item No. 13. Therefore, it is desirable that, for every negative or zero balance, the computer leave a blank space, which can be easily spotted when the record is examined. Thus the computer is expected to print, in the balance column, numbers and blanks. Keep in mind that, in FØRTRAN, blanks are alphameric characters that are described by the A specifications.

To make the computer mix numbers with blanks, we convey to it two items of instruction: First, we tell it that a negative balance is to be printed as a blank, and second, we furnish it with two different specifications, one for a numerical balance, the other for a blank balance.

Let us assign the following variable names to the quantities shown in the table above:

NØ   INSTØK   IØRDER   NET

One of the statements in the program will be

NET = INSTØK − IØRDER

For the case when NET is negative we shall need the statement

NET = BLANK

in which BLANK must be defined, ahead of the statement, as one or more blank spaces. One way to define BLANK is to read it in from a data card, as follows:

```
            READ(5,2) BLANK
      2  FØRMAT(A4)
```

DATA: Blank card

The machine will pick up four "blank" characters from the first four spaces on the card and store them under BLANK.

The program will conclude with

```
      WRITE(6,8) NØ,INSTØK,IØRDER,NET
```

If we knew NET to be positive we could continue with

```
      8 FØRMAT(1H0,4I11)
```

and obtain a printout of four numbers in eleven-space fields.

But we know that, occasionally, NET will be a blank, which is described by an A specification, and therefore the following set of specifications is required:

```
      8A FØRMAT(1H0,3I11,7X,A4)
```

Let us rewrite FØRMAT 8 as follows:

```
      8B FØRMAT(1H0,3I11,7X,I4)
```

Now FØRMATs 8A and 8B are nearly identical, except for I4 and A4 in the last two places.

We know from the first illustration in this article that FØRMAT specifications can be stored as arrays. Both sets of the specifications above, 8A and 8B, have 16 characters each, including the parentheses. Therefore, we can divide the specifications into four words of four characters each, and store *both* sets as an array FMT in four locations FMT(1), FMT(2), FMT(3), and FMT(4), exchanging I4 and A4 in the last location as the occasion demands it. Thus the first three locations will receive the following characters, common to both sets:

FMT(1)	FMT(2)	FMT(3)
(1H0	,3I1	1,7X

and the fourth location, FMT(4), will receive either ,I4) or ,A4), depending on the value of NET. Because of this expected variation in the fourth location, we fill it, in the beginning of the program, with blanks.

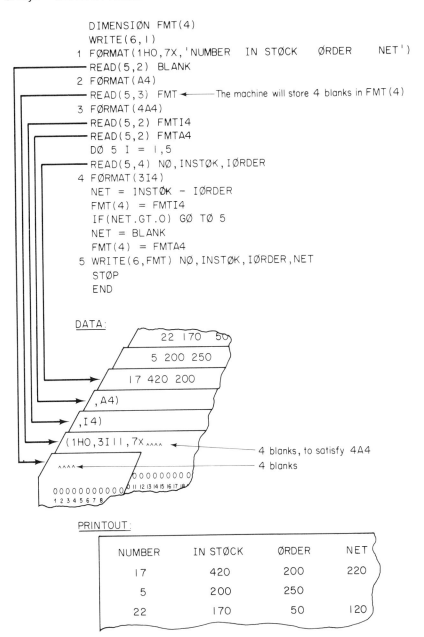

```
      DIMENSIØN FMT(4)
      WRITE(6,1)
    1 FØRMAT(1HO,7X,'NUMBER   IN STØCK    ØRDER    NET')
      READ(5,2)  BLANK
    2 FØRMAT(A4)
      READ(5,3)  FMT ◄────── The machine will store 4 blanks in FMT(4)
    3 FØRMAT(4A4)
      READ(5,2)  FMTI4
      READ(5,2)  FMTA4
      DØ 5 I = 1,5
      READ(5,4)  NØ,INSTØK,IØRDER
    4 FØRMAT(3I4)
      NET = INSTØK - IØRDER
      FMT(4) = FMTI4
      IF(NET.GT.O) GØ TØ 5
      NET = BLANK
      FMT(4) = FMTA4
    5 WRITE(6,FMT) NØ,INSTØK,IØRDER,NET
      STØP
      END
```

DATA:

```
          22 170  50
          5 200 250
        17 420 200
      ,A4)
    ,I4)
   (1HO,3I11,7X ^^^^  ◄────────── 4 blanks, to satisfy 4A4
 ^^^^ ◄────────────────────────── 4 blanks
              000000000
   0000000000 0 11 12 13 14 15 16 17 18
   1 2 3 4 5 6 7 8
```

PRINTOUT:

NUMBER	IN STØCK	ØRDER	NET
17	420	200	220
5	200	250	
22	170	50	120

Figure 10-7

Since ,I4) and ,A4) are parts of the specifications that require individual handling, we need to call them by names: let these be FMTI4 and FMTA4, respectively.

Having considered separately all the details of programming with variable FØRMAT, we are now ready to tie all the pieces together in the complete program: this is shown in Fig. 10-7. Study this program and review the discussion that precedes it.

We have now learned that FØRMAT specifications can be read in as data. In the preceding article we have also learned that data can be incorporated into a program by means of the DATA statement. Combining the two ideas, we can introduce FØRMAT specifications into a program via the DATA statement, and thereby eliminate READ statements that read FØRMAT specifications and the FØRMAT statements associated with these READ statements.

The following program shows the program of Fig. 10-7 modified to illustrate the use of the DATA statement to load FØRMAT specifications. The data deck associated with this program will show only inventory quantities.

```
      DIMENSIØN FMT(4)
      DATA BLANK, FMT,FMTI4,FMTA4/'ᴧᴧᴧᴧ','(1H0',',3I1','1,7X','ᴧᴧᴧᴧ',
     *',I4)',',A4)'/
      WRITE(6,1)
    1 FØRMAT(1H0,7X,'NUMBERᴧᴧᴧIN STØCKᴧᴧᴧᴧᴧ ØRDERᴧᴧᴧᴧᴧᴧᴧNET')
      DØ 5I = 1,5
      READ(5,4) NØ,INSTØK,IØRDER
    4 FØRMAT(3I4)
      NET = INSTØK − IØRDER
      FMT(4) = FMTI4
      IF(NET.GT.0) GØ TØ 5
      NET = BLANK
      FMT(4) = FMTA4
    5 WRITE(6,FMT) NØ,INSTØK,IØRDER,NET
      STØP
```

questions and problems

10-1/   Define and give an example of

    (a)   A one-dimensional array.
    (b)   A two-dimensional array.

10-2/   Which of the following DIMENSIØN statements are invalid and why?

(a) DIMENSIØN A(500)
(b) DIMENSIØN B(25 + 10)
(c) DIMENSIØN C(8.5)
(d) DIMENSIØN DATE (11)
(e) DIMENSIØN E(ARRAY)
(f) DIMENSIØN 5(F)

10-3/ Which of the following combinations of the DIMENSIØN and READ and WRITE statements are incorrect and why?

(a) DIMENSIØN S(10)
     READ(5,1) S
(b) DIMENSIØN CHECK(15)
     WRITE(5,2) (CHECK(I) = 1, 15)
(c) DIMENSIØN B(20)
     READ(5,3) (S(I),I = 1,20)
(d) DIMENSIØN DATA(100)
     READ(5,4) (DATA(I),I = 1,200)

10-4/ How many data cards have been read by the following programs when the STØP statement is executed?

(a)   READ(5, 1) (C(I),I = 1,10)
       1 FØRMAT(F5.1)
          STØP
(b)   READ(5,2) (C(I),I = 1,10)
       2 FØRMAT(3F5.1)
          STØP
(c)   READ(5,3) (C(I),I = 1,10)
       3 FØRMAT(2F5.1/4F5.1)
          STØP

10-5/ Figure 10-8 shows an irregular curve AB. To calculate the area between AB and the X-axis, the projection of AB on the X-axis has been divided into 20 equal segments, each segment being 0.25 in. long. The ordinates of the curve, in inches, are shown in the figure.
       Write a program that will

(1) Enter the ordinates into storage as a one-dimensional array Y; use one data card.
(2) Compute the area under the curve, considering each element of the area corresponding to a 0.25-inch segment as a trapezoid.

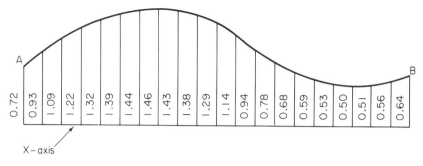

Figure 10-8

(3) Compute the mean ordinate of the curve, that is, the ordinate which, multiplied by the horizontal projection of the curve, would give the same area.

(4) Compute the average ordinate.

(5) Print AREA, MEAN, AVERAGE, with the results of (b), (c), and (d), on three separate lines.

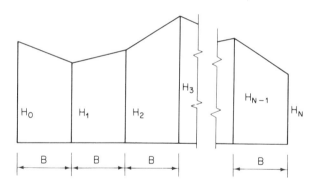

Figure 10-9

Analysis. In Fig. 10-8 assume each element of the area corresponding to a 0.25-inch segment to be a trapezoid, as shown in Fig. 10-9. Then:

$$\text{Area} = \frac{H_0 + H_1}{2}B + \frac{H_1 + H_2}{2}B + \frac{H_2 + H_3}{2}B + \ldots + \frac{H_{N-1} + H_N}{2}B$$

$$= B\left(\frac{H_0 + H_N}{2} + H_1 + H_2 + \ldots + H_{N-1}\right)$$

$$= B\left(\sum_{0}^{N} H - \frac{H_0 + H_N}{2}\right)$$

10-6/ Given the equation of the curve:

$$y = x^3 + 2x^2 + 5x + 6$$

write a program to find the area between the curve and the X-axis, between x = 3 and x = 10.

Make the computer use the trapezoidal formula and, for that purpose, divide the axis under the curve, consecutively, into 3, 4, ... , 10 equal segments, and obtain eight corresponding answers.

10-7/ A firm employing not over 100 persons keeps its payroll records in the following form:

Employee No.	Hours worked per week	Pay rate, $/hr.	Marital status	Exemp-tions
17	38.5	11.60	2	4
85	44.0	4.50	2	4
2	40.0	15.25	2	5
44	52.0	7.75	1	2
16	42.5	3.60	1	2
37	45.0	4.20	2	3
68	40.0	10.50	2	7
4	40.0	18.50	2	3
. .	. . . .	. . . . . .	.	.

Single employees are coded 1 and married ones 2.

The U.S. Internal Revenue Service requires the firm to withhold from the gross wages of each employee an amount sufficient to cover the employee's annual income tax obligation. If the payroll is met weekly, the amount to be withheld in 1977 (based on the *adjusted* wages of each employee) is given in Table 10-1.

Accordingly—if other deductions are ignored—the amount shown on an employee's check is determined as follows:

CHECK = GRØSS WAGES − WITHHØLDING

The gross wages are computed as follows:

Let R = regular rate of pay
H = total hours worked
G = gross wages

(a) Up to 40 hours per week:

$$G = R * H$$

Table 10-1. WEEKLY Payroll Period

(a) SINGLE person—including head of household:

If the amount
of wages is:

The amount of income tax
to be withheld shall be:

Not over $33 0

Over—	But not over—		of excess over—
$33	—$76 .....16%		—$33
$76	—$143 .....$6.88 plus 18%		—$76
$143	—$182 .....$18.94 plus 22%		—$143
$182	—$220 .....$27.52 plus 24%		—$182
$220	—$297 .....$36.64 plus 28%		—$220
$297	—$355 .....$58.20 plus 32%		—$297
$355 ....$76.76 plus 36%			—$355

(b) MARRIED person—

If the amount
of wages is:

The amount of income tax
to be withheld shall be:

Not over $61 0

Over—	But not over—		of excess over—
$61	—$105 .....15%		—$61
$105	—$223 .....$6.60 plus 18%		—$105
$223	—$278 .....$27.84 plus 22%		—$223
$278	—$355 .....$39.94 plus 25%		—$278
$355	—$432 .....$59.19 plus 28%		—$355
$432	—$509 .....$80.75 plus 32%		—$432
$509 ....$105.39 plus 36%			—$509

(b) Time over 40 hours is paid for at 1.5 times the regular rate. It follows that each hour of overtime is equal to 1.5 regular hours.

$$\text{Hours of overtime} = H - 40.$$

Then

$$
\begin{aligned}
G &= R * 40. + R * (1 + 0.5) * (H - 40.)\\
&= R * (40. + H - 40. + 0.5 * (H - 40.))\\
&= R * (H + 0.5 * (H - 40.))\\
&= R * (H + ADD)
\end{aligned}
$$

where

$$\text{ADD} = 0.5 * (H - 40.)$$

The adjusted wages are determined by the following formula:

$$\text{ADJUSTED WAGES} = \text{GRØSS WAGES} - 14.40 * \text{NØ.}$$
$$\text{ØF EXEMPTIØNS}$$

For the eight employees shown above, write a program that will produce a printout of the firm's payroll record as shown below:

EMPLØYEE NØ. GRØSS WAGES, \$ WITHHØLDING, \$ CHECK, \$

| 17 | ? | ? | ? |

. . .　　　. . .　　　. . .　　　. . .

10-8/ In statistics, the *average*, a, of a *number*, n, of *measurements*, x_1, x_2, . . . , x_n, is calculated by the equation

$$a = \frac{x_1 + x_2 + \ldots + x_n}{n} = \frac{\sum\limits_{x=1}^{x=n} x}{n}$$

(The average, a, is a *measure of the size* of measurements.)
The *variance*, v, is calculated by the equation

$$v = \frac{(x_1 - a)^2 + (x_2 - a)^2 + \ldots + (x_n - a)^2}{n} = \frac{\sum\limits_{x=1}^{x=n} (x - a)^2}{n}$$

where any $(x - a)$ is called a *deviation* from the average.
(The variance, v, is the average of the squares of the deviations from the average.)
The *standard deviation*, s, is calculated by the equation

$$s = \sqrt{v}$$

Given the following five numbers:

17　25　30　32　41

write a program that will produce a printout of the average, the variance, and the standard deviation of these numbers.

Note: In some cases, the variance is calculated with $(n-1)$ in the denominator instead of n.

10-9/ Write a program to produce a printout of a symmetrical triangle filled with X's, with the vertex at the top. The triangle is to have 25 rows, with one X in the first (top) row, three in the second, five in the third, and, finally, forty-nine in the last.

Analysis. The solution consists in making each row of the triangle contain an array of 49 elements, some of them X's, others blanks. As the first step, store an X and a blank under the variables X and B. Next, prepare an array consisting of 49 blanks. Then convert to X, consecutively, the middle element in the first row, the two elements flanking the middle one in the second row, the next two flanking elements in the third row, and so on, and print each array after each conversion.

10-10/ Rewrite the program of Problem 10-9 to produce the triangle of that problem with the vertex at the bottom.

10-11/ Explain each symbol in the following expressions for an array element.

(a) A(3)
(b) B(I,J)
(c) C(K+2,3*J)

10-12/ Which of the following expressions have incorrect forms of subscripts and why?

(a) A(2,4)
(b) B(I,K)
(c) CASH(3,J*L)
(d) DATA(I−1,3*L)
(e) EXAM(100,2+K)
(f) F(L,A+4)
(g) GAME(I+2,M(2))
(h) H(MIN,MAX)

10-13/ Which of the following DIMENSIØN statements are incorrect and why?

(a) A(5, 10),B(20)
(b) C(I,J), D(8,8)

(c) E(8, 10.), F(6,5+15)
(d) G(4,4), H(10), I(7,7)

10-14/ How many data cards will have been read by the following programs when the STØP statement is executed?

(a)   DIMENSIØN A(5,5)
       READ(5,1) A
    1 FØRMAT (F5.1)
       STØP

(b)   DIMENSIØN B(5,5)
       READ(5,2) B
    2 FØRMAT(5F5.1)
       STØP

(c)   DIMENSIØN C(6,6)
       READ (5,3) ((C(I,J),I = 1,6), J = 1,5)
    3 FØRMAT (4F6.2)
       STØP

(d)   DIMENSIØN D(8,10)
       READ(5,4) ((D(K,L),K=1,8), L=1,10)
    4 FØRMAT(4F6.2/2F5.2)
       STØP

10-15/ Bins are arranged on a warehouse floor as shown in Fig. 10-10.

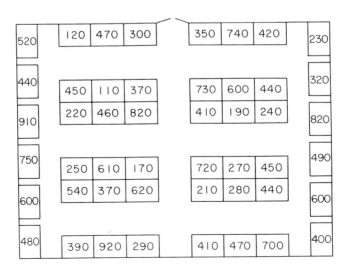

Figure 10-10

To check the load-carrying capacity of the floor, the weights of the bins and their contents were determined and recorded as shown on the figure. The weights were punched on six data cards, by rows, eight weights per card.

Write a program that will

(1)   Enter the array W of all the weights into the memory of the computer.
(2)   Find the total weight of the bins.
(3)   Find the total weight of the interior bins (those away from the walls).
(4)   Report the location and weight of the heaviest bin.
(5)   Print out the results in the following form:

```
TØTAL WEIGHT ØF BINS      =   ?   LB
WEIGHT ØF INTERIØR BINS   =   ?   LB
HEAVIEST BIN, W(?,?)       =   ?   LB
```

Question marks in parentheses on the last line should be replaced by appropriate subscripts.

10-16/   In road construction it is almost always necessary to *cut* or *fill*, that is, to remove soil or to deposit it, in order to create a smooth and reasonably level base for the road. Figure 10-11 shows a typical cross section in cut: *AGFE* is the original surface of the soil, and *ABCDE* is the outline of the cut that must be made in the soil to expose the predetermined base *BCD; C* is a point on the centerline of the road. The figure *ABCDEFG* is a view of one section taken across the prism of soil that must be excavated along the road; similar cross section views are obtained at other points on the centerline of the road, usually at equal intervals; and the areas of these cross section views are calculated.

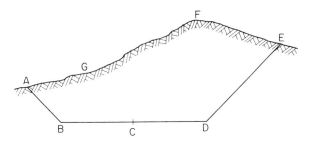

Figure 10-11

Let A_1 and A_2 be the areas of two consecutive cross sections a distance L apart. The volume of the soil prism to be excavated between A_1 and A_2 is given closely by the formula

$$\text{Volume} = \frac{A_1 + A_2}{2} \cdot L$$

The area A of an irregular cross section, such as $ABCDEFG$ in Figure 10-11, is obtained from the coordinates of the vertices of the cross section. Let V and H be the vertical and horizontal distances of any vertex from C. For calculation, these distances are arranged in the form of a matrix, with each vertical distance above the corresponding horizontal distance, and all the vertices in the consecutive order, *beginning and ending with the same vertex,* as shown below:

$$\begin{matrix} V_A & V_B & V_D & V_E & V_F & V_G & V_A \\ H_A & H_B & H_D & H_E & H_F & H_G & H_A \end{matrix}$$

(C is not included because it is not a vertex.)

To obtain the area of the cross section, multiply each V by the *following* H (V_A*H_B), and find the sum of the products, S_1; then multiply each H by the *following* V (H_A*V_B), and find the sum of the products, S_2. The area of the cross section,

$$A = \text{absolute value of } \frac{S_1 - S_2}{2}$$

The problem to be programmed is as follows. Four sections along the center line of the road-to-be have the coordinates of the vertices, measured from the road center in feet, as shown in the table below:

Section 1	V	5.0	0.0	0.0	9.2	11.2	7.3
	H	−18.2	−10.0	+10.0	+21.8	+11.2	−8.8
Section 2	V	4.6	0.0	0.0	10.4	12.7	6.1
	H	−16.9	−10.0	+10.0	+26.6	+12.0	−7.4
Section 3	V	2.9	0.0	0.0	13.2	13.5	
	H	−14.5	−10.0	+10.0	+30.2	+ 7.2	
Section 4	V	3.2	0.0	0.0	9.1		
	H	−15.1	−10.0	+10.0	+22.1		

Write a program that will make the computer store each set of coordinates as a two-dimensional array (two rows and six columns) and report each cross-sectional area in square feet and the total volume of excavation in cubic feet and in cubic yards. The cross sections are 200 feet apart.

10-17/ Given the following table of measurements, X:

VALUES OF X, FT.

9.2   6.1   12.3   5.2   9.0   10.7

and the equation

$$T = X - 9.0$$

write a program to compute the corresponding values of T and to print them in one line, replacing the negative values of T by blank spaces.

Arrange the printout in the following form:

X, FT. 9.2   6.1   12.3   5.2   9.0   10.7
T, FT. ?   ?   ?

10-18/ Given a two-dimensional array LI:

6	4	−10
7	−3	− 2
2	6	− 3
5	4	2

transform it into a two-dimensional array MI:

6	4
−10	7
− 3	−2
2	6
− 3	5
4	2

Submit the array LI to the machine on a single card, punched by columns, that is, 6, 7, 2, ...

10-19/ A single card is punched with nine elements of a one-dimensional array K, as follows:

$$6 \quad 10 \quad 2 \quad 7 \quad 5 \quad -6 \quad -10 \quad 4 \quad 3$$

Write a program that will make the computer

(1) Transform the array K into a two-dimensional array M and print it, double-spaced vertically, as follows:

6	10	2
7	5	-6
-10	4	3

(2) Skip three lines and print the following:

PRØDUCT ØF THE ELEMENTS ØN THE
DIAGØNAL FRØM TØP RIGHT = N

where N is to be a number determined by the computer from the values stored in its memory.

10-20/ A *matrix* is an array, or group, of numbers of the same type, usually arranged in rows and columns. The individual numbers in the matrix are called its *elements*. For their identification, the elements are subscripted: if the matrix is one-dimensional, that is, if it has only one row or column of elements, each element receives one subscript, in the order of its position in the matrix; if the matrix consists of several rows and columns of elements, each element receives two subscripts, the first for its row, the second for its column.

Write a program which will

(a) Generate a square matrix of 64 real elements, the value of each given by the expression:

$$\text{ELEMENT} = \frac{\text{ROW NUMBER} + 2\ (\text{COLUMN NUMBER})}{2.}$$

(b) Compute the sum of the elements on the *main diagonal*, that is, on the diagonal between the top left and the bottom right elements.

(c) Compute the sum of the elements in the first row.
(d) Compute the sum of the elements in the fourth column.

All results should appear with appropriate titles.

10-21/ Invoking the WATFIV compiler, write a program

(1) To generate a 3x2 matrix of the first six integer multiples of 5, arranged consecutively by rows;
(2) To dump the matrix;
(3) To write out the matrix;
(4) To change the elements to the real form;
(5) To dump the real matrix.

10-22/ Repeat Problem 10-21 with the G compiler and add a command to dump the second element in the second row of the real matrix.

10-23/ Write a program, invoking the G compiler, to dump the first 300 integers.

10-24/ Write a program that will duplicate the three initials shown below:

```
COL. 24
     RRRRR   W     W    M     M
     R   R   W     W    MM   MM
     RRRRR   W     W    M  M  M
     RR      W     W    M     M
     R R     W  W  W    M     M
     R   R   WW  WW     M     M
     R   R   W     W    M     M
```

Use the DATA statement to store the letters and blanks of RWM as the individual elements of a 7x19 array. Write the list of elements *by columns* to insure sequential storage; use repetition numbers whenever necessary.

To obtain the printout, begin the WRITE command as follows:

WRITE (6,FMT)

where FMT is the 10-character array (24X,19A1) punched on a data card.

10-25/ Write a program to find the value y of any polynomial in x written in the following form:

$$y = a_0 x^0 + a_1 x^1 + a_2 x^2 + \ldots \ldots + a_n x^n$$

Write the program in terms of X, A, the array of the coefficients, and N, the number of terms in the polynomial.

Find two values of Y, corresponding to the two sets of values given below:

	N	X	COEFFICIENTS, A				
SET 1	5	2.00	5.00	4.00	3.00	2.00	1.00
SET 2	4	1.67	1.35	−2.46	5.26	−1.62	

10-26/ Given the array K of seven elements:

$$-1 \quad 6 \quad 3 \quad -5 \quad 2 \quad 1 \quad 7$$

write a program which will identify the even elements (that is, the elements divisible by 2 without a fraction) and print them.

chapter 11

subprograms

11-1. the statement function

Consider the following segment of a program and note, in particular, the underlined expressions:

```
        . . . .
        U = U + 1.
     1  FØRMAT (1X, 3F10.5)
        READ(5,1) A, B, C
     2  D = A + 5.0*B + C/U − 7.2
        READ(5,1) E, F, G
     3  H = SQRT(ABS(E + 5.0*F + G/U))
        READ(5,1) Q, R, S
     4  P = (Q + 5.0*R + S/U)*3.2
        WRITE(6,1) D, H, P
        STØP
```

You must have observed that the underlined expressions in statements 2, 3, and 4 all have a similar makeup, which is of the form

$$X + 5.0*Y + Z/U$$

and that they occur either in arithmetical combinations with other terms or factors, as in statements 2 and 4, or are the object of a mathematical operation, as in statement 3 (extraction of the square root).

We can readily agree that writing and rewriting the expression $X + 5.0*Y + Z/U$ in the program in its several guises is both time-consuming and subject to error. This is even more so in the case of longer programs and more complex expressions. Thus it is only natural that a programmer should wish to adopt an abbreviation or a short name for the repeating expression, and to refer to this expression anywhere in the program by this short name.

FORTRAN permits such a substitution, provided the computer is informed about it. To do this, we write in the program a nonexecutable arithmetic statement, called a *statement function,* which has the following general form:

$$\text{NAME (X, Y, Z, . . .)} = \text{REX}$$

where:

REX ('arithmetic *e*xpression') is a formula that represents in one general form all similarly constructed arithmetic expressions in the program,

X,Y,Z, . . . are the *parameters* of REX, that is, inert or *dummy* arguments in REX which correspond, in all respects and in order, to the variables in the expressions upon which REX is modeled, and

NAME is a short name given to REX.

Thus, for the program segment above, we can write the following statement function:

$$\text{SF(X, Y, Z)} = X + 5.0*Y + Z/U$$

in which SF (statement function) is the name given to the expression $X + 5.0*Y + Z/U$, and X, Y, and Z are the *parameters* (dummy arguments) of SF that correspond to the *actual arguments* of the similarly constructed expressions in the program. For brevity and simplicity, we shall call the actual arguments of the program *arguments,* and the corresponding dummy arguments of the statement function *parameters.*

Once the statement function is introduced at the head of the program, it is no longer necessary to write out in full the actual expressions upon which the REX of the statement function is modeled; for example, Statement 2 can now be simplified to

$$D = \text{SF(A,B,C)} - 7.2$$

The computer will interpret this statement as a command to evaluate the expression $A + 5.0*B + C/U$ by substituting the numerical values of A, B, and C for the parameters X, Y, and Z in SF, then to subtract 7.2 from the result, and assign the difference to D.

Similarly, Statement 3 can be rewritten as

$$H = SQRT(ABS(SF(E,F,G)))$$

with E,F, and G replacing X,Y, and Z in SF, and so on.

Note that the variable U is not a parameter; it is defined, in the beginning of the program, by the statement

$$U = U + 1$$

and therefore it becomes, in effect, a constant, similar to 5.0. However, if U had not been mentioned at all earlier in the program, the value of U would have to be read into the memory in the same manner as the values of A,B,C or E,F,G, in order that the value of REX might be calculated. In that case, with four arguments being supplied to REX, the statement function would have to be written with four parameters, as follows:

$$SF(X,Y,Z,U) = X + 5.0*Y + Z/U$$

If, on the other hand, the first, second, and fourth parameters above (X, Y, and U) were predefined in the program, Z remaining as the only variable parameter, the statement function would be written

$$SF(Z) = X + 5.0*Y + Z/U$$

A program statement that refers to a statement function in the arithmetic expression on the right side of its equals sign is called the *calling statement* or the CALL; it *calls* for a single value of REX in the statement function. The statement function is said to be *called* by the calling statement.

It was stated earlier that a statement function is a nonexecutable statement. This is so because the function is, in effect, a formula, and its REX, though it describes a calculation, causes no calculation to occur. The parameters of the REX are not attached as addresses to storage locations in the memory, and no values are assigned to those parameters.

However, when a calling statement calls for the REX of the statement function by its name and supplies the arguments, control passes from the calling statement to the statement function, the stored values corresponding to the arguments are fetched from the memory and substituted for the parameters in the REX, the single value of REX is calculated, and that value and control are returned to the calling statement to continue the execution of the program.

Because the parameters play no part in the program and are always replaced by the values of the arguments before a calculation can take place, it makes no difference what letters are used to write a statement function; thus the two following statement functions are equivalent:

$$SF(X,Y,Z) = X + 5.0*Y + Z/U$$
$$SF(E,F,G) = E + 5.0*F + G/U$$

If we adopt the second form and then write in the program a statement

$$READ(5,4) \ F, \ E, \ G \qquad \text{(note the order!)}$$

and accompany it by the data

$$2.0 \quad 6.0 \quad 16.0$$

and then write

$$H = SQRT(ABS(SF(F,E,G)))$$

2.0, corresponding to the argument F, will replace the parameter E; 6.0, corresponding to the argument E, will replace the parameter F, and so on.

To summarize, the program segment presented in the beginning of this article may be rewritten, with the addition of the statement function, as follows:

```
  SF(X,Y,Z) = X + 5.0*Y + Z/U
  U = U + 1.
1 FØRMAT (1X, 3F10.5)
  READ(5,1) A, B, C
2 D = SF (A,B,C) − 7.2
  READ(5,1) E, F, G
3 H = SQRT(ABS(SF(E,F,G)))
  READ(5,1) Q, R, S
4 P = SF(Q,R,S)*3.2
  WRITE(6,1) D, H, P
  STØP
```

11-2. rules of the statement function

1/ The definition of a statement function must precede the first executable statement in the program.

2/ The name of the function must not exceed six characters in length and must be different from the names of the other variables in the program; the name must be integer if the function evaluates an integer quantity, and real if the function evaluates a real quantity.

3/ The parameters must be ordinary variables; they may not be constants, subscripted variables, or names of arrays; their modes may be different.

4/ The REX of a statement function may include combinations of the parameters, constants, and mathematical functions, as well as *other* statement functions and function subprograms† (both with constants or definable parameters in parentheses).

5/ The names of the parameters may be used elsewhere in the program.

6/ A statement function is called by writing its name in the REX of an assignment statement in the program; the name must be followed by the arguments separated by commas and enclosed in parentheses.

7/ The arguments may be constants, ordinary or subscripted variables, arithmetic expressions, and the names (with constants or definable parameters) of the called statement function itself, any other statement function, or a function subprogram.†

8/ The arguments must agree in number, mode, and order with the parameters of the statement function.

9/ The result of evaluating a statement function is a single value.

Statement functions and their calls are illustrated in the examples given below. In each example one or more arguments, their values, and the corresponding parameters are circled and connected to indicate the flow of information.

example 11-1.   Statement function RØØT evaluates a real quantity.

FUNCTION:	RØØT(A, B ,C) = B **2 − 4.*A*C
CALL:	Q = P + RØØT (5., 3. ,T) / 2.4
EQUIVALENT EXPRESSION:	Q = P + (3. **2 − 4.*5.*T)/2.4

example 11-2.   Statement function K evaluates an integer quantity.

FUNCTION:	K(I , J) = (I + 5*N)**2 − 4*J* I
CALL:	M = 2*L − K(3 ,L) / 4
EQUIVALENT EXPRESSION:	M = 2*L − ((3 + 5*N)**2 − 4*L* 3)/4

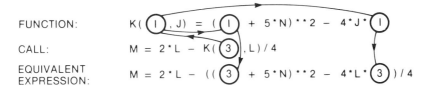

---

† Function subprograms are presented in Article 11-3.

example 11-3. Statement function SF1 contains in its REX a mathematical function and another statement function, SF2, with its parameters.

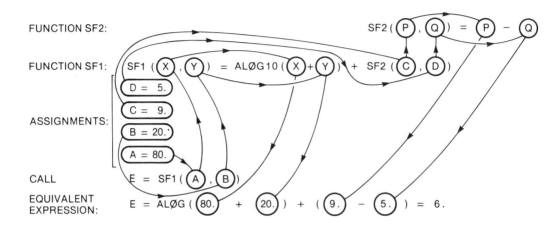

Function SF2, referred to in Function SF1, must precede SF1 in the program.

example 11-4. A call for statement function SF1 uses SF1 itself, twice, as an argument.

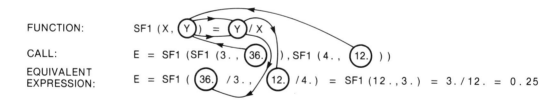

11-3. the function subprogram

A statement function is a useful device for simplifying the writing of programs, but its own simplicity limits its usefulness: it is only a one-line formula which can be called only when a program contains a REX patterned on that formula.

Many repetitive operations within a program cannot be represented by REXes and therefore by statement functions. Consider, for instance, the procedure of computing a factorial; a program to find the factorial K of any number N† may be written as follows:

Program	*Comments*
READ(5,1) N	N is the integer for which the factorial
	K = 2*3*4*. . . .*N is to be computed
1 FØRMAT(I5)	
K = 1	The factorial K is initialized at 1
DO 2 I = 2,N	Successive cycles produce the product
2 K = K*I	2*3*4*. . .*N
WRITE(6,3) K	
3 FØRMAT(1X,I7)	
STØP	

If the value of N punched on the data card is 5, the printout is 120.

Now it is possible that a program may require for its execution the computation of the factorials of several different numbers. In the absence of a handy shortcut we would have to include the above-shown factorial program in the main program every time we came to a statement calling for a factorial. But a shortcut is available in Fortran: It is called the *function subprogram.* In several ways the function subprogram is similar to the statement function; therefore, to make for an easier transition from the latter to the former, we shall examine their similarities first.

1/ Both a statement function and a function subprogram are assigned a name; the name generally conforms to the rules for naming variables: a maximum of six characters, and the first character alphabetic and in agreement with the mode of the value to be calculated.

2/ Both a statement function and a function subprogram are called into

---

† The IBM/360 computer cannot calculate the factorials of integers larger than 12. The factorials of 12 and 13 are 479,001,600 and 6,227,020,800, respectively, and the largest integer that a storage location may contain is 2,147,483,647 (see Article C-12 in Appendix C); when 1 is added to 2,147,483,647, the contents of the location are reset to 0, that is, 2,147,483,648 is stored as 0. A reset occurs after every accumulation of 2,147,483,648. Thus, after two resets, the factorial of 13 is stored as 6,227,020,800 − 2(2,147,483,648) = 1,932,053,504.

When factorials are computed as real numbers in double precision, that is, with storage locations of double capacity (Art. 12-5), the factorials are perfect through 17.; after 17. the less significant digits of the factorials become unreliable (See Problem 12-13).

action by having their name included in an expression on the right-hand side of an arithmetic statement in the calling program.

3/ In the declaration statements of the statement function and the function subprogram the names are followed by parameters in parentheses; the parameters form the general skeleton of the formula in the statement function or of the formularized solution in the function subprogram; when the name is called, the parameters are replaced by the values of the arguments that are listed, in parentheses and in corresponding order, after the name in the calling statement.

A review of the factorial subprogram above will show that that program represents a formulalike computation of the factorial in terms of the parameter N. This computation remains lifeless until it receives a numerical argument from the calling program. As soon as the calling program supplies the value of the argument, say 5, to the subprogram, 5 replaces N, the subprogram is activated, and its execution returns the factorial of 5, namely, 120, to the calling program.

Now we shall look at the differences between the statement function and the function subprogram.

1/ A statement function is a one-line statement, consisting of the name followed by the parameters of the function on the left and of the function formula on the right; a function subprogram is a full-fledged independent program, with its own END and with one or more RETURN statements generally replacing the STØP statement.

2/ A statement function calculates one value; a function subprogram calculates one value or an array of several values.

3/ A function subprogram is introduced by a FUNCTIØN statement of the form

FUNCTIØN NAME (X, Y, Z, . . .)

where

NAME is a name selected (as described above) to represent the value(s) to be returned by the subprogram to the calling program, and

(X,Y,Z, . . .) are the parameters of the subprogram to be replaced by the arguments from the calling program.

The factorial program above furnishes us with an example of the function statement:

FUNCTIØN   K (N)

4/ A statement function precedes the first executable statement in the program; a function subprogram may precede or follow the calling program, though usually it is written at the end of the calling program, after the STØP and END statements of that program.

5/ In the function subprogram the STØP statement is normally replaced by the RETURN statement; the RETURN statement is, in effect, both a STØP and a GØ TØ statement: It stops the execution of the subprogram and transfers the value(s) calculated by the subprogram to the calling statement. There may be more than one RETURN statement in the subprogram; for example, each branch of an IF instruction may end with its own RETURN.

6/ The name of the subprogram, NAME, must appear, without parameters, on the left side of an arithmetic statement in the subprogram, in order that the value(s) calculated by the subprogram may be assigned to NAME and transferred to the program which calls NAME.

11-4. rules of the function subprogram

The rules for writing function subprograms are, by and large, the same as those for writing statements functions. However, because of the increased scope of the function subprogram, there are additional rules:

1/ The parameters of a function subprogram may be ordinary variables, names of arrays, and, with associated parameters, names of other function subprograms and of subroutine subprograms;† the parameters may not be subscripted variables or constants.

2/ A parameter that represents an array must be dimensioned.

3/ The arguments that a function subprogram receives from the calling program as replacements for its parameters may be arithmetic, literal, or logical constants, ordinary and subscripted variables, REXes, array names, and names of subprograms (with defining arguments); arguments replacing parameter arrays must themselves be in the form of dimensioned arrays.

4/ The lists of parameters and arguments must each contain at least one element.

5/ A function subprogram called NAME must always contain a statement

$$NAME = REX$$

in order that the evaluated REX may be assigned to NAME and transferred to the program which has called NAME.

---

† Subroutine subprograms are presented in Article 11-5.

6/ A function subprogram may call other function subprograms or sub-routine subprograms, but it may not be recursive, that is, it may not call itself; if it might, the subprogram would resume its own execution after the call, would arrive again at the calling statement, and thus continue in a never-ending loop of calling itself.

7/ A function subprogram is compiled independently of the program which calls it; therefore, a function subprogram may be used with different programs.

The use of a function subprogram is demonstrated in Example 11-5.

example 11-5. Write a program that will use the series given in Article 9-2 (Rule 7) to find the value of *e*, and will use the factorial program of Article 11-3 as a function subprogram to supply the factorials to the series.

Program	Comments
E = 1.0	Beginning of the main program; *e* is initialized at 1.0, the first term of the series.
DØ 1 J = 1,9	9 additional terms of the series are arbitrarily decided upon.
R = K(J)	Statement calls the function subprogram K and supplies current argument J; the subprogram returns an integer factorial that is made real.
ADD = 1./R†	ADD is the term in the series corresponding to J.
E = E + ADD 3 FØRMAT(1H0,F10.8,5X,F10.8) 1 WRITE(6,3)ADD,E	Printout of consecutive increments and values of E.
STØP END FUNCTIØN K(N)	Beginning of the function subprogram.

† Most compilers will accept a single combined statement ADD = 1./K(J) as a substitute for the two statements R = K (J) and ADD = 1./R.

```
    K = 1
    DØ 2I = 1, N
```
When K is called, the current J in the main program is substituted for N, and the corresponding K is computed.

```
2   K = K * I
```
Name of the function appears on the left-hand side

```
    RETURN
```
Control and the value of K(J) are returned to the statement R = K(J)

```
    END
```

In the main program and the subprogram above there was no reason to use the index J in the one and the index I in the other, except to avoid confusion; the same letter, say I, could have been used in both programs, because the two programs are actually independent of each other; they happen to be linked together only when the parameter N is replaced by the argument J; the *value* of J, of course, is not affected by the letter we choose as the name for the index.

A rather dangerous capability of the function subprogram is that of changing the arguments of the calling program. This may happen if the parameters of the subprogram appear in the subprogram on the left of the equals sign in assignment statements, as, for example, in $I = I + 1$. When such statements are executed, the new values of the parameters, sent to the addresses of the corresponding arguments, erase the original values stored there. This is illustrated in Example 11-6.

example 11-6. Given the following main program and function subprogram, what values will be printed out when the WRITE statement in the main program is executed?

Program	Comments

```
    A = 4.
    B = 2.
    C = 3.
```
Begin the main program; A, B, and C are the arguments to be sent to the subprogram SØLVE

```
    RESULT = SØLVE(A,B,C)
```
Call function subprogram SØLVE

```
    WRITE(6,1)RESULT, A,B,C
1   FØRMAT(1H0,4F7.1)
    STØP
    END
```

FUNCTIØN SØLVE(X,Y,Z)	Beginning of the subprogram SOLVE; parameters X,Y,Z are to be replaced by the values of arguments A,B,C
X = X + 3. Z = Z*2.	Parameters X and Z are altered; consequently, A becomes 4. + 3. = 7., and C becomes 3.*2. = 6.
SØLVE = (X + Y)/Z	SØLVE = (7.+2.)/6. = 1.5
RETURN	Control returns to RESULT in the main program
END	

The command WRITE produces:

1.5	7.0	2.0	6.0
(RESULT)	(A)	(B)	(C)

Having been shown what may happen to the arguments of the calling program, the programmer is advised to avoid altering the parameters of the function subprogram. For if he does and forgets that the arguments may have been altered, the main program and the subprogram will complete the execution without issuing a single error message and will produce results that may be all wrong.

The programmer may obtain the value he is seeking for SØLVE—and yet avoid falling into the trap of changed arguments—by introducing into the subprogram *local variables*, say P and Q, as shown in the modified program below:

```
FUNCTIØN SØLVE(X,Y,Z)
P = X + 3.
Q = Z*2.
SØLVE = (P + Y)/Q
RETURN
END
```

Since the values of P and Q are stored locally in the subprogram, and X and Z are not affected, the printout will show the original values of A and C:

1.5	4.0	2.0	3.0
(RESULT)	(A)	(B)	(C)

A program that illustrates a return of multiple values by a function subprogram is shown in Example 11-7. The program is written to transpose two arrays, A and B, into arrays C and D. The transpose is obtained by interchanging the rows and columns; thus $A_{3,1}$ becomes $C_{1,3}$, etc.

example 11-7. Given two arrays, A and B:

Array A   *Array B*

3.2	−4.4	−2.0		17.6	42.3	−80.2	60.9
7.1	2.5	−0.7		52.4	−22.2	50.9	16.7
5.2	−4.7	9.2					

write a program which will call a function subprogram to return an array C as a transpose of A and an array D as a transpose of B.

Program:

```
  DIMENSIØN A(3,3),B(2,4),C(3,3),D(4,2)
  READ(5,1) A,B
1 FØRMAT(9F4.1,8F5.1)
  C(3,3) = TRANSP(A,3,3,C)
  D(4,2) = TRANSP(B,2,4,D)
  WRITE(6,2)((C(I,J),J=1,3),I=1,3),((D(I,J),J=1,2),I=1,4)
2 FØRMAT(1H0,9X,'ARRAY C'//3(1X,3F7.1/)/1H0,9X,
 *'ARRAY D'//4(1X,3X,2F7.1/))
  STØP
  END

  FUNCTIØN TRANSP(P,K,L,Q)
  DIMENSIØN P(K,L), Q(L,K)
  DØ 1 I=1,K
  DØ 1 J=1,L
1 Q(J,I) = P(I,J)
  TRANSP = Q(J−1,I−1)
  RETURN
  END
```

Printout:

ARRAY C

3.2	7.1	5.2
−4.4	2.5	−4.7
−2.0	−0.7	9.2

ARRAY D

17.6	52.4
42.3	−22.2
−80.2	50.9
60.9	16.7

Note the form of the calling statements, for example:

$$D(4,2) = TRANSP(B,2,4,D)$$

The array D to be received from the function subprogram TRANSP is dimensioned (4,2), and the arguments sent to TRANSP include the names of the original and transposed arrays, B and D, with the name B followed by the dimensions of B, (2,4). The returning values form the matrix of the array D.

Example 11-8 shows a program with the statement function SF1 whose parameters, X and Y, are replaced by the values generated by the function subprogram FSUB.

example 11-8.

```
      SF1(X,Y) = Y/X
      E = SF1(FSUB(7.,3.),FSUB(25.,5.))
      WRITE(6,1) E
   1  FØRMAT(1H0,F6.2)
      STØP
      END

      FUNCTIØN FSUB(E,F)
      FSUB = E + F
      RETURN
      END
```

Printout:

‸‸3.00

Example 11-9 shows the statement function SF1 whose REX contains the statement function SF2 and the function subprogram FSUB.

example 11-9.

```
      SF2(P,Q) = P − Q
      SF1(X,Y) = Y/X + SF2(C,D) + FSUB(C,D)
      C = 8.
      D = 5.
      E = SF1(3.,12.)
      WRITE(6,1) E
   1  FØRMAT(1H0,F6.2)
      STØP
      END

      FUNCTIØN FSUB(E,F)
      FSUB = E + F
      RETURN
      END
```

Printout:

20.00

Example 11-10 shows a transfer of the literal data from the calling program to a function subprogram. The literal data are expressed as an array LIT consisting of two 4-character groups, each group enclosed in apostrophes.

example 11-10.

```
      DIMENSIØN LIT (2)
      DATA A,K,LIT/5.,2,'SQUA','RE˄='/
      SQUARE = SQ(A,K,LIT)
      STØP                        ı
      END

      FUNCTIØN SQ (H,J,L)
      DIMENSIØN L (2)
      SQ = H**J
      WRITE (6,1) L,SQ
   1  FØRMAT (1H0,2A4,F5.1)
      RETURN
      END
```

Printout:

SQUARE⌄=⌄25.0

An identical printout, without a transfer of the literal data, is produced by the following combination of programs:

```
      DIMENSIØN LIT (2)
      DATA A,K,LIT/5.,2,'SQUA','RE⌄='/
      SQUARE = SQ (A,K)
      WRITE (6,1) LIT,SQUARE
   1  FØRMAT (1H0,2A4,F5.1)
      STØP
      END


      FUNCTIØN SQ (H,J)
      SQ = H**J
      RETURN
      END
```

11-5.   the subroutine subprogram

Just as the function subprogram is a broader extension of the statement function, the *subroutine subprogram* is a still broader extension of the function subprogram.

Like a function subprogram, a subroutine subprogram is called by a statement in the main program, but the nature of the call is different from the one used to call a function subprogram. This is so because a subroutine subprogram may return to the main program, on one hand, any number of values, and, on the other, *no values at all.* Because of this characteristic, the type of call, such as R = K(J) in Example 11-5, which asks for a value, is inappropriate for a subroutine subprogram. Instead, the subroutine subprogram is called by the following CALL statement in the main program:

CALL NAME (X, Y, Z, . . .)

where the word

CALL is mandatory.

NAME is a name for the subroutine subprogram which will be executed upon call; NAME may not have more than six alphameric characters and must begin with a letter.

(X, Y, Z, . . .) are the arguments that are passed from the calling statement to the subroutine as replacements for its parameters.

The subroutine subprogram usually follows the main program and always begins with the declaratory SUBRØUTINE statement, which has the following general form:

SUBRØUTINE NAME (P, Q, R, . . .)

where the word
SUBRØUTINE is mandatory.
NAME is the same name as that used in the CALL statement.
(P, Q, R, . . .) are the parameters upon which the subroutine subprogram is constructed and which are replaced by the arguments X, Y, Z, . . . sent in by the call statement.

The roles of the NAME and of the parameters are identical in the subroutine and function subprograms. Like the function subprogram, the subroutine subprogram may have several RETURN statements. And, being a complete and independent program, the subroutine subprogram always ends with the statement

END

To see how a subroutine subprogram receives arguments from the calling program and how it does or does not return values to the calling program, let us study the illustrative program of Example 11-11.

example 11-11. To simplify the financial bookkeeping, some organizations round off dollars and cents to the nearest dollars, by dropping 49 cents or less and by increasing 50 cents or more to a dollar.

In this example the main program reads two amounts (say, 16.22 and 8.47) on a data card and passes them on to the subroutine which adds them, rounds off the sum to the nearest dollar, and returns the rounded sum to the main program. The process is repeated three times, there being three data cards.

Program	Comments
DØ 2 J = 1,3	Main program begins, to be executed
READ(5,3) A, B	three times
3 FØRMAT(2F6.2)	Two values are stored at A and B
CALL ADD(A,B,SUM)	Subroutine ADD is called; the values of A and B are sent to define the parameters P and Q; ADD computes S and returns its value to SUM

```
2    WRITE(6,4) A,B,SUM
4    FØRMAT(1H0,2F8.2,F8.0)
     STØP
     END
```

```
     SUBRØUTINE ADD(P,Q,S)        Declaration statement of ADD with the
     S = P + Q                    list of parameters

     K = S                        S loses its decimals
     IF(S − K.GT.0.49) GØ TØ 1    If FALSE, S = K; if TRUE, S = K + 1
     S = K
     RETURN
1    S = K + 1
     RETURN
     END
```

Data cards:

```
⌐16.22⌐⌐8.47⌐
⌐⌐⌐5.78⌐⌐3.22⌐
⌐20.97⌐16.11⌐
```

Printout:

```
⌐⌐⌐16.22⌐⌐⌐⌐⌐8.47⌐⌐⌐⌐⌐⌐25.
⌐⌐⌐⌐⌐5.78⌐⌐⌐⌐⌐3.22⌐⌐⌐⌐⌐⌐⌐9.
⌐⌐⌐20.97⌐⌐⌐16.11⌐⌐⌐⌐⌐⌐37.
```

A more involved relationship between a main program and two subroutines is illustrated in Example 11-12.

example 11-12. Write a program to read three numbers on consecutive data cards, to compute the sum of the three numbers and the product of the last two numbers on each card, and to report the results by printing the positive values and X's for the negative and zero values.

Three variants of the program are presented, illustrating different interactions between the main program and the subroutine subprograms.

first variant

Program	*Comments*
READ(5,4) Y 4 FØRMAT(A1)	The main program begins; the machine reads the letter X on the first data card and stores it in Y with the A specification

1 READ(5,2) A,B,C 2 FØRMAT(3F5.1)	Three numbers are read on the second data card and stored under A,B,C
IF(A.EQ.999.0) STØP	A trailer card punched with 999.0 is placed at the back of the deck to stop the program
CALL ADD(Y,A,B,C,SUM)	Subroutine ADD is called; values of the arguments Y,A,B,C replace the parameters Z,P,Q,R; the subroutine computes the value of the parameter TØT, and returns it and control to the main program; SUM receives either a positive number or an X
CALL MULT(Y,A,B,C, PRØD)	Subroutine MULT is called; values of Y,A,B,C replace Z,T,U,V; UV is computed; PRØD receives either a positive number or an X
WRITE(6,3)A,B,C,SUM, PRØD 3 FØRMAT(1H0,3F5.1, 2F7.1)	If SUM and PRØD are both numbers, both are printed out; if SUM (or PRØD) is X, the field will show not X, which requires the A specification, but a line of asterisks
GØ TØ 1	The computer goes back to read the next data card
END	End of the main program; STØP is ordered in the fifth line of the program
SUBRØUTINE ADD(Z,P,Q,R,TØT)	The first subprogram begins; upon call, Z,P,Q,R receive the values of Y,A,B,C
TØT = P + Q + R	The value of TØT is computed
IF(TØT.LE.0.) TØT = Z	If TØT≤0., its value is changed to the value stored in Z (i.e., the letter X)
RETURN	SUM receives the value of TØT; control returns to the statement following the calling statement, i.e., to CALL MULT
END	End of subroutine ADD
SUBRØUTINE MULT (Z,T,U,V,UV)	The second subprogram begins; upon call, Z,T,U,V receive the values of Y,A,B,C

UV = U*V   The value of UV is computed

IF(UV.LE.0.) UV = Z   If UV≤0., its value is changed to the value stored
                            in Z (i.e., X)

RETURN   PRØD receives the value of UV; control returns
                            to WRITE in the main program

END   End of subroutine MULT

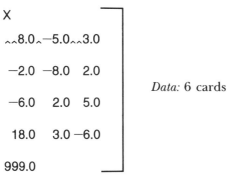

X

ᴧᴧ8.0ᴧ−5.0ᴧᴧ3.0

−2.0 −8.0 2.0

−6.0   2.0 5.0

18.0   3.0 −6.0   *Data:* 6 cards

999.0

The following printout is obtained:

ᴧᴧ8.0ᴧ−5.0ᴧᴧ3.0ᴧᴧᴧᴧ6.0*******

−2.0 −8.0 2.0*************

−6.0   2.0 5.0   1.0   10.0

18.0   3.0 −6.0   15.0*******

In the printout the negative and zero results are indicated not by X's which
were required by the statement of the problem but by lines of asterisks. This
is the reaction of the computer to an inappropriate specification: the alphameric
X requires an A specification, but the FØRMAT associated with the WRITE
statement has matched it with an F specification.

To obtain X's in the printout, the A specification must be introduced into
the program; this increases the complexity of the program, as may be seen
from the study of the second variant below. This variant shows four WRITE
commands, each with its FØRMAT, corresponding to the four possible combinations of positive and negative SUM and PRØD. Comments are shown only for
the subroutine ADD.

second variant

Program	Comments

```
   READ(5,4) Y
4  FØRMAT(A1)
1  READ(5,2) A,B,C
2  FØRMAT (3F5.1)
   IF(A.EQ.999.0) STØP
   CALL ADD(Y,A,B,C,SUM)
   CALL MULT(Y,A,B,C,PRØD)
   IF(SUM.EQ.Y.AND.PRØD.NE.Y)WRITE(6,5)A,B,C,SUM,PRØD
5  FØRMAT(1H0,3F5.1,4X,A1,2X,F7.1)
   IF(SUM.NE.Y.AND.PRØD.EQ.Y)WRITE(6,6)A,B,C,SUM,PRØD
6  FØRMAT(1H0,3F5.1,F7.1,4X,A1)
   IF(SUM.EQ.Y.AND.PRØD.EQ.Y)WRITE(6,7)A,B,C,SUM,PRØD
7  FØRMAT(1H0,3F5.1,4X,A1,6X,A1)
   IF(SUM.NE.Y.AND.PRØD.NE.Y)WRITE(6,3)A,B,C,SUM,PRØD
3  FØRMAT (1H0,3F5.1,2F7.1)
   GØ TØ 1
   END
```

Program	Comments
SUBRØUTINE ADD (Z,P,Q,R,TØT)	Upon call, Z,P,Q,R receive the values of Y,A,B,C
TØT = Z	TØT receives the value stored in Y (i.e., X)
T = P + Q + R	The sum of values in P, Q, R is stored under the local variable T
IF(T.LE.0.) RETURN	If T≤0., SUM receives X from TØT, and control returns to the main program; the rest of the sub-routine is ignored
TØT = T	If T>0., the preceding command is ignored; X in TØT is replaced by the positive value in T
RETURN	SUM receives the positive value from TØT, and control returns to the main program
END	End of subroutine ADD

```
SUBRØUTINE MULT(Z,T,U,V,UV)
UV = Z
S = U*V
IF(S.LE.0.) RETURN
UV = S
RETURN
END
```

With the same data as in the first variant, the printout is as follows:

```
^^8.0^−5.0^^3.0^^^^6.0^^^^X
−2.0 −8.0  2.0    X     X
−6.0  2.0  5.0   1.0  10.0
18.0  3.0 −6.0  15.0    X
```

It can be seen that the second variant of the main program is much longer and more awkward than the first because of the four IF statements and the four associated Format statements required to combine the numeric and alphameric values of SUM and PRØD in four different ways. However, the second variant is a more satisfactory solution in that it fulfills the requirements of the problem exactly; in addition, it serves to show that subroutines do not return all computed values to the main program (negative and zero values of T do not return), and that a subroutine may have more than one return to the main program.

The second variant may be streamlined by introducing the object-time Format, that is, by making the subroutines supply not only the values of SUM and PRØD but also the appropriate specifications. This is done in the third variant shown below. A review of the four output specifications in the second variant will show that the specifications may be distributed among the three programs as follows:

Portions of a Format Statement Stored by		
Main Program	*Subroutine ADD*	*Subroutine MULT*
(1H0,3F5.1,	F5.1, or 2X,A3, (to describe SUM)	F5.1) or 2X,A3) (to describe PRØD)

Specifications F7.1 and A1 of the second variant are changed to F5.1 and A3, and the spacer is changed to 2X, to make the printout more uniform and compact, as shown in the example below:

```
^−2.0^−8.0^^2.0^^X^^^^X
^−6.0^^2.0^^5.0^^1.0^10.0
```

Since the specifications are written in alphameric characters, they must be stored in groups of four (or fewer) characters. Obviously there will be several groups in every complete FORMAT; therefore these groups are properly stored as an array, say F.

To find the dimension of F, we divide the specifications in the table into groups and assign the groups to consecutive storage locations, as shown below; we see that there are seven groups and seven storage locations, and that, consequently, the dimension of F is 7.

Storing Program	Main			ADD		MULT	
Storage Location	F (1)	F (2)	F (3)	F (4)	F (5)	F (6)	F (7)
Contents	(1H0	,3F5	.1,	F5.1 or 2X,A	, or 3,	F5.1 or 2X,A	) or 3)

Beginning the process of forming a Format, the main program fills F(1), F(2), and F(3) with values from a data card and the remaining four locations with blanks, using the sequence:

```
        READ (5,7) F
    7   FØRMAT (2A4,A3,4A1)
```

and the data card:

```
(1H0,3F5.1,
```

The addition of 4A1 (or 4A4) in FØRMAT 7 is necessary in order to make the computer fill storage locations F(4), F(5), F(6), and F(7) with the blanks which follow (1H0,3F5.1, on the data card. An omission of 4A1 would make the computer re-use FØRMAT 7 and store values from the next cards in the deck.

Subroutine ADD assigns its four groups of values to the variables G, H, S, and T by means of the DATA statement:

```
    DATA G,H,S,T/'F5.1',',',',','2X,A','3,'/
```

and fills F(4) and F(5) with G and H if TØT is numeric or with S and T if TØT is alphameric.

Similarly, subroutine MULT assigns its four groups of values to the variables G, H, S, and T by the DATA statement:

```
    DATA G,H,S,T/'F5.1',')','2X,A','3)'/
```

and fills F(6) and F(7) with G and H if UV is numeric or with S and T if UV is alphameric.

Rewritten with the object-time Format, the main program and the two subprograms are shown in the third variant below, together with the resulting printout.

third variant

```
    DIMENSIØN F(7)
    READ(5,7) F
  7 FØRMAT(2A4,A3,4A1)
    READ(5,4)Y
  4 FØRMAT(A1)
  1 READ(5,2)A,B,C
  2 FØRMAT(3F5.1)
    IF(A.EQ.999.0)STØP
    CALL ADD (Y,A,B,C,SUM,F(4),F(5))
    CALL MULT(Y,A,B,C,PRØD,F(6),F(7))
    WRITE(6,F)A,B,C,SUM,PRØD
    GØ TØ 1
    END

    SUBRØUTINE ADD (Z,P,Q,R,TØT,D,E)
    DATA G,H,S,T/'F5.1',',',' 2X,A','3,'/
    D = G
    E = H
    TØT = P+Q+R
    IF(TØT.GT.0.) RETURN
    TØT = Z
    D = S
    E = T
    RETURN
    END

    SUBRØUTINE MULT (Z,W,U,V,UV,D,E)
    DATA G,H,S,T/'F5.1',')',' 2X,A','3)'/
    D = G
    E = H
    UV = U*V
    IF(UV.GT.0.) RETURN
    UV = Z
    D = S
    E = T
    RETURN
    END
```

Printout:

```
∧∧8.0∧−5.0∧∧3.0∧∧6.0∧∧X
−2.0 −8.0  2.0  X    X
−6.0   2.0  5.0  1.0 10.0
 18.0   3.0 −6.0 15.0   X
```

11-6. rules of the subroutine subprogram

The rules of the subroutine subprograms are generally the same as those of the function subprograms. In particular, by reviewing the three programs of Example 11-12, we may note the following points:

1/ The main program may have more than one subprogram.

2/ The subprograms may return all, some, or none of the results of their calculations, depending on the arguments of the call.

3/ The mode of the subroutine name (ADD, MULT) is immaterial, since no value is associated with the name.

4/ The name of the subroutine, unlike the name of the function in the function subprogram, may not appear as an independent variable in any arithmetic statement; for example, in the programs of Example 11-12 it is illegal to write a statement such as

$$MULT = 1.0$$

because the results of the subroutine computations are called by names such as SUM and PRØD (which appear in the lists of arguments) and not by the name of the subroutine.

5/ A subroutine may have more than one RETURN statement.

6/ The arguments and parameters must agree in number, mode, and order from left to right in their respective lists; for instance, CALL MULT(B,A,C,PRØD) would result in a product of A and C instead of B and C.

7/ The lists of arguments and parameters may have no elements at all (unlike those of the function subprogram, which must have at least one element).

8/ A subroutine subprogram may call on another subroutine subprogram, but it may not call on itself.

9/ Arguments and parameters that are names of arrays must be dimensioned.

11-7. subroutines with arrays—adjustable dimensions

Arrays or subarrays (parts of arrays) may be passed between a main program and a subroutine subprogram in the same manner as single variables, that is, by a CALL statement, but several precautions must be observed in writing the associated programs.

In the first place, both programs must have DIMENSIØN statements. If the dimension of the array W stored by the main program is (6,8), and the corresponding parameter in the subroutine SUB is A, then the two programs should begin as follows:

Main Program: SUBROUTINE SUB(A, ...)

    DIMENSIØN W(6,8)   DIMENSIØN A(6,8)

The elements of W are transferred to SUB to define A by the statement:

    CALL SUB(W, ...)

However, the (6,8) dimension of A limits the usefulness of the subroutine SUB; to enable SUB to operate on arrays of various sizes, we may write A with the *adjustable dimension* (M,N), as follows:

                  DIMENSIØN A(M,N)

In this case it is not enough to write in the main program

    CALL SUB (W, ...)

because such a call leaves the dimension (M,N) of A undefined; therefore the list of the call must be extended to include the (6,8) dimension of W and, to establish the connection between the programs, the parameters M,N must be added to the list of the subroutine declaration statement, thus:

                                SUBRØUTINE SUB (A,M,N, ...)
    DIMENSIØN W(6,8)   DIMENSIØN A(M,N)
    CALL SUB(W,6,8, ...)

Secondly, a general subroutine SUB may be constructed to operate not only on the entire array A but also on any subarray of A between rows KI and LI and between columns KJ and LJ, inclusive. In such a case these four limiting integer variables must appear in the list of SUB, and their defining values must be added to the list of the CALL. For example, if the main program desires the results of the operations on the subarray of W between rows 4 and 6 and between columns 5 and 8, inclusive, the CALL and the declaration statements must be written:

SUBRØUTINE SUB(A,M,N,KI,LI,KJ,
LJ, . . .)

CALL SUB(W,6,8,4,6,5,8, . . .)

These points are illustrated in Example 11-13.

example 11-13.   Write a subroutine which will find the total weight of any subarray of bins given in Problem 10-15; then write a program which will call on the subroutine to find the total weight of bins

(1)   Between rows 1 and 3 and columns 1 and 4, inclusive;
(2)   Between rows 4 and 6 and columns 5 and 8, inclusive.

Main Program:	*Comments*
DIMENSIØN W(6,8)	
READ(5,2) ((W(I,J),J=1,8),I=1,6)	The array W, punched by rows on 6 data cards, is stored
2 FØRMAT(8F6.1) CALL SUB(W,6,8,1,3,1,4,TØTAL1)	SUB is called to compute and return TØTAL1, the weight of bins between rows 1 and 3 and columns 1 and 4
CALL SUB(W,6,8,4,6,5,8,TØTAL2)	SUB is called to compute and return TØTAL2, the weight of bins between rows 4 and 6 and columns 5 and 8
WRITE(6,1) TØTAL1,TØTAL2	Values of TØTAL1 and TØTAL2 returned by SUB are printed on two lines
1 FØRMAT(1X,F6.0)	
STØP	
END	

```
SUBRØUTINE SUB(A,M,N,KI,LI,KJ,LJ,T)

DIMENSIØN A(M,N)

T = 0.

DØ 1 I = KI,LI
DØ 1 J = KJ,LJ
1   T = T + A(I,J)
    RETURN
    END
```

The list of SUB shows the array A, its overall dimension (M,N), the boundaries of a subarray (KI,LI,KJ,LJ), and the weight T of the subarray

T is found by summing up A(I,J)'s between rows KI and LI and columns KJ and LJ

The following rules apply to the adjustable dimensions:

1/ An adjustable dimension, such as DIMENSIØN A(M,N), may appear only in a subprogram; it may not appear in the main program.

2/ An adjustable dimension, occurring as a parameter in a subprogram, must appear in the list of parameters in the declaration statement of the subprogram. A corresponding argument must appear in the CALL statement of the main program. The argument may be a constant or a variable. A variable argument must be predefined.

3/ An adjustable dimension may not be redefined in the subprogram.

4/ Arrays with adjustable dimensions may not be listed in the COMMON statement of a subroutine (See Articles 11-10 and 11-11).

5/ An array that is not listed in the CALL statement of the main program or in the declaration statement of the subprogram may not have an adjustable dimension.

Rule 5 is illustrated in Example 11-14.

example 11-14. The main program below stores the array A of bank deposits and calls the subroutine DEBT to compute the interest, PAY, on those deposits. The subroutine DEBT creates the array RATE of variable rates of interest and uses it to compute the values of PAY. A and PAY in the subroutine have an adjustable dimension K. When the main program calls DEBT, it transmits the elements of A and the value of KØUNT (the number of deposits) to define K and, in return, receives the elements of PAY. The array RATE in the subroutine has a constant dimension 3.

Main Program:
```
DIMENSIØN A(100),PAY(100)
DØ 2 I = 1,100
READ(5,1) A(I)
```

```
1    FØRMAT(F10.2)
     IF (A(I).EQ.−500.00) GØ TØ 3
2    CØNTINUE
3    KØUNT = I − 1
     CALL DEBT (A,KØUNT,PAY)
     WRITE(6,4) (A(I),PAY(I),I = 1,KØUNT)
4    FØRMAT (1H0,2F10.2)
     STØP

     SUBRØUTINE DEBT (A,K,PAY)
     DIMENSIØN A(K),PAY(K),RATE(3)
     READ(5,1) BASE
1    FØRMAT(F5.2)
     DØ 2 I = 1,3
2    RATE(I) = BASE + I
     DØ 4 I = 1,K
     IF (A(I).LE.25000.)PAY(I) = A(I)*RATE(1)/100.
     IF (A(I).GT.25000..AND.A(I).LE.50000.)PAY(I) = A(I)
     *RATE(2)/100.
4    IF (A(I).GT.50000.)PAY(I) = A(I)*RATE(3)/100.
     RETURN
```

Data cards:

```
Card 1:    ^ ^20000.00
Card 2:    ^ ^60000.00
Card 3:    ^ ^10000.00
Card 4:    ^ ^40000.00
Card 5:    ^100000.00
Card 6:    ^ ^ ^−500.00
Card 7:    ^6.00
```

Printout:

20000.00	1400.00
60000.00	5400.00
10000.00	700.00
40000.00	3200.00
100000.00	9000.00

The array RATE in the subprogram may not have an adjustable dimension, say N, because a defining value for N may not be transmitted from the main program without an associated array, and the main program has no array corresponding to RATE: therefore the main program cannot send 3 to define N by a statement such as

CALL DEBT (A,KØUNT,PAY,3)

and N, without RATE in the list, may not appear in a subroutine declaration statement such as

SUBRØUTINE DEBT (A,K,PAY,N)

11-8. directed returns from a subroutine

Normally a subroutine subprogram returns control to the statement in the calling program which follows the CALL. The following scheme permits a return of control to *any* statement in the calling program:

(a) Include in the argument list of the CALL the numbers of the statements that are to receive control from the subroutine; precede each number by the ampersand (&); separate the numbers and the other arguments in the list by commas.

example: If the list contains the arguments A and K, and control may be returned to the statements 3 and 4, write the list as follows:

(A,K,&3,&4)

(b) Write the parameter list of the subroutine as follows:

(H,J,*,*)

In this list H and J will receive the values of A and K, the *first* asterisk will correspond to &3, and the *second* asterisk to &4.

(c) If control is to pass from some point in the subroutine to statement 3 in the calling program, write at the point in the subroutine RETURN 1; the subroutine will associate the integer 1 with the *first* asterisk in its list and with &3 in the CALL list, and will return control accordingly; if control is to return to statement 4, write RETURN 2; the subroutine will associate 2 with the *second* asterisk and with the corresponding &4; if control is to return to the statement that follows the CALL, write only RETURN.

The general form of the subroutine statement that makes control return to different statements in the calling program is RETURN i, where i is an integer. The operation of this statement is illustrated in Example 11-15, in which wages of employees in different tax brackets are sent by the subroutine to different points in the calling program for processing.

example 11-15.

```
6    READ(5,1,END=7) NØ,HØURS,RATE
1    FØRMAT(I3,F5.1,F6.2)
     CALL SUB(HØURS,RATE,WAGE,&3,&4)
     CHECK = 0.90*WAGE
     GØ TØ 5
3    CHECK = 0.80*(WAGE − 300.) + 270.
     GØ TØ 5
4    CHECK = 0.70*(WAGE − 500.) + 430.
5    WRITE(6,2) NØ,HØURS,RATE,WAGE,CHECK
2    FØRMAT(1H0,I3,F5.1,3F7.2)
     GØ TØ 6
7    STØP
     END

     SUBRØUTINE SUB(HØURS,RATE,WAGE,*,*)
     WAGE = HØURS*RATE
     IF (WAGE.LE.300.) RETURN
     IF (WAGE.GT.300..AND.WAGE.LE.500.) RETURN 1
     IF (WAGE.GT.500.) RETURN 2
     END
```

Data cards:

```
 17  36.0    4.50
102  40.0  11.50
 69  38.5  16.00
```

Printout:

```
 17  36.0    4.50  162.00  145.80
102  40.0  11.50  460.00  398.00
 69  38.5  16.00  616.00  511.20
```

11-9. transfer of the literal data to a subroutine

A transfer of the literal data from the calling program to a subroutine is illustrated in Examples 11-16 and 11-17. In Example 11-16 the four-character groups are listed in the CALL statement and transfer directly to the parameters P and Q in the subroutine. In Example 11-17 the four-character groups are expressed as an array LIT, dimensioned 2, LIT is stored by means of the DATA statement, and LIT is shown in the CALL list. To match LIT, the subroutine has L in its list of parameters, and L is also dimensioned 2.

example 11-16.

```
          A = 5.
          K = 2
          CALL WØRK(A,K,'SQUA','RE‸=')
          STØP
          END

          SUBRØUTINE WØRK(H,J,P,Q)
          S = H**J
          WRITE(6,1) P,Q,S
     1    FØRMAT(1H0,2A4,F5.1)
          RETURN
          END
```

Printout:

```
SQUARE‸=‸25.0
```

example 11-17.

```
          DIMENSIØN LIT(2)
          DATA A,K,LIT/5.,2,'SQUA','RE‸='/
          CALL WØRK(A,K,LIT)
          STØP
          END

          SUBRØUTINE WØRK(H,J,L)
          DIMENSIØN L(2)
          S = H**J
          WRITE(6,1) L,S
```

```
1    FØRMAT(1H0,2A4,F5.1)
     RETURN
     END
```

Printout:

SQUARE‸=‸25.0

11-10. the CØMMØN statement

A review of the interaction between the calling program and its subprograms will make it apparent that, once they are linked together in a single job, the calling program and the subprograms generally operate on the same information. We saw in Article 11-5 that the subroutine subprograms ADD and MULT became activated when their parameters Z, P, Q, R and Z, T, U, V received the values (strictly speaking, the addresses of the values) of the arguments Y, A, B, C from the main program. Having computed the values of TØT and UV, the subprograms sent these values back to the main program. It follows, then, that the interaction consists essentially of the transfer of values from the arguments in the calling program to the parameters in subprograms, and vice versa.

This transfer of values entails, first, the writing by the programmer of the lists of arguments and corresponding parameters in the linked programs and, second, the carrying out of a series of operations by the computer to effect the transfer of information between the programs. These tasks mean extra work for the programmer and for the computer. Therefore, if we make it possible for the parameters to receive their values directly from the storage of the main program, we can eliminate this work, that is, the writing of the lists and the transfer operations of the computer. We can establish direct communication between the parameters and the memory by placing the values of the arguments in CØMMØN storage, that is, storage common to the calling program and its associated subprograms. We accomplish this by writing in every program (the calling program and the subprograms) a *CØMMØN statement,* that is, a statement that contains the list of the variables in that program which have claim, in order from left to right, on the values in common storage.

Let us draw on Example 11-12 for the elements of information with which to construct CØMMØN statements for the programs of that example.

Considering only the main program and the subprogram ADD, we can write for the main program

CØMMØN Y, A, B, C, SUM

and for the subprogram ADD:

CØMMØN Z, P, Q, R, TØT

Note that the listed elements are separated by commas, but are not enclosed in parentheses.

Placing these statements at the beginning of the respective programs will cause the block of values that we wish to be shared by the arguments and parameters of the two programs to be placed in common storage. This storage is not a separate physical storage unit; it is simply a section of the computer memory reserved by the compiler for storing the data common to two or more programs.

The common storage established, a call from the main program for the subprogram ADD will cause the computer to reach directly in storage locations Y, A, B, C for the values of the parameters Z, P, Q, R, in that order, and subsequently, to return the computed value of TØT into the storage location SUM.

Now, if we pair the main program with the subprogram MULT, we can write for the main program

CØMMØN Y, A, B, C, PRØD

and for the subprogram MULT

CØMMØN Z, T, U, V, UV

and the computer will operate in the same manner as before.

Inspection of the two pairs of CØMMØN statements shows, first, that the main program has two CØMMØN statements and, second, that they are practically identical, except for the last argument. Two CØMMØN statements in a program are not prohibited, although their use is not recommended. Therefore, rather than write two CØMMØN statements, we combine them into a single statement, as follows:

CØMMØN Y, A, B, C, SUM, PRØD

Now we must modify the CØMMØN statement of one of the subprograms because the rules of the CØMMØN statement (see Article 11-11) require the parameters to match the arguments in mode and order, if not in number. We shall have no trouble with the CØMMØN statement for the subprogram ADD, because its five elements match correctly the first five elements of the new CØMMØN statement we have just written for the main program; ADD has no sixth element, and therefore PRØD, the sixth element of the new CØMMØN statement will not be used.†

However, the CØMMØN statement for the subprogram MULT has UV in the fifth place, and PRØD, which it should match, is in the sixth. We get around this difficulty by inserting in the CØMMØN statement of MULT a dummy *spacer-parameter*, E, in the fifth place, as follows:

CØMMØN Z, T, U, V, E, UV

Now UV matches PRØD, and E matches SUM; however, since E is not used in the subprogram, SUM gets no action.

The common storage arrangement, making the values of the arguments directly accessible to the parameters, makes for simpler writing of the CALL and SUBRØUTINE statements: The lists of the arguments and parameters are no longer necessary. Of course, the lists now appear in the CØMMØN statements; but there are usually more calls on the subprograms than there are CØMMØN statements, and thus a certain economy in writing is achieved.

With the provision of the common storage, the program of the first variant of Example 11-12 would read as follows:

Program	*Comments*
CØMMØN Y,A,B,C,SUM,PRØD	CØMMØN statement
READ(5,4)Y	
4 FØRMAT(A1)	
1 READ(5,2) A,B,C	
2 FØRMAT(3F5.1)	
IF(A.EQ.999.0) STØP	
CALL ADD	No list of arguments
CALL MULT	No list of arguments
WRITE(6,3)A,B,C,SUM,PRØD	
3 FØRMAT(1H0,3F5.1,2F7.1)	
GØ TØ 1	
END	
SUBRØUTINE ADD	No list of parameters
CØMMØN Z,P,Q,R,TØT	CØMMØN statement
TØT = P + Q + R	

---

† Some compilers issue a warning or error message when they find unequal lists in CØMMØN statements; in the present example things can be easily made right by adding a dummy parameter, D, in the sixth place to the list of ADD (see the next paragraph).

```
IF(TØT.LE.0) TØT = Z
RETURN
END

SUBRØUTINE MULT          No list of parameters
CØMMØN Z,T,U,V,E,UV      CØMMØN statement
UV = U*V
IF(UV.LE.0) UV = Z
RETURN
END
```

The printout is the same as that at the end of the first variant in Example 11-12.

11-11. rules of the CØMMØN statement

1/ The general form of the CØMMØN statement is

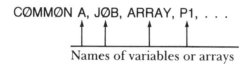

Locations in common storage are assigned to the elements in the list in the order of listing.

2/ The listed elements are separated by commas, but are not enclosed in parentheses.

3/ Arrays assigned to common storage must be dimensioned either in the DIMENSIØN statement or in the CØMMØN statement, but not in both. The DIMENSIØN statement precedes the CØMMØN statement. If the dimensions are shown in the CØMMØN statement, the DIMENSIØN statement is not necessary. Thus we may write

```
DIMENSIØN JØB(4), X(5,5)
CØMMØN A, C, JØB, X
```

or simply

```
CØMMØN A, C, JØB(4), X(5,5)
```

The listed elements would be placed in common storage in the following order: A in the first location, C in the second, the four-element array JØB in locations 3-6, and the 25-element array X in locations 7-31.

4/ Unless it is preceded by the DIMENSIØN statement, the CØMMØN statement begins the main program and follows the declaration statement of a subprogram.

5/ The elements in the CØMMØN statements of linked programs must match one another (1) in mode and (2) in order from left to right. Some compilers permit the number of elements listed in a subprogram to be shorter than the number in the main program, but not vice versa. Array sizes and dimensions may be different in the main program and in a subprogram, as long as they match sequentially in mode and order. Thus we may write:

Main program	*Subprogram*
CØMMØN J(3,4)	CØMMØN K(2), L(3,3)

The following pairs would share the same storage locations: J(1,1) and K(1), J(2,1) and K(2), J(3,1) and L(1,1), J(1,2) and L(2,1),etc.

6/ Dummy elements may be included in CØMMØN statements as spacers, to produce correct correspondence between actual elements.

7/ Elements listed in CØMMØN statements are not included in the lists of arguments or parameters.

8/ A DATA statement may not be used to load values into storage that is CØMMØN to a main program and a subprogram because the values in the CØMMØN storage may be altered by the subprogram and thus conflict with the values declared in the DATA statement.

9/ A DATA statement may be used in a subprogram but only for the values internal to the subprogram.

10/ Arrays with adjustable dimensions may not be listed in the CØMMØN statement of a subroutine (See Article 11-13).

11-12. labeled CØMMØN storage

Let us suppose that we have a main program with five arguments A, B, C, D, E, and two subprograms, SUB1, with three parameters, F, G, H, and SUB2, with four parameters, P, Q, R, S. Let us further suppose that, when we call

SUB1, we want the values of B, D, and E to be assigned to F, G, and H, respectively, and that, when we call SUB2, we want the values of A, C, D, and E to be assigned to P, Q, R, and S.

As shown in Article 11-10 we could make these assignments by writing:

In the main program: CØMMØN A, B, C, D, E
In SUB1:   CØMMØN X, F, Y, G, H
In SUB2:   CØMMØN P, T, Q, R, S

where X, Y, and T are dummy, or spacer, parameters, introduced to effect proper correspondence between the arguments and the real parameters.

The method above suffers from the need to write dummy parameters in the lists of the subprograms. Also, if SUB1 and SUB2 were to be used with another main program, which had a list of, say, six arguments, the lists of the subprograms would have to be revised, to effect the correct positioning of the interrelated variables.

We may eliminate the dummy parameters and the need for revisions by making use of the *labeled* CØMMØN storage.

We can see, in the example above, that the values of the arguments D and E are needed in both subprograms, the value of B only in SUB1, and the values of A and C only in SUB2. Therefore, we can place these three sets of values in three different blocks of CØMMØN storage: the values of D and E in *blank* CØMMØN storage, that is, storage common to all programs, the value of B in the *labeled* storage LST1, common only to the main program and SUB1, and the values of A and C in the *labeled* storage LST2, common to the main program and SUB2. The names, or labels, of the labeled blocks, LST1 and LST2, are selected arbitrarily and, usually, mnemonically; they may have from one to six alphameric characters, of which the first must be alphabetic. Blank CØMMØN storage is called simply CØMMØN storage: It has no label.

Now we can write the CØMMØN statements for the three programs by listing, for each program, the names of the pertinent storage blocks, between slashes, followed by the variables placed in those blocks. Blank CØMMØN block, which has no label, is indicated by two consecutive slashes (since no name goes between them); the two slashes may be omitted, if the blank CØMMØN is placed first in the list. Thus the CØMMØN statements above may be rewritten as follows:

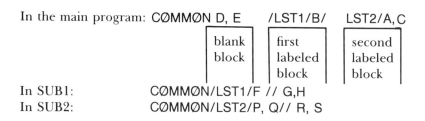

In the main program: CØMMØN D, E   /LST1/B/   LST2/A, C

| | blank block | first labeled block | second labeled block |

In SUB1:   CØMMØN/LST1/F // G,H
In SUB2:   CØMMØN/LST2/P, Q// R, S

During the execution of the program, a call for SUB1 will cause SUB1 to reach for the values of G and H in locations D and E in common storage and for the value of F in location B in labeled common storage LST1; then a call for SUB2 will make SUB2 obtain the values of R and S in locations D and E in common storage and the values of P and Q in locations A and C in labeled common storage LST2.

As stated in Article 11-10, compilers generally take an exception to the lists of variables in COMMON statements of associated programs that are of unequal lengths; the exception takes the form of a warning diagnostic, although the program is usually executed.

For example, were we to place all the arguments and parameters of the first paragraph of this article in *blank common* in the following order, with a single dummy parameter X in SUB2:

Main program:	CØMMØN D, E, B, A, C
SUB1:	CØMMØN G, H, F
SUB2:	CØMMØN R, S, X, P, Q

the computer would execute the program, but would issue a message to the effect that the CØMMØN of SUB1 is shorter than those of the other two programs.

Returning to Article 11-10, we may write the CØMMØN statements for the main program and the subprograms ADD and MULT, utilizing the idea of the labeled CØMMØN storage, as follows:

In the main program:	CØMMØN Y, A, B, C/ST/SUM/PU/PRØD
In ADD:	CØMMØN Z, P, Q, R/ST/TØT
In MULT:	CØMMØN Z, T, U, V/PU/UV

where ST is the name of the block common to SUM and TØT, and PU is the name of the block common to PRØD and UV.

The names assigned to labeled storage blocks may not be used for any other purpose in any of the related programs.

Labeled storage may be common to two or more subroutines without being common to the main program.

11-13. roots of a polynomial by the Newton-Raphson method

A polynomial, or a function, in x, usually abbreviated $f(x)$, has *roots*, that is, values of x which, substituted into the function, make the function equal to zero; for example,

$$f(x) = x^2 - 4x - 5$$

has the roots 5 and -1.

The roots of a function can be found by the Newton-Raphson method as follows:

1/ Assume any value of x to be a root and substitute it into the function, obtaining a numerical value of the function.
Example. Given the function above, assume $x = 3$. Then:

$$f(3) = 3^2 - 4(3) - 5 = -8$$

If $f(3)$ came out to be 0, 3 would be one of the roots.

2/ Take the first derivative of the function and evaluate it, using the same assumed root as before.

$$\frac{df(x)}{dx} = f'(x) = 2x - 4$$
$$f'(3) = 2(3) - 4 = 2$$

3/ Find the next approximation to the root, x_n (new x), by evaluating the expression:

$$x_n = x - \frac{f(x)}{f'(x)}$$

Continuing with the example above:

$$x_n = 3 - \frac{-8}{2} = 3 + 4 = 7$$

4/ Return to Step 1, use the value of x_n as x, and cycle through Steps 2-4, until x_n very nearly equals the preceding x.

Second cycle: Substitute 7 for x:

$$f(7) = 7^2 - 4(7) - 5 = 16$$
$$f'(7) = 2(7) - 4 \qquad = 10$$
$$x_n = 7 - \frac{16}{10} = 5.4$$

and so on.

The calculations shown above are displayed graphically on the right. The roots of an equation are the abscissas of the points at which the graph of the equation crosses the X axis, that is, the values of x corresponding to $y = 0$.

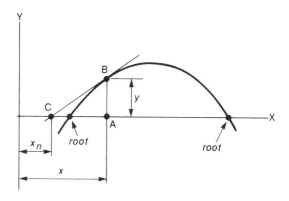

In Step 1 we assume a value of x (any point A on the X axis) and compute the corresponding ordinate y; unless we are lucky, y will be different from 0 and will establish a point B on the graph above A.

In Step 2 we compute the corresponding derivative,

$$\frac{dy}{dx} = \frac{df(x)}{dx},$$

which is the slope $\dfrac{AB}{CA}$ of the graph at B.

In Step 3 we divide the ordinate y, AB, of Step 1 by the slope $\dfrac{dy}{dx}$, $\dfrac{AB}{CA}$, of Step 2, and subtract the quotient from the x of Step 1:

$$x - \frac{AB}{AB/CA} = x - CA$$

Inspection of the diagram shows that the difference $x - CA = x_n$ is a closer approximation to a root value of the equation.

A program and the associated subroutine which find a root of an equation are shown below.

```
        X = 3.
        WRITE (6,1) X
    1   FØRMAT (1X,F7.4)
        DØ 2 I = 1,20
        F = X**2 − 4.*X − 5.
        DER = 2.*X − 4.
        CALL NEWT (X,F,DER,X,DIFF)
        WRITE (6,1) X
        IF (DIFF.LE.0.00001) GØ TØ 3
```

```
2    CØNTINUE
3    STØP
     SUBRØUTINE NEWT (X,F,DER,XN,DIFF)
     XN = X − F/DER
     DIFF = ABS (XN − N)
     RETURN
```

Printout:

```
3.0000
7.0000
5.4000
5.0235
5.0001
5.0000
5.0000
```

The programs above do not work for all polynomials. Some polynomials have imaginary roots. In some cases, an assumed root may make the derivative of a function equal to zero and cause x_n to become infinite. Therefore the program contains a DØ statement which stops the computer after 20 iterations and prevents an endless search of the root.

For polynomials with several roots, begin the program with another initial value of x, selected outside the range revealed by the calculations of the preceding root(s).

11-14.   the EQUIVALENCE statement

The EQUIVALENCE statement provides a means of avoiding revising large programs or of reducing demands on the computer's memory.

Consider a deck of several hundred data cards in a bank, each of which shows a customer's deposit in the savings account. Two persons, independently, write two programs, one to find the total amount on deposit, the other to find the total amount of interest, at 6 percent, owed the customers. The two programs are shown below.

Money on deposit	*Interest*
DIMENSIØN DEP (1000)	DIMENSIØN BAL (1000)
SUM = 0.	TØTINT = 0.

```
    DØ 5 I = 1,1000                      DØ 5 I = 1,1000
    READ (5,1) DEP (I)                   READ (5,1) BAL (I)
1   FØRMAT (F8.2)                    1   FØRMAT (F8.2)
    IF (DEP (I).EQ.−999.00) GØ TØ 2      IF (BAL (I).EQ.−333.33) GØ TØ 2
5   SUM = SUM + DEP (I)                  RINT = BAL (I)*6./100.
2   WRITE (6,4) SUM                  5   TØTINT = TØTINT + RINT
4   FØRMAT (1H0,F10.2)               2   WRITE (6,4) TØTINT
    STØP                             4    FØRMAT (1H0,F8.2)
                                         STØP
```

The two programmers, it can be seen, used two different names for the deposits, DEP in the first program, BAL in the second. It can also be seen that the results of the two programs can be produced by a single program formed by moving a few statements from the second program to the first and changing BAL in those statements to DEP. However, the change from BAL to DEP can be obviated by the statement

```
            EQUIVALENCE (DEP,BAL)
```

included in the combined program immediately after the DIMENSIØN statement. The EQUIVALENCE statement is a nonexecutable statement which informs the compiler that the elements of BAL are identical with those of DEP and occupy the same storage locations. This statement permits a transfer of cards from the second program to the first without changing BAL to DEP. The resulting combined program is shown below.

```
        DIMENSIØN DEP (1000),BAL (1000)
        EQUIVALENCE (DEP,BAL)
        SUM = 0.
        TØTINT = 0.
        DØ 5 I = 1,1000
        READ (5,1) DEP (I)
1       FØRMAT (F8.2)
        IF (DEP (I) .EQ.−999.00) GØ TØ 2
```

        SUM = SUM + DEP (I)

        RINT = BAL(I)*6./100.

5   TØTINT = TØTINT + RINT

2   WRITE (6,4) SUM,TØTINT

4   FØRMAT (1H0,2F10.2)

        STØP

Note that the DIMENSIØN statement lists both DEP and BAL, but only 1000 storage locations are required for the elements of the two arrays.

Looking over the combined program one might sensibly conclude that the EQUIVALENCE statement and the BAL dimension could be left out of the program if BAL were changed to DEP in the statement

$$RINT = BAL(I)*6./100.$$

But the program above was made simple in order to demonstrate simply and quickly the EQUIVALENCE principle. If the second program had a dozen statements with BAL in them, a programmer would not hesitate to use a single EQUIVALENCE statement rather than make a dozen revisions in the program.

As stated in the beginning of the article, the EQUIVALENCE statement also helps to lighten the load on the memory of the computer. This is done by making different sets of data occupy the same locations in the memory. How this is done is illustrated in Example 11-18.

example 11-18.   Given two one-dimensional arrays, K and L,

			K						L	
10	20	30	40	50	60	70		21	22	23

write a program that will

1/   Store the array K.

2/   Store the array L in the locations occupied by the K elements 30 40 50.

3/   Write out the last four elements of K (after the inclusion of L) as a one-dimensional array M.

The program is shown first; the explanation follows it.

```
       DIMENSIØN K(7),L(3),M(4)
       EQUIVALENCE (K(3),L(1)),(K(4),M(1))
       READ(5,1) K
  1    FØRMAT(7I3)
       READ(5,1) L
       WRITE(6,2) M
  2    FØRMAT(1H0,4I3)
       STØP
```

Data cards:

/ ˌ21 ˌ22 ˌ23 ⌐
/ ˌ10 ˌ20 ˌ30 ˌ40 ˌ50 ˌ60 ˌ70 ⌐

Printout:

ˌ22ˌ23ˌ60ˌ70

Now, the explanation.

Arrays are always stored in consecutive locations. The EQUIVALENCE statement says that, after K has been stored, L is to be stored so that the first element of L, L(1), lands in the location occupied by the third element of K, K(3); this *automatically* puts L(2) into the location of K(4) and L(3) into the location of K(5); in the process, the values of K(3), K(4), and K(5) are erased. The equivalence of K(4) and M(1) says that the array M is to come out of the four consecutive locations beginning with the location originally occupied by K(4) and now occupied by L(2).

Example 11-18 shows that, even though the three arrays require $7 + 3 + 4 = 14$ storage locations for the data, the EQUIVALENCE statement makes it possible to store all three arrays in seven locations. This, of course, is possible only if one array, say K, has been used in some calculation and is no longer needed in the program when it is modified by the inclusion of another array, such as L.

Note some of the points about the EQUIVALENCE statement:

1/ An EQUIVALENCE statement may be used to store *any* number of variables in a single location.

2/ In an EQUIVALENCE statement the group of variables stored in a single location is enclosed in parentheses, and the variables are separated by commas.

3/ An EQUIVALENCE statement may contain several groups of equivalenced variables, all groups enclosed in pairs of parentheses, and the groups separated by commas.

4/ Names of subprograms may not be equivalenced.

In Article 10-8 it was stated that we may write

```
        DATA K /'DEAF'/
   and  L = K
```

but we may not write

```
        A = K
```

because the computer does not accept a mixed-mode assignment of the alphameric data.

The EQUIVALENCE declaration permits us to get around this obstacle, as the program below shows.

```
        EQUIVALENCE (K,A)
        DATA K /'DEAF'/
        WRITE (6,1) K,K,A,A
   1    FØRMAT(1H0,A4,I10/1H0,A4,E15.5)
        STØP
```

Printout:

```
DEAF-993672762
DEAF    -0.50626E+05
```

The results of the example show that the output from a single string of 0's and 1's in a storage location may have three different forms, such as the word DEAF, the integer number −993672762, and the real number

−0.50626E+05. This is the meaning of the EQUIVALENCE statement: the contents of a storage location may have several interpretations. If the computer encounters the statement WRITE K, accompanied by the specification I10, it interprets the combination of K with I10 as a request for an integer number and prints −993672762.

problems

11-1/ Study the following sequences of statements, correct those that are incorrect, and evaluate the last statement, using the given data.

(a) 1 FØRMAT(3F6.1)
        H(E,F,G) = E*F + G
        READ(5,1) A, B, C   (Data: 4.0 2.5 5.0)
        D = H(A,B,C)*2.

(b) 1 FØRMAT(3F6.1)
        Q(E,F) = E*F + G
        READ(5,1) A, B, G   (Data: 4.0 2.5 8.0)
        P = Q(A,B)/2.

(c) 1 FØRMAT(3F6.1)
        R(E,F,G) = (E + G)*F
        READ(5,1) S,T,U   (Data: 6.0 2.0 4.5)
        V = 2.0*R(S,T,U)

(d) 1 FØRMAT(3F6.1)
        W(E,F,G,H) = E*G + F*H
        READ(5,1) A, B, C   (Data: 5.0 3.0 4.5)
        X = W (A,B,C)/3.

11-2/ In physical mechanics it is shown that when a force P acts on the boom shown in Fig. 11-1, the cable *OA* develops the tensile force

$$T = \frac{P\cos(Y-Z)}{\sin(X+Y)}$$

and the rod *OB* develops the compressive force

$$C = \frac{P\cos(X+Z)}{\sin(X+Y)}$$

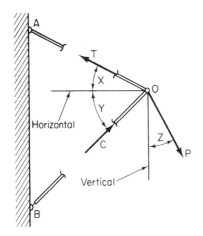

Figure 11-1

Given P = 1000 lb, write a program that will produce tabulations of the values of T and C corresponding to various combinations of the angles X, Y, and Z.

Include the expressions for T and C in the form of statement functions.

The printout should appear in the following form:

. . . .
2 spaces

              P = 1000.0 POUNDS

2 spaces

Z	X	Y	C	T
DEGREES	DEGREES	DEGREES	POUNDS	POUNDS

2 spaces

Z	X	Y	C	T
0.	0.	15.	?	?
0.	0.	30.		
0.	0.	45.		
0.	0.	60.		

2 spaces

0.	15.	15.		
0.	15.	30.		

. . . .

To obtain the printout above, make the computer set Z = 0., vary X from 0. to 45. at intervals of 15. degrees, and, for every X, vary Y from 15. to 60. at intervals of 15. degrees, and compute the corresponding C and T in each case; then change Z respectively to 15., 30., and 45., and repeat as for Z = 0..

11-3/ Transverse loads placed on a beam (Fig. 11-2) produce in it internal forces whose moments oppose the moments of the applied loads. As the loads increase, both sets of moments increase. Eventually, the internal moment attains its ultimate value, represented by the strength of the material(s) of the beam. If the beam is loaded beyond this value, it fails.

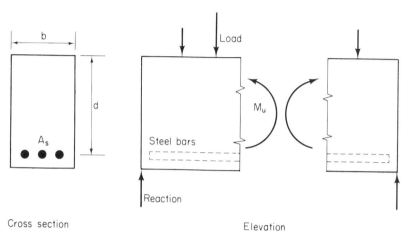

Cross section   Elevation

Figure 11-2

In reinforced concrete design, the ultimate resisting moment of a beam, based on the strength of concrete and steel bars of which it is made and on its dimensions, is given by the expression

$$M_u = 0.075\, A_s f_y \left(d - \frac{A_s f_y}{1.7\, b f_c{}'} \right)$$

where

M_u = ultimate resisting moment, kip-feet
b = width of the rectangular beam, in.
d = distance from the top of the beam to the tension steel, in.
A_s = area of the tension steel, sq in.
$f_c{}'$ = compressive strength of concrete, kips per sq in (ksi)
f_y = yield strength of steel, kips per sq in.

The area of steel, A_s, may have any value between the following limits:

$$\text{Minimum } A_s = \frac{0.2\,bd}{f_y}$$

$$\text{Maximum } A_s = \frac{55.4625\,bdk_1 f_c}{f_y(87 + f_y)}$$

where k_1 = a factor depending on the strength of concrete.

The number of combinations of the strengths of steel and concrete and of the dimensions and reinforcement of the beam is infinite. In this problem you are asked to investigate only three combinations of strengths and beam dimensions, and for every combination to determine the ultimate resisting moments corresponding to uniformly varying areas of reinforcement. The following three combinations will be investigated:

f_y, ksi.	f_c', ksi.	k_1	b, in.	d, in.
60.0	3.0	0.85	10.0	20.0
60.0	4.0	0.85	12.0	24.0
50.0	5.0	0.80	12.0	26.0

The numerical data above will be punched, line by line, on three data cards. Suggested storage addresses for the data, in consecutive order, are FY, FC, Q1 (why not K1?), B, and D.

Write a program that will produce, for every card, a table similar to the one below:

. . . .
2 spaces

	FY	FC	K1	B	D

1 space

	60.0 KSI.	3.0 KSI.	0.85	10.0 IN.	20.0 IN.

2 spaces

	AREA OF STEEL		ULTIMATE MOMENT

1 space

	SQ. IN.		KIP-FEET

2 spaces

	0.67	57.65
	0.80	. . .
Single	1.00	
spaces	. . .	
	3.20	
	3.21	

2 spaces

In the table above, 0.67 is the minimum area of steel and 3.21 the maximum; the intermediate areas are to be multiples of 0.20.

suggestions:

a/ Use the following additional notation for coding:

M_u = UM; max M_u = UMMAX; min M_u = UMMIN

A_s = AS; max A_s = ASMAX; min A_s = ASMIN

b/ Write a nest of two DØ's: The outer DØ will write the fixed data, such as FY, FC, etc., the titles, and the minimum and maximum values of AS and UM; the inner DØ will vary the values of AS by increments of 0.20 sq in. between the minimum and maximum values of AS, will calculate the corresponding values of UM, and will print out AS and UM.

c/ The expression for M_u may be written

$$M_u = (0.075 f_y d) A_s - \left(\frac{0.075 f_y{}^2}{1.7 \ bf_{c'}} \right) A_s{}^2$$

$$= P A_s - Q A_s{}^2$$

which suggests a statement function of the form

$$S(AS) = P*AS - Q*AS**2$$

This function may be called by a statement such as

$$UMMIN = S(ASMIN)$$

Do not fail to include the expressions for P and Q in the program.

d/ To vary AS by 0.20 you may use the following sequence:

```
DØ 7 I = 1,100
RI = I
AS = RI/5.
7 . . . . .
```

11-4/ The equation of a curve is:

$$Y = 1 + X^2$$

and the limits of X are A and B.

Assume that the area between the curve and the X axis is divided by equally spaced vertical lines into a series of trapezoids with the base D and the variable sides Y.

Write a program, employing a statement function, to find the area under the curve as the sum of the areas of the trapezoids. Use the following five sets of data:

A	B	D
0.	2.	1.00
0.	2.	0.10
0.	2.	0.01
2.	4.	0.10
0.	4.	0.10

Hint. The vertical sides corresponding to any two abscissas X and X+D are $1 + X^2$ and $1 + (X+D)^2$. Therefore the area of the trapezoid between these abscissas is:

$$\frac{1 + X^2 + 1 + (X+D)^2}{2} \cdot D$$

11-5/ The sine of an angle X, expressed in radians, is given by the series:

$$\sin X = \frac{X}{1!} - \frac{X^3}{3!} + \frac{X^5}{5!} - \frac{X^7}{7!} + \ldots$$

Write a program, with a function subprogram, which will evaluate the sine of $A = 50.0°$.

11-6/ Using the data of the illustrative program in Example 11-12 write a program, with common storage for the subroutines, which will

a/ Divide the sum of the first two numbers by the third.
b/ Subtract the third number from the sum of the first two.
c/ Cube the third number.
d/ Print the negative results and asterisks for the positive and zero results.

11-7/ Rewrite the program of Example 11-7 utilizing a subroutine subprogram instead of a function subprogram.

11-8/ a/ Write a main program and a subroutine subprogram, in which the main program supplies to the subprogram the values of P and Q, and the subprogram computes and returns to the main program the following values of R, S, and T:

R = P + Q;   S = P/Q;   T = Q**S − R

Let P = 12. and Q = 6.

b/ Revise the programs of (a) to make the subprogram return only the value of T.

11-9/ Write a program to find the average and variance of the first 42 numbers (See Problem 10-8).

a/ Make the program general for any array A of up to 100 elements;

b/ Show the actual number, N, of elements (42) and the values of the elements (1., 2., ... 41., 42.) on data cards;

c/ Have the elements read in by an implied DØ;

d/ Have the average of the elements calculated by a function subprogram;

e/ Have the variance calculated by a subroutine;

f/ Place N and A, the number and the values of the elements, in CØMMØN;

g/ Obtain a printout of A, N, the average, and the variance.

11-10/ For an array of bins, such as is given in Problem 10-15, write a general subroutine which will find the heaviest bin in each quadrant of the floor and will print its weight and its location, as indicated by subscripts; then write the main program calling on the subroutine to produce the values corresponding to the array of Problem 10-15.

11-11/ Find by the Newton-Raphson method both roots of the polynomial

$$f(x) = x^2 - 2x - 3$$

11-12/ Write a program that will store any 140 consecutive alphameric characters and then call a subroutine to print them, 132 on the first line and 8 on the second.

11-13/ Write a program which will generate the factorials of all consecutive integers from 1 to 14. Compare the results with the true factorials given in Problem 12-13 and explain the discrepancies.

chapter 12

type statements

12-1. introduction

So far in this book we have dealt only with real and integer numbers, such as 1.23 (real) and 45 (integer), and with real and integer variables, having names such as SUM (real) and ITEM (integer), whose first letter defined the type of the variable. Now, in some calculations, there may occur numbers and/or variables that do not fit—or fit awkwardly—in the categories described above. For instance, a common symbol for the electric current is i; therefore, I is a natural for the name of a variable current; yet I is an integer name, whereas the current, in amperes, is a real quantity. Therefore, the programmer, forced to match the modes of the name and of the value, names the current RI or XI. This practice is annoying, because it appears to be redundant; besides, a name such as XI obscures the familiar symbol i.

To take a different case, in Article 2-5 it was shown that the WATFIV compiler stores only 7 significant digits of a real number, and the G compiler only 9; the rest of the digits are truncated. This limitation on the number of digits in real numbers may be the cause of a serious lack of precision in some computations. Consider the addition of a large number and a small number, such as 1234567. and 0.1234567: their exact sum, 1234567.1234567, cannot be normally stored by either compiler; therefore, to avoid a truncation, a special provision must be made for storing the complete number.

Another quantity that has not been considered so far is the imaginary number $\sqrt{-1}$ or its combination with real numbers to form a complex number, such as $2. + 5.*\sqrt{-1}$.

Again, there are quantities, known as logical quantities, which require no numerical representation; it is necessary only to know whether these quantities are true or false. An example of a problem involving such quantities is furnished by a table lamp with a switch and a plug: if the plug P is plugged into an outlet (true) and the switch S is turned on (true), the lamp will light (true); but if either P or S is false, the lamp will remain dark (false).

Finally, there are *names* of subprograms, such as SIN and CØS, which may be conveyed from the main program as arguments to a principal subprogram, such as SUBR. The arguments SIN and CØS are *not* names of the variables, numerically defined in the main program; they are names of subprograms that the main program wants SUBR to use in its operations on a certain variable. For example, it may pass to SUBR an angle θ and, with it, the name of the subprogram SIN, expecting SUBR to return sin θ; at another time, it may send to SUBR the angle θ and the name CØS, in order to receive back cos θ. But SIN, CØS, etc., may also be used as the names of variables, even though such usage is not recommended. Unless SUBR is informed that SIN is the name of a subprogram and not of a variable, SUBR will treat SIN as the name of a variable, and will look for a number defining it; not finding it, it will stop the execution.

It can be seen, from the discussion above, that some calculations may involve numbers, variables, and names (of functions) that do not fall readily within the framework of regular real and integer numbers and variables. The characteristics and use of such numbers, variables, and names will be described in the following articles.

12-2. type statements

The special numbers, variables, and names discussed in the preceding article require special provisions for their storage and manipulation. For instance, the computer must be informed that a sum of two numbers will require more than one location for its storage; or that only real values will be assigned to the variable I; or that a variable P may have only logical values TRUE or FALSE; or that the name ALØG in a program is not the name of a variable but that of a subprogram.

Such information is conveyed to the computer by *type statements*. A type statement consists of one or two words declaring the special characteristic of the variable(s) or name(s) and of a list of the variables or names covered by the declaration; the listed variables or names are separated by commas.

There are seven type statements. They are shown below, with examples of variables and names and pertinent remarks.

1/ REAL I, KØUNT

This statement will override the integer nature of the first letters (I and K) of the two names; the two variables I and KØUNT will be treated as real variables associated with real values.

2/   INTEGER SUM, TØTAL

The two variables, in spite of the first letters S and T, will be treated as integer variables associated with integer values.

3/   DØUBLE PRECISIØN PI, CIRCLE

The values of PI and CIRCLE will be stored in two storage locations each, to accommodate nearly twice the usual number of significant digits.

4/   CØMPLEX X, Y, Z

The complex values of X, Y, and Z will be stored in two locations each, one location for the real (first) part of the number, the second for the real multiplier of $\sqrt{-1}$.

5/   LØGICAL P, S

The variables P and S will assume only the values TRUE and FALSE.

6/   EXTERNAL SIN, CØS

SIN and CØS are the names of subprograms, not of variables; they will be passed as functions, not as variables, to the principal subprogram.

7/   IMPLICIT REAL (I-K)
     INTEGER ITEM

The IMPLICIT statement declares all variables beginning with the letters I,J,K to be REAL; in other words, it overrides the predefining convention that makes variables beginning with those letters integer. However, the explicit statement INTEGER ITEM excludes the variable ITEM from the effect of the IMPLICIT statement: ITEM remains integer.

Type statements are governed by the following rules:

1/   The type statement(s) for a variable must appear prior to the first use of the variable in an executable statement.

2/ The type statement nullifies (or restores) the type of a variable implicit in the first letter of its name.

3/ The type statements permanently establish the type of a variable; it may not be changed later in the program by other type statements.

4/ The list of a type statement may contain the names of several variables, statement functions, and function subprograms, separated by commas.

5/ The list of a type statement may contain names of variables that need no typing; for instance, it is permissible to write

REAL ITEM,KØUNT,SUM

even though SUM is already typed real by its first letter.

6/ A variable typed by a statement may be assigned only values of the same type; it follows that it must be described by a specification of the same type.

7/ An array name appearing in a type statement may have its dimension specified in the statement; thus, it is permissible to write

INTEGER TØTAL (20, 15)

In such a case the DIMENSIØN statement is not necessary, though it is still permissible. If a type statement for an array is used jointly with the DIMENSIØN statement, or the CØMMØN statement, or both, the dimension(s) of the variable(s) may appear in *only one* statement, normally in the DIMENSIØN statement:

INTEGER TØTAL
DIMENSIØN TØTAL (20,15)

8/ To satisfy all compilers, statements should appear in the following order:

TYPE
DIMENSIØN
CØMMØN

9/ A variable may appear in only one type statement. The only exception occurs when a type statement is followed by an EXTERNAL type statement; thus, it is permissible to write

```
REAL      MATRIX
EXTERNAL  MATRIX
```

The two statements indicate that MATRIX is the *real* name of a function subprogram that will be sent as an argument from the main program to a principal subprogram.

12-3. INTEGER type statement

The INTEGER type statement has the form

```
INTEGER BØYS, GIRLS, MEN, WØMEN, TØTAL
```

where the word INTEGER is mandatory and the words BØYS, GIRLS, MEN, WØMEN, TØTAL (separated by commas) form the name list of the variables that are declared to be of the integer type. No harm results from the inclusion in the list of MEN which is implicitly an integer name. Only integer values may be assigned to the variables declared integer by the statement.

example 12-1. Find the total number of persons, given the following data: boys, 7; girls, 4; men, 2; women, 10.

Program:

```
      INTEGER BØYS,GIRLS,MEN,WØMEN,TØTAL
      READ(5,1) BØYS,GIRLS,MEN,WØMEN
   1  FØRMAT(4I3)
      TØTAL = BØYS + GIRLS + MEN + WØMEN
      WRITE(6,2) TØTAL
   2  FØRMAT(1H0, 'TØTAL⌃=',I4)
      STØP
```

Data card:

Output:

```
TØTAL⌃=⌃⌃23
```

The integer type statement eliminates the necessity of prefixing real names by I, J, etc., in order to make their mode match the integer mode of the data.

If a real variable X is declared INTEGER, and a program contains a sequence such as

INTEGER X
READ(5,1) X
1 FØRMAT(F5.2)

Data card:

the machine will declare an error, because the variable and the specification do not match in type.

But if the sequence reads

INTEGER X
X = 91.80

the machine will store 91 (integer) at X.

12-4. REAL type statement

The REAL type statement has the form

REAL MATRIX (4,3)

where the word REAL is mandatory and the word MATRIX, followed by (4,3), is the name of an array of *real* numbers, arranged in four rows and three columns. No DIMENSIØN statement is necessary if the array is dimensioned in the type statement.

example 12-2. Find the sum of all the terms in the array MAT below:

2.7	−7.5	6.1
−3.1	0.2	4.6

Program:

```
      REAL MAT(2,3)
      READ(5,1) MAT
    1 FØRMAT(6F4.1)
      SUM = 0.
      DØ 2I = 1,2
      DØ 2 J = 1,3
    2 SUM = SUM + MAT(I,J)
      WRITE(6,3) SUM
    3 FØRMAT(1H0,'SUM‸=',F5.1)
      STØP
```

Data card:

$$2.7-3.1-7.5‸0.2‸6.1‸4.6$$

Output:

SUM‸=‸‸3.0

The real type statement eliminates the necessity of prefixing integer names by real initials, such as A, R, etc., in order to make their mode match the real mode of the data.

12-5.   DØUBLE PRECISIØN type statement

The DØUBLE PRECISIØN type statement has the form

DØUBLE PRECISIØN RADIUS, ALPHA, DSIN

where the two words, DØUBLE PRECISIØN, are mandatory, and the words RADIUS, ALPHA, DSIN form the name list of the variables and functions that are declared to be of the double-precision type. The variables RADIUS and ALPHA will be assigned double-precision values; the function DSIN will be recognized as a function for evaluating the sine of an angle in double precision.[†]

[†] The recognition will be effected by an EXTERNAL statement (Article 12-8).

The purpose of the statement is to make the computer link up two storage locations for each variable declared to be in double precision.[†]

Regardless of the initial letter of the variable to which it is assigned, a double-precision number is a *real* number which may (but need not) have up to eighteen significant digits [††] with the G compiler and up to sixteen significant digits with the WATFIV compiler. The number is written formally in the exponential form (like an E number), but with a D instead of an E. Examples of formally written double-precision numbers are:

$$4.123D+02 = 412.3$$
$$0.123456789D-03 = 0.000123456789$$
$$-25.987654321D+00 = -25.987654321$$

As with E-numbers, the D-part of a double-precision number (the D and the exponent) may be abbreviated in a number of ways; thus:

$$4.123D+02 = 4.123D2 = 4.123+2$$

One reason for writing a number such as 4.123D+02 as a double-precision number is the impossibility of representing most fractions exactly in the binary system; thus eighteen digits give a closer approximation to the actual value than nine digits.

Input:

To receive a double-precision value, a variable V must be listed in a DØUBLE PRECISIØN statement placed first in the program:

DØUBLE PRECISIØN V

A double-precision value, such as 0.123D+00 may be stored at V in one of three ways:

[†] The statement declaring a number to be in double precision has an alternate form; instead of writing:

DØUBLE PRECISIØN A,K

we may write:

REAL*8 A,K

For an explanation of the latter form, see Article 12-10.

[††] For a discussion of the significant figures see Appendix B.

1/ By an assignment statement:

$$V = 0.123D+00$$

2/ By a DATA statement:

$$DATA\ V\ /0.123D+00/$$

3/ By a READ sequence with a D specification in the Format statement:

```
        READ (5,1) V
1       FØRMAT (D9.3)
```

Data card:

```
 0.123D+00
```

A D specification is written in the same manner as an E specification, but with a D instead of an E.

In the third case, that of storage by reading a data card during the execution of the program, the number and the specification may be in the F or E form; it is all right to write:

```
        READ (5,1) V           or           READ (5,2) V
1       FØRMAT (F5.3)                 2      FØRMAT (E8.2)
```

Data card: *Data card:*

```
 0.123                            1.23E-01
```

In both cases above, 0.123 will be stored in double precision.
But it is wrong to write:

$$V = 0.123 \qquad or \qquad DATA\ V\ /0.123/$$

because in these two cases the numbers will be loaded with the program as constants, and these constants will be stored in single precision.

One exception occurs with the WATFIV compiler if a number has more than seven significant digits; in this case the compiler recognizes the number as a double-precision number and stores it accordingly; for example, encountering the following sequence:

```
DØUBLE PRECISIØN X,Y
DATA X /0.12345678/
Y = 0.987654321
```

and counting eight digits in one number and nine in the other, the WATFIV compiler stores both numbers in double precision. Furthermore, the WATFIV compiler declares an error if a variable, declared to be in double precision, has a value in a DATA statement that has fewer than eight significant digits and has no D.

In all cases the safe thing to do is to write double-precision numbers with a D.

Operations:

An arithmetic expression may contain both single-precision and double-precision constants and variables combined in operations involving addition, subtraction, multiplication, and division. A double-precision quantity may be raised to an integer power. All operations on mixed-type expressions are performed in double-precision arithmetic, and the results that are declared to be in double precision are printed in the D form. However, the product of A in single precision and B in double precision does not have the double-precision accuracy of the product when both A and B are in double precision.

Mathematical (or library) functions, similar to those developed for single-precision quantities, are available for double-precision quantities and may be used in arithmetic expressions involving double-precision quantities. The distinguishing mark of a double-precision function is the letter D in front of its name. Table 12-1 gives the names of some of the available functions, with a typical argument X, and the operations that the functions perform on X. The argument X may be a variable, a constant, or a complicated arithmetic expression, all of them in double precision.

Table 12-1. Double Precision Functions

Function and argument	Function calculates
DSIN(X)	Sine of X
DCØS(X)	Cosine of X
DTAN(X)	Tangent of X
DATAN(X)	Arctangent of X
DABS(X)	Absolute value of X
DSQRT(X)	Square root of X
DLØG(X)	Natural logarithm of X
DLØG10(X)	Logarithm of X to base 10
DEXP(X)	e^X

The name list associated with a DØUBLE PRECISIØN type statement must include not only the names of the variables which are to be evaluated in double precision, but also the names of the functions that are brought into play in the course of the evaluation. Thus, if an angle α and X = sin α are both to be evaluated in double precision, the type statement should read

DØUBLE PRECISIØN ALPHA, X, DSIN

example 12-3. Calculate the double-precision value of the square root of 7.

Program:

```
    DØUBLE PRECISIØN A,B,DSQRT
    A = 7.  ← (A whole number is always stored exactly)
    B = DSQRT(A)
    WRITE(6,1) B
  1 FØRMAT(1H0,D23.16)
    STØP
```

Printout:

∧0.2645751311064591D∧01

When an arithmetic expression on the right side of an arithmetic statement is evaluated, the resulting double-precision number is assigned to the variable on the left side in accordance with the type of the variable. If the variable on the left is R, listed in the DØUBLE PRECISIØN statement, the G compiler sends eighteen digits to R, and the WATFIV compiler sixteen; if the variable on the left is V, not declared to be in double precision, but real by virtue of the letter V, the compiler truncates the right half of the number stored in the *16-character hexadecimal form,*† and converts the remaining eight characters into a 7- or 9-digit single-precision value; if the variable on the left is an unlisted integer M, the single-precision value is reduced to its integer part, and only this part is stored under M.

An assignment of the double-precision value of a variable S to an integer variable N may occasionally produce a value at N which has no resemblance to the value at S. This happens when the value of S exceeds the integer capacity of a storage location ($2^{31} - 1 = 2,147,483,648 - 1$); when 1 is added to $2^{31} - 1$ in the location, the sum resets to zero, and the location continues to accumulate the value of S (and reset to zero) until the value of S is reached; at that time the number in storage is equal to the integral part of the value of S minus 2^{31} times the number of resets. It is this difference that is stored under N.

---

† The hexadecimal system of numbers is described in Appendix C.

Output:

On output a double-precision number may be printed in the D form or the F form, depending on the specification.

The standard form of a printout in the D form consists of three parts: (1) ±0., in a 3-space field, (2) the decimal part, *beginning with a significant digit*, and (3) the 4-character exponent, such as D-03. An illustration of the output of two numbers is given below.

```
        DØUBLE PRECISIØN P,Q
        P = 12.34D+00
        Q = −0.000567D−02
        WRITE (6,1) P,Q
  1     FØRMAT (1H0,2D13.5)
        STØP
```

Printout:

˄˄0.12340D˄02˄−0.56700D−05

In the illustration both specifications call for numbers with five decimal digits; therefore the minimum field is $3 + 5 + 4 = 12$ spaces; however, both fields are made 13, mainly to insert a space between the two numbers.

A printout of a double-precision number in the F form contains all the significant digits of the number, provided that the specified F field has sufficient room for the digits on each side of the decimal point.

If the value of a double-precision variable R is assigned to a single-precision variable V, the value of V (limited to nine or seven significant digits, depending on the compiler) may be printed out in the F form or E form, depending on the specification, as has been done heretofore in the book.

Values stored under integer variables may be called out only by an I specification.

All the varieties of assignment and output discussed above are illustrated in the program of Example 12-4 below.

example 12-4. Store in double precision the following values:

R = −12.34567891234567D+00   S = 0.6D+10   K = 0.0000000700

and make the computer report them out as follows:

(1)   R in D form.

(2)   R in double precision, in F form.

(3)   R in single precision, in F form.

(4)   R in single precision, in E form.

(5)   R as an integer.

(6)   S as an integer.

(7)   K in D form.

Program:

```
   DØUBLE PRECISIØN R,S,K
   READ(5,1) R,S,K
 1 FØRMAT(D22.14,D10.1,F14.10)
   V = R
   M = R
   N = S
   WRITE(6,2) R,R,V,V, M,N,K
 2 FØRMAT(1H0,'OUTPUT'/1H0,D25.18/1X,F19.14/1X,F15.10/
  *1X,E25.18/1X,I12/1X,I12/1X,D13.4)
   STØP
```

Data card:

```
-12.34567891234567D+00 ^^^0.6D+10 ^^0.0000000700
```

Printout:

```
-0.123456789123456701D+02
 -12.34567891234567
 -12.3456783
-0.123456783           E+02
          -12
 1705032704
  0.7000D-07
```

Note the following points about the output:

—   The first two lines give the double-precision-values of R in the D form and the F form, in each case with sixteen original significant digits.
—   The third line gives only the single-precision value of V (nine significant digits), in spite of the more than ample width of the specified F field.
—   The fourth line gives the value of V in the E form; note the nine blanks skipped to satisfy the 18-decimal field.

- In the fifth line, the value of R, assigned to M, is truncated to −12.
- In the sixth line, the value of N is not 6,000,000,000 (the value of S), but 6,000,000,000 − 2(2,147,483,648) = 1,705,032,704.
- In the seventh line K appears in the D form.

an illustrative program

Double-precision quantities are often needed in the solutions of certain simultaneous equations.

Consider the following two equations:

$$AX + BY = E$$
$$CX + DY = F$$

in which A, B, C, D, E, F represent numerical constants.

The values of X and Y that satisfy both equations are given by the Cramer's expressions

$$X = \frac{DE - BF}{AD - BC}$$

and

$$Y = \frac{AF - CE}{AD - BC}$$

Both expressions have the same denominator, AD − BC. This denominator has a powerful effect on the values of X and Y when the products AD and BC are nearly equal, that is, when AD − BC approaches zero. When this is the case, a slight change in one or both products—due to imprecision in calculations—may seriously alter the results. To observe this effect, let us substitute into the expression for X a set of assumed simple values:

$$X = \frac{6.224 - 1.266}{2.642 - 2.508} = \frac{4.958}{0.134} = 37.$$

Now let us round off the values above at two significant digits (instead of four). Then

$$X = \frac{6.2 - 1.3}{2.6 - 2.5} = \frac{4.9}{0.1} = 49.$$

If we imagine the values in the first illustration to be in double precision and in the second in single precision, we can see that a loss of precision can cause the result to change from 37 to 49. With actual single- and double-precision numbers—which, of course, run to nine and eighteen digits—the change can be equally drastic. Accuracy is further reduced by the fact that, when a double precision value is truncated to a single precision value, the last digit of the latter is not increased by 1 even if the truncated part begins with a digit higher than 4.

The solutions of simultaneous equations in double-precision and single-precision are illustrated—and may be compared—in Example 12-5.

example 12-5. Find the (a) double-precision, and (b) single-precision values of X and Y that satisfy the simultaneous equations

$$278,335X + 70,340Y = 73,360$$
$$160,559X + 40,576Y = 42,320$$

Use the WATFIV compiler.

(a) *Program in Double Precision*

```
DØUBLE PRECISIØN A,B,C,D,E,F,H,R,S,T,U,V,G,P,Q,X,Y
  READ(5,1)A,B,C,D,E,F
1 FØRMAT(6F8.0)
  H = A*D
  R = B*C
  S = D*E
  T = B*F
  U = A*F
  V = C*E
  G = H−R
  P = S−T
  Q = U−V
  X = P/G
  Y = Q/G
  WRITE(6,2)H,R,G,S,T,P,U,V,Q,X,Y
2 FØRMAT(1H0,'H∧=',D23.16/1X,'R∧=',D23.16/1X,'G∧=',
 *D23.16/1H0,'S∧=',D23.16/1X,'T∧=',D23.16/1X,'P∧=',
 *D23.16/1H0,'U∧=',D23.16/1X,'V∧=',D23.16/1X,'Q∧=',
 *D23.16/1H0,'X∧=',D23.16/1H0,'Y∧=',D23.16)
  STØP
```

Data card:

```
/ 278335. ∧∧ 70340. ∧ 160559. ∧∧ 40576. ∧∧ 73360. ∧∧ 42320. /
  ∧                              ∧∧∧          ∧∧∧          ∧∧∧
```

Printout:

```
H.= .0.1129372096000000D.11
R.= .0.1129372006000000D 11
G.= .0.9000000000000000D 03

S.= .0.2976655360000001D 10
T.= .0.2976788800000001D 10
P.= −0.1334400000000000D 06

U.= .0.1177913720000000D 11
V.= .0.1177860824000000D 11
Q.= .0.5289600000000000D 06

X.= −0.1482666666666667D 03

Y.= .0.5877333333333333D 03
```

(b) *Program in Single Precision*

```
   READ(5,1)A,B,C,D,E,F
 1 FØRMAT(6F8.0)
   H = A*D
   R = B*C
   S = D*E
   T = B*F
   U = A*F
   V = C*E
   G = H−R
   P = S−T
   Q = U−V
   X = P/G
   Y = Q/G
   WRITE(6,2)H,R,G,S,T,P,U,V,Q,X,Y
 2 FØRMAT(1H0,'H.=',E23.16/1X,'R.=',E23.16/1X,'G.=',
  *E23.16/1H0,'S.=',E23.16/1X,'T.='E23.16/1X,'P.=',
  *E23.16/1H0,'U.=',E23.16/1X,'V.=',E23.16/1X,'Q.=',
  *E23.16/1H0,'X.=',E23.16/1H0,'Y.=',E23.16)
   STØP
```

Data card:

```
.278335. .. 70340. 160559. .. 40576. .. 73360. .. 42320.
```

Printout:

H.= ⌃0.1129372000000000E⌃11
R.= ⌃0.1129371000000000E 11
G.= ⌃0.4096000000000000E 04

S.= ⌃0.2976655000000000E 10
T.= ⌃0.2976788000000000E 10
P.= −0.1333760000000000E 06

U.= ⌃0.1177913000000000E 11
V.= ⌃0.1177860000000000E 11
Q.= ⌃0.5283840000000000E 06

X.= −0.3256250000000000E 02

Y.= ⌃0.1290000000000000E 03

For comparison, the values of X and Y given by the two solutions are tabulated below:

	Double precision	*Single precision*
X	−148.27	− 32.56
Y	587.73	129.00

Obviously, the two sets of values are entirely different. What is the cause? An inspection of the two printouts reveals that the culprit is the denominator G: in double precision, G = 900.; in single precision, it is 4096.

To determine which of the two is right, we examine the difference H-R:

In double precision:
$$G = \frac{\begin{array}{r} 11{,}293{,}720{,}960. \\ \underline{11{,}293{,}720{,}060.} \end{array}}{900.}$$

In single precision:
$$G = \frac{\begin{array}{r} 11{,}293{,}720{,}000. \\ \underline{11{,}293{,}710{,}000.} \end{array}}{10{,}000.}$$

Yet, in the latter case, the computer has printed G = 4096., and used it to compute the values of X and Y.

One may be tempted to accuse the computer of making a mistake in subtraction. But the computer makes no mistakes. The explanation lies in the hexadecimal system which the computer uses in its operations and which is described in Appendix C.[†]

From the erratic performance of the computer in single precision above, we may conclude that single-precision results are always suspect. This is far from being so. Errors in single precision occur in cases of division by numbers approaching zero or when numerators of fractions are 50 to 100 times larger than denominators. When numerators and denominators are of the same order of magnitude, single precision is accurate. Double precision values do have nearly twice as many digits as single precision values, but the computer's time required to process a double precision value is up to eight times longer than the time required for a single precision value, and, normally, the extra precision is unnecessary.

12-6. COMPLEX type statement

The COMPLEX type statement has the form:

COMPLEX A, B, K

where the word COMPLEX is mandatory and the letters A,B,K form the name list of the variables that are declared to be of the complex type. These variables will each be assigned a pair of values corresponding to the two parts of a complex number. The name of a complex number may begin with any letter.

A typical complex number has the form:

$$3.0 + 4.0\sqrt{-1}$$

in which 3.0 is said to be the real part and $+4.0\sqrt{-1}$ the imaginary part; the

---

[†] For those who are curious, in the hexadecimal system the double-precision values of H, R, and G appear as

$$
\begin{array}{rl}
H = & 2A1,288,180 \\
R = & \underline{2A1,287,DFC} \\
G = & 384 = 3(16)^2 + 8(16) + 4 = 900
\end{array}
$$

Operating in single precision, the computer saves only the six leftmost significant digits of the numbers; thus:

$$
\begin{array}{rl}
H = & 2A1,288,000 \\
R = & \underline{2A1,287,000} \\
G = & 1,000 = 1(16)^3 = 4096
\end{array}
$$

imaginary part is the product of a real number (+4.0) and $\sqrt{-1}$, and the part of the product which is really imaginary is $\sqrt{-1}$, because a square root of a negative number does not exist; every number, positive or negative, multiplied by itself, forms a positive product. In mathematics, the factor $\sqrt{-1}$ is denoted by i; in electrical engineering, by j, to avoid confusion with i used as the symbol for the electric current. Thus the number above is usually written:

$$3.0 + 4.0i \quad \text{or} \quad 3.0 + 4.0j$$

A complex number may be represented graphically by a point in a plane. Fig. 12-1 shows the X and Y axes intersecting at right angles at O. Let us call the X axis the *axis of real numbers or reals,* and the Y axis the *axis of imaginary numbers or imaginaries.* Then the number $3.0 + 4.0i$ may be represented by a point P which is +3.0 units (to the right) from the Y axis and +4.0 units (up) from the X axis.

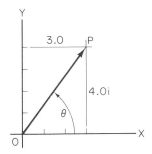

Figure 12-1

The plane of the axis of reals and the axis of imaginaries is called the *complex plane.* Every point in the plane represents a complex number; every complex number is represented by a point in the plane. Two complex numbers are equal only if their real parts are equal and their imaginary parts are equal.

The complex number $3.0 + 4.0i$, represented by the point P in Fig. 12-1, may also be represented by the directed line (or vector) *OP;* not by the length of *OP,* but by the *length and direction of OP.* The length of the vector *OP* is called the *modulus* of the complex number and is equal to the absolute value of the square root of the sum of the squares of the two *real* factors of the complex number; that is, in Fig. 12-1:

Modulus or absolute value of $3.0 + 4.0i = OP = \sqrt{3^2 + 4^2} = 5.$

The imaginary i is not considered in the computation of the modulus. The angle θ, measured counterclockwise from the positive direction of the X axis, is called the *argument* or *amplitude* of the complex number. From Fig. 12-1:

$$\sin \theta = \frac{4.0}{5.0} = 0.8 \quad \text{and} \quad \cos \theta = \frac{3.0}{5.0} = 0.6$$

addition and subtraction of complex numbers

The real and the imaginary parts of a complex number are two distinct entities; it might be said that the real part of a number is its width, and the imaginary part its height. Therefore, when two complex numbers are to be added together, the proper operation is to add the width of one number to the width of the other and the height of one number to the height of the other. From this conclusion follows the rule:

To add (or subtract) two complex numbers, add (or subtract) the real and imaginary parts separately.

example 12-6.

Addition	Subtraction
$\begin{aligned}+\ & 6. + 3.i \\ & 2. - 4.i \\ \hline & 8. -\ i \end{aligned}$	$\begin{aligned}-\ & 6. + 3.i \\ & 2. - 4.i \\ \hline & 4. + 7.i \end{aligned}$

The separate addition of the real and imaginary parts, characteristic of complex numbers, is analogous to the process of addition that is used in combining vectors employed in many branches of physical and engineering sciences. Vectors, for instance, are commonly used to represent forces (Fig. 12-2). Every force vector has a horizontal and a vertical component; two force vectors P and Q are added by adding together, first, their horizontal components and, second, their vertical components; the two sums form the horizontal and vertical components of the resultant force vector R (that is, of the sum of the two force vectors P and Q); the square root of the sum of the squares of the two components gives the magnitude of the resultant force R, and the ratio of the vertical component to the horizontal component gives the tangent of the angle θ between the resultant and the X axis.

The similarity between forces and complex numbers is obvious: The horizontal component of a force is analogous to the real part of a complex number, and the vertical component to the imaginary part. The only difference is that there is nothing imaginary about the vertical component of a force. The resultant force and its angle are analogous to the modulus and amplitude of a complex number.

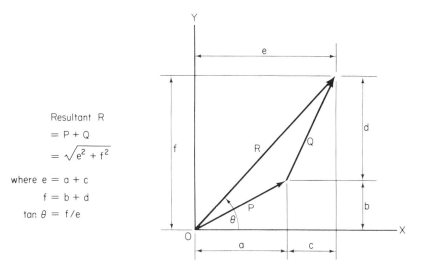

$$\text{Resultant } R$$
$$= P + Q$$
$$= \sqrt{e^2 + f^2}$$
$$\text{where } e = a + c$$
$$f = b + d$$
$$\tan \theta = f / e$$

Figure 12-2

input and output of complex numbers

Since the two real values of a complex number cannot be combined, and i is the fixed component of every complex number, complex numbers are always submitted to—and reported by—the computer as two real numbers, the same two real numbers that make up the complex number, and in the same order in which they appear in the complex number, and i is omitted. The two numbers retain their signs.

A complex number may be stored in the computer's memory in a number of ways.

Direct Assignment

CØMPLEX A
A = (2.4, − 4.7)

In the first statement the variable A (which is to receive a complex value) is declared CØMPLEX; in the second statement the real values 2.4 and −4.7 are separated by a comma and enclosed in parentheses. The machine stores $2.4 - 4.7i$.

READ a Complex Number

CØMPLEX B
READ(5,1) B
1   FØRMAT(F4.1,E10.2)

Data card:

```
10.7ʌʌ0.62E+01
```

In the first statement B is declared CØMPLEX; therefore the machine, told to READ a complex B, seeks *two* numbers on the data card; it finds them in the two fields described in the FØRMAT statement. One number is punched in the F form, the other in the E form, to show that both forms are acceptable. The comma and the parentheses do not appear on the data card. The machine stores $10.7+6.2i$.

READ Two Real Numbers

```
      CØMPLEX C, CMPLX
      READ(5,2) D,E
   2  FØRMAT (2E11.4)
      C = CMPLX (D,E)
```

Data card:

```
ʌ0.0123E+03-0.6250E+02
```

The machine reads and stores two distinct real numbers D and E. Then, in the statement C = CMPLX(D,E), the function CMPLX converts the real values of D and E into the real components of the complex number $C = D + Ei$. The list of the CØMPLEX type statement includes not only C, but also the converting function CMPLX.†

On output, the computer generally reports only the two real components of a complex number:

```
      CØMPLEX A
      WRITE(6,3) A
   3  FØRMAT (1H0,2F6.1)
```

Printout:

ʌʌʌ2.4ʌʌ−4.7

---

† Some versions of FORTRAN do not require CMPLX in the list; however, they always accept it. Therefore, unless one is sure, it is always a good idea to include CMPLX in the list.

If one wishes to see the actual complex number, the following program will produce it:

```
      COMPLEX B
      WRITE(6,4) B
    4 FØRMAT (1H0,F6.1,'+(',F5.1,')I')
```

Printout:

ᴧᴧ10.7+(ᴧᴧ6.2)I

The Hollerith specifications produce the plus sign, which the computer often omits, and the parentheses, which help to keep $6.2i$ from looking like 6.21.

operations with complex numbers

Complex and real numbers may be mixed in an arithmetic expression: a real number, after all, is a complex number with the imaginary part equal to $0.*i$. The evaluated result of a mixed expression is always complex. A complex number may be raised to an integer power; this is the only time an integer may be used in a complex expression. It is important to note that

$$i^2 = \sqrt{-1} \quad * \quad \sqrt{-1} = -1$$

example 12-7. Write a program that will make the computer

(1) Store the following numbers: $6.5-2.0i, \quad 2.5 + 4.0i, \quad 4.5, \quad 2$

(2) Add the first three numbers together.

(3) Multiply the first number by the second.

(4) Raise the second number to the power of the fourth.

(5) Print the given values and the results.

Program:

```
      CØMPLEX P,K,D,F,N
      READ(5,1)P,K,A,J
    1 FØRMAT(5F4.1,I2)
      D = P + K + A
      F = P * K
      N = K ** J
      WRITE(6,2) P,K,A,J,D,F,N
    2 FØRMAT(1H0,2(2F5.1,3X),F5.1,3X,I3/(1H0,2F6.2))
      STØP
```

Data card:

P	K	A J

⌒6.5–2.0⌒2.5⌒4.0⌒4.5⌒2

Printout:

⌒⌒6.5⌒–2.0⌒⌒⌒⌒⌒2.5⌒⌒4.0⌒⌒⌒⌒⌒4.5⌒⌒⌒⌒⌒2

13.50   2.00

24.25 21.00

–9.75 20.00

modulus and amplitude of a complex number

The modulus and amplitude of a complex number were defined and illustrated (Fig. 12-1) in the beginning of this article. Their values may be calculated in a straightforward fashion from the properties of the triangle formed by the two real factors of the complex number and their resultant vector. There is also a CØMPLEX function CABS which, given the name of the complex number as an argument, produces its modulus directly.

If we denote the real factor of the imaginary (vertical) part of the number by V and the real (horizontal) part by H, then

$$\text{Modulus} = \sqrt{H^2 + V^2}$$

and

$$\text{Amplitude} = \arctan \frac{V}{H}$$

Different programs may be written, depending on whether the complex number is submitted as a pair of real factors or a single complex number. In the latter case the complex number must be separated into its real and imaginary parts, and both parts converted into real numbers for use in the computations; the separation and conversion are carried out by two complex functions: REAL for the horizontal (real) component and AIMAG for the vertical (imaginary) component; both functions use the name of the complex number as their argument. It is not necessary to list the names REAL and AIMAG in the CØMPLEX type statement.

Different procedures for finding the modulus and amplitude of a complex number are illustrated in the three programs of Example 12-8.

example 12-8.   Find the modulus and amplitude of

$$P = 3.0 + 4.0i$$

PROGRAM I. The components are submitted as two real numbers.

```
  READ(5,1) H,V
1 FØRMAT(2F3.1)
  AMØDUL = SQRT(H*H + V*V)
  AMPLIT = ATAN(V/H)*57.3
  WRITE(6,2) AMØDUL,AMPLIT
2 FØRMAT(1H0,'MØDULUS⌃⌃⌃= ',F5.1/1H0,'AMPLITUDE⌃= ',F5.1)
  STØP
```

Data card:

```
/3.04.0⌡
```

Printout:

MODULUS⌃⌃⌃=⌃⌃5.0

AMPLITUDE = 53.1

PROGRAM II. The complex number is submitted as a unit.

```
  CØMPLEX P
  READ(5,1) P
1 FØRMAT(2F3.1)
  H = REAL(P)
  V = AIMAG(P)
  AMØDUL = SQRT(H*H + V*V)
  AMPLIT = ATAN(V/H)*57.3
  WRITE(6,2)AMØDUL,AMPLIT
2 FØRMAT(1H0,'MØDULUS⌃⌃⌃=',F5.1/1H0,'AMPLITUDE⌃=',F5.1)
  STØP
```

Data card:

```
/3.04.0⌡
```

Printout:

MODULUS ˄ ˄ ˄ = ˄ ˄ 5 . 0

AMPLITUDE ˄ = ˄ 53 . 1

As stated earlier, the modulus of a complex number is also given directly by the complex function CABS: its application is demonstrated in Program III below. CABS is not listed in the type statement.

PROGRAM III.

```
   CØMPLEX P
   READ(5,1) P
1  FØRMAT(2F3.1)
   AMØDUL = CABS(P)
   WRITE(6,2)AMØDUL
2  FØRMAT(1H0,'MØDULUS˄=',F4.1)
   STØP
```

Data card:

3 . 04 . 0

Printout:

MØDULUS˄=˄5.0

addition of force vectors

As stated earlier, force vectors are analogous to complex numbers. They have horizontal and vertical components that are similar to the real factors in the real and imaginary terms of complex numbers. Consequently, forces may be submitted to the computer as pairs of components, just like the pairs of real factors in complex numbers. Then the computer operates on the forces in the same manner as it operates on complex numbers. Commanded to add forces together, it adds the horizontal and vertical components of the forces separately, and obtains a complex sum, which consists of two terms, the first representing the horizontal component of the resultant and the second its vertical component. These two terms of the complex sum must now be separated and converted into real components, for the purpose of computing the values of the resultant force and of its angle. The separation and conversion are carried out by the functions REAL and AIMAG, described in the section on modulus and amplitude; their argument is the name of the complex sum. The angle is placed in the proper quadrant by the library function ATAN2; its argument (in parentheses) consists of the names of the vertical and horizontal components, in that order, separated by a comma. The computer measures the angle from the positive end of the X axis, counterclockwise if the vertical component is positive, clockwise if the vertical component is negative, and assigns to the clockwise angle a minus sign. Since an angle may have any value up to −180. degrees, its specification must provide for at least four spaces before the decimal point.

Numerous forces should generally be handled as an array. The procedure is illustrated in Example 12-9.

example 12-9.   Four forces have their components, in pounds, as shown in Fig. 12-3 and in the table below:

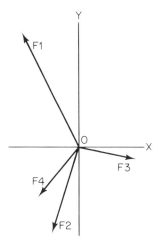

Figure 12-3

Force	Components	
	Horizontal	*Vertical*
F1	−100.	200.
F2	− 50.	−150.
F3	100.	− 20.
F4	− 70.	− 80.

(A negative sign means that the component acts either to the left or downward.)

Find the resultant of the forces, R, and its angle, θ, from the X axis.

Program:

```
C THE FØRCES ARE TREATED AS AN
      ARRAY F ØF FØUR CØMPLEX NUMBERS
C THE TYPE STATEMENT LISTS THE DIMENSIØNED
      ARRAY F AND THE CØMPLEX SUM

    CØMPLEX F(4), SUM
    READ(5,1) F
 1  FØRMAT(8F5.0)
C INITIALIZE SUM AT (0.,0.)

    SUM = (0.,0.)
    DØ 2 I = 1,4
 2  SUM = SUM + F(I)
C THE CØMPLEX SUM IS CØNVERTED INTØ
      REAL CØMPØNENTS H AND V

    H = REAL(SUM)
    V = AIMAG(SUM)
    R = SQRT(H*H + V*V)
    THETA = ATAN2(V,H)*57.3
    WRITE (6,3) F,H,V,R,THETA
 3  FØRMAT(1H0,8F5.0/1H0,2F6.0/1H0,'RESULTANT⌃⌃⌃=',
   *F7.1,'⌃LB.'/1H0,'ANGLE THETA⌃=',F7.1,'⌃DEG.')
    STØP
```

Data card:

```
−100.⌃200.⌃−50.−150.⌃100.⌃−20.⌃−70.⌃−80.
```

Printout:

```
−100.⌃200.⌃−50.−150.⌃100.⌃−20.⌃−70.⌃−80.
⌃−120.⌃⌃−50.
RESULTANT⌃⌃⌃=⌃⌃⌃130.0⌃LB.
ANGLE⌃THETA⌃=⌃⌃−157.4⌃DEG.
```

Fig. 12-4 shows the resultant of the four forces shown in Fig. 12-3 and its angle from the X axis.

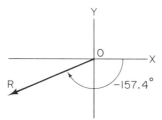

Figure 12-4

quadratic equations

A quadratic equation of the form

$$ax^2 + bx + c = 0$$

has two values of x, known as the *roots*, which satisfy the equation. The values of the roots are given by the expressions

$$x = \begin{cases} \text{Root } 1 = -\dfrac{b}{2a} + \dfrac{\sqrt{b^2 - 4ac}}{2a} \\[2em] \text{Root } 2 = -\dfrac{b}{2a} - \dfrac{\sqrt{b^2 - 4ac}}{2a} \end{cases}$$

For the purpose of programming we can reduce these expressions to:

$$\text{RØØT1} = \text{FIRST} + \text{SECØND}$$
$$\text{RØØT2} = \text{FIRST} - \text{SECØND}$$

where
$$\text{FIRST} = -\frac{b}{2a}$$

and
$$\text{SECOND} = \frac{\sqrt{b^2 - 4ac}}{2a}$$

It can be seen that the difference between the two roots is entirely due to the different signs between FIRST and SECØND.

The expression under the radical, $b^2 - 4ac$, is called the *discriminant*. If the discriminant is positive, SECØND is a real (i.e., not imaginary) number, and the two roots are two different real numbers; if the discriminant is zero, SECØND = 0, and the two roots are equal; finally, if the discriminant is negative, SECØND is an imaginary number, and the two roots are two different complex numbers.

Quadratic equations may be solved by real or complex arithmetic. The two methods are illustrated in Examples 12-10 and 12-11; the programs of both examples are written to solve three quadratic equations,

$$2.5x^2 - 6.0x + 5.2 = 0$$
$$2.5x^2 - 6.0x + 3.2 = 0$$
$$5.0x^2 + 8.0x + 3.2 = 0$$

example 12-10. solution by real arithmetic An important step in the solution is the determination of the sign and magnitude of the discriminant; depending on the sign, the computer is directed to take one of two routes: one route for a positive or zero discriminant, the other for a negative discriminant.

If the discriminant is positive, say, $+36$, the numerator of SECOND is $\sqrt{36} = 6$; if the discriminant is negative, say, -36, the numerator is $\sqrt{-36} = \sqrt{36(-1)} = 6i$. In both cases the numerator of SECOND is a positive number multiplied either by $+1$ or by i, where the positive number is equal to the square root of the absolute value of the discriminant $= \sqrt{|b^2 - 4ac|}$.

Thus, in writing a program to determine the roots of a quadratic equation by real arithmetic, we ask the computer, first, to evaluate

$$\text{FIRST} = -\frac{b}{2a} \text{ and SEC\O{}ND} = \frac{\sqrt{|b^2 - 4ac|}}{2a}$$

and, then, to establish whether the discriminant, $b^2 - 4ac$, is negative, zero, or positive.

If the discriminant is negative and therefore SEC\O{}ND is imaginary, FIRST and SEC\O{}ND cannot be added; consequently we ask the computer to

WRITE(6,5) FIRST, SEC\O{}ND

The two numbers, say, 2.6 and 4.2, will be printed separately; however, by skillful formatting, the numbers can be joined to appear as

R\O{}\O{}T1 = 2.6 + (4.2)I

Following up with the repeat command

WRITE(6,6) FIRST, SEC\O{}ND

we can obtain

$$RØØT2 = 2.6 - (4.2)I$$

If the discriminant is zero or positive, that is, if SECØND is either 0 or real, we write in the program:

$$RØØT1 = FIRST + SECØND$$
$$RØØT2 = FIRST - SECØND$$

and ask the computer to WRITE RØØT1 and RØØT2 directly.
The procedure is illustrated in the following program.

Program:

```
   DØ 8I = 1,3
   READ(5,1) A,B,C
 1 FØRMAT(3F5.1)
   WRITE(6,2) I
 2 FØRMAT(/1H0,'CARD∧',I1)
   FIRST = -B/(2.*A)
   DISCR = B*B - 4.*A*C
   SECØND = SQRT(ABS(DISCR))/(2.*A)
   IF(DISCR) 3,4,4
 3 WRITE(6,5) FIRST, SECØND
 5 FØRMAT (1H0,'RØØT∧ØNE∧=',F7.3,'∧+∧(',F7.3,')I')
   WRITE(6,6) FIRST, SECØND
 6 FØRMAT(1H0,'RØØT∧TWØ∧=',F7.3,'∧-∧(',F7.3,')I')
   GØ TØ 8
 4 RØØT1 = FIRST + SECØND
   RØØT2 = FIRST - SECØND
   WRITE(6,7) RØØT1, RØØT2
 7 FØRMAT(1H0,'RØØT∧ØNE∧=',F7.3/1H0,'RØØT∧TWØ∧=',F7.3)
 8 CØNTINUE
   STØP
```

Data cards:

```
∧∧2.5∧-6.0∧∧5.2
∧∧2.5∧-6.0∧∧3.2
∧∧5.0∧∧8.0∧∧3.2
```

Printout:

CARD˄1
ROOT˄ONE˄=˄˄1.200˄+˄(˄˄0.800)I
ROOT TWO =   1.200 − (0.800)I

CARD 2
ROOT ONE =   1.600
ROOT TWO =   0.800

CARD 3
ROOT ONE = −0.800
ROOT TWO = −0.800

example 12-11. solution by complex arithmetic   In a solution by complex arithmetic, there is no need to distinguish between positive, zero, or negative discriminants; in either case, a complex square root function, CSQRT, may be used to extract a real or imaginary root of the discriminant, the root divided by *2a* to give the value of SECØND, and SECØND added to or subtracted from FIRST to give the two RØØTs. Since either RØØT may be complex, both ROOTS must be listed in the CØMPLEX declaration statement, together with the discriminant, SECØND, and the function CSQRT. Real roots may always be output as complex numbers with the imaginary term equal to 0.0*i.

As an illustration of what happens in a solution by complex arithmetic, consider the equation

$$2x^2 + 6x + 6 + 2i = 0$$

$$\text{FIRST} = -\frac{6}{2(2)} = -1.5$$

$$\text{SECØND} = \frac{\sqrt{36 - 8(6 + 2i)}}{2(2)} = \frac{\sqrt{36 - 48 - 16i}}{4} = \frac{\sqrt{-12 - 16i}}{4}$$

$$= \frac{-2 + 4i}{4} = -0.5 + i$$

$$\text{RØØT1} = -1.5 + (-0.5 + i) = -2 + i$$
$$\text{RØØT2} = -1.5 - (-0.5 + i) = -1 - i$$

Program:

```
   CØMPLEX DISCR, SECØND, RØØT1, RØØT2,CSQRT
   WRITE(6,3)
 3 FØRMAT(1H0,18X,'WITH^I',16X,'WITHOUT^I')
   DØ 8 I = 1,3
   READ(5,1) A,B,C
 1 FØRMAT(3F5.1)
   WRITE(6,2) I
 2 FØRMAT(/1H0,'CARD^',I1)
   FIRST = -B/(2.*A)
   DISCR = B*B -4.*A*C
   SECØND = CSQRT(DISCR)/(2.*A)
   RØØT1 = FIRST + SECØND
   RØØT2 = FIRST - SECØND
   WRITE(6,7) RØØT1, RØØT1,RØØT2,RØØT2
 7 FØRMAT(1X,'RØØT^ØNE^=',F7.3,'^+^(',F7.3,')I^^^ØR^^',
  *2F7.3/1X,'RØØT TWØ^=',F7.3,'^+^(',F7.3,')I^^^ØR^^',2F7.3)
 8 CØNTINUE
   STØP
```

Data cards:

```
^^2.5^-6.0^^5.2
^^2.5^-6.0^^3.2
^^5.0^^8.0^^3.2
```

Printout:

```
                    WITH I              WITHOUT I

CARD^1
ROOT^ONE^=^^1.200^+^(^^0.800)I^^^OR^^^^1.200^^0.800
ROOT TWO =  1.200 + (-0.800)I   OR    1.200 -0.800

CARD 2
ROOT ONE =  1.600 + (  0.000)I   OR    1.600  0.000
ROOT TWO =  0.800 + (-0.000)I   OR    0.800 -0.000

CARD 3
ROOT ONE = -0.800 + (  0.000)I   OR   -0.800  0.000
ROOT TWO = -0.800 + (-0.000)I   OR   -0.800 -0.000
```

12-7. LØGICAL type statement

In the introductory article to this chapter (Article 12-1) we mentioned a table lamp with a switch and a plug and the associated problem of determining whether the lamp is on or off. In this simple case, it is obvious that the light will be on only if the plug is in an outlet and the switch is on. Now, how can we get this answer from the computer?

We may proceed as follows. We command the computer to READ the values of the two variables PLUG and SWITCH. On the associated data card we punch, for each variable, not a numerical value (of which there is none) but one or the other of the two words, TRUE or FALSE: TRUE if the plug is in, or the switch is on, FALSE otherwise. With these values stored in the memory, we can write the assignment statement:

LAMP = PLUG.AND.SWITCH

The object of this statement is to assign a TRUE or FALSE value to the variable LAMP. Executing this statement, the computer fetches the TRUE/FALSE values from its memory and substitutes them for PLUG and SWITCH: if both PLUG *and* SWITCH are TRUE, the expression on the right side of the equals sign is evaluated to be TRUE, and the computer assigns the value TRUE to LAMP: the light is on; if either PLUG or SWITCH is FALSE, or both of them are FALSE, LAMP will be FALSE: no light. The values TRUE and FALSE are stored in the memory with periods preceding and following them, thus: .TRUE., .FALSE..

In the discussion above we have introduced a new type of values: TRUE and FALSE. They are obviously not numeric; we call them *logical values*. Lest the computer falter in its execution of a program involving logical values, we must inform it, in the beginning of the program, that some of the values it will deal with will be logical. This information is conveyed by the LØGICAL type statement, which has the form

LØGICAL LAMP, RADIØ

To the computer this will mean that the variables LAMP, RADIØ will be assigned only TRUE/FALSE values. The names of the logical variables, like those of the real and integer variables, may not have more than six alphameric characters; however, they may begin with *any* letter of the alphabet.

Logical values are described by the L specification; for example, L5 is the specification that will describe FALSE, punched in five spaces on a data card. Actually, the computer pays attention only to the first letter of a logical value: the value FALSE may be punched as F in one space on a card, and described by L1. If the described field is blank, the computer stores the value FALSE. On data cards TRUE/FALSE are punched without periods.

On output, the computer prints only one letter, T or F; therefore, L1 is sufficient to describe the printout of a logical value; if a printout specification is L7, the computer will print T (or F) right-justified in a field of seven spaces.

Now we can write the LAMP program as follows:

```
  LØGICAL LAMP,PLUG,SWITCH
  READ(5,1)PLUG,SWITCH
1 FØRMAT(2L4)
  LAMP = PLUG.AND.SWITCH
  WRITE(6,2)LAMP
2 FØRMAT(1H0,L3)
  STØP
```

Data card:

Printout:

∧∧F

In the program above the values of PLUG and SWITCH, T and F, instead of being read from a data card, could have been input by the DATA statement

DATA PLUG, SWITCH /T,F/

without apostrophes enclosing T or F.

A numerical value may not be assigned to a variable declared to be logical; we may not write:

LØGICAL K
DATA K/25/ ⎫ ◀───── NO!

However, if the value is submitted in the hexadecimal form[†], the compiler

---

[†] See Article C-6 in Appendix C.

accepts it, and the computer, if asked, will print the value in the hexadecimal form, the decimal form, and the logical form, the last one always being T (true).

> LØGICAL K
> DATA K/Z19/ (19 is the hexadecimal equivalent of 25)
> WRITE(6,1) K,K,K
> 1   FØRMAT(1H0,Z8,I5,L4)
> STØP

Printout:

00000019   25   T

A T or F value stored at logical K may be assigned to N (or P) and retrieved from it as T or F, provided (1) N (or P) is declared logical, or (2) N (or P) is equivalenced with K. A hexadecimal value stored at logical K may be retrieved from N (or P) in the hexadecimal, decimal or T form if N (or P) is equivalenced with K or K is assigned to N (or P) and N (or P) is declared logical. Thus we may write:

LOGICAL K,N DATA K /F/ N = K WRITE(6,1)K,N 1 FØRMAT(1H0,2L3) *Printout:* ∧∧F∧∧F	LØGICAL K,P DATA K /F/ P = K WRITE(6,1)K,P 1 FØRMAT(1H0,2L3) ∧∧F∧∧F
LØGICAL K EQUIVALENCE (K,N) DATA K /F/ WRITE(6,1)K,N 1 FØRMAT(1H0,2L3) ∧∧F∧∧F	LØGICAL K EQUIVALENCE (K,N) DATA K /Z19/ WRITE(6,1)N,N,N 1 FØRMAT(1H0,Z8,I4,L3) 00000019∧∧25∧∧T

In the program with PLUG, SWITCH and LAMP the statement

$$LAMP = PLUG.AND.SWITCH$$

is called the *logical statement* or the *logical assignment statement;* the expression on the right side of the equals sign is called the *logical expression, LEX,* and the word .AND. is called the *logical operator;* it must always be preceded and followed by periods.

In all, there are three logical operators:

$$.AND. \quad .OR. \quad .NOT.$$

If, in the program above, .AND. were changed to .OR. (though it would make no physical sense), the printout for the value of LAMP would be T. The computer would evaluate the expression on the right as TRUE, because TRUE would satisfy the stipulated requirement that only one of the two variables, either PLUG *or* SWITCH, should be TRUE.

.NOT. reverses the value of a variable. If a logical variable B has the value .TRUE. stored in its memory register, then the statement

$$A = .NOT.B$$

would cause A to receive the value .FALSE..

To borrow an illustration from the world of finance, consider a stock broker who receives numerous orders to buy or sell stocks at specified prices. Since prices continually move up and down, he wants to be aware at any given time whether the price of a stock is right for the execution of an order.

Stocks are identified by ticker symbols of from one to three characters. Prices of stocks are quoted in dollars and fractions of a dollar, with denominators of 2, 4, and 8 (rarely 16); for example:

$$30\frac{1}{8}, \ 17\frac{3}{4}$$

Let us suppose that the broker has orders to:

	BUY	BOEING (BA)	at 62½
		CHRYSLER (C)	at 10
		GULF OIL (GO)	at 26
and	SELL	RCA (RCA)	at 25¼
		UNIROYAL (R)	at 10

He writes the following program:

```
      LØGICAL BUYBA,BUYC,BUYGØ,SELRCA,SELR
      READ(5,1)BA,C,GØ,RCA,R
1     FØRMAT(5F8.3)
      BUYBA = BA.LE.62.5
      BUYC = C.LE.10.
      BUYGØ = GØ.LE.26.
      SELRCA = RCA.GE.25.25
      SELR = R.GE.10.
      WRITE(6,2)BUYBA,BUYC,BUYGØ,SELRCA,SELR
2     FØRMAT(1H0,' BUYBA BUYC BUYGØ SELRCA SELR'/
     *1H0,5L8)
      STØP
```

At specified intervals of time a data card is punched with the current values of the stocks and submitted with the program to the computer. Let us assume a data card punched as follows:

```
 ∧∧63.125∧∧∧9.5∧∧∧∧26.∧∧∧∧∧∧24.5∧∧∧∧10.
```

The computer stores these values and begins to execute the assignment statements. These statements are logical statements, because the expressions on their right are logical expressions: the latter can be evaluated only as .TRUE. or .FALSE., depending on the numbers on the data card. The first and fourth expressions are found to be .FALSE., and thus BUYBA and SELRCA become .FALSE.; the other three become .TRUE.. The printout that the computer produces is

BUYBA	BUYC	BUYGØ	SELRCA	SELR
F	T	T	F	T

and the broker is informed that the time is right to buy Chrysler and Gulf Oil and sell Uniroyal.[†]

It should be noted that in this program the data consist of real values that are assigned to real variables, such as BA, in the expressions; it is the

---

[†] One should be careful with ticker symbols beginning with I, J, K, L, M, N; thus Memorex, with a ticker symbol MRX, should be named XMRX or YMRX in the READ statement and in the logical expressions, although it is safe to write BUYMRX.

logical expressions, such as BA.LE.62.5, that receive the logical values .TRUE. or .FALSE., depending on whether BA is equal to, less than, or greater than 62.5.

The symbols .LE. and .GE. are called *relational operators.* Six relational operators are used in logical expressions; they are

.EQ.   .NE.   .GT.   .LT.   .GE.   .LE.

They are the same as the relational operators described in connection with the logical IF statement in Chapter 8. As shown above, they must be preceded and followed by periods.

12-8.   EXTERNAL type statement

A program to find the sine, cosine, and tangent of the sum of two angles, A and B, may be written as follows:

```
  READ(5,1) A,B
1 FØRMAT(2F4.0)
  P = SIN((A + B)/57.3)
  Q = CØS((A + B)/57.3)
  R = TAN((A + B)/57.3)
  WRITE(6,2) P,Q,R
2 FØRMAT(1H0,3F8.4)
  STØP
```

Data card:

```
/ ˄30.˄45./
```

Printout:

˄˄0.9659˄˄0.2589˄˄3.7306

In the three statements that assign values to P, Q, and R, the functions SIN, CØS, and TAN all have the same argument, (A + B)/57.3. To avoid writing this argument three times, we may transfer it to a function subprogram, write it there only once, and then vary the function that is to operate on it. The function subprogram may be written as follows:

```
FUNCTIØN SICØTA(F,S,T)
SICØTA = F((S + T)/57.3)
RETURN
```

The name of the subprogram, SICØTA, is made up from the first two letters of SIN, CØS, and TAN; the parameter F represents the function that is to operate on the sum of the dummy angles S and T. The relationship is shown in the second line of the subprogram.

Now in the main program, instead of writing

$$P = SIN ((A + B)/57.3)$$

we can write

$$P = SICØTA(SIN,A,B)$$

and the three arguments, SIN, A, B will flow to the subprogram and replace the corresponding parameters F, S, T; SICØTA will be evaluated, and its value returned to the main program for assignment to P.

As it is shown, however, the transfer of the arguments SIN, A, B from the main program to the subprogram has a fatal flaw in it. SIN, A, and B are acceptable variable names; but the computer has in storage only values for A and B; there is no value for SIN; thus the computer would be compelled to declare an error.

To prevent it from doing this, we must inform the computer that SIN is not the name of a variable, but an external function that will be passed to the subprogram. This information is conveyed to the computer by the EXTERNAL type statement, which has the form

EXTERNAL͜SIN

Adding CØS and TAN to the list of the type statement above, we can write the combined program and subprogram as follows:

```
  EXTERNAL SIN, CØS, TAN
  READ(5,1) A,B
1 FØRMAT(2F4.0)
  P = SICØTA(SIN,A,B)
  Q = SICØTA(CØS,A,B)
  R = SICØTA(TAN,A,B)
  WRITE(6,2)P,Q,R
2 FØRMAT(1H0,3F8.4)
  STØP
```

```
FUNCTIØN SICØTA(F,S,T)
SICØTA = F((S + T)/57.3)
RETURN
```

Data card:

Printout:

∧∧0.9659∧∧0.2589∧∧3.7306

The combined program and subprogram are, indeed, longer than the original program, but the combination illustrates the principle of the EXTERNAL type statement. And even though the combination is longer, it is simpler to write. It would be quite in order with an expression more complicated than (S + T)/57.3, and with more frequent calls on the subprogram.

The passing of the names of the subprograms written together with the main program is illustrated in Example 12-12.

example 12-12.   A circular disk, with a triangle and a rectangle cut out of it, is shown on the right.

To find the area of the disk, the main program calls the function subprogram CIR. CIR calculates the gross area of the disk and calls the function subprograms HØLE1 and HØLE2 to give it the areas of the cutouts. However, HØLE1 and HØLE2 are general subprograms for cutouts of unspecified shape or size. To define HØLE1 and HØLE2 and their parameters, CIR must receive from the main program the names of the function sub-

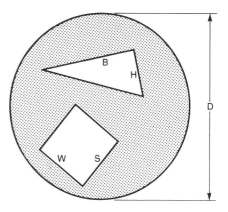

programs TRI and REC that describe the shapes and calculate the areas of the cutouts. Accordingly, the main program is written together with three function subprograms: TRI, REC, and CIR. TRI finds the area of a right-angled triangle, B*H/2, and REC finds the area of a rectangle, S*W. When the main program calls CIR, it passes to it the diameter of the circle, D, the name TRI with its arguments B and H, to define HØLE1 and its parameters P1 and Q1, and the name REC with its arguments S and W, to define HØLE2 and its parameters P2 and Q2.

Since TRI and REC in the call for CIR are the names of the subprograms and not of variables, both must be listed in the EXTERNAL statement of the program.

Programs:

```
        EXTERNAL TRI, REC
        D = 6.
        B = 1.5
        H = 4.
        S = 2.
        W = 2.5
        AREA = CIR(D,TRI,B,H,REC,S,W)
    1   FØRMAT(1H0,F8.3)
        STØP

        FUNCTIØN TRI (P,Q)
        TRI = P*Q/2.
        RETURN

        FUNCTIØN REC(P,Q)
        REC = P*Q
        RETURN

        FUNCTIØN CIR(DIA,HØLE1,P1,Q1,HØLE2,P2,Q2)
        CIR = 3.14*DIA**2/4. − HØLE1(P1,Q1) − HØLE2(P2,Q2)
        RETURN
```

A hole can be eliminated by making its arguments 0.,0..

12-9. IMPLICIT type statement

According to the predefining convention, the first letter R in the name RADIUS makes RADIUS the name of a *real* variable, and the first letter I in the name ITEM makes ITEM the name of an *integer* variable. The IMPLICIT type statement overrides this convention.

A typical IMPLICIT statement is of the form

$$\text{IMPLICIT REAL(I,N), INTEGER(A-D,H)}$$

This statement declares that the variables whose names begin with I and N are real and that those whose names begin with A, B, C, D, and H are integer. Note that the range A, B, C, D is abbreviated to A-D: only the first and the last characters of the range are shown, separated by a dash. Also note that the lists for each type are enclosed in parentheses, that the types are separated by commas, and that the single characters and ranges in each list are separated by commas.

The effect of the IMPLICIT statement above is to make the variables such as ISUM, ITEM, NØ, and NUMBER real, and the variables such as AREA, ARC, BASE, CHØRD, DIA, and HEIGHT integer. However, if the programmer wants to exclude ITEM and AREA from the effect of the IMPLICIT statement, he can write, at the head of the program, the following sequence:

```
IMPLICIT REAL(I,N), INTEGER(A-D,H)
INTEGER ITEM
REAL AREA
```

example 12-13.

```
        IMPLICIT INTEGER(A,D), REAL(I-K)

        INTEGER ITEM

        REAL DIA

        READ(5,1) ARC,DIST,DIA,ISUM,ITEM,JØB,KIP

    1   FØRMAT(2I2,2F5.1,I3,2F5.1)

        WRITE(6,2) ARC,DIST,ITEM,DIA,ISUM,JØB,KIP

    2   FØRMAT(1H0,3I3,4F6.1)

        STØP
```

Data card:

$$\overline{\left|\begin{array}{l} \wedge 5 \wedge 8 \wedge \wedge 2.5 \wedge 57.0 \wedge 15 \wedge 22.2 \wedge 44.4 \end{array}\right.}$$

Printout:

∧∧5∧∧8∧15∧∧∧2.5∧∧57.0∧∧22.2∧∧44.4

12-10.   size of a storage location

An IBM/360 storage location consists of 32 ferrite rings (or other devices), called *bits;* each group of 8 bits is called a *byte.*

Normally the values of the integer, real, and logical variables are stored in single locations of 4 bytes each; such storage assignments are said to be made by *default.* However, a programmer has it within his power to change the size of a storage location to suit the size of the value he may want to place in it. He does this, for instance, when he declares a value to be in double precision, because such a value requires two normal storage locations or 8 bytes.

Complex numbers automatically require two normal storage locations, one for the real part of the number, the other for the real multiplier of $\sqrt{-1}$; however, the programmer may express both parts in double precision, requiring four normal storage locations or 16 bytes.

On the other hand, he may want to store a logical value, such as T (the first letter of TRUE), in a single byte.

The storage defaults may be overridden by means of the following typical statements:

Statement	Comments
INTEGER*2 K	The integer value of K will be stored in 2 bytes, instead of 4.
REAL*8 A	The real value of A will be stored in 8 bytes, that is, in two normal storage locations; REAL*8 A is equivalent to DØUBLE PRECISIØN A.
LOGICAL*1 C	The logical value of C will be stored in 1 byte.
CØMPLEX*16 P(3)	Each of the 3 complex elements of the array P will be stored in 16 bytes.

The last statement, in effect, puts the complex P in double precision. However, we may not write

```
DØUBLE PRECISIØN P(3)
CØMPLEX P
```

because mentioning P in two type statements contradicts Rule 9 in Article 12-2.

The default and alternate storage sizes for the variables of various types are summarized in Table 12-2.

Table 12-2. Storage Location Sizes, in Bytes

Type of variable	Default size	Alternate size
INTEGER	4	2
REAL	4	8
LOGICAL	4	1
COMPLEX	8	16

Type, size, and data statements may be combined, as shown in the following examples.

Statement	*Comments*
INTEGER*2 ITEM/7/,SET(3)	ITEM, initialized to 7, and the 3 elements of SET will be stored as integers, each in 2 bytes
REAL A(2,2)/1.,2.,3.,4./,K*8/1.7/	The 4 elements of A will be stored normally as real values in 4-byte locations; the value of K, declared to be real, will be stored in 8 bytes; in order not to affect A, *8 is placed not after REAL, but after K
IMPLICIT REAL*8(G-I),INTEGER(C,N-P), LØGICAL*1(S)	The variables beginning with G,H,I will have their real values stored in 8 bytes each; the variables beginning with C,N,O,P will have their integer values stored in 4 bytes each; S will have its logical value stored in 1 byte

example 12-14.

```
      IMPLICIT REAL*8(G-I),INTEGER(C,N-P),LØGICAL*1(S)
      INTEGER IX
      REAL PART(2)
      DATA GAS,HØT,IK,IX,CØST,NET,ØFF,PART,PIECE,S /0.1D-3,
     *0.2D-2,0.3D-1,4,10,9,5,17.25,98.76,15,'T'/
      WRITE(6,1) GAS,HØT,IK,IX,CØST,NET,ØFF,PART,PIECE,S
    1 FØRMAT(1H0,3D13.4/1H0,4I5/1H0,2F6.2,I4,A3)
      STØP
```

Printout:

```
 0.1000D-03    0.2000D-02    0.3000D-01
    4    10    9    5
17.25 98.76   15   T
```

The linking of two storage locations associated with double precision makes it possible to store alphameric and special characters in groups of 8 instead of the usual 4. Heretofore, to store PØRTLAND and to have it printed, we had to write:

```
    DIMENSIØN A(2)
    DATA A /'PØRT','LAND'/
    WRITE(6,1) A
1   FØRMAT(1H0,2A4)
```

But we can also write:

```
    REAL*8 A
    DATA A /'PØRTLAND'/
    WRITE(6,2) A
2   FØRMAT(1H0,A8)
```

and obtain a printout of the entire word.

The same effect is produced if REAL*8 is replaced by DØUBLE PRECISIØN.

12-11. packing and unpacking

(Before reading this article one should become familiar with the hexadecimal system and its conversions, described in Articles C-6, 7, and 8 in Appendix C).

When the computer is given, say, eight numbers to store, it stores them in eight separate storage locations. For example, if we write:

```
    DIMENSIØN K(8)
    DATA K /1,2,3,4,5,6,7,8/
    WRITE(6,1) K
1   FØRMAT(1X,Z8)
```

Printout:

```
00000001
00000002
00000003
00000004
00000005
00000006
00000007
00000008
```

the computer stores in eight locations the eight integers listed in the DATA statement and then prints them out in the hexadecimal form, as shown here.

The printout shows two things: first, that a digit corresponds to every 4-bit half-byte in a storage location and, second, that only the last (rightmost) half-byte in every storage location was used to store a number; the other seven half-bytes were not used. This is a wasteful use of the computer memory.

To use the memory space more economically we *pack* numbers; that is, we crowd the eight integers in the example above into a single storage location, so that a printout from that storage location appears as 12345678.

A glance at the eight-line printout above will show what we have to do: we have to shift 1 from its eighth place in the storage location seven places to the left, 2 six places, 3 five places, and so on. In the decimal system we shift a digit one place to the left by multiplying it by 10^1, two places by multiplying it by 10^2, and so on. In the hexadecimal system we shift digits by multiplying them by the powers of 16. Thus in the example above we multiply 1 by 16^7, 2 by 16^6, and so on, producing the following separate numbers in storage:

$$
\begin{array}{ll}
1000 & 0000 \\
0200 & 0000 \\
0030 & 0000 \\
0004 & 0000 \\
0000 & 5000 \\
0000 & 0600 \\
0000 & 0070 \\
0000 & 0008 \\
\end{array}
$$

These numbers are no longer the elements of the original array K; they are the elements of a new 8-element array L. We create L by the following sequence:

```
      DIMENSIØN L(8)
      DØ 2 I = 1,8
   2  L(I) = K(I)*16**(8 − I)
```

The eight elements of L are still distinct from one another. So we add them together as shown in the next sequence:

```
      ISUM = 0
      DØ 3 I = 1,8
   3  ISUM = ISUM + L(I)
```

The two sequences above may be combined into a single sequence:

$$\text{ISUM} = 0$$
$$\text{DØ } 4 \text{ I} = 1,8$$
$$\text{L(I)} = \text{K(I)}*16**(8 - \text{I})$$
$$4 \quad \text{ISUM} = \text{ISUM} + \text{L(I)}$$

If we continue with

$$\text{WRITE(6,5) ISUM}$$
$$5 \quad \text{FØRMAT(1H0,Z8)}$$

the machine prints:

12345678

that is, it prints all the elements of the original array K from a single storage location.

The complete program for packing eight integers is written as follows:

```
      DIMENSIØN K(8), L(8)
      DATA K /1,2,3,4,5,6,7,8/
      WRITE(6,1) K
1     FØRMAT(1X,Z8)
      ISUM = 0
      DØ 4 I = 1,8
      L(I) = K(I)*16**(8—I)
4     ISUM = ISUM + L(I)
      WRITE(6,5) ISUM
5     FØRMAT(1H0,Z8)
      STØP
```

It must be clearly understood that the digits in the last one-line printout above are the *images* of the elements of K, and not the elements themselves: 1 is not 1 but $1*16^7$.

To separate a packed number into its elements we reverse the process. Consider the eight hexadecimal digits packed into the number 47B28A93. Remember that 47B28A93 is the ISUM of the eight elements of the array L. We must now strip the eight elements of L, one after the other, from ISUM and convert them into the elements of K. We accomplish it as follows. We divide 47B28A93, that is, ISUM, by 16. The division being in the integer mode, the fraction $\frac{3}{16}$ is lost. Therefore we can write:

$$N = \frac{\text{ISUM}}{16} = \frac{47B28A93}{16} = 047B28A9$$

Next, we multiply N back by 16, obtaining 47B28A90, and subtract the product from ISUM, obtaining the last, eighth, element of K:

$$K(8) = \text{ISUM} - N*16 = 47B28A93 - 47B28A90 = 00000003$$

To find the next, seventh, element, we repeat the process above with N as ISUM; that is, we set:

$$\text{ISUM} = N = 047B28A9$$

compute the new $N = \frac{\text{ISUM}}{16} = \frac{047B28A9}{16} = 0047B28A$

and find $K(7) = \text{ISUM} - N*16 = 047B28A9 - 047B28A0 = 00000009$

A program to unpack eight digits packed into a single storage location may be written as follows:

```
        DIMENSIØN K(8)
        DATA ISUM /Z47B28A93/
        DØ 6 I = 1,8
        N = ISUM/16
        K(9-I) = ISUM - N*16
6       ISUM = N
        WRITE(6,1) K
1       FØRMAT(1X,Z8)
        STØP
```

Printout:

00000004
00000007
0000000B
00000002
00000008
0000000A
00000009
00000003

If the integers to be packed are large, naturally enough, fewer of them can be packed into a single storage location. To find out how much we can pack, we must first express the integers in the hexadecimal form. Let us suppose that we have been given 507, 4748, and 822 to pack. The hexadecimal equivalents of these numbers are 1FB, 128C, and 336. Since a half-byte can store one digit, and a storage location has eight half-bytes, obviously enough we can pack only the first two numbers into a storage location. We shall put the first number into the left half and the second number into the right half. The following program will do it.

```
      DATA I,J /507,4748/
      WRITE(6,1) I,J
 1    FØRMAT(1X,Z8)
      IPACK = I*16**4
      ISUM = IPACK + J
      WRITE(6,5) ISUM
 5    FØRMAT(1H0,Z8)
      STØP
```

Printout:

000001FB
0000128C

01FB128C

To unpack the number 013579BD into its two halves, we write:

DATA ISUM /Z013579BD/

$I = ISUM/16**4$

$J = ISUM - I*16**4$

WRITE(6,1) I,J

1   FØRMAT(1X,Z8)

STØP

Printout:

00000135
000079BD

One must be cognizant of the fact that the largest digit storable in the leftmost half-byte of a storage location is 7 and not F, because the first bit in that half-byte is reserved for the sign of the number.

12-12.   masking

In the IBM System/360 every value is stored as a string of thirty-two 0's and 1's. *Masking* is an operation that erases some of the 1's, that is, alters some of the 1's to 0. The operation is performed by the *logical* statement

$$N = L.AND.M$$

in which L = the original *logical* value in storage
    M = the *logical* value of the *mask* designed to alter L
and N = the altered *logical* value of L.

The operation of the statement is analogous to the operation of a light bulb, N, on a line with two switches, L and M, in series (Fig. 12-5).

Let 0 represent an open switch or the dark bulb and 1 a closed switch or the lighted bulb. If either L or M or both are 0, that is, open, the bulb will be dark, 0. If both switches are 1, that is, closed, the bulb will be lighted, 1.

The four possible combinations are shown in the table.

L	M	N
0	0	0
1	0	0
0	1	0
1	1	1

The table shows that if the mask M is 1, N has the value of L; if M is 0, N is 0.

The variables L, M, N can represent whole words, that is, entire strings of 0's and 1's in storage locations. For example, if a segment of the L string is stored as

$$\ldots 0 0 1 1 0 1 1 1 \ldots \quad (L)$$

and we decide to delete the last two 1's from the segment above, we create a mask M containing the corresponding segment

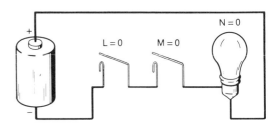

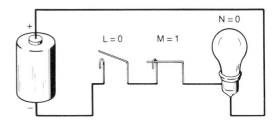

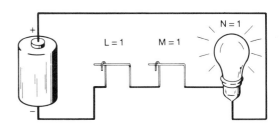

Figure 12-5

$$\ldots 1 1 1 1 1 1 0 0 \ldots \quad (M)$$

and make the computer compare the two segments, creating a segment of N in the process; the 1's in M will protect the corresponding digits in L, and the 0's will convert the corresponding digits to 0, producing

$$\ldots 0 0 1 1 0 1 0 0 \ldots \quad (N)$$

As stated earlier, the statement N = L.AND.M is a *logical* statement. The computer regards the values 0 and 1 as the *logical* values FALSE and TRUE. Therefore the statement must always be preceded by the declaration

LØGICAL L,M,N

Thus the statement N = L.AND.M may be restated as follows: If both L and M are TRUE (1), N is TRUE (1); in all other cases N is FALSE (0).

Numbers to be stored are normally submitted in the decimal form; occasionally they are submitted in the hexadecimal form; but once they are stored, they must be made *logical* in order to undergo a masking operation. The conversion from the numerical mode to the logical mode is a formality demanded by the computer; the string of 0's and 1's in storage remains unchanged. The conversion effect is produced by the LØGICAL declaration.

The procedure of masking is illustrated in Example 12-15.

example 12-15. Write a program that will store the hexadecimal L = 5780AB61 and will create the hexadecimal N by deleting every even digit from L.

We create the mask M by putting 0000 (0 hexadecimal) opposite every half-byte containing an even digit and 1111 (F hexadecimal) opposite every half-byte with an odd digit.

```
        LØGICAL L,M,N
        DATA L,M /Z5780AB61, ZFF000F0F/
        N = L.AND.M
        WRITE(6,1) N
   1    FØRMAT(1H0,Z8)
        STØP
```

Printout:

57000B01

problems

12-1/   Rewrite the program below to produce the same results without type statements. Change the names wherever necessary.

```
        INTEGER A,P
        REAL I
        A = 27.2
        B = 4.5
        I = 46
        J = 2
        P = - 5.75
        D = I*B
```

```
            L = J − P
            M = A*J
            WRITE(6,1)D,L,M
          1 FØRMAT(1X,F6.1,2I5)
            STØP
```

12-2/ A store's daily sales of cases of soft drinks are shown, for one week, in the table below:

Coca-Cola	Seven-Up	Dr. Pepper	Pepsi-Cola
67	39	20	58
50	35	22	62
58	40	20	60
70	36	24	64
66	32	21	57
70	30	25	63
40	10	15	30

Write a program that will print the number of cases of each drink, and also the total number of cases, sold during the week.

For easier identification, assign to storage locations the names of the drinks, modified as little as possible.

12-3/ If M is nearly equal to N, then $\sqrt{MN}$ is approximately equal to

$$\frac{M + N}{2}$$

Write a program that will reproduce the table below and fill the blank columns with values (with 5 decimal digits).

M	N	SQRT(MN)	(M+N)/2	(M+N)/2/SQRT(MN)
2.060	2.490			
10.310	10.124			
6.723	6.921			
6.379	6.921			

Use M and N in writing the program, and precede their use with a REAL type declaration.

12-4/ The value of π can be established from the relation

$$\frac{\pi^2}{6} = 1 + \frac{1}{2^2} + \frac{1}{3^2} + \frac{1}{4^2} + \cdots$$

The accuracy of the result depends on the length of the series used in the summation.

Write a program that will evaluate π in double precision. Select your own cut-off point; or try two different cut-off points for comparison.

Arrange the printout in the following form:

NØ. OF TERM	VALUE ØF TERM	SUM
1	. . .	. . .
. .	. . .	. . .

$$PI_\wedge =$$

12-5/ A bank pays compound interest on a deposited SUM of money at RATE percent per year. The year is divided into CI compounding intervals, so that the rate per interval is RATE/CI.

An expression for the compounded VALUE of the SUM at the end of NI compounding intervals is:

$$VALUE = SUM \; (1 + \frac{RATE}{100 \; (CI)})^{NI}$$

(See Problem 8-11)

Write a general program that will produce a tabulation of the compounded values of any sum corresponding to any rate of interest at the end of every consecutive compounding interval during the time that the sum is on deposit. To make the computation possible, submit as data the following values:

SUM = 100.00   RATE = 6.
CI   = 365.   NI   = 501

Use the flow chart on the right as a guide in writing the program.

To make the tabulated values accurate for large sums, such as $1,000,000., have the computer print the values with 8 decimal places; this will require operations in double precision.

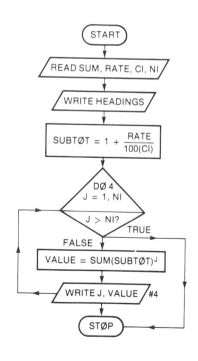

The results are to appear in the following form:

DAILY VALUES OF 100.00 COMPOUNDED DAILY

AT THE RATE OF 6.00 PER CENT PER YEAR

DAY	VALUE, $	DAY	VALUE, $	DAY	VALUE, $
1	?	2	?	3	?
4	?	5	?	. . .	. . .

12-6/   Given the following three forces:

Force, lb.	Counterclockwise angle from the +X axis, deg.
65	60
120	220
92	310

write a program to find their resultant and its angle from the +X axis.

12-7/   The resultant of two forces, P and Q, is R. If R, inclined 45 deg. clockwise from the +X axis, is 50 lb, and P, inclined 60 deg. counterclockwise from the +X axis, is 80 lb, write a program to find the magnitude and inclination of Q.

12-8/   Write a program to find the roots of the following quadratic equations:

(a) $3.5x^2 - 6.1x + 12.0 = 0$
(b) $x^2 + 7x + 3.2 = 0$
(c) $4.5x^2 - 16.4 = 0$
(d) $3.2x^2 + 6.9x = 0$
(e) $2.2x^2 - (2.5 + i)x + 9.2 = 0$
(f) $x^2 + 7.2x - 2.4 + 4.2i = 0$
(g) $(2 - 4.7i)x^2 - 3.4x + 6.2 = 0$

12-9/   The values of x and y in the two simultaneous equations

$$ax + by = e$$
$$cx + dy = f$$

are given by the Cramer's expressions:

$$x = \frac{de - bf}{ad - bc}$$

$$y = \frac{af - ce}{ad - bc}$$

Write a program that will produce the values of x and y corresponding to the following three sets of values:

Set	a	b	c	d	e	f
1	2	$5 - i$	$4 - 2i$	3	7	$2 + i$
2	i	-4	$-3i$	5	2	6
3	$2 + 3i$	3	4	-i	$-4 + 2i$	2

12-10/ The following six sketches show pipe systems with valves. Water will flow out at the right end only if one or more valves are open. For each sketch write a logical assignment statement, such as

$$FL\emptyset W = A.AND.(B.\emptyset R.C)$$

which will describe the conditions necessary for the flow of water to occur. The meaning of the statement above is that FL∅W will be .TRUE. (water will flow) if A is .TRUE. (valve A is open) and either B or C is .TRUE..

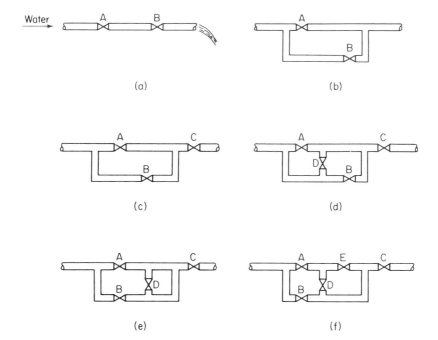

If valves are compared in groups against other valves or groups of valves, enclose the specific groups in parentheses for clearness.

Write a program for the case (d) to determine the values of FLØW (.TRUE. or .FALSE.) corresponding to the following sets of data:

SET	A	B	C	D
1	F	F	T	T
2	T	T	F	F
3	F	T	T	T

12-11/ Write the program of Problem 12-6, using a subroutine to evaluate the force components.

This means that SIN and CØS must be included among the arguments passed to the subroutine and must be listed in the EXTERNAL statement.

12-12/ Write a program that will store a two-dimensional array, A, of logical elements, T and F, count the T elements, and print the number of the T elements and the array itself.

Make the program general for all arrays not exceeding the 35x35 size.

The data card for a specific array should show its dimensions and all its elements.

Use the L format to input/output the elements.

To count the T elements use the sequence:

$$K = 0$$

$$IF\ (A(I,J))\ K = K + 1$$

where K = K + 1 will be executed only if A(I,J) is TRUE.

12-13/ Write a program which will generate, in double precision, the factorials of all consecutive real numbers from 1 to 23.

Compare the results with the factorials in the table shown on the right (see the footnote in Article 11-3).

Factorial $n!$ of n

$$n! = 1 \cdot 2 \cdot 3 \cdot \ldots \cdot n$$

n	$n!$
0	1 (by definition)
1	1
2	2
3	6
4	24
5	120
6	720
7	5,040
8	40,320
9	362,880
10	3,628,800
11	39,916,800
12	479,001,600
13	6,227,020,800
14	87,178,291,200
15	1,307,674,368,000
16	20,922,789,888,000
17	355,687,428,096,000
18	6,402,373,705,728,000
19	121,645,100,408,832,000
20	2,432,902,008,176,640,000
21	51,090,942,171,709,440,000
22	1,124,000,727,777,937,680,000
23	25,852,016,738,892,566,840,000

12-14/ Write a program that will pack 100,500, and 900 into one storage location and print the original values and the packed value in the hexadecimal form.

12-15/ Write a program that will unpack 24680BDF, consecutively, from the first three half-bytes, the next three half-bytes, and the last two half-bytes, and print the unpacked values in the hexadecimal and integer forms.

12-16/ Write a program that will store the hexadecimal 5780AB61 and will delete every odd digit.

appendix a

the ibm 29
card punch

A-1. introduction

A punched card is the most familiar means for entering information into a computer. A card, known as an IBM, or Hollerith, card (Fig. A-1), is a thin piece of cardboard that has room on it for eighty printed characters in the top row and, below them, for punched holes anywhere in twelve rows and eighty columns.

The IBM 29 Card Punch (or key punch) is a machine that punches information on a card in the form of holes; simultaneously with punching the holes, the machine commonly prints characters at the top of the card that are code related to the punched holes and can be read by the operator of the machine.

There may be one, two, or three holes in a column corresponding to a

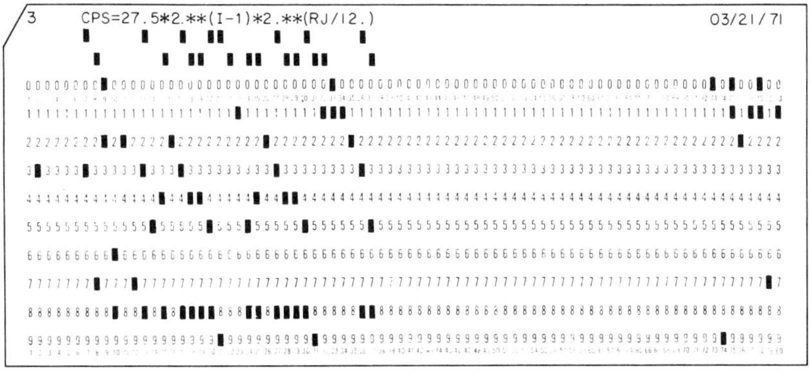

Figure A-1

character at the top. It is not important or necessary to know the code which relates these holes to the character.

A-2. the card punch

The IBM 29 Card Punch is shown in Fig. A-2. It functions much like a typewriter, except that depressions of the keys on the keyboard cause holes to be punched in a card; in addition, if the PRINT switch on the switch panel above the keyboard is ON, key depressions cause characters to be printed above the holes.

The machine is mounted on a desk, with the card processing mechanism on the back half of the desk and the keyboard on the right side of the work space in front. The main line switch for starting the machine is in the knee space under the desk, in the top right corner of the cabinet front.

A-3. the keyboard

The keyboard of the IBM 29 Card Punch is shown in Fig. A-3. In the picture, the keys are numbered, from 1 to 49, above each key.

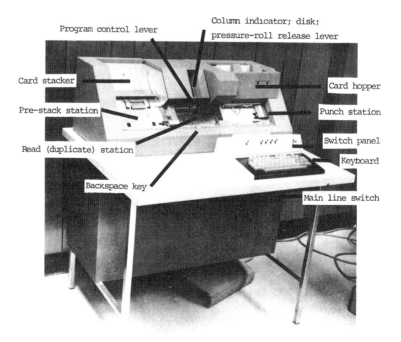

Figure A-2

Figure A-3

This is a combination keyboard: 32 keys on the board combine two characters; for example, K and 5 are combined on key #33 and , (comma) and 8 on key #45. To operate the dual keys, the keyboard has two shifts or positions: the ALPHA or normal shift and the NUMERIC shift. The lower characters on the keys are punched from the ALPHA shift and the upper characters from the NUMERIC shift. The keyboard is normally in the ALPHA shift: Depressing a character key—alone—produces a punch of the lower character shown on the key; thus depressing key #33 produces a punch (and print) of K. To obtain the upper character, the keyboard must be placed in the NUMERIC shift by depressing the NUMERIC key (#37) before depressing the character key; thus depressing, first, the NUMERIC key and, then, key #33 produces a punch of 5. The NUMERIC key cannot be locked in position; it must be held down to produce a string of upper characters.

The keyboard has several special characteristics that should be noted:

1/ The alphabetic characters are printed in *capital* letters; there are no small letters.

2/ Keys #26 and #38 have only one character each, A and Z; these characters are punched and printed when the keyboard is in the normal (ALPHA) shift; if the keyboard is in the NUMERIC shift, depressing the A and Z keys causes the keyboard to lock up.

3/ The locked keyboard is unlocked by pressing the ERROR RESET key (#13).

4/ The minus sign is in both the lower and the upper positions on key #8 (not in the upper position on key #30).

5/ The numerals 0 (zero) and 1 are in the upper positions on keys #9 and #20; the lower character on key #22 is O (oh), and the lower character on key #21 is I; the upper character on key #19 *is not* 1 (one).

A-4. the switch panel

There are six switches on the panel above the keyboard (Fig. A-3). The purpose and use of three of these switches—AUTO FEED, PRINT, and CLEAR—will be explained further on in this discussion. The other three switches have special functions that will not be gone into here; they should be set or ignored as follows:

> AUTO SKIP DUP (auto skip/duplicate): OFF (down)
> PROG SEL (program selection): ignore
> LZ PRINT (left-zero print): ON (up).

A-5. the card processing mechanism

In the normal course of operation, a card occupies five successive positions in the machine: (1) the *card hopper* at the upper right of the machine, (2) the *punch station* below the hopper, (3) the *read* (or *duplicate*) *station* to the left of the punch station (in the middle of the machine), (4) the *prestack station* to the left of the read station, and (5) the *card stacker* above the prestack station.

The card hopper can hold up to 500 blank cards. If, prior to punching, it is observed that the hopper is empty or nearly empty, a package of cards sufficient for the job at hand should be placed in the hopper between the pressure plate, which can be pulled back, and the front of the hopper. The cards are placed in the hopper with the 9-edge down, their face forward, and all edges even. The cards are fed from the hopper to the punch station below it by pressing the FEED key (#24) on the keyboard.

A card fed down to the punch station occupies initially the *preregister* position; in this position it cannot be punched. To allow punching, the card must be *registered;* this is done by pressing either the *register* (REG) key (#36) on the keyboard or the FEED key for the second time; in the latter case a second card will drop from the hopper into the preregister position behind the first card.

The registering operation moves the first card slightly to the left and places it in position for punching a character in Column 1 on the card. This column, or any other column that is to be punched, is always indicated by the red *pointer* (or *column indicator*) located opposite a numbered disk inside the cover above the read station; the disk is numbered from 1 to 80, one number for each column on the card. If it is desired to skip a number of columns on the card, that is, to leave them unpunched, the long space bar (#49) in front of the keyboard is depressed, moving the card to the left until the desired column is in the punching position, as shown on the disk by the red pointer. If the card moves too far to the left, it can be brought back to the correct position for punching by means of the *backspace key* located just below the read station.

After the card has been punched, the procedure depends on whether this is the only card being punched or whether it is being followed by other cards. In the former case it is only necessary to raise the CLEAR switch at the right end of the switch panel. The card will advance without stopping through the read and prestack stations and will be lifted into the card stacker. If, on the other hand, the card is followed by another card at the punch station, raising the CLEAR switch will send both cards into the stacker. Therefore, in the latter case, the CLEAR switch should not be used; instead, the *release* (REL) key (#11) should be pressed.

Pressing the REL key has two different effects, depending on the position of the AUTO FEED switch on the switch panel. If the AUTO FEED switch is down, and there are two cards at the punch station, pressing the REL key will simply advance the first card to the read station; it will not register either the first card at the read station or the second card at the punch station, and it will not bring the third card down from the hopper; these three latter effects are produced by pressing the FEED key after pressing the REL key. If the AUTO FEED switch is up, pressing the REL key will produce simultaneously the combined effects of depressing the REL and FEED keys described above.

As stated earlier, characters corresponding to the holes punched in the card are printed along the top edge of the card if the PRINT switch on the switch panel is in the ON position. If the PRINT switch is down, the characters are suppressed.

A-6. duplication

A card to be duplicated (known as the *master card*) must be stationed at the read (duplication) station; a blank card which is to become a duplicate of the master card must be located at the punch station.

Normally, the blank card is fed to the punch station from the hopper by pressing the FEED key, and the master card is inserted at the read station manually. In manual insertion the card is held in the right hand by its right edge, its left edge is inserted from the right between the feed rolls near the middle of the station, and the card is pushed in until it stops against the left end of the station. With the blank and the master cards in place, before the duplication can begin, both cards must be registered by pressing the REG key once.

The purpose of duplication may be (1) to produce an exact replica of the master card, or (2) to produce a card on which one or more characters differ from those on the master card (usually to correct errors on the mispunched master card). The two objectives are gained most efficiently with the proper setting of the two-wing grey lever (program control lever), which is located just below the cover on the red column indicator. If the *left wing* of the lever is pressed down, a single touch of the *duplicate* (DUP) key (#7) causes the master and the blank cards to move synchronously across their stations, the blank card to be punched automatically with holes identical with those on the master card, and both cards to be lifted into the stacker.

If the *right wing* of the lever is pressed down, pressing the DUP key causes duplication to occur only as long as the DUP key is held down. Therefore, if the object of the duplication is to correct errors on the master card, the DUP key is released when the red indicator points at the column containing the wrong character; then the correct key is pressed, and the duplication of the correct information is resumed until the next wrong character is encountered.

The newly punched card becomes the master card, and the original (incorrect) card is discarded.

A-7. jammed cards

If a card jams under the post between the punch and read stations (or, more rarely, under the post to the left of it), do not assault the machine or the card.

If a part of the card extends to the left of the post, tear off the extension along the post; next, open the center cover on the red pointer (from the back) and press the shiny pressure-roll release lever in the lower right corner; then grasp the right edge of the jammed card and pull to the right.

If the card does not move easily, press all the numeric keys, then, holding down the shiny lever, pull on the card again.

If the card tears, hold the shiny lever down and push the torn pieces from under the post with a smooth-edge metal blade or with a strip of another card cut or torn lengthwise.

If nothing works, leave an "out of order" note on the machine and report the trouble to the clerk on duty.

A-8. punching cards without the automatic card feed

step-by-step procedure with five cards

1/ Make sure that there is a sufficient supply of blank cards in the card hopper; then start the machine by turning up the main line switch.

2/ On the switch panel above the keyboard turn the PRINT switch ON; this will cause characters to be printed at the top edge of the card as the holes are punched on the card; if the AUTO FEED switch is ON, turn it down.

3/ Press the FEED key; this will bring Card 1 from the hopper to the punch station.

4/ Press the FEED key the second time; this will bring Card 2 from the hopper to the punch station (behind Card 1) and will register Card 1 for punching.

5/ Punch Card 1; to punch the upper characters shown on the keys, depress the NUMERIC key on the left of the keyboard before depressing the character key; to space between characters and words, depress the long space bar in front of the keyboard.

6/ Press the REL (release) key; this will advance Card 1 to the read station in the middle.

7/ Press the FEED key; this will bring Card 3 down behind Card 2 in the punch station and will register automatically Card 1 for duplication (if necessary) and Card 2 for punching.

8/ Punch Card 2.

9/ Press the REL key; this will advance Card 1 to the prestack station, and Card 2 to the read station.

10/ Press the FEED key; this will send Card 1 to the stacker, will register Cards 2 and 3 for duplicating and punching, and will bring Card 4 down behind Card 3.

11/ Punch Card 3.

12/ Press the REL key; this will advance Card 2 to the prestack station and Card 3 to the read station.

13/ Press the FEED key; this will send Card 2 to the stacker, will register Cards 3 and 4, and will bring Card 5 behind Card 4.

14/ Punch Card 4.

15/ Press the REL key; this will advance Card 3 to the prestack station and Card 4 to the read station.

16/ Press the REG (register) key; this will register Cards 4 and 5, but will not bring down another card from the hopper.

17/ Punch Card 5.

18/ Turn the CLEAR switch ON; this will advance Cards 3, 4, and 5 to the stacker and clear the machine.

19/ Turn down the main line switch to stop the machine.

With more than five cards to punch *after Step 15,* repeat Steps 13-15 until Step 13 brings down to the punch station the last card to be punched; then finish with Steps 14-19.

To put it another way, after the last card has been brought to the punch station by the FEED key, and the preceding card has been punched and released, press the REG key instead of the FEED key, punch the last card, clear the machine, and stop.

A-9. punching cards with the automatic card feed

step-by-step procedure with five cards

1/ Make sure that there is a sufficient supply of blank cards in the card hopper, then start the machine by turning up the main line switch.

2/ On the switch panel above the keyboard turn both the PRINT switch and the AUTO FEED switch ON.

3/ Press the FEED key; this will bring Card 1 from the hopper to the punch station.

4/ Press the FEED key the second time; this will bring Card 2 from the hopper to the punch station (behind Card 1) and will register Card 1 for punching.

5/ Punch Card 1.

6/ Press the REL (release) key; this will advance Card 1 to the read station in the middle, will bring Card 3 down behind Card 2 in the punch station and will register automatically Card 1 for duplication (if necessary) and Card 2 for punching.

7/ Punch Card 2.

8/ Press the REL key; this will send Card 1 to the stacker and Card 2 to the read station, will register Cards 2 and 3 for duplicating and punching, and will bring Card 4 down behind Card 3.

9/ Punch Card 3.

10/ Press the REL key; this will send Card 2 to the stacker and Card 3 to the read station, will register Cards 3 and 4, and will bring Card 5 behind Card 4.

11/ Turn down the AUTO FEED switch.

12/ Punch Card 4.

13/ Press the REL key; this will send Card 3 to the prestack station and Card 4 to the read station; Card 5 will remain where it was.

14/ Press the REG (register) key; this will send Card 3 to the stacker and will register Cards 4 and 5, but will not bring down another card from the hopper.

15/ Punch Card 5.

16/ Turn the CLEAR switch ON; this will advance Cards 4 and 5 to the stacker and clear the machine.

17/ Turn down the main line switch to stop the machine.

With more than five cards to punch, *after Step 10*, repeat Steps 9-10 until Step 10 brings down to the punch station the last card to be punched; then finish with Steps 11-17.

A-10. duplication (with corrections)

step-by-step procedure

1/ Make sure that there are blank cards in the card hopper and that the right wing of the grey lever is down; then start the machine by turning up the main line switch.

2/ On the switch panel above the keyboard turn the PRINT switch ON and the AUTO SWITCH down.

3/ Press the FEED key; this will bring a blank card from the hopper to the punch station.

4/ Insert the card to be duplicated (the master card) at the read station.

5/ Press the REG key; this will register both cards.

6/ Press and hold the DUP (duplicate) key; this will duplicate the master card on the blank card.

7/ If the master card has errors, release the DUP key at the points of errors (watch the red pointer) and punch the correct characters; re-press the DUP key to duplicate between errors.

8/ Upon completing the duplication, turn the CLEAR switch ON; this will advance the two cards to the stacker and clear the machine.

9/ Discard the card with errors.

10/ Turn down the main line switch to stop the machine.

appendix b

significant figures

Physical quantities, be they lengths, weights, or pressures, are measured by various instruments, each of which has a scale with divisions. The digits that are read and estimated on a scale are called *significant figures;* these include all the certain digits and *one* additional doubtful digit based on the observer's estimate of a fractional part of the smallest scale subdivision. For example, let the length of an object be measured with a rule whose smallest subdivision is 1 cm (Fig. B-1). Since the right end of the object falls between the 10- and 11-cm marks, we are sure of the number of whole centimeters in the length of the object (10 marked on the scale), but we are doubtful of the digit that represents the fractional part of the centimeter that extends to the end of the object.

Figure B-1

A reasonable estimate is that the object's end lies at a distance of 0.6 cm beyond the 10 cm mark. Therefore, the length of the object, to three significant figures, is 10.6 cm; of these three figures the first two are certain, and the third one is doubtful. The rule to remember is that the digit preceding the doubtful digit represents the smallest subdivision of the scale (1 cm). Were the observer to record this reading as 10.58, he would convey an impression that his scale was divided into tenths of a centimeter; and that the object's end lay between the 10.5- and 10.6-cm marks.

A question arises: If the object's end lay exactly at the 10-cm mark, would the correct record of the reading be 10 cm or 10.0 cm? The correct answer is

10.0 cm, because it conveys the information that the smallest subdivision is a centimeter, and that the dimension is closer to 10.0 than to 9.9 or 10.1, just as 10.6 above was a closer reading than 10.5 or 10.7. To write just 10 would imply that the scale is divided into units 10 cm long, and that the length of the object is closer to 10 than to 9 or 11, whose positions might be estimated on such a scale.

The number of significant figures in a measurement can be ascertained by the use of the following rules:

1/ All digits between, and including, the leftmost and the rightmost *nonzero* digits are significant figures.

examples.

$$29.04 = \text{four significant figures}$$
$$32 = \text{two significant figures}$$
$$0.000204 = \text{three significant figures}$$

In the last example the zeros to the left of 2 are not significant; the information this number conveys is that the measurement is closer to 204 millionths than to 203 or 205 millionths. (The dial must have markings of 190, 200, 210 millionths, corresponding to a unit division of 10 millionths.

2/ Zeros to the right of the decimal point are significant only if they are preceded on the left by nonzero digits to the left or right of the decimal point; in the former case zeros to the left of the decimal point are also significant.

examples.

$$10.0 = \text{three significant figures}$$
$$10.00 = \text{four significant figures}$$

In the second example, the rightmost 0 is the doubtful significant figure; it shows that the measurement is closer to 10.00 than to 9.99 or 10.01.

$$0.0002040 = \text{four significant figures}$$

The measurement is closer to 2040 than to 2039 or 2041 ten-mil-lionths.

$$3200.060 = \text{seven significant figures}$$

3/ In integral numbers, zeros to the right of nonzero digits are significant only if specially indicated.

$$3200 = \text{two significant figures}$$

It is not indicated that this number is anything but a rounded-off measurement closer to 3200 than to 3100 or 3300; the unit division is 1000; the doubtful digit is 2; the zeros are not significant; the number may be written 3200 ± 50.

$$3200 \pm 5 = \text{three significant figures}$$

This measurement is closer to 3200 than to 3190 or 3210; the unit division is 100; the doubtful digit is the left zero and is, therefore, significant.

$$3200 \pm 0.5 = \text{four significant figures}$$

Both zeros are significant.

appendix c

number systems

C-1.   introduction

A *number system* is a system of representing a quantity by means of a limited number of *digits,* the digits being written in a string and each digit in the string *weighted* in accordance with its *position.*

The system most familiar to us is the *decimal* system, which employs ten digits, from 0 to 9. A typical number in this system is 20795.46 .

In the decimal system, the two digits, 2 and 4, written 24, represent twenty-four units; that is, 4 in the first position (counting from the right) represents four units, and 2 in the second position represents $2 \times 10 =$ twenty units. If 2 and 4 exchange their positions, becoming 42, the number represents forty-two units, because 4 in the second position represents $4 \times 10 =$ forty units.

In Chapter 3 it is shown that a typical computer memory consists of iron rings which can be magnetized to represent either 0 or 1. The other eight digits of the decimal system cannot be represented by individual iron rings, and therefore numbers written in the decimal system cannot be stored in a typical computer memory directly. Thus the decimal system is not compatible with the design and construction of computers.

The number system that is singularly suitable to computers is the *binary* system. This system has only two digits, 0 and 1; a typical number in this system is 11101.001 .

The third number system which we encounter in dealing with computers is the *hexadecimal* system, which has 16 digits, 0, 1, 2, . . . , 8, 9, A, B, C, D, E, F; a typical number in this system is 4A0.E5 . The Central Processing Unit (CPU) of the IBM System/360 performs all its operations in the hexadecimal system.

The three number systems described above have three things in common: they have a *base* or *radix*, they have *digits*, and they rely on *positional representation* to express the magnitude of a quantity. These concepts, the systems themselves, and their relationships to one another are described in the following sections.

C-2. the decimal system

When we see a number such as 245, we normally say, "two hundred and forty-five." Speaking in this manner we employ the concept of the positional representation: we assign to 2 (in position 3 from the right) the positional weight of 100 (or 10^2), to 4 (in position 2) the positional weight of 10 (or 10^1), and to 5 (in position 1) the positional weight of 1 (or 10^0). Note that the powers of 10 are 1 less than the position. If the digits are rearranged to form 524, we say "five hundred and twenty-four," assigning the weight of 100 to 5, of 10 to 2, and of 1 to 4.

The number 10, raised to various powers and forming the positional weights of digits, is called the *base* or *radix* of the decimal system.

The *digits* of the decimal system are 0, 1, 2, 3, 4, 5, 6, 7, 8, and 9. The maximum digit, 9, is 1 less than the base, 10. There is no need for a digit, such as X in the Roman system, to represent ten, because in the decimal system ten is written 10, where 1 in position 2 does represent ten.

A decimal number may be displayed on an *abacus* built as an image of the decimal system. An abacus is a device consisting of beads strung on wires held in a frame. Fig. C-1(A) shows a *decimal abacus;* it has six wires,* with nine beads on each wire. The consecutive beads on a wire are marked 1 to 9 on the left of the abacus. When n beads are shifted toward the near side of the abacus (the bottom of the figure), they represent the digit n in the decimal system. The absence of beads on the near side represents 0.

As described briefly in the first paragraph of this section, the magnitude of a number is obtained by multiplying the consecutive digits of the number by the values, or weights, associated with the positions of the digits. The scheme for assigning the values is shown in Fig. C-1(A), where the wires of the abacus correspond to the digit positions, P, of a number. The positions, beginning with the rightmost digit and wire and proceeding to the left, are shown in the top line of the figure. The second line shows the base 10 raised to the power of P-1, and the third line shows the numbers equivalent to the powers of the

---

* The range or capacity of an abacus can be extended indefinitely by increasing the number of wires.

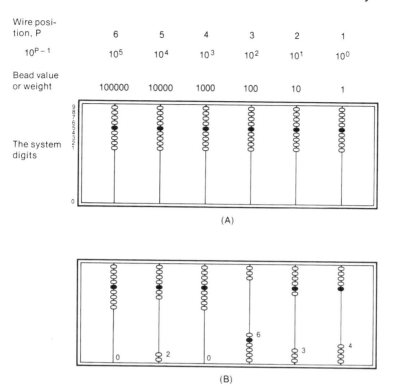

Figure C-1. The decimal abacus

base. These numbers are the values, or weights, of the digits and beads in those positions. Thus the magnitude of the number shown in Fig. C-1(B) is

$$0\times100000 + 2\times10000 + 0\times1000 + 6\times100 + 3\times10$$
$$+ 4\times1 = 20000 + 600 + 30 + 4 = 20634.$$

This number can be read easily on the abacus by counting the beads on the near side of the abacus and paying strict attention to their weights shown at the top of the figure.

Obviously enough, Fig. C-1(A) shows the number 000000, whose magnitude is 0.

It can be seen that the largest number that can be displayed on the abacus of Fig. C-1 is $999999 = 10^6 - 1$.

It should be noted that the number of beads on a wire is one less than the base of the system.

C-3. the binary system

The next number system to be considered is the *binary system*, with the base 2 (the Latin word for 2 is *binarius*). The binary system forms the basis of construction of most digital computers. The abacus which illustrates the binary system is shown in Fig. C-2. There is only one bead on each wire of this abacus; this is consistent with the observation made in the last paragraph of the preceding section, namely, that the number of beads on a wire is one less than the base of the system. The single bead on a wire can represent only two quantities, 0 and 1, depending on the position of the bead on the wire. Thus the binary system has only two digits, 0 and 1. They are called *binary digits*, or *bits*.

As in Fig. C-1(A), Fig. C-2(A) shows, on the three lines above it, the positions of the wires and digits, the powers of the base 2, and the numbers equivalent to these powers. These numbers are the values, or weights, of the digits and beads in those positions in the binary system. Thus the number displayed as 110011 in Fig. C-2(B) has the magnitude given by the expression

$$1\times32 + 1\times16 + 0\times8 + 0\times4 + 1\times2 + 1\times1 = 32 + 16 + 2 + 1 = 51$$

The number 000000 displayed in Fig. C-2(A) has the magnitude 0.

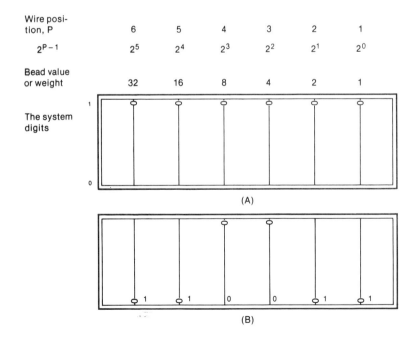

Figure C-2. The binary abacus

The largest number that can be shown on the abacus of Fig. C-2 is 111111. Converted to the decimal notation, this number is

$$1 \times 32 + 1 \times 16 + 1 \times 8 + 1 \times 4 + 1 \times 2 + 1 \times 1 = 63 = 2^6 - 1$$

Fractions can be expressed in the binary system by using the negative powers of 2. We know that whole numbers end at position $P = 1$, corresponding to 2^0. If we separate the whole part of the number from its fraction by the *binary point* (analogous to the decimal point), we can denote positions to the right of the binary point by -1, -2, etc., as shown in Table C-1, assign the corresponding powers of 2, 2^{-1}, 2^{-2}, etc., to the positions, and thus establish the values or weights of those positions.

Thus a binary 1 in position -1 represents 0.5; 1 in position -2 represents 0.25, etc. The binary number $0.1101 = 0.5 + 0.25 + 0.0625 = 0.8125$ in the decimal system.

Table C-1

Position, P, to the right of the binary point	-1	-2	-3	-4
2^P	2^{-1}	2^{-2}	2^{-3}	2^{-4}
Position value or weight	0.5	0.25	0.125	0.0625

It can be seen from Table C-1 that a decimal such as 0.3 cannot be expressed exactly in the binary form because 0.3 cannot be made up of any summation of the negative powers of 2. The latter all end with the rightmost digit of 5, successively one position farther to the right, and therefore any summation of terms will have an outermost 5 dangling at the end; but, by lengthening the string of 1's and 0's, a close approximation can be obtained.

A real number is said to be *normalized* when, its value remaining unchanged, it is represented as the product of a power of the base and a *fraction*, or *mantissa*, the fraction beginning with a nonzero digit after the point. Thus, in the decimal system, 12.39 is normalized to $10^2 \times 0.1239$, by moving the decimal point of 12.39 two places to the left, creating the fraction or mantissa 0.1239, and then multiplying the mantissa by 10^2, where the power of 10 is equal to the *number of places* the point has moved to the left. If the point moves to the right, the power is negative; thus 0.000427 is normalized to $10^{-3} \times 0.427$.

A binary number is normalized by substituting the base 2 for the base 10. Thus 111.01 is normalized to $2^3 \times 0.11101$, and 0.001101 is normalized to $2^{-2} \times 0.1101$.

C-4. binary arithmetic

addition

Before tackling the binary addition, let us review the decimal addition.

In the decimal system the base is 10. Therefore the addition of several decimal numbers is carried out as follows:

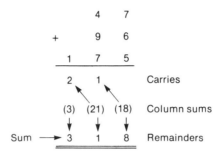

We add the digits in the first column on the right, obtain 18, divide 18 by the base 10, obtaining the whole quotient, 1, and the remainder, 8, write 8 under the first column and carry the quotient 1 to the second column (which has the position weight of 10 relative to the preceding column); add the digits and the carried 1 in the second column, obtain 21, divide 21 by 10, obtaining 2 as the whole quotient and 1 as the remainder, write 1 under the second column and carry 2 to the third column; then add all the digits in the third column and write the sum, 3, underneath.

Another example:

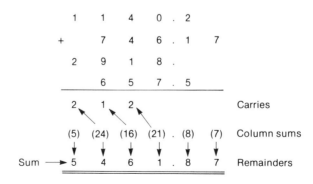

The base of the binary system is 2. Therefore when the sum of digits in a binary column equals or exceeds 2, we divide the sum by the base 2, write the remainder, 0 or 1, under the column, and carry the whole quotient to the next column on the left, repeating the process from column to column, as shown in the following examples.

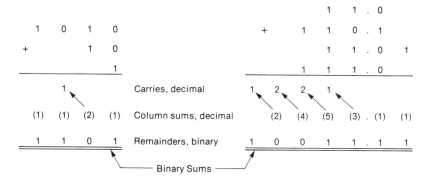

										1	1 . 0		
1	0	1	0			+		1	1	0 . 1		
+		1	0					1	1 . 0	1		
			1					1	1	1 . 0		

	Carries, decimal	Column sums, decimal	Remainders, binary
(addition example 1)			

Carries, decimal

(1) (1) (2) (1) Column sums, decimal (2) (4) (5) (3) . (1) (1)

1 1 0 1   Remainders, binary   1 0 0 1 1 . 1 1

Binary Sums

subtraction

Subtraction involves only two numbers. Subtracting 0 from 1 gives 1 and subtracting 1 from 1 gives 0. To subtract 1 from 0, it is necessary to borrow from the column(s) on the left. Since the base is 2, 1 unit borrowed from any column provides 2 units for the column on its right (just as 1 unit borrowed in the decimal system provides 10 units for the column on its right). Obviously, a borrow from a column reduces the count in that column by 1. The following examples illustrate the subtraction of binary numbers. The 1's from which borrows of 2 are made are circled to indicate that these 1's have become 0's.

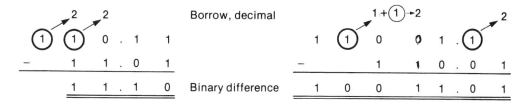

Borrow, decimal

Binary difference

multiplication

Multiplication is simple because, all digits being either 0 or 1, the process is reduced to writing the multiplicand once for every 1 in the multiplier, and then adding all the numbers below the multiplier, as shown in the examples below.

		1	0	0	1
×			1	0	1
		1	0	0	1
1	0	0	1		
1	0	1	1	0	1

			1	0	1	1
	×		1	0	1	1
			1	0	1	1
		1	0	1	1	
	1	0	1	1		
1	0	1	1			
1	1	1	1	0	0 . 1	

division

Division is carried out by subtracting the divisor from the dividend, once for every 1 in the quotient, as shown in the following examples.

```
Divisor        1111← Quotient   Divisor           10 0.01← Quotient
  └→1000 |1111000                 └→110.1,  |11011.1,01
          1000                               1101
          1110                               1 1 01
          1000                               1 1 01
           1100
           1000
            1000
            1000
```

In the second example, the comma (,) marks the shift of the binary point to make the divisor a whole number.

C-5. conversion between the decimal and binary systems

conversion of a decimal number to a binary number

Read the following instructions together with the conversion of 45.64 in Example C-1.

For tabulating the calculations, form a cross on the paper by drawing a horizontal line across the page and a short vertical line near its middle.

Write the decimal number above the horizontal line in two parts, the integer part (45) immediately to the left of the vertical line and the fraction part (.64) immediately to the right of it.

Integer Conversion

1. Divide the integer (45) by 2, obtaining the first quotient (22) and the first remainder (1); write the quotient (22) to the left of the integer and the remainder (1) below the integer, in the first binary position to the left of the vertical line; mark the binary point on the vertical line.

Fraction Conversion

1. Multiply the (first) fraction (.64) by 2, obtaining the first product (1.28); write the integer part of the product (1) below the first fraction in the first binary position to the right of the vertical line; write the fraction part of the first product (the second fraction, .28) to the right of the first fraction.

Integer Conversion

2. Divide the first quotient (22) by 2, obtaining the second quotient (11) and the second remainder (0); write the second quotient to the left of the first quotient and the second remainder below the first quotient, in the second binary position.

3. Repeat the process of dividing consecutive quotients by 2 and writing down the resulting quotients and remainders, moving left in the table; do this until the quotient has become 1.

4. When a quotient has become 1, it is also the last remainder of the division by 2 (with a 0 quotient); write 1 below the last quotient (1), and stop; the line of the remainders (101101) is the integer part of the binary number.

Fraction Conversion

2. Multiply the second fraction (.28) by 2, obtaining the second product (0.56); write the integer part of the product (0) below the second fraction, in the second binary position, and the fraction part of the product (the third fraction, .56) to the right of the second fraction.

3. Repeat the process of multiplying the consecutive fractions by 2 and writing down the resulting integers and fractions, moving right in the table. Do this until the fraction of a product becomes .0, or the product itself becomes 1 or close to 1.

4. When a fraction has become .0, or the product has become 1 or close to 1, write 1 below the product, and stop; the line of digits to the right of the binary point (.101001) is the binary fraction. It is exact if the last fraction is .0, and approximate if it is not.

example C-1.   Convert 45.64 to the binary form.

Quotients/2					Integer/2	Fraction*2	Fractions*2				
1/2	2/2	5/2	11/2	22/2	45/2	.64*2	.28*2	.56*2	.12*2	.24*2	.48*2
$=0\frac{1}{2}$	=1	$=2\frac{1}{2}$	$=5\frac{1}{2}$	=11	$=22\frac{1}{2}$	=1.28	=0.56	=1.12	=0.24	=0.48	=0.96
1	0	1	1	0	1	1	0	1	0	0	1

Therefore the decimal 45.64 = the binary 101101.101001 (approx.)

With experience, one can simplify the work of conversion as shown below:

1	2	5	11	22	45	.64	.28	.56	.12	.24	.48
1	0	1	1	0	1	1	0	1	0	0	1

conversion of a binary number to a decimal number

Read the following instructions together with the conversion of 101110.1011 in Example C-2.

For tabulating the calculations, draw two vertical lines down the page, to form spaces for three columns of numbers.

1. In the left column write the binary number vertically, with the leftmost digit at the top; include the point.
2. In the second column, opposite each binary 1, write 2 to the power corresponding to the position of the binary 1 in the number; for integer 1's the power is 1 less than the position, counting from the point; for fraction 1's the power is minus the position.
3. In the third column write the decimal equivalents of the powers of 2 in the second column.

4. Add up the values in the third column to obtain the decimal equivalent of the binary number.

example C-2. Convert 101110.1011 to the decimal form.

Binary digit	Corresponding power of 2	Column 2 in decimal form
1	2^5	32
0		
1	2^3	8
1	2^2	4
1	2^1	2
0		
.		
1	2^{-1}	0.5
0		
1	2^{-3}	0.125
1	2^{-4}	0.0625
		Sum = 46.6875

Therefore the binary $101110.1011 =$ the decimal 46.6875.

C-6. the hexadecimal system

The users of the IBM System/360 use the hexadecimal system to avoid writing long binary strings of 0's and 1's.

Like the decimal and the binary systems the hexadecimal system is illustrated by means of the hexadecimal abacus shown in Fig. C-3.

The base of the hexadecimal system is 16. Therefore the number of beads on each wire is 15. We want to identify every one of the 15 beads by a single character, just as the nine beads on the decimal abacus are identified by the individual digits 1-9. We use these nine digits of the decimal system for the first nine beads on a hexadecimal wire; for the remaining six beads, by common usage, we use the first six letters of the alphabet: thus A identifies the 10th bead and becomes the 10th digit of the hexadecimal system, B the 11th, and so on, through F, the 15th. The digits of the hexadecimal system are shown on the left side of the abacus in Fig. C-3(A).

The values of the beads are indicated on the last line above Fig. C-3(A).

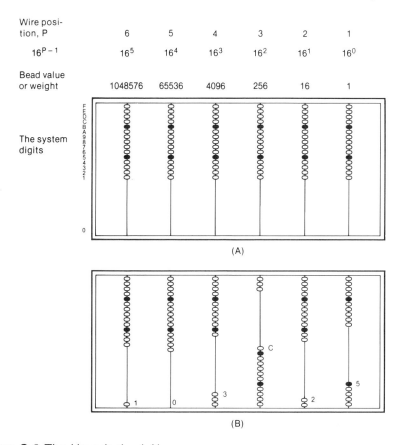

Figure C-3 The Hexadecimal Abacus

Thus the number shown in Fig. C-3(A) is 0., while the number shown in Fig. C-3(B) is:

$$1\times1,048,576 + 3\times4,096 + C\times256 + 2\times16 + 5\times1$$
$$(\overset{\cdot}{=}12)$$
$$= 1,048,576 + 12,288 + 3,072 + 32 + 5 = 1,063,973$$

The largest number that can be displayed on the abacus of Fig. C-3 is FFFFFF. This number is $16^6 - 1 = 16,772,215$.

Hexadecimal numbers are normalized in the manner analogous to that described for the binary numbers in Sec. C-3: the hexadecimal point is shifted n places, and the result is multiplied by 16^n, where n is positive if the shift is to the left. Thus C2.4 is normalized to $0.C24 \times 16^2$, and 0.05A is normalized to $0.5A \times 16^{-1}$.

A hexadecimal number is stored either from a data card or by means of a DATA statement. A hexadecimal number cannot be stored by an assignment statement; for instance, we cannot write:

$$K = AB \quad \text{(where AB is equivalent to the decimal 171)}$$

because the compiler will regard AB as a *variable*, without a value in storage to define it; nor can we write:

$$K = ZAB \quad \text{(where Z is the code for identifying}$$
$$\text{hexadecimal numbers)}$$

because the compiler will refuse to accept the identification and will still interpret ZAB as another undefined variable. However, an assignment statement may be used to copy a hexadecimal number from one storage location into another. For example, if a hexadecimal number is already stored in location A, we may write:

$$P = A$$

and the same number will be stored at P.

The name under which a hexadecimal number is stored may begin with *any letter*, and, regardless of the mode of the name, the number may be output in the hexadecimal, real, or integer form. However, if a hexadecimal number is stored under K, it is incorrect to mix modes and to write an assignment statement such as

$$P = K$$

A hexadecimal number may have any number of digits from 1 to 8: eight is the number of half-bytes in a storage location. Thus a number may be submitted as B1A2 or 00123456. Its storage or its output is effected by means of a Z specification; the specification is Z4 for B1A2 and Z8 for 00123456.

The various input/output operations with the hexadecimal numbers are illustrated in the following examples.

example C-3.

```
      READ(5,1) K
   1  FØRMAT(Z8)
      N = K
      WRITE(6,2) K,K,N,N
   2  FØRMAT(1H0,Z8,I7)
      STØP
```

Data card:

```
0001A025
```

Printout:

0001A025   106533

0001A025   106533

The computer copies the contents of K into N, and then prints the contents of both locations in the original hexadecimal form and in the integer form:

$$1*16^4 + 10*16^3 + 2*16^1 + 5*16^0 = 106533$$

Note the Z specification informing the compiler that the number on the data card is hexadecimal.

example C-4.

```
        DATA A /Z0001A025/
        P = A
        WRITE(6,2) A,A,P,P
    2   FØRMAT(1H0,Z8,E15.6/1H0,Z8,I7)
        STØP
```

Printout:

0001A025   0.054838E-78

0001A025   106533

The contents of A and P are identical with those at K and N in Example C-3. The specification I7 outputs, even from P, the same integer number, 106533, as in Example C-3. However, to satisfy the specification E15.6, the computer converts the number at A into the real number 00.01A025, with the decimal point between the second and third digits, and then calculates it as:

$$16^{-64}(\frac{1}{16^2} + \frac{10}{16^3} + \frac{2}{16^5} + \frac{5}{16^6}) = 0.054838*10^{-78}$$

An explanation of this calculation is given in Article C-13. Note in the DATA statement that Z before the number makes it hexadecimal. Also note that there is no Z on the data card in Example C-3.

example C-5.

```
      READ(5,1) K
  1   FØRMAT(Z8)
      P = K
      WRITE(6,2) K,K,P,P
  2   FØRMAT(1H0,Z8,E15.6/1H0,Z8,I11)
      STØP
```

Data card:

```
/ 0001A025 \
```

Printout:

0001A025   0.054838E-78

451A0250   1159332432

In this example the mixed mode assignment, P = K, introduces an error. The number at K is 0001A025. Assigning it to P makes the computer convert the number to 0001A025., with the point at the end of the number. Then it normalizes the number to $00.1A0250*16^5$, introduces the *bias* of 16^{64}, producing $00.1A0250*16^{69}$, converts 69 into the hexadecimal 45, and ends up with 451A0250, whose integer equivalent is 1159332432.

Again, the explanation of these operations is given in Article C-13. However, do not spend much time or thought on the explanation. Just remember not to mix modes when storing hexadecimal numbers.

C-7.   conversion between the decimal and hexadecimal systems

conversion of a decimal number to a hexadecimal number

Read the instructions below along with the conversion of 2621.95 in Example C-6.

For tabulating the calculations, form a cross on the paper by drawing a horizontal line across the page and a short vertical line near its middle.

Write the decimal number above the horizontal line in two parts, the integer part (2621) immediately to the left of the vertical line and the fraction part (.95) immediately to the right of it.

Integer Conversion

1. Divide the integer (2621) by 16, obtaining the first quotient (163) and the first remainder (13); convert the remainder into a hexadecimal (D); write the quotient (163) to the left of the integer and the remainder (D) below the integer, in the first hexadecimal position to the left of the vertical line; mark the hexadecimal point on the vertical line.

2. Divide the first quotient (163) by 16, obtaining the second quotient (10) and the second remainder (3); write the second quotient to the left of the first quotient and the second remainder below the first quotient, in the second hexadecimal position.

3. Repeat the process of dividing consecutive quotients by 16 and writing down the resulting quotients and remainders, moving left in the table. Do this until a quotient has become 15 or less.

4. When a quotient has become 15 or less (10 in the example), it is also the last remainder of the division by 16 (with a 0 quotient); write it as a hexadecimal (A) below itself, at the head (the left end) of the line of remainders, and stop; the line of the remainders (A3D) is the integer part of the hexadecimal number.

Fraction Conversion

1. Multiply the (first) fraction (.95) by 16, obtaining the first product (15.2); convert the integer part of the product (15) into a hexadecimal (F) and write it below the first fraction, in the first hexadecimal position to the right of the vertical line. Write the fraction part of the first product (the second fraction, .2) to the right of the first fraction.

2. Multiply the second fraction (.2) by 16, obtaining the second product (3.2); write the integer part of the product (3) below the second fraction, in the second hexadecimal position, and the fraction part of the product (the third fraction, .2 again) to the right of the second fraction.

3. Repeat the process of multiplying the consecutive fractions by 16 and writing down the resulting integers and fractions, moving right in the table; do this until the fraction of a product becomes zero or a group of hexadecimal digits (or a single digit) in the lower line begins to repeat itself.

4. When a fraction has become .0, stop; the digits in the lower line to the right of the hexadecimal point are the hexadecimal fraction. If the digits in the lower line begin to repeat, mark the repeating part by dots above it, and stop; the digits to the right of the hexadecimal point (.F$\dot{3}$) are the hexadecimal fraction.

example C-6. convert 2621.95 to the hexadecimal form.

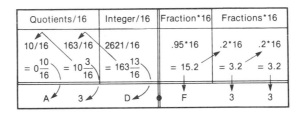

Therefore the decimal $2621.95 =$ the hexadecimal A3D.F$\overset{.}{3}$.
  The work of conversion can be simplified to:

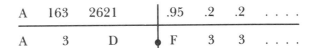

conversion of a hexadecimal number to a decimal number

Read the following instructions together with the conversion of 2E0.A8 in Example C-7.

For tabulating the calculations, draw two vertical lines down the page, to form spaces for three columns of numbers.

1. In the left column write the hexadecimal number vertically, with the leftmost digit at the top; include the point.
2. In the second column, opposite each digit, write 16 to the power corresponding to the position of the digit in the number. For integer digits the power is 1 less than the position, counting from the point. For fraction digits the power is minus the position.
3. In the third column write the decimal product of the digit in the first column and the corresponding power of 16 in the second column ($2*16^2 = 2*256 = 512$).
4. Add up the products in the third column to obtain the decimal equivalent of the hexadecimal number.

example C-7. convert 2E0.A8 to the decimal form.

Hexa-decimal digit	Correspond-ing power of 16	Product of columns 1 and 2
2	16^2	512.
E	16^1	224.
0	16^0	0.
.		
A	16^{-1}	0.625
8	16^{-2}	0.03125
	Sum $= 736.65625$	

Therefore the hexadecimal 2E0.A8
= the decimal 736.65625.

C-8.   conversion between the binary and hexadecimal systems

Table C-2 on the right shows that every hexadecimal digit can be represented by a combination of four binary digits. Therefore, to
convert a binary number to the hexadecimal
form, separate the number into groups of four
digits, proceeding in both directions from the
binary point. Replace each group by the corresponding hexadecimal digit. If an end
group has fewer than four digits, add leading
or trailing zeros to make the count four.

Thus to convert 1101101.1 to the hexadecimal form, write it in four-digit groups,
as follows:

Table C-2

Binary Group	Hexadecimal Digit
0001	1
0010	2
0011	3
0100	4
0101	5
0110	6
0111	7
1000	8
1001	9
1010	A
1011	B
1100	C
1101	D
1110	E
1111	F

$$0110 \quad 1101.1000$$

and replace each group by the corresponding
hexadecimal digit:

$$6 \quad D.8$$

The conversion can be checked by comparing the values of the separate
binary groups with those of the corresponding hexadecimal digits:

First group: Binary:
$1\times2^6 + 1\times2^5 = (2^2+2)2^4 = (4+2)16 = 6(16) = 96$
Hexadecimal: $6\times16^1 = 96$
Second group: Binary: $1\times2^3 + 1\times2^2 + 1\times2^0 = 8+4+1 = 13$
Hexadecimal: $D = 13$
Third group: Binary: $1\times2^{-1} = 1/2 = 0.5$
Hexadecimal: $8\times16^{-1} = 8/16 = 0.5$

Reversing the procedure, we convert the hexadecimal 4A7.06 to the binary
0100 1010 0111.0000 0110, or 10010100111.0000011.

Conversion to the decimal form can be made from either the binary or
hexadecimal form; conversion from the hexadecimal form is by far the simpler
of the two, as is demonstrated in the two examples below.

(a) Binary 0100.0001 = hexadecimal 4.1

Conversion from the binary form:

$$0100.0001 = 1 \times 2^2 + \frac{1}{2^4} = 4 + 0.0625 = 4.0625$$

Conversion from the hexadecimal form:

$$4.1 = 4 \times 16^0 + \frac{1}{16} = 4 + 0.0625 = 4.0625$$

(b)   Binary 1111 1100.0100 1100 = hexadecimal FC.4C

Conversion from the binary form:

$$1111\ 1100.0100\ 1100 = 1 \times 2^7 + 1 \times 2^6 + 1 \times 2^5 + 1 \times 2^4$$
$$+ 1 \times 2^3 + 1 \times 2^2 + \frac{1}{2^2} + \frac{1}{2^5} + \frac{1}{2^6}$$
$$= 128 + 64 + 32 + 16 + 8 + 4 + 0.25 + 0.03125 + 0.015625$$
$$= 252.296875$$

Conversion from the hexadecimal form:

$$FC.4C = 15 \times 16^1 + 12 \times 16^0 + \frac{4}{16^1} + \frac{12}{16^2}$$
$$= 240 + 12 + 0.25 + 0.046875 = 252.296875$$

C-9.   tens and twos complement notation

In the IBM System/360 arithmetic operations on negative integers are performed in the *twos complement* notation. To understand this concept, let us first study the *tens complement* notation, as it is used in the more familiar decimal system.

The tens complement, C_{10}, of any number, N, is given by the equation:

$$C_{10} = 10^d - N$$

where d is the number of digits in N. Examples:

N	d	10^d	10's complement, C_{10}
20	2	100	$100 - 20 = 80$
435	3	1000	$1000 - 435 = 565$
1111	4	10000	$10000 - 1111 = 8889$

To illustrate the use of the 10's complement notation, let us subtract 20 from 57. Commonly we write:

$$\begin{array}{r} 57 \\ -20 \\ \hline 37 \end{array}$$

But $20 = 100 - 80$. Therefore we can also write:

$$\begin{array}{r} 57 \\ -(100 - 80) \\ \hline \end{array}$$ which is the same as: $$\begin{array}{r} 57 \\ -100 + 80 \\ \hline -100 + 137 = 37 \end{array}$$

Thus we obtain the same result, 37, because the carry of +100 (from 137) is canceled by −100, the negative component which makes 80 the 10's complement of 20.

From the equation for C_{10} we have: $N = 10^d - C_{10}$. We can express the operation of subtraction in general terms as follows:

$$\begin{array}{r} M \\ -N \\ \hline \end{array}$$ is the same as $$\begin{array}{r} M \\ -(10^d - C_{10}) \\ \hline \end{array}$$ which is the same as $$\begin{array}{r} M \\ -10^d + C_{10} \\ \hline -10^d + (M + C_{10}) \end{array}$$

Thus we can subtract N from M by converting −N to $-10^d + C_{10}$ and adding it to M.

Let us now carry out the subtraction on a hypothetical calculator which has an accumulator register with two round windows for the numbers entered on the keyboard and a square window on their left which shows whether a number is accompanied by −100 or not. If yes, the square window shows −1; if no, +0. In effect, +0 and −1 in the square window are the indicators that the corresponding numbers, properly interpreted, are, respectively, positive and negative.

When we enter 57 on the keyboard, we see on the accumulator register:

$$\boxed{+0} \quad \circled{5} \;\circled{7}$$

and when we enter −100 + 80 (= −20), we see:

$$\boxed{-1} \quad \circled{8} \;\circled{0}$$

When the add button is pressed, 57 and 80 add up to 137, the carry of 1 (actually $+100$) cancels -1 (actually -100) in the square window, and the result reads:

$$\boxed{+0} \quad ③ \quad ⑦$$

Calculators with square windows for the negative components of the tens complements do not exist. However, some binary computers possess a mechanism which plays the part of the square window. We shall show how this is done by turning to the binary arithmetic.

When a binary computer is instructed to subtract N from M, it first subtracts N from 2^d, where d is the number of digits in N, and obtains the twos complement of N, C_2:

$$C_2 = 2^d - N$$

then it stores $-2^d + C_2 \ (= -N)$ in this form: $\overline{2^d}C_2$, and adds $\overline{2^d}C_2$ to M because

$$M + (\overline{2^d}C_2) = M + (-2^d) + (2^d - N) = M - N$$

The computer, of course, stores $\overline{2^d}$ and C_2 in the binary form, as shown in Table C-3, where $\overline{2^d}$ appears as $\overline{1}$ in the last column of the table in position $d + 1$ from the right; spaces between $\overline{1}$ and C_2, if any, are filled by zeros.

Table C-3

N	Number of digits in N, d	2^d, in binary form	Twos complement of N, in binary form, $C_2 = 2^d - N$	$-N$, stored as $\overline{2^d}C_2$
1	1	10	$10 - 1 = 1$	$\overline{1}1$
10	2	100	$100 - 10 = 10$	$\overline{1}10$
101	3	1000	$1000 - 101 = 11$	$\overline{1}011$
1010	4	10000	$10000 - 1010 = 110$	$\overline{1}0110$
10011	5	100000	$100000 - 10011 = 1101$	$\overline{1}01101$

Any number of consecutive 1's may be inserted, or dropped, immediately to the right of $\overline{1}$, without changing the stored value of $-N$:

$$\overline{1} \ 1 \ 0 \quad = \quad \overline{1} \ 1 \ 1 \ 1 \ 0 \quad = \quad \overline{1} \ 0$$
Decimal equivalent: $-4+2+0 = -2; -16+8+4+2+0 = -2; -2+0 = -2$

The insertion of 1's is occasionally necessary to align $\overline{1}$ with the leftmost digit of the minuend (the number from which N is to be subtracted).

Subtraction of a number by adding its twos complement is illustrated in the two examples below.

example C-8.   Subtract 101 from 1011.
Table C-3 shows that, for subtraction, 101 is stored as $\overline{1}011$.

Operation: 1011
                +$\overline{1}011$
Difference: 0110

example C-9.   Subtract 10 from 101001.
Table C-3 shows that 10 is stored as $\overline{1}10$; this is expanded to $\overline{1}11110$.

Operation: 101001
               +$\overline{1}11110$
Difference: 100111

In treatises on geometric series it is shown that

$$r^{n-1} + r^{n-2} + \ldots + r^2 + r^1 + r^0 = \frac{r^n - 1}{r - 1} \qquad \text{(C-1)}$$

where n is the number of terms in the series, counting r^0 as the first term.
    Substituting 2 for r, we obtain:

$$2^{n-1} + 2^{n-2} + \ldots + 2^2 + 2^1 + 2^0 = 2^n - 1$$

Thus, if $n = 4$:

$$2^3 + 2^2 + 2^1 + 2^0 = 2^4 - 1$$

which we can write in the binary form:

$$1111 = 10000 - 1$$

An interesting relationship exists between the binary numbers which are the exact opposites of one another, that is, in which the 0's of one are the 1's of the other, and vice versa: such numbers, added together, always form a string of 1's, as shown below:

          0001   10100
        + 1110   + 01011
          1111   11111

But, as shown above, a string of 1's is always equal to $2^n - 1$, where n is the number of digits in the sum of the two binary opposites. It follows that, if one binary opposite is increased by 1, it becomes the twos complement of the other opposite, since the sum of the two becomes 2^n; we can illustrate this by increasing either opposite in the examples above:

$$0001 + 1 = 0010$$
$$+\underline{1110}$$
$$10000 = 2^4$$

$$10100$$
$$+\underline{01100} = 01011 + 1$$
$$100000 = 2^5$$

Conversely, subtracting 1 from a twos complement and reversing the 1's and 0's gives the number itself. However, it can be easily shown that reversing, first, the 1's and 0's of the twos complement and then *adding* 1 also produces the number; this latter method will be used in the illustrations to follow.

We can take advantage of the relationship between the binary opposites to find directly the values of the negative integers that correspond to the twos complement values which the computer stores. In the last column of Table C-3 each value appears as $\bar{1}$ followed by the twos complement of N. Recalling an earlier remark in this section, we can interpret $\bar{1}$ as an indicator that N is negative, since $\bar{1}$ is always larger than the twos complement. Therefore, if we change $\bar{1}$ to the minus sign, $-$, write the binary opposite of the twos complement, and add to it 1, we obtain the value of $-N$. This method is used in Table C-4 to change the values of $-N$ in the last column of Table C-3 to their direct form.

Table C-4

Stored value of $-N$	Change $\bar{1}$ to $-$ and write the binary opposite of the twos complement	Add 1 to find $-N$
$\bar{1}1$	-0	-1
$\bar{1}10$	-01	-10
$\bar{1}011$	-100	-101
$\bar{1}0110$	-1001	-1010
$\bar{1}01101$	-10010	-10011

C-10. storage and processing of data

In the IBM System/360 a storage location consists of 32 iron rings or *bits*. Each group of eight bits is called a *byte*, and each byte consists of two *half-bytes*.

Each of the iron rings may be magnetized in one direction to represent a 0 and in the opposite direction to represent a 1. Thus a storage location may contain the number A:

Byte

$$\overbrace{\text{A} = 1111 \quad 1111 \quad \overbrace{1111 \quad 1111}}^{} \quad 1111 \quad \underbrace{1111}_{} \quad 1111 \quad 1111$$

Half-byte

or the number B:

$$B = 0000 \quad 0000 \quad 0000 \quad 0000 \quad 0000 \quad 0000 \quad 0000 \quad 0000$$

or any mixture of 1's and 0's forming the number C:

$$C = 1001 \quad 0010 \quad 1000 \quad 0000 \quad 1111 \quad 1010 \quad 0100 \quad 0101$$

It was shown in Table C-2 in Article C-8 that every hexadecimal digit, from 0 to F, can be represented by a combination of four binary digits. Since each half-byte contains four binary digits, the contents of the half-byte can be represented by a single hexadecimal digit. Referring to Table C-2 we can write the numbers A, B and C in the hexadecimal notation as follows:

$$A = FFFF \quad FFFF$$
$$B = 0000 \quad 0000$$
$$C = 9280 \quad FA45$$

Obviously, a number is shorter and easier to read, write and even to remember in the hexadecimal form. However, it must be kept in mind that the hexadecimal notation is only a convenient notation, and that numbers are actually stored in the binary form.

Numbers stored in 32-bit locations are said to be in *single precision*. Single precision numbers may be integer or real. The *integer* number represented by any given configuration of 1's and 0's in a location is different from the *real* number represented by the same configuration. The reasons for the difference are given in the following articles.

The computer has the ability of linking together two storage locations to form a double storage location of 64 bits, or 8 bytes, or 16 half-bytes. Only real numbers can be stored in double storage locations and, when so stored, such numbers are said to be in *double precision*. An example of a double precision number is 4012 C0B4 1004 A027. Double precision numbers have 16 hexadecimal digits, a digit for every half-byte.

Integer numbers can be stored only in single precision.

The computer processes (adds, multiplies, etc.) single and double precision real numbers in *calculating registers*. These registers have 64 bits; that is, the result of operations performed on real numbers in a calculating register is always in double precision and has 16 digits. Depending on the storage instructions it receives, the computer stores the result either in a double storage location, with all of its 16 digits, or in a single location. In the latter case it drops the right half of the double precision result and stores only the 8 digits of the left half. It also rounds up the last digit of the stored left half if the truncated right half is equal to or greater than 8000 0000.

The digit sequence 8000 0000 forms the right half of the *middle number* between any two consecutive numbers exactly storable in single precision. In the example below P and R are two consecutive single precision numbers and Q is the middle number between them. One should recall that, in the hexadecimal notation, 8 is the middle number between 0 and 10 (= 16, decimal), just as in the decimal notation 5 is the middle number between 0 and 10.

P = 4000 0005

4000 0005 8000 0000 = Q, middle number

R = 4000 0006

If the result in a calculation register lies between P and Q, the computer stores it as P; if the result is Q or lies between Q and R, the computer stores it as R. It can be seen that, in general, single precision numbers are the approximations of the calculated results.

Because of the loss of digits caused by the fixed capacity of the calculating registers and by the truncation of the double precision results when they are squeezed into single precision locations, it is unproductive to write data numbers with too many digits. Compilers take care of the excesses automatically: the G compiler disregards all significant digits in excess of 9 in single precision numbers written in the decimal notation, and the digits in excess of 18 in double precision numbers; the WATFIV compiler cuts off at 7 and 16, respectively.

C-11. representation of integer numbers in the memory

In every storage location of the IBM System/360 the first (leftmost) ring plays the role of a square window in the hypothetical decimal calculator described in Section C-9: that is, the first ring is used to store the sign of a number. If the number is a positive integer, the first ring is magnetized to represent 0, and the number is stored, right-justified, on the remaining rings of the location; if the number is a negative integer, the first ring is magnetized to represent 1, which is interpreted as $\bar{1}$, and the rest of the location is filled with the twos complement of the positive value of the number. Thus every number that begins with a 0 is positive and is read directly; every number that begins with a 1 is negative and must be converted from its twos complement form, as explained in Section C-9. The procedure is illustrated in Examples C-10 and C-11, assuming eight rings per storage location.

example C-10.

Positive Numbers

Location contents	Binary number	Decimal equivalent
00000111 00101010 01101101	111 101010 1101101	7 42 109

example C-11.

Negative Numbers

Location Contents	Change the first 1 to − and reverse the remaining 1's and 0's	Add 1 to obtain −N	Decimal equivalent
11111111 10000001 10011010	−0000000 −1111110 −1100101	−0000001 −1111111 −1100110	−1 −127 −102

C-12. the subroutines DUMP and PDUMP

If a program does not run, we can speed up its debugging by examining the values stored in the memory of the computer. A means to make this inspection is provided by the subroutines DUMP and PDUMP available in the IBM System/ 360 library of subprograms. When called, these subroutines *dump*, that is, print the values from a specified area of storage and thereby make these values available for inspection.

The general form of the CALL statement is:

$$\text{CALL DUMP} \quad (A_1, B_1, F_1, \ldots \ldots, A_n, B_n, F_n)$$

where A and B are the variables that indicate the limits of the dump and F is the code for the format of the dump. For example, if the variables I, J, K, and ISUM are stored in the memory in that order, and it is desired to examine all their values, the subroutine DUMP is called as follows:

$$\text{CALL DUMP} \quad (\text{I,ISUM,0})$$

and the four values, from I through ISUM, will be printed in the *hexadecimal* format, which is indicated by the code integer 0. The default code for the format is 0, so that, if the argument F is omitted, the computer prints the dump in the hexadecimal notation.

If it is desired to see only the value of J, in the hexadecimal form, the call is written:

CALL DUMP   (J,J,0)

and only the value of J is printed.

If the call is written:

CALL DUMP   (J,ISUM,0)

the values of J, K, and ISUM are printed.

If the second argument, B, is omitted, the subroutine may print additional and unrelated values stored in the locations which follow the locations used by the program.

The execution of a program is terminated after a call for DUMP. For the execution of the program to continue, PDUMP should be substituted for DUMP.

As an exercise in using the PDUMP subprogram and in interpreting the hexadecimal output, consider the following program:

```
I = 4
J = −16
K = 0
CALL PDUMP (I,K,0)
CALL PDUMP (K,0)
ISUM = I + J + K
CALL PDUMP (I,ISUM,0)
STØP
END
```

Since the calls have been made for PDUMP, the program is executed to the end, and there are three lines of printout, one for each call:

```
00000004 (I)    FFFFFFF0 (J)    00000000 (K)

                     Values unrelated to the program
00000000 (K)    5810C034      1861182D      00000000
00000004 (I)    FFFFFFF0 (J)    00000000 (K)    FFFFFFF4 (ISUM)
```

In the first line, the listed values are those of I, J, and K, as specified by the range from I through K in the call. In the second line, since the upper limit was not specified, the value of K is followed by three unrelated values from the adjacent locations. The third line shows the values of I, J, K, and ISUM, included in the specified range from I to ISUM.

It can be seen that the numbers are written in the hexadecimal form, and that each number has 8 digits. In Section C-10 it was shown that these digits correspond to the 8 half-bytes of a 32-bit location in the IBM System 360: each half-byte consists of 4 bits and can store any one of the 16 hexadecimal digits, from 0 to F, in the binary form; for example, 2 is stored as 0010, C (= 12) as 1100, and F (= 15) as 1111 (See Table C-2).

Now we shall interpret the numbers in the printout, one by one.

Variable ⟶ I
Hexadecimal form ⟶ 00000004
Convert each hexadecimal digit to binary   0000 0000 0000 0000 0000 0000 0000 0100
The number begins with 0, therefore it is positive;
the decimal equivalent of the underlined portion, with sign: +4

Variable ⟶ J
Hexadecimal form ⟶ FFFFFFF0
Convert to binary   1111 1111 1111 1111 1111 1111 1111 0000
The number begins with 1, therefore it is negative;
change the first 1 to − and exchange 0's and 1's:
−000 0000 0000 0000 0000 0000 0000 1111
Add 1:   −000 0000 0000 0000 0000 0000 0001 0000
The decimal equivalent of the underlined portion, with sign: −16

Variable ⟶ K
Hexadecimal form ⟶ 00000000
Obviously, the decimal equivalent is: 0

Variable ⟶ ISUM
Hexadecimal form ⟶ FFFFFFF4
Convert to binary   1111 1111 1111 1111 1111 1111 1111 0100
The number begins with 1, therefore it is negative;
change the first 1 to − and exchange 0's and 1's:
−000 0000 0000 0000 0000 0000 0000 1011
Add 1:   −000 0000 0000 0000 0000 0000 0000 1100
The decimal equivalent of the underlined portion, with sign: −12.

A short reflection will show that, generally, the work of writing out the entire binary string may be avoided. A hexadecimal string of 0's, ending with significant digits, represents a positive integer, whose value resides in those digits. Thus we need to work only with the underlined portions of such hexadecimal words:

$$0000002\underline{C} = + (2\times16 + 12\times1) = +44$$
$$00004\underline{BA2} = + (4\times4096 + 11\times256 + 10\times16 + 2\times1) = +19,362$$

A hexadecimal word that begins with a string of F's (that is, with the binary 1111. . .) represents a negative integer. From the examples in the box above it can be seen that only the digits to the right of the last F (underlined in the two examples below) need to be converted to the binary form, their 0's and 1's reversed, and 1 added to find the integer.

FFFFFF$\underline{24}$	← Hexadecimal word →	FFFFF$\underline{D05}$
0010 0100	Convert to binary	1101 0000 0101
1101 1011	Reverse 0's and 1's	0010 1111 1010
1101 1100	Add 1	0010 1111 1011
$-(13\times16 + 12\times1)$	Decimal number	$- (2\times256 + 15\times16 + 11\times1)$
$= -220$		$= -763$

The largest positive integer that can be stored in a 32-bit location is represented in binary by

$$0 \;\; 111 \;\; 1111 \;\; 1111 \;\; 1111 \;\; 1111 \;\; 1111 \;\; 1111 \;\; 1111$$

and in hexadecimal by 7FFFFFFF.
Its decimal value

$$= 7\times16^7 + 15(16^6 + 16^5 + 16^4 + 16^3 + 16^2 + 16^1 + 16^0)$$

which, by Equation C-1 in Section C-9, is:

$$7\times16^7 + \frac{15(16^7 - 1)}{16 - 1} = 16^7\times8 - 1 = 2^{31} - 1 = 2,147,483,647$$

The largest negative integer has the same absolute value as the largest positive integer, and the minus sign, namely:

$$-111 \;\; 1111 \;\; 1111 \;\; 1111 \;\; 1111 \;\; 1111 \;\; 1111 \;\; 1111$$

Its decimal equivalent, of course, is $-2,147,483,647$.
To find its hexadecimal form, first find its twos complement by changing the 1's to 0's:

$$-000 \;\; 0000 \;\; 0000 \;\; 0000 \;\; 0000 \;\; 0000 \;\; 0000 \;\; 0000$$

then replace — by 1 and add 1:.

$$1000 \quad 0000 \quad 0000 \quad 0000 \quad 0000 \quad 0000 \quad 0000 \quad 0001$$

Therefore the hexadecimal equivalent of the largest negative integer is:

80000001

A count of digits in 2,147,483,647 shows that 10 is the maximum number of significant digits in an integer number in the decimal form.

C-13.   representation of real numbers in the memory

Real, or floating-point, numbers, that is, numbers with a decimal point are stored in the memory of a computer in a manner entirely different from that used for integer numbers. While it is true that they are stored as the binary strings of 0's and 1's—there is no other way—the strings generally have an appearance different from that of the integer number strings.

The following scheme is employed for representing real numbers in the memory of the IBM System/360.

A number is expressed in the normalized hexadecimal form, for example, $-0.C052 \times 16^2$, where C052 is the mantissa beginning with a nonzero digit, 16 is the hexadecimal base, and 2 is the exponent of the base. The sign, —, is stored in the first (leftmost) bit of a 32-bit location, the exponent, 2, in the next 7 bits, and the mantissa, C052, in the remaining 24 bits or 6 half-bytes, a hexadecimal digit in every half-byte. Thus the mantissa C052 is stored as follows:

$$
\begin{array}{cccccc}
\text{C(=12)} & 0 & 5 & 2 & 0 & 0 \\
\hline
1100 & 0000 & 0101 & 0010 & 0000 & 0000 \\
\hline
\end{array}
$$

$$\texttt{24 bits}$$

The 7 bits reserved for the base exponent are divided into the left group of 3 and the right group of 4. The highest hexadecimal digits that can be stored in these two groups are 7 (111) in the left group and F (1111) in the right group; thus we may store exponents of 16 varying from 00 (0 decimal) to 7F ($7 \times 16 + F \times 1 = 112 + 15 = 127$ decimal). But all these exponents are positive. To provide for the negative exponents, the following scheme is used: a constant positive *bias quantity*, or simply *bias*, is added to the true exponent, and it is the *sum* of the bias and the true exponent, called *characteristic*, that is stored in the seven bits reserved for the exponent; that is:

characteristic = stored exponent = true exponent + bias

from which:

$$\text{true exponent} = \text{characteristic} - \text{bias}$$

The bias used in the IBM System/360 is 100 0000 (40 hexadecimal, 64 decimal). Therefore if the stored exponent is 111 1111 (7F hexadecimal, 127 decimal), the true exponent is 111 1111 − 100 0000 = 11 1111 (7F − 40 = 3F hexadecimal, 127 − 64 = 63 decimal); if the stored exponent is 000 0000 (00 hexadecimal, 0 decimal), the true exponent is 000 0000 − 100 0000 = − 100 0000 (00 − 40 = − 40 hexadecimal, 0 − 64 = − 64 decimal). This scheme provides for exponents ranging from −64 to +63.

As stated earlier, the sign is stored in the first bit; as with integers, + is stored as 0 and − as 1. For purposes of the hexadecimal representation the digit (0 or 1) stored in the first bit is combined with the binary digits of the exponent stored in the next 3 bits. For an illustration, let us return to −0.C052 × 16^2 as an example. The exponent of 16 is 2; in binary this is 10, which is stored in bits 7 and 8. The bias of 100 0000 is added to the exponent of 10, producing the characteristic of 100 0010 in bits 2-8. The − sign of the number is stored as 1 in the first bit. Thus the string in the first 8 bits is

$$1100 \quad 0010$$

which is represented hexadecimally by C2.

If the number were positive, the first eight bits would contain the string

$$0100 \quad 0010$$

equal, hexadecimally, to 42.

The entire number, −0.C052×16^2, is stored in a 32-bit register as the string

1	100 0010	1100 0000 0101 0010 0000 0000
Sign	Characteristic	Mantissa

Hexadecimally this string is written C2C05200.

C-14. interpretation of a dump of real numbers

Let us assume that a call for PDUMP produces a printout of two hexadecimal numbers 42508000 and C2396000. To find their decimal values we proceed as follows.

Hexadecimal number	42508000	C2396000
Convert the first two digits to binary and separate the sign and the characteristic	0 | 100 0010	1 | 100 0010
Replace the first digit by a sign, subtract the bias of 100 0000 from the characteristic, and write the remainder—the exponent of 16—in decimal form	Sign: + Exponent: 2	Sign: − Exponent: 2
Decimal number	$+ (\dfrac{5}{16} + \dfrac{8}{16^3})$ $\times 16^2$ $= + (80+0.5)$ $= + 80.5$	$- (\dfrac{3}{16} + \dfrac{9}{16^2} + \dfrac{6}{16^3})$ $\times 16^2$ $= - (48 + 9 + 0.375)$ $= - 57.375$

The largest positive real number that can be stored in a 32-bit location is represented in binary by

$$0111 \quad 1111 \quad 1111 \quad 1111 \quad 1111 \quad 1111 \quad 1111 \quad 1111$$

and in hexadecimal by 7FFF FFFF.

The exponent is 7F − 40 (bias) = 3F in hexadecimal and 3(16) + 15 = 63 in decimal.

The mantissa is

$$15 \left(\frac{1}{16^1} + \frac{1}{16^2} + \frac{1}{16^3} + \frac{1}{16^4} + \frac{1}{16^5} + \frac{1}{16^6} \right)$$

which, substituting $\dfrac{1}{16}$ for r in eq. (C-1) in Section C-9, is:

$$1 - \frac{1}{16^6}$$

Therefore, in decimal notation, the largest positive real number storable in a 32-bit location is

$$\left(1 - \frac{1}{16^6}\right) \times 16^{63} = 16^{63} - 16^{57} = 0.7237 \times 10^{76}$$

The largest negative real number is equal to the largest positive real number with the negative sign, that is, its value is -0.7237×10^{76}, because both numbers have the same maximum characteristic and mantissa. Since the minus sign is represented by 1 in the first bit, the largest negative real number appears in binary as:

$$1111 \quad 1111 \quad 1111 \quad 1111 \quad 1111 \quad 1111 \quad 1111 \quad 1111$$

and in hexadecimal as:

FFFF   FFFF

The smallest positive real number appears in the binary form as:

$$0000 \quad 0000 \quad 0000 \quad 0000 \quad 0000 \quad 0000 \quad 0000 \quad 0001$$

and in the hexadecimal form as:

0000   0001

The exponent of the smallest positive number is $00 - 40 = -40$ in hexadecimal and -64 in decimal. Thus the smallest positive real number storable in a 32-bit location is

$$\frac{1}{16^6} * 16^{-64} = \frac{1}{16^{70}}$$

Its decimal equivalent is $0.515 * 10^{-84}$.

The smallest negative number has the same magnitude, with the negative sign; it is stored in the binary form as:

$$1000 \quad 0000 \quad 0000 \quad 0000 \quad 0000 \quad 0000 \quad 0000 \quad 0001$$

its hexadecimal form is:

8000   0001

C-15. recognizing numbers in hexadecimal notation

The recognition of a number in the hexadecimal form depends principally on its name, that is, on its storage address. If the address is integer, the word must be read as integer; if the address is real, the word must be interpreted as real. Thus the word 42012000, dumped from the address K, is interpreted as an integer number:

Binary: 0 100 . . . . . .

Decimal: $+ 4(16^7) + 2(16^6) + 1(16^4) + 2(16^3)$
          $= 1,107,369,984$

The same word, dumped from the address P, is real; therefore:

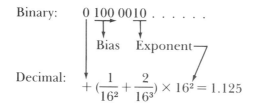

Binary: $0\ \underset{\text{Bias}}{\underline{100}}\ \underset{\text{Exponent}}{\underline{0010}}\ \ldots\ldots$

Decimal: $+ (\frac{1}{16^2} + \frac{2}{16^3}) \times 16^2 = 1.125$

The bias of 100 0000 incorporated in the characteristics of real numbers generally provides a clue for distinguishing between positive and negative real numbers. If the bias is preceded by a 0 for a positive number, the sign-characteristic string is stored as 0100 0000, which is 40 in hexadecimal. If the bias is preceded by 1 for a negative number, the sign-characteristic string is 1100 0000, which is C0 in hexadecimal.

Most of the real numbers one deals with consist of a few digits, with the decimal point somewhere among them. Such numbers, when normalized, rarely require multiplication by anything larger than 10^4 or 16^3 or smaller than 10^{-4} or 16^{-3}. In other words, their hexadecimal exponents are seldom in excess of ± 3. Hence the basic sign-bias of C0 may assume values of C1, C2, C3 on the high side and BF ($= C0 - 1$), BE, BD on the low side; similarly, the sign-bias of 40 may increase to 41, 42, 43 or decrease to 3F, 3E, 3D.

It follows from these observations that real hexadecimal words that begin with 3 or 4 generally represent *positive real* numbers and those that begin with B or C represent *negative real* numbers.

A review of Section C-11 will reveal that integer hexadecimal words that begin with 0 to 7 represent *positive integer* numbers and those beginning with 8 to F represent *negative integer* numbers.

Hexadecimal words may also represent literal data.

C-16. additional DUMP formats

In Section C-12 it was shown that data can be submitted in decimal form and the results dumped in hexadecimal form; the latter form was obtained by specifying F = 0 in the call for DUMP or PDUMP.

The operation can be reversed or carried out in various combinations. For example, data can be submitted in hexadecimal form by means of the Z specification and recovered in decimal form by specifying F = 4 for integer numbers and F = 5 for real numbers, as shown in the following sequence:

```
      READ(5,1) K, P
  1   FØRMAT(2Z9)
      CALL PDUMP(K,P,0)
      CALL PDUMP(K,K,4)
      CALL DUMP(P,P,5)
      END
```

Data card:

42012000 42012000

The first call produces a printout of K and P in the original—hexadecimal—form:

42012000   42012000

The second call produces the integer K in the decimal form:

1107369984

The last call produces the real number P in the decimal form and stops the execution:

0.112500000E+01

This example substantiates the statement made in Section C-15 that the types of address assigned to hexadecimal words guide the computer in interpreting them as integer or real numbers.

C-17. powers of 16

16^{-7}	0.000 000 003 725 290 298 461 914 062 5	1	16^{0}
16^{-6}	0.000 000 059 604 644 775 390 625	16	16^{1}
16^{-5}	0.000 000 953 674 316 406 25	256	16^{2}
16^{-4}	0.000 015 258 789 062 5	4 096	16^{3}
16^{-3}	0.000 244 140 625	65 536	16^{4}
16^{-2}	0.003 906 25	1 048 576	16^{5}
16^{-1}	0.062 5	16 777 216	16^{6}
		268 435 456	16^{7}
		4 294 967 296	16^{8}
		68 719 476 736	16^{9}
		1 099 511 627 776	16^{10}
		17 592 186 044 416	16^{11}
		281 474 976 710 656	16^{12}
		4 503 599 627 370 496	16^{13}
		72 057 594 037 927 936	16^{14}
		1 152 921 504 606 846 976	16^{15}

C-18.   double precision numbers

From Section C-13 we know that the mantissa of a real number is stored in the rightmost six half-bytes (24 bits) of a storage location. The two half-bytes on the left contain the sign and the characteristic (the power of 16 plus the bias) of the number. Since a half-byte can store only one hexadecimal digit, it follows that the mantissa of a number stored in a single location can have a maximum of six hexadecimal digits. Numbers with 6-digit mantissas are said to be in *single precision*.

Some numbers, like π (PI), have more digits than can be represented accurately by a mantissa with six hexadecimal digits. When such numbers, put in the hexadecimal form, are stored in single precision, they lose all the mantissa digits in excess of six, and their accuracy is diminished.

The exactness of a long number may be increased by declaring it to be in *double precision*. For example, the declaration statement:

DØUBLE PRECISIØN PI

makes the computer store and print out PI with as many as 18 digits.

The computer can do this, first, because it operates on all real values in calculating registers of 64-bit (16-half-byte) capacity, that is, in double precision; and, second, because, if directed to do so by the DOUBLE PRECISION declaration, it can link together two storage locations, each of 32 bits, to form a double, 64-bit location, and to store in it the results of its double precision operations (see Section C-10). When the computer links two 32-bit locations, it increases the length of the mantissa from 6 digits to 14, because, as in single precision, it needs only the two leftmost half-bytes of the double location for the sign and characteristic of a number: the remaining 6 half-bytes of the first location and the 8 half-bytes of the second location provide the space for the 14 digits of the mantissa.

Fig. C-4 shows the 16 half-bytes of two linked storage locations occupied by a number in double precision. The leftmost two half-bytes contain the sign and the characteristic of the number; the remaining 14 half-bytes contain the mantissa; the mantissa is understood to be preceded by the hexadecimal point.

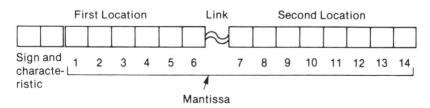

Figure C-4

In Section C-13 it was shown that the characteristics that may be stored in bits 2-8 may vary from the minimum of 000 0000 to the maximum of 111 1111. By design, these characteristics include the bias of 100 0000. Reduced by the bias, the characteristics become the exponents of 16, which may vary from −100 0000 to 011 1111, or from −40 to +3F in hexadecimal, and from −64 to +63 in decimal.

The smallest mantissa that may be stored in the 14 half-bytes reserved for mantissas is 1 in the last half-byte (14 in Fig. C-4) preceded by 13 zeros; it is also the smallest change that may occur in a mantissa. The largest mantissa is 14 F's.

Thus the smallest number of either sign that the computer can store in double precision is $\frac{1}{16^{14}} * 16^{-64} = \frac{1}{16^{78}}$. The largest number of either sign is equal to the mantissa of 14 F's multiplied by 16^{63}. To evaluate this number let us increase the mantissa by 1 in the last half-byte; this will change all the F's to 0's and produce 1 to the left of the mantissa's hexadecimal point; the resulting number is $1.* 16^{63}$ or, simply, 16^{63}. To find the number corresponding to the mantissa with 14 F's, we must reduce 16^{63} by the amount corresponding to the increase of 1 in the last half-byte: this increase is $\frac{1}{16^{14}} * 16^{63} = 16^{49}$. Therefore the largest number of either sign that the computer can store in double precision is $16^{63} - 16^{49}$; this compares with $16^{63} - 16^{57}$, the largest number storable in single precision. Since the difference between these two numbers begins in the umpteenth decimal place, both numbers have the same approximate value of $0.7237 * 10^{76}$.

Between the extremes of the largest positive number, $16^{63} - 16^{49}$, and the largest negative number, $-(16^{63} - 16^{49})$, consecutive numbers may vary only by 1 in the 14th half-byte of the mantissa. This does not mean that the difference between any two consecutive numbers is a constant. Consider the consecutive mantissas

$$10 \quad 0000 \quad 0000 \quad 0000$$

$$\text{and} \quad 10 \quad 0000 \quad 0000 \quad 0001$$

If the power of 16 stored in the bits 2-8 is 14, the two corresponding consecutive numbers are:

$$16^{14}*(\frac{1}{16}) \qquad = 16^{13} \qquad = \qquad 4 \; 503 \; 599 \; 627 \; 370 \; 496$$

$$\text{and } 16^{14}*(\frac{1}{16} + \frac{1}{16^{14}}) = 16^{13} + 16^0 = \qquad \underline{4 \; 503 \; 599 \; 627 \; 370 \; 497}$$

$$\text{Difference:} \qquad\qquad\qquad\qquad 1$$

But if the power of 16 in the bits 2-8 is 16, the two numbers are:

$$16^{16}*(\frac{1}{16}) \qquad = 16^{15} \qquad = 1\ 152\ 921\ 504\ 606\ 846\ 976$$

$$\text{and } 16^{16}*(\frac{1}{16} + \frac{1}{16^{14}}) = 16^{15} + 16^2 = \underline{1\ 152\ 921\ 504\ 608\ 847\ 232}$$

$$\text{Difference:} \qquad\qquad\qquad\qquad 256$$

These examples also show that the computer cannot store exactly any numbers intermediate between two consecutive exactly storable numbers; for example, the computer cannot store exactly any number between 1 152 . . . . . .6 976 and 1 152 . . . . . .7 232; the *middle* number between these two numbers is 1 152 . . . . . .7 104; any number between 1 152 . . . . .6 976 and 1 152 . . . . .7 104 is stored as 1 152 . . . . .6 976; numbers between 1 152 . . . . . .7 104 and 1 152 . . . . .7 232 are stored as 1 152 . . . . .7 232. It follows that the maximum possible error in a number is equal to one-half the difference between the two exactly storable numbers preceding and following the number.

We can develop a general expression for the difference, Δ, between any two consecutive exactly storable numbers. Let E be the exponent, or power, of 16 stored in the bits 2-8. If the 14th digit of the mantissa is increased by 1, the number increases by

$$\Delta = \frac{1}{16^{14}}*16^E = 16^{E-14} \tag{C-3}$$

Thus if E = 16, $\Delta = 16^{16-14} = 256;$
        if E = 14, $\Delta = 16^{14-14} = \quad 1.$

The maximum possible error in any number printed by the computer is

$$\sigma = \frac{\Delta}{2} = \frac{16^{E-14}}{2} \tag{C-4}$$

The preceding discussion shows that consecutive mantissas, in combinations with powers of 16, give rise to certain consecutive numbers which the computer can store exactly; that each exact number differs from the next larger (or smaller) exact number by Δ; and that any number which differs from the preceding (or following) exact number by less than Δ cannot be stored exactly. For every pair of consecutive exact numbers there is a *middle number*, differing from either exact number by σ. The computer rounds down to the lower exact number all the numbers between the lower number and the middle number. It rounds up to the upper exact number all the numbers between the upper number and the middle number. It follows that a number printed by the computer may have a maximum error equal to σ.

Table C-5 shows groups of numbers and the maximum possible errors in the numbers within these groups.

Table C-5

Powers of 16	Range of numbers	Maximum error, σ, in the value of a number
15	1152921504606846976 − 72057594037927936	8.
14	72057594037927936 − 4503599627370496	0.5
13	4503599627370496 − 281474976710656	0.03125
12	281474976710656 − 17592186044416	0.001953125
11	17592186044416 − 1099511627776	0.0001220703125
10	1099511627776 − 68719476736	0.00000762939453125

The ratio of the maximum possible error in any group to the smallest number in that group is always

$$\frac{16^{E-14}}{2} : 16^{E-1} = 1 : 2(16^{13}) = 1 : 9 \;\; 007 \;\; 199 \;\; 254 \;\; 740 \;\; 992$$

or 1 to 9 quadrillions or to 9 million billions. This error is equivalent to the error of 1/50th of an inch in the distance of 2 700 000 000 miles between the orbits of the Earth and Neptune.

Operating with the G1 compiler, the computer prints a double precision number in the decimal notation with a maximum of 18 significant digits†. The decimal number may be in the D form or the F form. The minimum specification for an 18-digit number in the D form is D25.18. The F specification is affected by the position of the decimal point in the number. Both the D and the F forms may be shortened by reducing the number of decimals in the specification. The number may also be obtained in the hexadecimal form; the specification which fetches 16 hexadecimal digits from the 16 half–bytes of a double storage location is Z16.

The variable names given to double precision numbers may begin with *any letter* of the alphabet; thus the declaration statement:

DØUBLE PRECISIØN   K

explicitly makes the number stored at K a real number in double precision.

Without a DØUBLE PRECISIØN declaration, names beginning with I, J, K, L, M, N identify integer numbers; such numbers, naturally, are in single precision. The DØUBLE PRECISIØN mechanism does not apply to integer numbers, but an integer number may be converted into a double precision number by a DØUBLE PRECISIØN declaration and an appropriate assignment, as shown in Example C-12.

---

† With the WATFIV compiler, the computer prints only 16 significant digits.

example C-12.

```
      DØUBLE PRECISIØN   A
      DATA   K /123/
      A = K
      WRITE(6,1) A
  1   FØRMAT(1H0,D25.18)
```

Printout:

0.123000000000000000D+03

In the paragraphs above it was not shown what the computer does with the middle numbers located halfway between two exactly storable numbers. Intriguingly enough, the computer sometimes rounds them down, and at other times rounds them up, as can be seen in Example C-13.

Example C-13 shows a program which stores, via the DATA statement, two groups of numbers, one based on 16^{13}, the other on 16^{14}, and prints them out in four different forms: (1) as a full-sized F number, (2) as a truncated F number, (3) as a full-sized D number, and (4) as a hexadecimal number. The data in the program contain several middle numbers which are related to the other numbers as described on the right of the program.

example C-13.

```
           DOUBLE PRECISION A,B,C,D,E,F,G,H,O,P,Q,R
           DATA              A,B,C,D,E,F,G,H,O,P,Q,R
Line  1  */0.4503599627370496    D16,  ◄──────────────── 16¹³
      2  * 0.45035996273704965   D16,  Middle number between Lines 1 and 5
      3  * 0.450359962737049650  D16,  "        "        "      "   "  " " "  +0
      4  * 0.450359962737049651  D16,
      5  * 0.4503599627370497    D16,  ◄──────────────── 16¹³+  1
      6  * 0.72057594037927935   D17,                        16¹⁴─   1
      7  * 0.720575940379279355  D17,  Middle number between Lines 6 and 9
      8  * 0.720575940379279356  D17,
      9  * 0.72057594037927936   D17,  ◄──────────────── 16¹⁴
     10  * 0.72057594037927944   D17,  Middle number between Lines 9 and 12
     11  * 0.720575940379279440  D17,  "        "        "      "   "  " " "  +0
     12  * 0.72057594037927952   D17/  ◄──────────────── 16¹⁴+   16
           WRITE(6,1)A,A,A,A,B,B,B,B,C,C,C,C,D,D,D,D,E,E,E,E,F,F,F,F,G,G,G,G,
      *           H,H,H,H,O,O,O,O,P,P,P,P,Q,Q,Q,Q,R,R,R,R
    1 FORMAT(1H0,F21.2,D11.4,D27.20,Z18)
           STOP
```

Printout:

```
 1  ..4503599627370496.00.0.4504D+16..0.450359962737049600..D+16..4E1000000000000
 2    4503599627370496.00 0.4504D+16 0.450359962737049600  D+16  4E1000000000000
 3    4503599627370496.00 0.4504D+16 0.450359962737049600  D+16  4E1000000000000
 4    4503599627370497.00 0.4504D+16 0.450359962737049700  D+16  4E1000000000001
 5    4503599627370497.00 0.4504D+16 0.450359962737049700  D+16  4E1000000000001
 6    7205759403792793.5.0 0.7206D+17 0.720575940379279350  D+17  4EFFFFFFFFFFFFFF
 7    7205759403792793.5.0 0.7206D+17 0.720575940379279350  D+17  4EFFFFFFFFFFFFFF
 8    7205759403792793.6.0 0.7206D+17 0.720575940379279360  D+17  4F1000000000000
 9    7205759403792793.6.0 0.7206D+17 0.720575940379279360  D+17  4F1000000000000
10    7205759403792795.2.0 0.7206D+17 0.720575940379279520  D+17  4F1000000000001
11    7205759403792793.6.0 0.7206D+17 0.720575940379279360  D+17  4F1000000000000
12    7205759403792795.2.0 0.7206D+17 0.720575940379279520  D+17  4F1000000000001
```

Observe a number of points in the printout:

1/ Even though the program stores and calls for ten different numbers, only five different values are printed; the numbers between the exactly storable numbers are rounded either up or down;

2/ Written in full in the F and D forms, the numbers are padded with zeros on the right to make the count of digits equal to 18; the count begins with the first significant digit on the left.

3/ Complying with the specification D27.20, the computer provides a field of 20 spaces for the decimals, but, limited to 18 digits, leaves 2 blank spaces in front of D.

4/ The specification F21.2 calls for 2 decimals, but only one is shown on Lines 6-12 because of the 18-digit limitation.

5/ When it truncates numbers to fit shorter specifications, the computer rounds up the last remaining digit if the truncated portion is greater than a 5 followed by zeros.

Observe also a peculiarity. The DATA numbers on Lines 10 and 11 are middle numbers which are identical, except for a zero added at the end of the number on Line 11. The computer rounds *up* the number on Line 10 and rounds *down* the number on Line 11. At the same time two identical middle numbers which differ by a zero appear on Lines 2 and 3, and the computer rounds both of them *down*.

Finally, note that in the DATA statement the double precision numbers are written in the D form. Double precision numbers in the F form are treated differently by different compilers. If the mantissa of an F number overflows into the half-bytes 7-14 on the right, the WATFIV compiler accepts the overflow and stores it. The G compiler, on the other hand, examines the overflow: if it begins with the hexadecimal 8 or higher, it increases the sixth digit of the mantissa by 1 and fills the half-bytes 7-14 with zeros; if the overflow begins with less than 8, the G compiler replaces it by eight zeros.

The effects of the two compilers are illustrated in Example C-14.

example C-14.   Given below are five numbers in the F form and in their equivalent hexadecimal form.

A	16	777	216.	4710	0000	0000	0000
B	16	777	223.	4710	0000	7000	0000
C	16	777	224.	4710	0000	8000	0000
D	16	777	225.	4710	0000	9000	0000
E	16	777	232.	4710	0001	0000	0000

The following program declares these numbers to be in double precision, stores them in the F form, and prints them in the F form, the short and long D forms, and the Z form.

```
  DOUBLE PRECISION A,B,C,D,E
  DATA A,B,C,D,E/16777216.,16777223.,16777224.,16777225.,16777232./
  WRITE(6,1) A,A,A,A,B,B,B,B,C,C,C,C,D,D,D,D,E,E,E,E
1 FORMAT(1H0,F10.1,D12.4,D16.8.Z18)
```

WATFIV compiler printout:

16777216.0	0.1678D 08	0.16777216D 08	4710000000000000
16777223.0	0.1678D 08	0.16777223D 08	4710000070000000
16777224.0	0.1678D 08	0.16777224D 08	4710000080000000
16777225.0	0.1678D 08	0.16777225D 08	4710000090000000
16777232.0	0.1678D 08	0.16777232D 08	4710000100000000

G compiler printout:

16777216.0	0.1678D+08	0.16777216D+08	4710000000000000
16777216.0	0.1678D+08	0.16777216D+08	4710000000000000
16777232.0	0.1678D+08	0.16777232D+08	4710000100000000
16777232.0	0.1678D+08	0.16777232D+08	4710000100000000
16777232.0	0.1678D+08	0.16777232D+08	4710000100000000

If a data number has more than 18 significant digits, the computer ignores the digits on the right in excess of 18, and does not round up the 18th digit.

It was stated, in Item 5 above, that the computer rounds up the last digit remaining after a truncation if the truncated part is greater than a 5 followed by zeros. Occasionally, but not always, the computer rounds up the last remaining digit if it truncates a single 5, as shown in Example C-15.

example C-15.

```
DOUBLE PRECISION A,B,C,D,E,F,G,H,O,P
DATA              A,B,C,D,E,F,G,H,O,P
*/0.015625D0,0.0078125D0,0.00390625D0,0.001953125D0,0.0009765625D0,
*              0.001953125D3,0.0009765625D3,0.00048828125D3,
* 0.000244140625D3,0.0001220703125D3/
WRITE(6,1)A,A,A,B,B,B,C,C,C,D,D,D,E,E,E,F,F,F,G,G,G,H,H,H,O,O,O,
* P,P,P
1 FORMAT ( 1H0,F19.7,F19.5,Z18/1H0,F19.8,F19.6,Z18/1H0,F19.9,F19.7,Z18
*          /1H0,F19.10,F19.8,Z18/1H0,F19.11,F19.9,Z18)
STOP
```

Printout:

0.0156250	0.01563	3F40000000000000
0.00781250	0.007813	3F20000000000000
0.003906250	0.0039062	3F10000000000000
0.0019531250	0.00195312	3E80000000000000
0.00097656250	0.000976562	3E40000000000000
1.9531250	1.95313	411F400000000000
0.97656250	0.976563	40FA000000000000
0.488281250	0.4882812	407D000000000000
0.2441406250	0.24414062	403E800000000000
0.12207031250	0.122070312	401F400000000000

A double precision number may always be retrieved from storage by a dump. A hexadecimal dump always has 16 digits. A decimal dump is always in the D form and has 18 digits following the decimal point.

questions and problems

C-1/ What is the base of the decimal system? How many digits are used in the system? What are they?

C-2/ What is the base of the binary system? How many digits are used in the system? What are they?

C-3/ Normalize the following binary numbers:

(a)   11.11   (b)   0.00101   (c)   101.   (d)   1010.101

C-4/   Perform the following binary arithmetic:

(a) $101 + 1001$ (b) $11.11001 + 10.10111 + 11.01111$
(c) $1001 - 110$ (d) $110.01 - 11.10$
(e) 111×101 (f) 11.01×1.011
(g) $1011011 \div 111$ (h) $100.0001 \div 1.01$

C-5/   Convert the following decimal numbers to the binary form:

(a)   45   (b)   3056   (c)   112:4   (d) -0.0725

C-6/   Convert the following binary numbers to the decimal form:

(a)   1000110   (b)   110.111   (c)   1101001.0011
(d) -0.11011

C-7/   What is the base of the hexadecimal system? How many digits are used in the system? What are they?

C-8/   Convert the following hexadecimal numbers to the decimal form:

(a)   19.2   (b)   439B   (c) -0.24 (d)   E.E

C-9/   Normalize the following hexadecimal numbers:

(a)   12.0   (b)   1C4.2   (c)   0.001A   (d)   B.0FF

C-10/   Convert the following hexadecimal numbers to the binary form:

(a)   E.E   (b) $-6C08$ (c)   C349.2F   (d)   1.3

C-11/   Convert the following binary numbers to the hexadecimal form:

(a)   101.1   (b)   10.01   (c) -11101111110
(d)   11.1011101

C-12/   Write the tens complements of the following decimal numbers:

(a)   46 ;   (b)   6402 ;   (c)   12345 ;   (d)   584673

C-13/   Write the twos complements of the following binary numbers:

(a)   11 ;   (b)   1001 ;   (c)   11010 ;   (d)   1100111

C-14/ What decimal numbers are represented by the following hexadecimal words dumped from the indicated locations in the IBM System/360?

(a) K: 0000000A ; (b) L: 00003BCD ;
(c) M: FFFFF117 (d) A: 42F12000 ;
(e) B: 3E900000 ; (f) C: 479312CF

C-15/ Write the following two decimal numbers in the hexadecimal form:

(a) 0.11, in single precision;
(b) 0.655362968750000000D+05, in double precision.

answers and solutions to the odd questions and problems

chapter 1

1-1/   A digital electronic computer is an automatic device which (1) accepts data and instructions on how to manipulate these data, and stores both in its magnetic memory in the form of digits; (2) performs step-by-step operations on the data in accordance with the instructions; and (3) issues the results of these operations.

1-3/   A program is the sequence of instructions that guide the computer in the processing of the data.

1-5/   A digital computer works with information expressed in the form of digits which are created in its memory by discrete electrical pulses; an analog computer operates on physical quantities, such as voltages and currents, which represent numbers by analogy.

1-7/   The most popular medium for recording computer programs and data is a punched card.

1-9/   FORTRAN is a programming language which combines the English language with mathematical and logical (or assertive) expressions to form standardized instructions to the computer; FORTRAN is called a problem-oriented language, because it consists of words, numbers and symbols which the programmer normally uses in solving a problem. The name FORTRAN is coined from the first syllables of FORmula TRANslation.

1-11/   A compiler is a program, written in a machine language, which translates a program written in a programming language into the machine language intelligible to the computer.

1-13/ The WATFIV compiler is a FORTRAN-to-machine translating program developed for educational purposes; it requires less compilation time than other compilers and issues numerous diagnostics.

chapter 2

2-1/ A data card, a business card, an IBM card, a Hollerith card.

2-3/ Print-punch a card as instructed and duplicate it.

2-5/ The two forms of a real number acceptable to the computer are the ordinary form and the exponential form; in the ordinary form the number has the whole and/or the fractional parts, and the decimal point. In the exponential form, the number, which may be in the ordinary form described above, is followed by the letter E and an exponent in the integer form.

> ***examples.*** Ordinary form: 123.00 ;   0.456;   −0.00078
> Exponential form: 12.3E 01 ;   0.456E 00 ;
> −0.78E−03

2-7/ A data field is the number of spaces on a data card allocated to a number or a combination of alphameric characters to be stored in one memory location.

2-9/ A FØRMAT statement consists of the word FØRMAT followed by parentheses containing a descriptive specification for every item to be stored from a data card or for every item to be printed on paper. In the latter case a carriage control specification must appear first in the statement. It will be shown later that a FØRMAT statement may also contain inner parentheses, carriage control specifications and slashes.

A FØRMAT statement may begin in any column between 7 and 72.

Each FØRMAT statement must have a unique statement number; the number must appear in columns 1-5.

2-11/

1	2	3	4	5	6	7	8	9	10	11	12	13	14	15	16	17	18	19	20	21	22	23	24	25	26	27
2	7		6	.	4		0	.	2	E	−	0	2													
				2		F	O	R	M	A	T	(	I	2	,	F	4	.	1	,	E	8	.	1	)	

2-13/ +0.93E 08

E9.2

2-15/ (a) The input unit is to bypass the first six columns on the data card.
(b) The output unit is to advance the sheet vertically one line (1X)

and to ride horizontally over the first five spaces (5X) on the line in front of it.

(c)   After performing the operation corresponding to the specification preceding 6X, the output unit is to ride horizontally over the six spaces on the line of the printout.

chapter 3

3-1/   The five functional components of a digital electronic computer are:

(1)   The input unit: it reads the information submitted to the computer on punched cards or paper tape or on magnetized tape or disks.

(2)   The memory unit: it holds the information received from the input unit or from the computing unit.

(3)   The arithmetic-logic, or computing, unit: it performs the mathematical and logical operations on the information which it receives from the memory unit.

(4)   The output unit: it reports the computed results as a printout on paper, as holes punched on cards or paper tape, or as magnetized spots on a tape or a disk.

(5)   The control unit: it coordinates the operations of the other four units.

The combination of the arithmetic-logic unit and the control unit is commonly referred to as the central processing unit or CPU.

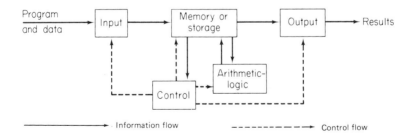

3-3/   Data and instructions for processing the data.

3-5/   When a punched card is processed by a card reader, electricity flows through the holes to the memory and magnetizes the cores.

3-7/   (a)   Executable; input.
       (b)   Executable; output.
       (c)   Non-executable; specification.

3-9/   The letter C, in the first column.

chapter 4

4-1/   (a)   Advance to the next page.
       (b)   Advance one line.
       (c)   Advance one line.
       (d)   Advance two lines.
       (e)   Do not advance.
       (f)   Advance three lines.

4-3/   The specification will make the printer advance the sheet two lines, skip the first five spaces on the line, and then print PI = 3.1416

4-5/
```
        WRITE(6,1)
      1 FORMAT(1H0,18X,'WEIGHT CHANGES, GRAMS')
        WRITE(6,2)
      2 FORMAT(1H0,12X,'SAMPLE A  SAMPLE B  SAMPLE C')
        READ(5,3)A,B,C
      3 FORMAT(3F6.2)
        WRITE(6,4)A,B,C
      4 FORMAT(1H0,'TEST 1 ',3F12.2)
        READ(5,3)A,B,C
        WRITE(6,5)A,B,C
      5 FORMAT(1X,'TEST 2',3F12.2)
        READ(5,3)A,B,C
        WRITE(6,5)A,B,C
        STOP
```

Data cards:

```
 -2.47 -1.59 +1.12
 ██    ██   ██ ██
 +4.17 -0.05 +0.62
██ ██     ██   ██ ██
 +5.26 +2.17 -1.05
 1 2 3 4 5 6 7 8 9 10 11 12 13 14 15 16 17 18
```

4-7/   (a)
```
        READ(5,1) P,N,Q,R
      1 FORMAT(-2PF7.3,I2,F7.4,E12.5)
```

       (b)
```
        WRITE(6,2) P,N,Q,R
      2 FORMAT (1H0,'P =',2PF9.0/1H0,'N =',I2/1H0,'Q =',
       *0PF6.2/1H0,'R =',3PE11.2)
```

Data card:

```
-12.345 6 0.8765 0.56789E+02
1 2 3 4 5 6 7 8 9 10 11 12 13 14 15 16 17 18 19 20 21 22 23 24 25 26 27 28
```

Printout:

P = −123450.

N = 6

Q = 87.65

R = 567.89E−01

chapter 5

5-1/ (a) Three cards: A and B on the first, C on the second, I on the third.

(b) Five cards: the first card will be ignored, D will be read on the second, the third card will be ignored, E will be read on the fourth card, and F on the fifth.

(c) Seven cards: P on the first, Q on the second, nothing on the third, R on the fourth, nothing on the fifth and sixth, S on the seventh.

5-3/ (a) A, K and L will be printed on the first line, right-justified, in consecutive fields of six, three and six spaces, and M and N will be printed on the second line, right-justified, in the fields of *two* and six spaces.

(b) All five numbers will be printed on the first line, A in the first six spaces, K in the next three, L in the next six, M in the next three, and N in the next six, right-justified in every case.

(c) B, I1, I2, I3 and I4 will be printed on the second line, consecutively, in six, three, five, three and five spaces; I5, I6, I7 and I8 will be printed on the fourth line, consecutively, in three, five, three and five spaces; and I9 and I10 will be printed on the sixth line in three and five spaces, all numbers right-justified in their fields.

5-5/ (a)
```
READ, X,Y,I
PRINT, X, Y, I
STOP
```

Data card:

```
5.23 10.45 12345
1 2 3 4 5 6 7 8 9 10 11 12 13 14 15 16
```

Printout:

```
^^^0.5230000E  01^^^^^0.1045000E  02^^^^^^^^^^12345
```

(b) PRINT, 5.23,10.45,12345

5-7/   1   READ, X,Y,N   *Data cards:*
               IF (X.EQ.0.) GO TO 2
               W = X**N + Y**N
               PRINT, X,Y,N,W
               GO TO 1
         2   STOP

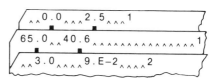

Printout:

    0.3000000E 01   0.8999997E-01   2   0.9008100E 01
     0.6500000E 02   0.4060001E 02   1   0.1056000E 03

5-9/

```
PRINT, 'ONCE UPON A SUNNY MORNING A MAN WHO SAT IN A BREAKFAST NOO
*K  LOOKED UP FROM HIS SCRAMBLED EGGS TO SEE A WHITE UNICORN WITH A
*GOLDEN', 'HORN QUIETLY CROPPING ROSES IN THE GARDEN.    THE MAN WEN
*T  UP TO THE BEDROOM WHERE HIS WIFE WAS STILL ASLEEP AND WOKE HER.
*   ''THERE''S',      'A UNICORN IN THE GARDEN,'' HE SAID.    ''EATING ROSES.''
*    SHE OPENED ONE UNFRIENDLY EYE AND LOOKED AT HIM. ''THE UNICORN I
*S  A MYTHICAL',    'BEAST,'' SHE SAID, AND TURNED HER BACK ON HIM.
*
*'                                   THURBER, THE UNICORN IN THE GARDEN'
 STOP
```

5-11/   READ (5,*)   A,B,C,D,K,L
                   WRITE (6,*)   A,B,C,D,K,L
                   STOP

Data card:

```
3*2.5 0.456E4 4 -105
```

Printout (in one line):

  2.50000000   2.50000000   2.50000000   4560.00000   4   -105

chapter 6

6-1/   I, J, K, L, M and N.

6-3/   Integer numbers are used primarily for counting; they are also used to identify statements and operational components of the system, such as a printer; and they are used as array subscripts.

     Real numbers are used principally to represent measured or measurable quantities, since such quantities normally have fractional parts.

6-5/ (a) A + B**2   (b) B + (C − D)/A

      (c) (A + B)/(C + D)   (d) A** (−B)

      (e) (I**2 + K**2)**2 + 2*J*K + J

      (f) 1. + A + A**2/2. + A**3/3./2.   (g) A*B/(C + 2.)

      (h) (A/B)**(C − 1.)   (i) 2.*3.14*R**2

      (j) K**3 + (M*N/2/I)**(2*K)

6-7/ (a) (1. + CØS(Y))/(1. − CØS(Y))   (b) −0.5/A + SIN (A/2.)

      (c) (2.*3.14)**0.5*D**(D + 1.)*EXP(−D)
      (d) ALØG10((A − B)/(C + D)) − F
      (e) ALØG(EXP(F + G) + SQRT(CØS(X)))
      (f) X*ALØG10(ABS(ATAN(X/2.)))

6-9/
```
        READ(5,1) B,J,HAT,MONTH,A5,L2N
      1 FORMAT(F10.3,I5,E12.5,I6,E14.3,I6)
        WRITE(6,2) B,J,HAT,MONTH,A5,L2N
      2 FORMAT(1H0,F10.3,I5,E12.5,I6,E14.3,I6)
        WRITE(6,3) HAT,L2N,J,A5,B,MONTH,B,J
      3 FORMAT(1H0,F10.7,I8,I5,F10.6,F10.6,I12,E10.3,I10)
        WRITE(6,4) J,MONTH,L2N
      4 FORMAT(1H0,3I12)
        WRITE(6,5) B,HAT,A5
      5 FORMAT(1H0,3F12.5)
        STOP
```

Data card:

```
      12.496   12723.15412E+01   1664    976.245E−024 57662
  1 2 3 4 5 6 7 8 9 10 11 12 13 14 15 16 17 18 19 20 21 22 23 24 25 26 27 28 29 30 31 32 33 34 35 36 37 38 39 40 41 42 43 44 45 46 47 48 49 50 51 52 53
```

Printout:

```
   12.496   127 0.23154E+03   1664       0.976E+01 457662
********** 457662 127   9.762450 12.496000        1664 0.125E+02
       127       1664       457662                 127
   12.49600   231.54120      9.76245
```

The printer fails to print the first number in Line 2, the value of HAT, which must be printed as 231.5412000 and cannot fit in the field of 10 spaces; this is a case of FØRMAT overflow.

6-11/   (a) $2/3 = 0$ (b) $3/2 + 2.5 = 3$

       (c) $2. - 3.2/8. + 2.5 = 4.1$ (d) $\dfrac{(2.)^3(2.)(3.2)}{3.2} = 16.$

       (e) $(8. + (2.)(2.))^2 = 144$ (f) $(2.)(3.14)(5.) = 31.4$

       (g) $(2.)(8.)/2. = 8.$ (h) $\left(\dfrac{8.}{2.}\right)^{(3-1)} = 16.$

6-13/

```
       READ(5,1)X,Y,A,B,I
1      FORMAT(2F6.2/2F6.2/I4)
       C=I
       SOLN=A*X+B*Y+C
       WRITE(6,2)X,Y,A,B,I,SOLN
2      FORMAT(1H0,7X,4HX‸=‸,F6.2,5X,4HY‸=‸,F6.2//8X,4HA‸=‸,
      1 F6.2,5X,4HB‸=‸,F6.2//8X,3HI‸=,I4///5X,6HSOLN‸=,E15.6)
       WRITE(6,3) X, Y, A, B, I, SOLN
C      REPEAT WITH QUOTATION MARKS
     3 FORMAT(1H0,7X,'X = ',F6.2,5X,'Y = ',F6.2//8X,'A = ',F6.2,5X,'B = '
      1 ,F6.2//8X,'I =',I4///5X,'SOLN =',E15.6)
       STOP
```

Data cards: *Printout:*

‸250	
‸‸5.00‸‸2.00	
100.00 70.00	
1 2 3 4 5 6 7 8 9 10 11 12	

X = 100.00	Y = 70.00
A = 5.00	B = 2.00
I = 250	
SOLN = 0.890000E+03	
X = 100.00	Y = 70.00
A = 5.00	B = 2.00
I = 250	
SOLN = 0.890000E+03	

chapter 7

7-1/   The unconditional GØ TØ statement directs the computer to go to *one* statement in the program; the computed GØ TØ statement lists several statements that the computer may be directed to go to and contains an index whose value gives the position in the list of the statement that the computer is to execute next.

7-3/ (a) The statement number must be an integer constant (say, 6), not a variable (K).
   (c) The comma after the right (closing) parenthesis is missing.
   (d) The index must be an integer variable, not a real variable.

7-5/

```
            WRITE(6,2)
2           FORMAT(//3X,6HCARD *,15X,13HN U M B E R S,14X,9H*        SUM)
6           READ(5,1)KARD,A,B,C,D
1           FORMAT (I2,4F8.3)
            SUM=A+B+C+D
            WRITE(6,3)KARD, A, B, C, D, SUM
3           FORMAT (1H0,I5,2X,1H*,4(2X,F8.3),3H∧∧*,2X,F8.3)
            GOTO6
```

Data cards:

```
 ∧5 ∧600.45∧∧∧∧∧7.236∧∧ 11.11∧∧ 199.42
 ∧41000. ∧∧∧∧822.6∧∧∧∧∧∧6.32∧∧240.56
 ∧3 ∧∧∧1.123∧∧∧4.06∧∧∧∧∧0.002∧∧79.12
 ∧2 ∧∧99.0∧∧∧∧16.05∧∧954.263∧∧ ∧7.15
 ∧1 ∧∧∧7.60∧∧∧18.010∧100.2∧∧∧∧∧∧0.20
```

Flow chart:

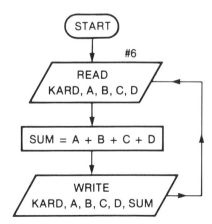

Printout:

CARD	*		NUMBERS			*	SUM
1	*	7.600	18.010	100.200	0.200	*	126.010
2	*	99.000	16.050	954.263	7.150	*	1076.463
3	*	1.123	4.060	0.002	79.120	*	84.305
4	*	1000.000	822.600	6.320	240.560	*	2069.480
5	*	600.450	7.236	11.110	199.420	*	818.216

IH0900I EXECUTION TERMINATING DUE TO ERROR COUNT FOR ERROR
NUMBER 217

7-7/


```
        WRITE(6,1)
  1   FORMAT(1H0,10X,'ITEM NO.      GROSS PRICE      DISCOUNT      NET PRICE'/)
  5   READ(5,2) ITEM,NUM,PRICE,KLIENT
  2   FORMAT (2I5,F8.2,I3)
        GROSS = PRICE*NUM
        GO TO(7,8),KLIENT
  7   DISC = 0.40*GROSS
        ANET = GROSS − DISC
        WRITE(6,3) ITEM,GROSS,DISC,ANET
  3   FORMAT(12X,I5,4X,F9.2,5X,F7.2,4X,F8.2)
        GO TO 5
  8   WRITE(6,3) ITEM,GROSS
        GO TO 5
        STOP
```


Data cards:

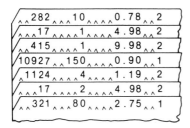

Printout:

ITEM NO.	GROSS PRICE	DISCOUNT	NET PRICE
321	220.00	88.00	132.00
17	9.96		
1124	4.76		
10927	135.00	54.00	81.00
415	9.98		
17	4.98		
282	7.80		

IH0900I EXECUTION TERMINATING DUE TO ERROR COUNT FOR ERROR
NUMBER   217

chapter 8

8-1/   (c)   One statement number is missing.
      (e)   The comma between (K + L) and 7 is an error.
      (g)   C= 5. is not an arithmetic expression.
      (h)   The last comma (after 5) is an error.

8-3/   (a)   30   (b)   6   (c)   5   (d)   3   (e)   8   (f)   4

8-5/

```
      WRITE(6,1)
1     FORMAT (1H0,15X,'DELTA,IN./IN.',6X,'STRESS,LB./SQ.IN.'/)
      DELTA=0.
7     IF(DELTA-0.00105)10,10,30
10    STRESS=0.3E+08*DELTA
      GOTO4
30    STRESS=0.2E+07*DELTA+0.28E+05
4     WRITE(6,2)DELTA,STRESS
2     FORMAT(19X,F6.4,15X,F7.1)
      DELTA=DELTA+0.0001
      IF(DELTA-0.00205)7,7,8
8     STOP
```

FLOW CHART

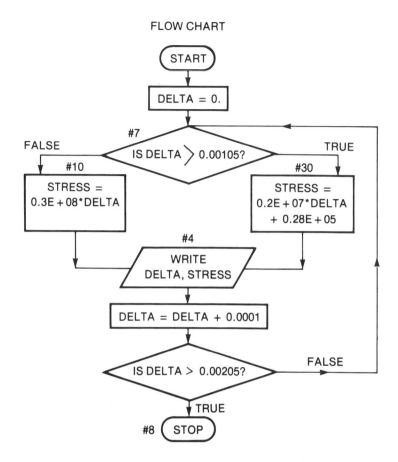

Printout:

DELTA,IN./IN.	STRESS,LB./SQ.IN.
0.0	0.0
0.0001	3000.0
0.0002	6000.0
0.0003	9000.0
0.0004	12000.0
0.0005	15000.0
0.0006	18000.0
0.0007	21000.0
0.0008	24000.0
0.0009	27000.0
0.0010	30000.0
0.0011	30200.0

DELTA,IN./IN.	STRESS,LB./SQ.IN.
0.0012	30400.0
0.0013	30600.0
0.0014	30800.0
0.0015	31000.0
0.0016	31200.0
0.0017	31400.0
0.0018	31600.0
0.0019	31800.0
0.0020	32000.0

8-7/   (a)   A.GT.2.*B.AND.A.LT.3.*C

    (b)   D.GT.A.AND.D.GT.B.AND.D.GT.C

    (c)   D.GT.A.ØR.D.GT.B.ØR.D.GT.C

    (d)   A.GT.B.AND.A.LT.2.*C

    (e)   A.NE.B.AND.C.NE.D.AND.C.NE.E

8-9/

```
       WRITE(6,1)
1      FORMAT(1H0,10X,7HX, FEET,4X,16HMOMENT, KIP-FEET/)
       X=0.
       READ(5,3)S,A,B,W
       RL=W*B*(2.*(S—A)—B)/(2.*S)
50     IF(X.LE.A)GOTO10
       IF(X.LE.A+B)GOTO20
       IF(X.GT.A+B)GOTO30
10     BM=RL*X
       GOTO40
20     BM=RL*X—W*(X—A)**2/2.
       GOTO40
30     BM=RL*X—W*B*(X—A—B/2.)
40     WRITE(6,2)X,BM
2      FORMAT(11X,F5.1,10X,F6.2)
       X=X+0.5
       IF(X.LE.S)GOTO50
3      FORMAT(4F4.1)
       STOP
```

Data card:

15.0ₓ5.0ₓ6.0ₓ0.8

Printout:

X, FEET	MOMENT, KIP-FEET
0.0	0.0
0.5	1.12
1.0	2.24
1.5	3.36
2.0	4.48
2.5	5.60
3.0	6.72
3.5	7.84
4.0	8.96
4.5	10.08
5.0	11.20
5.5	12.22
6.0	13.04
6.5	13.66
7.0	14.08
7.5	14.30
8.0	14.32
8.5	14.14
9.0	13.76
9.5	13.18
10.0	12.40
10.5	11.42
11.0	10.24
11.5	8.96
12.0	7.68
12.5	6.40
13.0	5.12
13.5	3.84
14.0	2.56
14.5	1.28
15.0	−0.00

8-11/

```
   WRITE(6,1)
 1 FORMAT(1H0,5X,'INTERVAL       VALUE, $'/)
   READ(5,2) SUM,RATE,C,T
 2 FORMAT (F6.2,2F3.0,F5.0)
   CI = 365./C
   N = T/C
```

```
   SUBTOT = 1. + RATE/100./CI
   NI = 1
4  VALUE = SUM*SUBTOT**NI
   WRITE(6,3) NI,VALUE
3  FORMAT(1X,I10,F14.2)
   NI = NI + 1
   IF(NI.EQ.N+1) STOP
   GO TO 4
```

Data card:

100.00ˏ6.ˏ5.ˏ450.

Printout: (in two columns)

INTERVAL	VALUE, $				
1	100.08	31	102.58	61	105.13
2	100.16	32	102.66	62	105.22
3	100.25	33	102.74	63	105.30
4	100.33	34	102.83	64	105.39
5	100.41	35	102.91	65	105.48
6	100.49	36	103.00	66	105.56
7	100.58	37	103.08	67	105.65
8	100.66	38	103.17	68	105.74
9	100.74	39	103.25	69	105.82
10	100.82	40	103.33	70	105.91
11	100.91	41	103.42	71	106.00
12	100.99	42	103.50	72	106.08
13	101.07	43	103.59	73	106.17
14	101.15	44	103.67	74	106.26
15	101.24	45	103.76	75	106.34
16	101.32	46	103.84	76	106.43
17	101.40	47	103.93	77	106.52
18	101.49	48	104.02	78	106.61
19	101.57	49	104.10	79	106.69
20	101.65	50	104.19	80	106.78
21	101.74	51	104.27	81	106.87
22	101.82	52	104.36	82	106.96
23	101.90	53	104.44	83	107.04
24	101.99	54	104.53	84	107.13
25	102.07	55	104.61	85	107.22
26	102.16	56	104.70	86	107.31
27	102.24	57	104.79	87	107.40
28	102.32	58	104.87	88	107.48
29	102.41	59	104.96	89	107.57
30	102.49	60	105.04	90	107.66

chapter 9

9-1/   (d) The index A must be an integer variable.
      (f) The parameter I+7 contains an arithmetic operation which is forbidden.
      (g) 6.5 is not an integer.
      (h) The statement number N must be an integer constant.

9-3/   (a) 2   (b) 20.   (c) 80, 90, 30   (d) 70, 90, 30   (e) 3
      (f) 9.0; 90, 30, 100   (g) 100; 8 or 11, depending on the compiler.

9-5/

```
      SUM=0.
      DO7I=1,100
      READ(5,1)NO,SCO
1     FORMAT(1X,I4,5X,F4.0)
      IF(NO.EQ.399) GO TO 8
7     SUM=SUM+SCO
   8  AVE = SUM/(I−1)
      WRITE(6,2)AVE
2     FORMAT(1X,F6.2)
      STOP
```

Data cards:

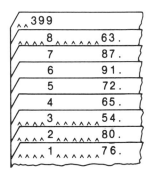

Printout:

73.50

9-7/

```
      DIMENSION C(6,7)
      READ(5,21) NN
21    FORMAT(I2)
      LL = NN + 1
      DO 1 I = 1,NN
 1    READ(5,2) (C(I, J),J = 1,LL)
 2    FORMAT( 7F5.1)
      DO 11 J = 1,NN
      PIVOT = C(J,J)
      MAXRO = J
      IF(J.EQ.NN) GO TO 13
      MM = NN − 1
      DO 3 I = J,MM
      IF(ABS(PIVOT) − ABS(C(I+1,J))) 4,3,3
```

```
   4   PIVOT = C(I+ 1,J)
       MAXRO = I + 1
   3   CONTINUE
  13   IF(ABS(PIVOT) − 0.00001) 7,8,8
   7   WRITE(6,9) PIVOT
   9   FORMAT(1H0,'PIVOT =',E10.3,', TOO SMALL/CHECK EQUATIONS')
       STOP
   8   IF(MAXRO.EQ.J) GO TO 6
       DO 5 K = 1,LL
       TEMP = C(MAXRO,K)
       C(MAXRO,K) = C(J,K)
   5   C(J,K) = TEMP
   6   DO 10 L = 1,LL
  10   C(J,L) = C(J,L)/PIVOT
       DO 11 M = 1,NN
       IF(M.EQ.J) GO TO 11
       COEFJ = −C(M,J)
       IF(ABS(COEFJ).LT.0.00001) GO TO 11
       DO 20 N = 1,LL
  20   C(M,N) = C(M,N) + C(J,N)*COEFJ
  11   CONTINUE
       WRITE(6,12) (C(I,LL), I = 1,NN)
  12   FORMAT(1H0,'A = ',E10.3/1H0,'B = ',E10.3/1H0,'C = ',E10.3/
       *          1H0,'D = ',E10.3/1H0,'E = ',E10.3/1H0,'F = ',E10.3)
       STOP
```

Data cards: *Printout:*

3.0	−4.0	−2.0	0.0	1.0	−2.0	21.8	
0.0	−8.0	6.4	−3.0	−2.5	2.0	−55.0	
0.0	0.0	3.0	2.0	1.0	0.0	5.7	
1.0	1.0	1.0	1.0	1.0	1.0	5.4	
1.0	−1.0	1.0	−1.0	1.0	−1.0	6.4	
−2.0	−7.0	1.0	−2.0	−1.0	2.0	−29.6	
6							

A =   0.120E+01

B =   0.500E+00

C = −0.250E+01

D =   0.300E+01

E =   0.720E+01

F = −0.400E+01

9-9/

```
       DIMENSION K(10),KDES(10)
       READ(5,6) K
   6   FORMAT(10I3)
       WRITE(6,5) K
```

```
      N = 10
      L = N - 1
  4   J = 1
  2   ILAST = 0
      DO 1 I = J,L
      IF(K(I).LE.K(I+1)) GO TO 1
      KEEP = K(I)
      K(I) = K(I+1)
      K(I+1) = KEEP
      IF(ILAST.EQ.0) ISTART = I - 1
      ILAST = I
  1   CONTINUE
      IF(ILAST.EQ.0) GO TO 3
      L = ILAST
      IF(ISTART.EQ.0) GO TO 4
      J = ISTART
      GO TO 2
  3   WRITE(6,5) K
  5   FORMAT(1H0,10I3)
      DO 8 I = 1,N
  8   KDES(I) = K(N - I + 1)
      WRITE(6,5) KDES
      STOP
```

Data card:

```
 -2   6   4   1   7  -1   9   3   4   5
```

Printout:

-2	6	4	1	7	-1	9	3	4	5
-2	-1	1	3	4	4	5	6	7	9
9	7	6	5	4	4	3	1	-1	-2

chapter 10

10-1/ (a) A one-dimensional array is a group of elements of the same type arranged in a single row or column.

Example: The hourly outdoor temperatures observed throughout a day form a one-dimensional array T of 24 elements.

(b)   A two-dimensional array is a group of elements of the same type arranged in a matrix, that is, in a table of several rows and columns.

Example: The hourly outdoor temperatures observed throughout a day in Atlanta, Denver, New York and Seattle form a two-dimensional array TEMP of four rows and twenty-four columns (or vice versa).

10-3/   (b)   Line 2 should read: WRITE(6,2)   (CHECK(I),I = 1,15)
     (c)   Line 2 should read: READ (5,3)   (B(I),I = 1,20)
     (d)   The dimension of DATA is 100, but READ calls for 200 elements.

10-5/

```
      DIMENSION Y(21)
      READ(5,1)Y
    1 FORMAT(21F3.2)
      SUM1=(Y(I)+Y(21))/2.
      SUM2=0.
      DO2I=1,21,1
    2 SUM2=SUM2+Y(I)
      AREA=0.25*(SUM2-SUM1)
      RMEAN=AREA/(20.*0.25)
      AVERGE=SUM2/21.
      WRITE(6,3)AREA,RMEAN,AVERGE
    3 FORMAT(1H0,10X,'AREA      =',F7.4,' SQ. IN.'/1H0,10X,
     *'MEAN      =',F7.4,' IN.'/1H0,10X,'AVERAGE =',F7.4,' IN.')
      STOP
```

Data card:

$$\overline{)07209310912213213914414614313381291140940780680590530500051056064}$$

Printout:

```
AREA      = 4.9650 SQ. IN.
MEAN      = 0.9930 IN.
AVERAGE = 0.9781 IN.
```

10-7/

```
C    NO=EMPLOYEE NUMBER / HRS=TOTAL HOURS WORKED/
C    MAR=MARITAL STATUS / ADD=HOURS ADDED TO HRS
C    TO PRODUCE THE SAME INCOME AT REGULAR RATE /
C    IX=EXEMPTION / PAY=GROSS INCOME / A=ADJUSTED INCOME /
C    DED=WITHHOLDING
          DIMENSION NO(100),HRS(100),RATE(100),MAR(100),IX(100)
          DIMENSION PAY(100),DED(100),CHEK(100)
          WRITE(6,1)
     1    FORMAT(1H1,'EMPLOYEE NO.^^GROSS PAY,^$^^WITH',
     *    'HOLDING,^$^^CHECK,^$')
          DO 2 J = 1,100
          READ(5,3) NO(J),HRS(J),RATE(J),MAR(J),IX(J)
     3    FORMAT(I3,F5.1,F6.2,I2,I3)
          IF(NO(J).EQ.200) GO TO 4
     2    CONTINUE
     4    K = J − 1
          DO 9 I = 1,K
          ADD = (HRS(I) − 40.)*0.5
          IF(ADD) 10,10,20
    10    PAY(I) = HRS(I)*RATE(I)
          GO TO 6
    20    PAY(I) = (HRS(I) + ADD)*RATE(I)
     6    A       = PAY(I) − 14.40*IX(I)
          IF(A.LE.11.) DED(I) = 0.
          L = MAR(I)
          GO TO(7,8),L
     7    IF(A.GT. 11..AND.A.LE. 35.) DED(I)=(A− 11.)*0.14
          IF(A.GT. 35..AND.A.LE. 73.) DED(I)=(A− 35.)*0.18+  3.36
          IF(A.GT. 73..AND.A.LE.202.) DED(I)=(A− 73.)*0.21+ 10.20
          IF(A.GT.202..AND.A.LE.231.) DED(I)=(A−202.)*0.23+ 37.29
          IF(A.GT.231..AND.A.LE.269.) DED(I)=(A−231.)*0.27+ 43.96
          IF(A.GT.269..AND.A.LE.333.) DED(I)=(A−269.)*0.31+ 54.22
          IF(A.GT.333.)               DED(I)=(A−333.)*0.35+ 74.06
          GO TO 9
     8    IF(A.GT. 11..AND.A.LE. 39.) DED(I)=(A− 11.)*0.14
          IF(A.GT. 39..AND.A.LE.167.) DED(I)=(A− 39.)*0.16+  3.92
          IF(A.GT.167..AND.A.LE.207.) DED(I)=(A−167.)*0.20+ 24.40
          IF(A.GT.207..AND.A.LE.324.) DED(I)=(A−207.)*0.24+ 32.40
          IF(A.GT.324..AND.A.LE.409.) DED(I)=(A−324.)*0.28+ 60.48
          IF(A.GT.409..AND.A.LE.486.) DED(I)=(A−409.)*0.32+ 84.28
          IF(A.GT.486.)               DED(I)=(A−486.)*0.36+108.92
     9    CHEK(I) = PAY(I) − DED(I)
          WRITE(6,11)(NO(I),PAY(I),DED(I),CHEK(I),I=1,K)
    11    FORMAT(1H0,I7,F16.2,F15.2,F13.2)
          STOP
```

Data cards:

```
200
^^4^40.0^18.50^2^^3
68  40.0  10.50  2    7
37  45.0    4.20  2    3
16  42.5    3.60  1    2
44  52.0    7.75  1    2
^^2^40.0^15.25^2^^5
^85^44.0^^4.50^2^^4
^17^38.5^^1.60^2^^4
```

Printout:

EMPLOYEE NO.	GROSS PAY, $	WITHHOLDING, $	CHECK, $
17	61.60	0.0	61.60
85	207.00	21.58	185.42
2	610.00	127.64	482.36
44	449.50	104.75	344.74
16	157.50	21.90	135.60
37	199.50	22.69	176.81
68	420.00	59.33	360.67
4	740.00	184.81	555.19

10-9/

```
      DIMENSION TR(49)
      M = 49
      N = (M+1)/2
      READ(5,1) X,B
 1    FORMAT(2A1)
      DO 2 JB = 1,M
 2    TR(JB) = B
      DO 3 I = 1,N
      K = N − (I − 1)
      L = N + (I − 1)
      TR(K) = X
      TR(L) = X
 3    WRITE(6,4) (TR(J), J = 1,M)
 4    FORMAT(5X,49A1)
      STOP
```

Data card:

Printout:

```
                            X
                           XXX
                          XXXXX
                         XXXXXXX
                        XXXXXXXXX
                       XXXXXXXXXXX
                      XXXXXXXXXXXXX
                     XXXXXXXXXXXXXXX
                    XXXXXXXXXXXXXXXXX
                   XXXXXXXXXXXXXXXXXXX
                  XXXXXXXXXXXXXXXXXXXXX
                 XXXXXXXXXXXXXXXXXXXXXXX
                XXXXXXXXXXXXXXXXXXXXXXXXX
               XXXXXXXXXXXXXXXXXXXXXXXXXXX
              XXXXXXXXXXXXXXXXXXXXXXXXXXXXX
             XXXXXXXXXXXXXXXXXXXXXXXXXXXXXXX
            XXXXXXXXXXXXXXXXXXXXXXXXXXXXXXXXX
           XXXXXXXXXXXXXXXXXXXXXXXXXXXXXXXXXXX
          XXXXXXXXXXXXXXXXXXXXXXXXXXXXXXXXXXXXX
         XXXXXXXXXXXXXXXXXXXXXXXXXXXXXXXXXXXXXXX
        XXXXXXXXXXXXXXXXXXXXXXXXXXXXXXXXXXXXXXXXX
       XXXXXXXXXXXXXXXXXXXXXXXXXXXXXXXXXXXXXXXXXXX
      XXXXXXXXXXXXXXXXXXXXXXXXXXXXXXXXXXXXXXXXXXXXX
     XXXXXXXXXXXXXXXXXXXXXXXXXXXXXXXXXXXXXXXXXXXXXXX
    XXXXXXXXXXXXXXXXXXXXXXXXXXXXXXXXXXXXXXXXXXXXXXXXX
```

10-11/
   (a)   A is the name of a one-dimensional array; (3) is the subscript indicating the third element of the array.
   (b)   B is the name of a two-dimensional array; (I,J) are the subscripts of the element in row I and column J.
   (c)   C is the name of a two-dimensional array; (K+2,3*J) are the subscripts of the element in row K+2 and column 3*J.

10-13/
   (b)   The subscripts of C must be constants, not variables.
   (c)   The second subscript of E must be 10, not 10.; the second subscript of F must be 20, not 5+15; arithmetic operations are not allowed in subscripts.

10-15/

```
        DIMENSION W(6,8)
        READ(5,2)((W(I,J),J=1,8),I=1,6)
2       FORMAT(8F6.1)
```

```
            TOTAL=0.
            DO3J=1,8
            DO3I=1,6
3           TOTAL=TOTAL+W(I,J)
            WRITE(6,4)TOTAL
4           FORMAT(1H0,5X,'TOTAL WEIGHT OF BINS      =',F8.1,' LB.')
            BINSIN=0.
            DO5L=2,7
            DO5K=2,5
5           BINSIN=BINSIN+W(K,L)
            WRITE(6,6)BINSIN
6           FORMAT(1H0,5X,'WEIGHT OF INTERIOR BINS  =',F8.1,' LB.')
            BIG=0.
            DO9J=1,8
            DO9I=1,6
            IF(W(I,J).LE.BIG)GOTO9
            BIG=W(I,J)
            KI = I
            KJ = J
9           CONTINUE
            WRITE(6,10)KI,KJ,BIG
10          FORMAT(1H0,5X,'HEAVIEST BIN, W(',I1,',',I1,')      =',F8.1,' LB.')
            STOP
```

Data cards:

```
   480.    390.    920.    290.    410.    470.    700.    400.
   600.    540.    370.    620.    210.    280.    440.    600.
   750.    250.    610.    170.    720.    270.    450.    490.
   910.    220.    460.    820.    410.    190.    240.    820.
   440.    450.    110.    370.    730.    600.    440.    320.
   520.    120.    470.    300.    350.    740.    420.    230.
```

Printout:

```
TOTAL WEIGHT OF BINS      = 22110.0 LB.

WEIGHT OF INTERIOR BINS =   9970.0 LB.

HEAVIEST BIN, W(6,3)      =   920.0 LB.
```

10-17/

```
    DIMENSION X(6),T(6),F(17),FFIELD(2),AFIELD(2)
    DATA F1,F2,F3,F4,F17,FFIELD,AFIELD,A/'(1H0',',',5X,',',''' T, ',
   *'FT.''',',')',',',F6.',',1',',',2X,',','A4','^^^^'/
```

```
      F(1) = F1
      F(2) = F2
      F(3) = F3
      F(4) = F4
      F(17) = F17
      READ(5,1) X
   1  FORMAT(6F5.1)
      WRITE(6,8) X
   8  FORMAT(1H0,5X,'X, FT.',6F6.1)
      DO 2 I = 1,6
      T(I) = X(I) − 9.0
      F(2*I+3) = FFIELD(1)
      F(2*I+4) = FFIELD(2)
      IF(T(I).GE.0.) GO TO 2
      T(I) = A
      F(2*I+3) = AFIELD(1)
      F(2*I+4) = AFIELD(2)
   2  CONTINUE
      WRITE(6,F) T
      STOP
```

Data card:

```
⌐  9.2ᴧᴧ 6.1ᴧ 12.3ᴧᴧ 5.2ᴧᴧ 9.0ᴧ 10.7 ⌐
 ᴧᴧ
```

Printout:

X, FT.	9.2	6.1	12.3	5.2	9.0	10.7
T, FT.	0.2		3.3		0.0	1.7

10-19/

```
          DIMENSION K(9), M(3,3)
          READ(5,1) K
       1  FORMAT(9I3)
   C            TRANSFORM THE ONE-DIMENSIONAL ARRAY K
   C            INTO A SQUARE ARRAY M BY ROWS,
   C            THAT IS, INTO M(1,1), M(1,2), M(1,3), M(2,1), ETC.
          I = 0
          DO 7 J = 1,3
          DO 7 L = 1,3
          I = I + 1
       7  M(J,L) = K(I)
   C            NOW ORDER THE PRINTOUT BY ROWS
          WRITE(6,2) ((M(J,L),L = 1,3), J = 1,3)
       2  FORMAT(1H0,20X,3I5)
```

```
C                AS A CHECK, ORDER A PRINTOUT OF M(1,3)
        WRITE(6,6) M(1,3)
    6   FORMAT(1H0,15X,I5)
C                THE PRINTOUT IS 2, WHICH WAS STORED AS M(1,3) AND
C                APPEARS IN THE PRINTED MATRIX IN LOCATION (1,3)
C                NOW FIND THE DIAGONAL PRODUCT
        IPROD = 1
        DO 3 I = 1,3
    3   IPROD = IPROD*M(I,(4−I))
        WRITE(6,4) IPROD
    4   FORMAT(//1H0,'PRODUCT OF THE ELEMENTS ON THE ˄',
       *'DIAGONAL FROM TOP RIGHT˄=', I5)
        STOP
```

Data card:

```
⌐    6ˬ10ˬˬ2ˬˬ7ˬˬ5ˬ−6−10ˬˬ4ˬˬ3     ⌐
```

Printout:

```
        6       10       2

        7        5      −6

      −10        4       3
2
```

PRODUCT OF THE ELEMENTS ON THE DIAGONAL FROM TOP RIGHT = −100

10-21/

1		DIMENSION K(3,2), C(3,2)
2		DO 1 I = 1,3
3		DO 1 J = 1,2
4	1	K(I,J) = 10*(I−1) + 5*J
5		DUMPLIST/L1/K
6		WRITE(6,3) ((K(I,J),J=1,2),I=1,3)
7	3	FORMAT(1H0,2I5)
8		DO 2 I = 1,3
9		DO 2 J = 1,2
10	2	C(I,J) = K(I,J)
11		DUMPLIST/L2/C
12		END
WARNING		END STATEMENT NOT PRECEDED BY A TRANSFER

Printout:

5	10
15	20
25	30

ERROR   AN END STATEMENT WAS USED TO TERMINATE
EXECUTION

PROGRAM WAS EXECUTING LINE   12 IN ROUTINE
M/PROG WHEN TERMINATION OCCURRED

**** DUMPLIST FOR ROUTINE M/PROG FOLLOWS ****
&L2

C=	0.5000000E 01,	0.1500000E 02,	0.2500000E 02,	
&L1	0.1000000E 02,	0.2000000E 02,	0.3000000E 02,&END	

K=	5,	15,	25,	10,
		20,	30,&END	

10-23/

```
    DIMENSION J(300)
    DO 1 I = 1,300
1   J(I) = I
    CALL DUMP(J(1),J(300),4)
    END
```

The printer prints 300 integers in 30 rows and 10 columns, as shown partially below. The first number on a line is in a 9-space field, all the others in 12-space fields.

```
~~~~~~~~~1~~~~~~~~~~~2~~~~~~~~~~~3~~~~  · · ·~~9~~~~~~~~~~~10
    11          12          13
        . . . . . . . . .
    291         292         293   . . . 299          300
```

10-25/

```
    DIMENSION A(10)
5   READ(5,1,END=3) N,X,(A(I),I = 1,N)
1   FORMAT(I2,10F6.2)
    Y = 0.
    DO 2 J = 1,N
```

2   Y = Y + A(J)*X**(J−1)
    WRITE(6,4) Y
4   FORMAT (1H0,F10.4)
    GO TO 5
3   STOP

Data cards:

| 4   1.67   1.35   −2.46   5.26   −1.62 |
| 5ᴧᴧ2.00ᴧᴧ5.00ᴧᴧ4.00ᴧᴧ3.00ᴧᴧ2.00ᴧᴧ1.00 |

57.0000

4.3663

chapter 11

11-1/   (a) $D = (A*B + C)*2. = (4.0*2.5 + 5.0)*2. = 30.0$

(b) $P = (A*B + G)/2. = (4.0*2.5 + 8.0)/2. = 9.0$

(c) $V = 2.0*(S + U)*T = 2.0*(6.0 + 4.5)*2.0 = 42.0$

(d)   Change the last two lines to:

READ (5,1) A,B,C,D   (Data: 5.0 3.0 4.5 2.0)

X = W (A,B,C,D)/3.

Then:

$X = (A*C + B*D)/3. = (5.0*4.5 + 3.0*2.0)/3. = 9.5$

11-3/

```
        SF(AS) = P*AS −Q*AS**2
        DO8J=1,3
        READ(5,1)FY,FC,Q1,B,D
        P = 0.075*FY*D
        Q = 0.075*FY**2/(1.7*B*FC)
        ASMIN = 0.2*B*D/FY
        UMMIN = SF(ASMIN)
1       FORMAT (5F6.2)
2       FORMAT (1H0,6X,'FY',9X,'FC',8X,'K1',7X,'B',10X,'D'/4X,F4.1,
        1'ᴧKSI.',3X,F3.1,' KSI.',3X,F4.2,3X,F4.1,' IN.',3X,F4.1,' IN.'
        2/1H0,10X,'AREAᴧOFᴧSTEEL',6X,'ULTIMATE MOMENT'
```

```
      3/14X,'SQ. IN.',13X,'KIP-FEET'/1H0,14X,F5.2,14X,F7.2)
      WRITE(6,2)FY,FC,Q1,B,D,ASMIN,UMMIN
      ASMAX=55.4625*B*D*Q1*FC/(FY*(87.+FY))
      UMMAX = SF(ASMAX)
      DO7 I=1,100
      RI = I
      AS=RI/5.
      IF(AS.LT.ASMIN)GOTO7
      UM = SF(AS)
      IF(UM.GT.UMMAX)GOTO8
      WRITE(6,3)AS,UM
3     FORMAT (15X,F5.2,14X,F7.2)
7     CONTINUE
8     WRITE(6,3)ASMAX,UMMAX
      STOP
```

Data cards:

```
/ 50.0    5.0   0.80 12.0   26.0 /
/ 60.0    4.0   0.85 12.0   24.0 /
/ 60.0    3.0   0.85 10.0   20.0 /
```

Printout (partial):

FY	FC	K1	B	D
60.0 KSI.	3.0 KSI.	0.85	10.0 IN.	20.0 IN.

AREA OF STEEL SQ. IN.	ULTIMATE MOMENT KIP-FEET
0.67	57.65
0.80	68.61
1.00	84.71
1.20	100.38
. . . .	. . . . .
2.20	172.38
2.40	185.51
2.60	198.21
2.80	210.49
3.00	222.35
3.20	233.79
3.21	234.18

FY	FC	K1	B	D
60.0 KSI.	4.0 KSI.	0.85	12.0 IN.	24.0 IN.

AREA OF STEEL SQ. IN.	ULTIMATE MOMENT KIP-FEET
0.96	100.63
1.00	104.69
1.20	124.84
1.40	144.71
. . . .	. . . . . .
5.20	472.13
5.40	486.71
5.60	501.03
5.80	515.09
6.00	528.88
6.16	539.55

FY	FC	K1	B	D
50.0 KSI.	5.0 KSI.	0.80	12.0 IN.	26.0 IN.

AREA OF STEEL SQ. IN.	ULTIMATE MOMENT KIP-FEET
1.25	118.82
1.40	132.90
1.60	151.29
1.80	169.54
. . . .	. . . . . .
9.40	754.07
9.60	766.59
9.80	778.96
10.00	791.18
10.10	797.51

11-5/

```
        READ(5,1)X
1       FORMAT (F6.2)
        RAD=X*3.1416/180.
        SINX=0.
        DO2I=1,49,4
        RI=I
        SINX=SINX+RAD**I/FAC(RI)−RAD**(I+2)/FAC(RI+2.)
3       FORMAT (1X,I3,5X,E15.8)
```

```
2       WRITE(6,3)I,SINX
        STOP

        FUNCTION FAC(P)
        FAC=1.0
        N=P
        DO2 I=1,N
        RI=I
2       FAC=FAC*RI
        RETURN
```

Data card:

/ 50.00 /

Printout:

1	0.76190376E+00
5	0.76604480E+00
9	0.76604551E+00
13	0.76604551E+00
17	0.76604551E+00
21	0.76604551E+00
25	0.76604551E+00
29	0.76604551E+00
33	0.76604551E+00
37	0.76604551E+00
41	0.76604551E+00
45	0.76604551E+00
49	0.76604551E+00

11-7/

```
        DIMENSION A(3,3),B(2,4),C(3,3),D(4,2)
        READ(5,1) A,B
1       FORMAT (9F4.1,8F5.1)
        CALL TRANSP(A,C,3,3)
        CALL TRANSP(B,D,2,4)
        WRITE(6,2)((C(I,J),J=1,3),I=1,3),((D(I,J),J=1,2),I=1,4)
2       FORMAT (1H0,9X,'ARRAY C'//3(1X,3F7.1/)/1H0,9X,
       *'ARRAY D'//4(1X,3X,2F7.1/))
        WRITE(6,2)A,B
        STOP

        SUBROUTINE TRANSP(P,Q,K,L)
        DIMENSION P(K,L), Q(L,K)
        DO 1 I = 1,K
        DO 1 J = 1,L
1       Q(J,I) = P(I,J)
        RETURN
```

Data card:

3.2 7.1 5.2−4.4 2.5−4.7−2.0−0.7 9.2 17.6 52.4 42.3−22.2−80.2 50.9 60.9 16.7

Printout:

ARRAY C

3.2	7.1	5.2
−4.4	2.5	−4.7
−2.0	−0.7	9.2

ARRAY D

17.6	52.4
42.3	−22.2
−80.2	50.9
60.9	16.7

ARRAY C

3.2	7.1	5.2
−4.4	2.5	−4.7
−2.0	−0.7	9.2

ARRAY D

17.6	52.4
42.3	−22.2
−80.2	50.9
60.9	16.7

11-9/

```
  DIMENSION A(100)
  COMMON N,A
  READ(5,1) N,(A(I),I=1,N)
1 FORMAT(I4,38F2.0/40F2.0/22F2.0)
  AV = AVER(N,A)
  CALL VAR(AV,V)
  WRITE(6,2)(A(I),I=1,N)
2 FORMAT(5(/1H0,20F4.0))
  WRITE(6,3) N,AV,V
3 FORMAT(1H0,I5,2F8.3)
  STOP

  FUNCTION AVER(K,B)
  DIMENSION B(100)
  SUM = 0.
  DO 1 I = 1,K
```

```
1   SUM = SUM + B(I)
    AVER = SUM/K
    RETURN

    SUBROUTINE VAR(AVE,VARI)
    COMMON J,C(100)
    SUM = 0.
    DO 1 I = 1,J
1   SUM = SUM + (C(I) −AVE)**2
    VAR I = SUM/J
    RETURN
```

Data cards:

```
39404142
  42010203040506070809101112131415161718192021222324252627282930313233343536373 8
```

Printout:

```
 1.    2.    3.    4.    5.    6.    7.    8.    9.   10.
11.   12.   13.   14.   15.   16.   17.   18.   19.   20.

21.   22.   23.   24.   25.   26.   27.   28.   29.   30.
31.   32.   33.   34.   35.   36.   37.   38.   39.   40.

41.   42.

    42   21.500   146.917
```

11-11/

```
SUBROUTINE NEWT(X,F,DER,XN,DIFF)
XN = X − F/DER
DIFF = ABS(XN − X)
RETURN
```

```
    X = 4.                                     X = −4.
    WRITE(6,1) X                               WRITE(6,1) X
1   FORMAT (1X,F7.4)                       1   FORMAT (1X,F7.4)
    DO 2 I = 1,20                              DO 2 I = 1,20
    F = X**2 − 2.*X − 3.                       F = X**2 − 2.*X − 3.
    DER = 2.*X − 2.                            DER = 2.*X − 2.
    CALL NEWT (X,F,DER,X,DIFF)                 CALL NEWT(X,F,DER,X,DIFF)
    WRITE(6,1) X                               WRITE(6,1) X
    IF (DIFF.LE.0.00001) GO TO 3              IF (DIFF.LE.0.00001) GO TO 3
2   CONTINUE                               2   CONTINUE
3   STOP                                   3   STOP
```

Printout:

4.0000
3.1667
3.0064
3.0000
3.0000

Printout:

−4.0000
−1.9000
−1.1397
−1.0046
−1.0000
−1.0000

11-13/

```
    DO 4 J = 1,14
    K = 1
    DO 5 I = 1,J
5   K = K*I
4   WRITE(6,3) J,K
3   FORMAT (1X,I2,I14)
    STOP
```

Printout:

1	1
2	2
3	6
4	24
5	120
6	720
7	5040
8	40320
9	362880
10	3628800
11	39916800
12	479001600

True Factorial

13   1932053504 + 2 (2147483648) = 6227020800
14   1278945280 + 40 (2147483648) = 87178291200

chapter 12

12-1/

```
    K = 27
    B = 4.5
```

```
     C = 46.
     J = 2
     N = − 5
     D = C*B
     L = J − N
     M = K*J
     WRITE(6,1) D,L,M
  1  FORMAT (F6.1,2I5)
     STOP
```

Printout:

207.0   7   54

12-3/

```
     REAL M(4), N(4)
     DIMENSION ROOT(4),HAFSUM(4),DIV(4)
     READ(5,1) M,N
  1  FORMAT (8F7.3)
     WRITE(6,2)
  2  FORMAT(1H0,5X,'M∧∧∧∧∧∧∧∧∧∧N∧∧∧∧∧∧∧SQRT(MN)∧∧∧∧∧∧(M+N)/2',
    *6X,'(M+N)/2/SQRT (MN)')
     DO 4 I = 1,4
     ROOT(I) = SQRT. (M(I)*N(I))
     HAFSUM(I) = (M(I) + N(I))/2.
     DIV (I) = HAFSUM(I)/ROOT (I)
  4  WRITE(6,3) M(I),N(I),ROOT (I),HAFSUM (I),DIV(I)
  3  FORMAT(1H0,2X,F6.3,F10.3,2F13.5,F17.5)
     STOP
```

Data card:

 ∧∧2.060∧10.310∧∧6.723∧∧6.379∧∧2.490∧10.124∧∧6.921∧∧6.921

Printout:

M	N	SQRT(MN)	(M+N)/2	(M+N)/2/SQRT(MN)
2.060	2.490	2.26482	2.27500	1.00449
10.310	10.124	10.21658	10.21700	1.00004
6.723	6.921	6.82128	6.82200	1.00010
6.379	6.921	6.64447	6.65000	1.00083

12-5/

```
      DOUBLE PRECISION CI,SUBTOT,VALUE
      DIMENSION N(3), VALUE(3)
      READ(5,1) SUM,RATE,CI,NI
  1   FORMAT (3F5.0,I4)
      NCI = CI
      WRITE(6,2) SUM,RATE
  2   FORMAT (1H1,16X,'DAILY VALUES OF',F7.2,' COMPOUNDED DAILY'/
     *18X,'AT THE RATE OF',F5.2,' PER CENT PER YEAR'/
     *1H0,2X,3(4X,'DAY',6X,'VALUE, $')/)
      SUBTOT = 1. + RATE/100./CI
      L = NI/3
      DO 4 J = 1,L
      K = J - 1
      DO 5 I = 1,3
      N(I) = I + 3*K
  5   VALUE(I) = SUM*SUBTOT**N(I)
  4   WRITE(6,3) (N(I), VALUE(I), I = 1,3)
  3   FORMAT (5X,3(2X,I3,4X,F12.8))
      STOP
```

Data card:

```
 ┌─────────────────────────────────┐
/  100.^^^6.^365.^501              │
~~~~~~~~~~~~~~~~~~~~~~~~~~~~~~~~~~~~~~~
```

Printout (partial):

DAILY VALUES OF 100.00 COMPOUNDED DAILY
AT THE RATE OF 6.00 PER CENT PER YEAR

DAY	VALUE, $	DAY	VALUE, $	DAY	VALUE, $
1	100.01643836	2	100.03287941	3	100.04932317
4	100.06576964	5	100.08221881	6	100.09867068
7	100.11512525	8	100.13158253	9	100.14804252
10	100.16450521	11	100.18097061	12	100.19743871
13	100.21390952	14	100.23038304	15	100.24685927
16	100.26333821	17	100.27981985	18	100.29630420
..	....	..	....	..	....
487	108.33392981	488	108.35173813	489	108.36954937
490	108.38736354	491	108.40518064	492	108.42300067
493	108.44082363	494	108.45864952	495	108.47647834
496	108.49431009	497	108.51214477	498	108.52998238
499	108.54782293	500	108.56566640	501	108.58351281

12-7/

```
  READ(5,1) R,P,AR,AP
1 FORMAT (4F5.0)
  VQ = R*SIN(AR/57.3) − P*SIN(AP/57.3)
  HQ = R*COS(AR/57.3) − P*COS(AP/57.3)
  Q = SQRT(VQ**2 + HQ**2)
  AQ = ATAN2(VQ,HQ)*57.3
  WRITE(6,2) Q,AQ
2 FORMAT (1H0,5X,'FORCE Q^^^^=^',F7.1,'^LB.'/1H0,5X,
 *'ANGLE^OF^Q^=^',F7.1,'^DEG.')
  STOP
```

Data card: *Printout:*

50.^^80.^315.^^60.

FORCE Q   =   104.8 LB.

ANGLE OF Q=   −92.6 DEG.

12-9/

```
  COMPLEX A,B,C,D,E,F,DENOM,X,Y
  WRITE(6,1)
1 FORMAT (1H0,5X,'SET              X              Y')
  DO 4 I = 1,3
  READ(5,2) A,B,C,D,E,F
2 FORMAT (6(F3.0,F3.0))
  DENOM = A*D − B*C
  X = (D*E − B*F)/DENOM
  Y = (A*F − C*E)/DENOM
4 WRITE(6,3) I,X,Y
3 FORMAT (1H0,6X,I1,2(5X,F8.3,'+(',F8.3,')I'))
  STOP
```

Data cards:

```
2   3   3   0   4   0   0  −1  −4   2   2   0
0   1  −4   0   0  −3   5   0   2   0   6   0
2   0   5  −1   4  −2   3   0   7   0   2   1
```

Printout:

SET	X	Y
1	−0.476+(−0.306)I	1.506+(0.424)I
2	0.0 +(4.857)I	−1.714+(0.0)I
3	0.329+(−0.518)I	−2.071+(0.682)I

12-11/

```
    EXTERNAL SIN,COS
    DIMENSION F(3),A(3),V(3),H(3)
    READ(5,1) F,A
1   FORMAT (6F5.0)
    SUMV = 0.
    SUMH = 0.
    DO 2 I = 1,3
    CALL COMP(F(I),A(I),SIN,V(I))
    CALL COMP(F(I),A(I),COS,H(I))
    SUMV = SUMV + V(I)
2   SUMH = SUMH + H(I)
    R = SQRT(SUMV**2 + SUMH**2)
    THETA = ATAN2(SUMV,SUMH)*57.3
    WRITE(6,3) R,THETA
3   FORMAT (1H0,'RESULTANT٨٨٨=',F7.1,'٨LB.'/1H0,'ANGLE THETA٨=',
   *F7.1,' DEG.')
    STOP

    SUBROUTINE COMP(F,A,TRIG,C)
    C = F*TRIG(A/57.3)
    RETURN
```

Data card:

```
 ٨٨65.٨120.٨٨٨92.٨٨60.٨220.٨310.
```

Printout:

```
RESULTANT   = 91.3 LB.
ANGLE THETA = −90.2 DEG.
```

12-13/

```
   DOUBLE PRECISION F
   DO 4 J = 1,25
   F = 1.
   DO 5 I = 1,J
 5 F = F*I
 4 WRITE(6,3) J,F
 3 FORMAT (1X,I2,F30.0)
   STOP
```

Printout:

1	1.
2	2.
3	6.
4	24.
5	120.
6	720.
7	5040.
8	40320.
9	362880.
10	3628800.
11	39916800.
12	479001600.
13	6227020800.
14	87178291200.
15	1307674368000.
16	20922789888000.
17	355687428096000.
18	6402373705728000.
19	121645100408832000.
20	2432902008176640000.
21	51090942171709440000.
22	1124000727777607680000.
23	25852016738884976100000.
24	620448401733239427000000.
25	15511210043330985500000000.

12-15/

```
   DATA ISUM /Z24680BDF/
   I = ISUM/16**5
   N = ISUM − I*16**5
   J = N/16**2
   K = N − J*16**2
   WRITE(6,1) I,I,J,J,K,K
 1 FORMAT (1H0,Z8,I6)
   STOP
```

Printout:

00000246	582
0000080B	2059
000000DF	223

appendix c

C-1/ The base of the decimal system is 10.
Ten.
0 1 2 3 4 5 6 7 8 9 .

C-3/ (a) 0.1111×2^2 (b) 0.101×2^{-2}
(c) 0.101×2^3 (d) 0.1010101×2^4

C-5/ (a) 101101.   (b) 101111110000.
(c) 1110000.<u>01100110</u> . . .   (d) $-0.000100101001.$ . . .
repeating group↘

C-7/ The base of the hexadecimal system is 16.
Sixteen.
0 1 2 3 4 5 6 7 8 9 A B C D E F .

C-9/ (a) 0.12×16^2 (b) $0.1C42 \times 16^3$
(c) $0.1A \times 16^{-2}$ (d) $0.B0FF \times 16$

C-11/ (a) 5.8   (b) 2.4
(c) 77E.   (d) 3.BA

C-13/ (a) 01   (b) 0111
(c) 00110   (d) 0011001

C-15/ (a) 0.1C28F6 (6 digits)   (b) 10000.4C0000000 (14 digits)

index